Grateful acknowledgement is made to the following sources:

"Baoche's Universal Action," from Dogen Zenji's *Genjokoan,* is based on a translation by Anzan Hoshin Roshi and Yasuda Joshu Dainan Roshi from the forthcoming book *Dogen: Zen Writings on the Practice of Realization.* Text © 2017 White Wind Community (wwzc.org). Used with permission.

"Pai Chang's No Tools" is based on an excerpt from Zoketsu Norman Fischer's essay *On Zen Work.* Text © 1997 Zoketsu Norman Fischer (everydayzen.org). Used with Permission.

"Do Not Stand at My Grave and Weep" is based on a poem by Mary Elizabeth Frye. (Public Domain).

Special thanks to Ven. Anzan Hoshin Roshi and Zoketsu Norman Fischer; Mishin at the White Wind Zen Community, Ottawa, ON; and Luke Howard for help with the Pascal quote.

drawnandquarterly.com
For more information about King-Cat Comics, please visit king-cat.net.

First edition: April 2018
Printed in China
10 9 8 7 6 5 4 3 2 1

Library and Archives Canada Cataloguing in Publication. Porcellino, John, author, illustrator. *From Lone Mountain* / John Porcellino. ISBN 978-1-77046-295-3 (softcover). 1. Comics (Graphic works). I. Title. PN6727.P67F76 2017   741.5'973 C2017-901677-6.

Published in the USA by Drawn & Quarterly, a client publisher of Farrar, Straus and Giroux. Orders: 888.330.8477. Published in Canada by Drawn & Quarterly, a client publisher of Raincoast Books. Orders: 800.663.5714. Published in the United Kingdom by Drawn & Quarterly, a client publisher of Publishers Group UK. Orders: info@pguk.co.uk

FROM LONE MOUNTAIN

King-Cat Comics and Stories 2003-2007

BY JOHN PORCELLINO

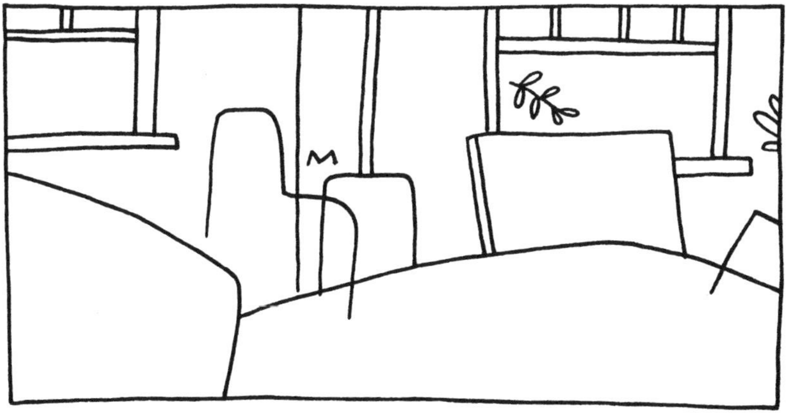
M

Drawn and Quarterly
Montréal

HIPPIE♥GIRL

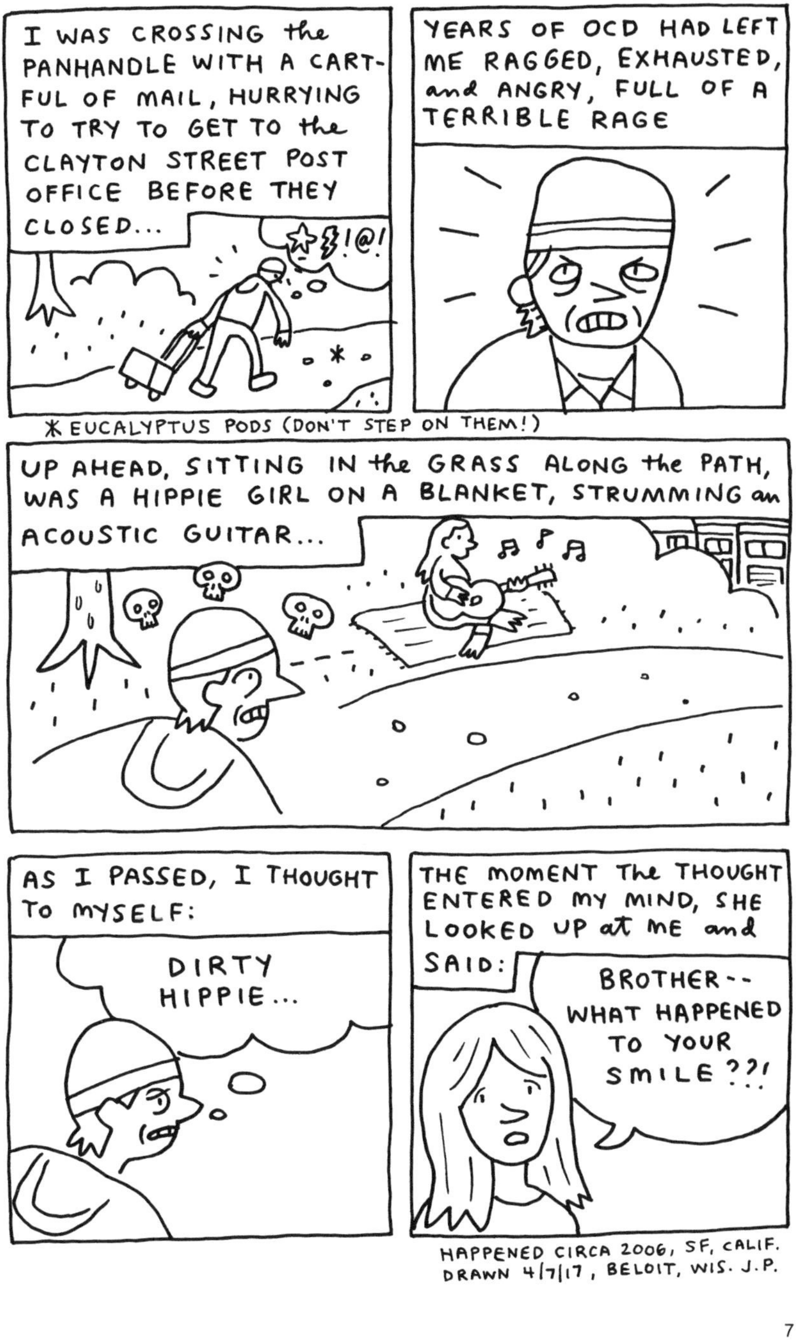
I WAS CROSSING the PANHANDLE WITH A CART-FUL OF MAIL, HURRYING TO TRY TO GET TO the CLAYTON STREET POST OFFICE BEFORE THEY CLOSED...
!@!
*
* EUCALYPTUS PODS (DON'T STEP ON THEM!)
YEARS OF OCD HAD LEFT ME RAGGED, EXHAUSTED, and ANGRY, FULL OF A TERRIBLE RAGE
UP AHEAD, SITTING IN the GRASS ALONG the PATH, WAS A HIPPIE GIRL ON A BLANKET, STRUMMING an ACOUSTIC GUITAR...
AS I PASSED, I THOUGHT TO MYSELF:
DIRTY HIPPIE...
THE MOMENT The THOUGHT ENTERED MY MIND, SHE LOOKED UP at ME and SAID:
BROTHER-- WHAT HAPPENED TO YOUR SMILE??!
HAPPENED CIRCA 2006, SF, CALIF.
DRAWN 4/7/17, BELOIT, WIS. J.P.

KING-CAT

COMICS and STORIES

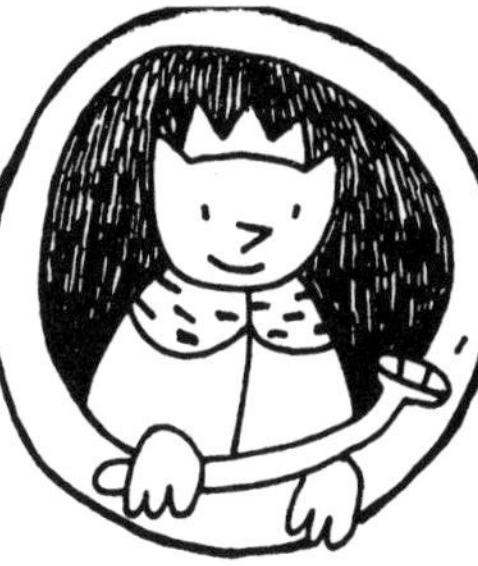

NUMBER 62 $2.00

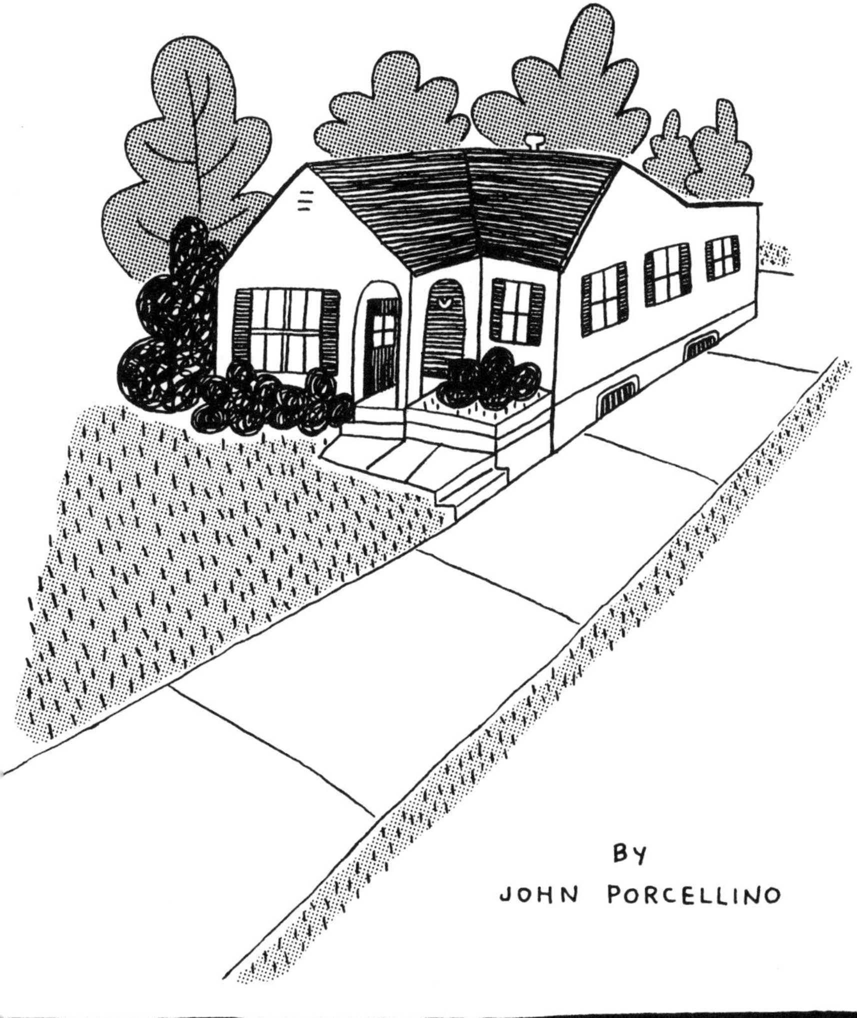

BY

JOHN PORCELLINO

KING-CAT SNORNOSE, 62 ☆

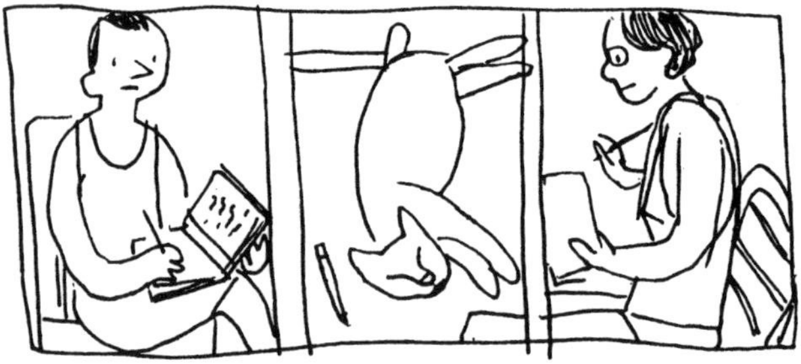

WE LEFT ELGIN on Monday December 2nd, in the afternoon, in the middle of a snowstorm. The truck was packed up, my shoes were wet; I was sad. Maisie was in her carrier. I put on my boots, picked her up, and we walked out the back door, down the back steps, into the snow. Misun closed the door behind us and we crossed the snowy driveway, climbed up into the truck, and pulled out, going slow on slushy streets, heading west – Larkin to 20 to Plank Road to 47 and onto the interstate. I didn't have the time, or the heart, to look back then, but I can see it now in front of me, quite clearly: all of us, together, going down those snow-covered steps in Illinois.

* * *

Denver is a place that exists in my mind, but I guess it's also real. To get there you head west through cornfields and the expanse of Midwestern sky. The road bends and you cross the river into green Iowa hills, Des Moines, and the road bends again before the border. Then it's Omaha – and the red-dirt gold-light sunset. The world is very large. →

KING-CAT COMICS and STORIES Number 62
Published by SPIT and a HALF: [redacted]
Denver, Colorado [redacted] Please write!
Catalog online at: www.king-cat.net

Printed in August.
with thanks to Jordan Crane and Souther Salazar!

At Ogallala the Road bends again into empty hills—
Colorado scrub and brush — Sterling, Ft. Morgan, and
the long, slow ride into Denver. The traffic builds, the
mountains appear... Suddenly — you're there. You pull
up, step out, onto Red slate sidewalks, gaze up at the
blue sky and wonder — You just came a thousand miles,
so where are you now?

✳ ✳ ✳

Misun and I were married on Sunday, June 29th,
2003, at the Botanic Gardens in Denver. It was hot—
it was very beautiful — and it was hot. It's still hot as
I write this, it's been hot for weeks.

One evening, after the wedding, we went to return
Leona's iron and ironing board. We were walking up
her front porch stairs when I noticed the iron,
which Misun was carrying, was dripping water. I said:
"Misun — it's dripping water." We looked down and a
water drop splashed onto Leona's front porch, right in
front of where a Daddy-Long-Legs was walking. When it
saw the splash, the Daddy-Long-Legs paused, ran over,
and in the heat of a hot summer night, it drank from
the drop of water.

Here's King-Cat 62. Love,
        John P.

CORRECTIONS & CLARIFICATIONS
– – – – – – – – – – – – – – –
✳ It was incorrectly reported in Issue Sixty-one
  that my mother will not drive west of Roselle
  Road... In fact, she will not drive EAST
  of Roselle Road.
✳ Fabyan "Street" is really Fabyan Parkway, which
  crosses the Fox River at Batavia, Illinois.
✳ "the LOOP" = WLUP, 97.9 F.M. – "Where Chicago Rocks"
            ◦ ◦ ◦
(Front cover is 212 N. Melrose, Elgin, Illinois—
  where I lived from Nov. 1998 to Dec. 2002 ♡)

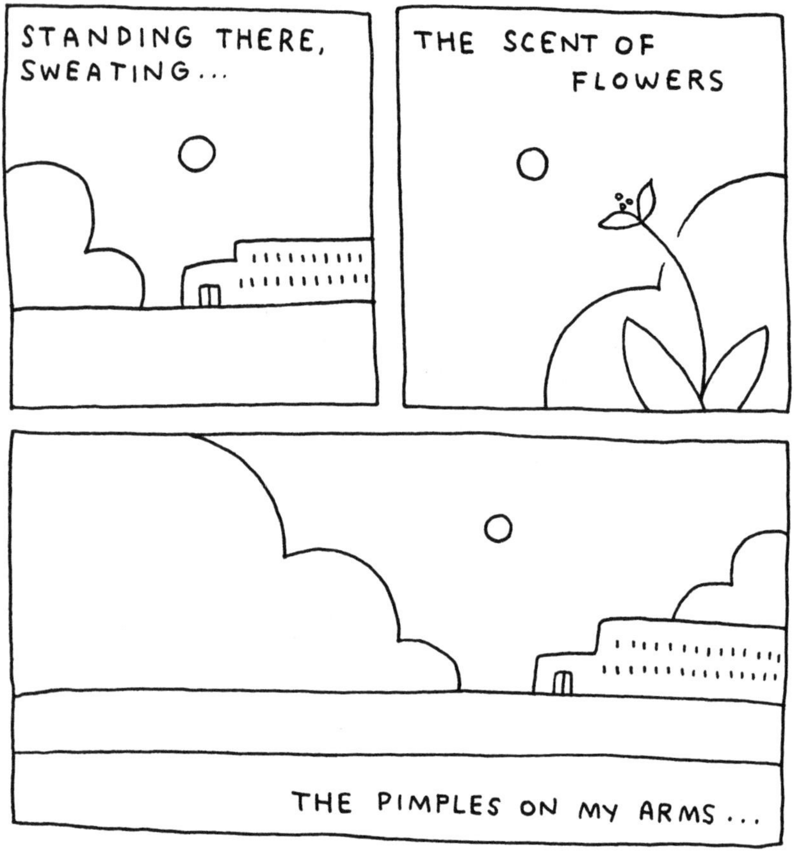
STANDING THERE, SWEATING...
THE SCENT OF FLOWERS
THE PIMPLES ON MY ARMS...

JULY NIGHT - PALATINE, ILL.
FEB. 12, 2003

March.

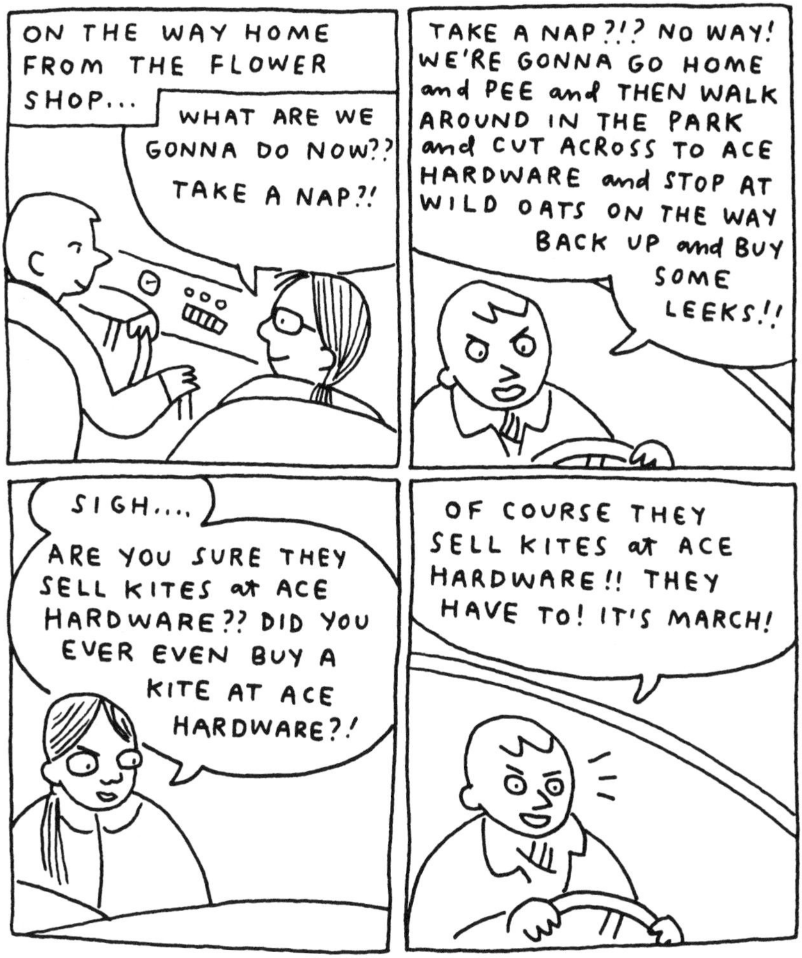

ON THE WAY HOME FROM THE FLOWER SHOP...
WHAT ARE WE GONNA DO NOW?? TAKE A NAP?!
TAKE A NAP?!? NO WAY! WE'RE GONNA GO HOME and PEE and THEN WALK AROUND IN THE PARK and CUT ACROSS TO ACE HARDWARE and STOP AT WILD OATS ON THE WAY BACK UP and BUY SOME LEEKS!!
SIGH.... ARE YOU SURE THEY SELL KITES at ACE HARDWARE?? DID YOU EVER EVEN BUY A KITE AT ACE HARDWARE?!
OF COURSE THEY SELL KITES at ACE HARDWARE!! THEY HAVE TO! IT'S MARCH!

HAPPENED MARCH 7, 2003
DRAWN 3/12/03

LONG DAY

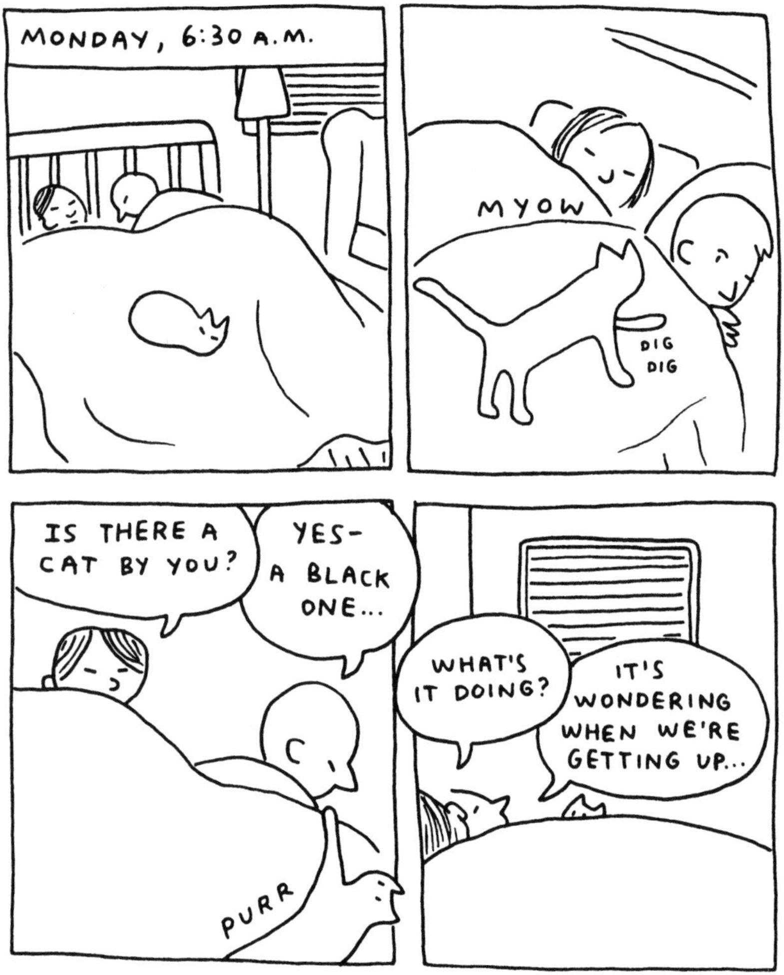

MONDAY, 6:30 A.M.
MYOW
DIG DIG
IS THERE A CAT BY YOU?
YES- A BLACK ONE...
PURR
WHAT'S IT DOING?
IT'S WONDERING WHEN WE'RE GETTING UP...

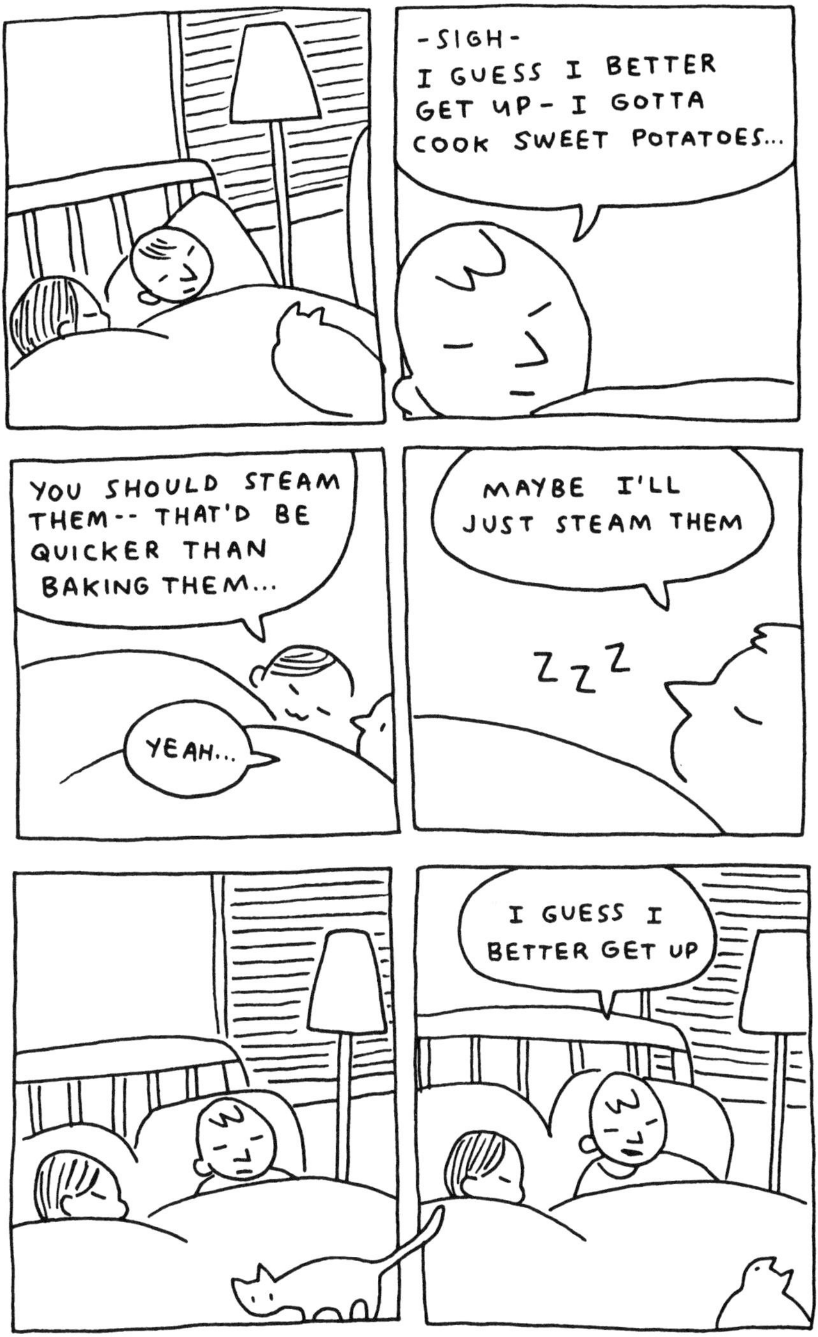
-SIGH-
I GUESS I BETTER GET UP- I GOTTA COOK SWEET POTATOES...
YOU SHOULD STEAM THEM-- THAT'D BE QUICKER THAN BAKING THEM...
YEAH...
MAYBE I'LL JUST STEAM THEM
ZZZ
I GUESS I BETTER GET UP

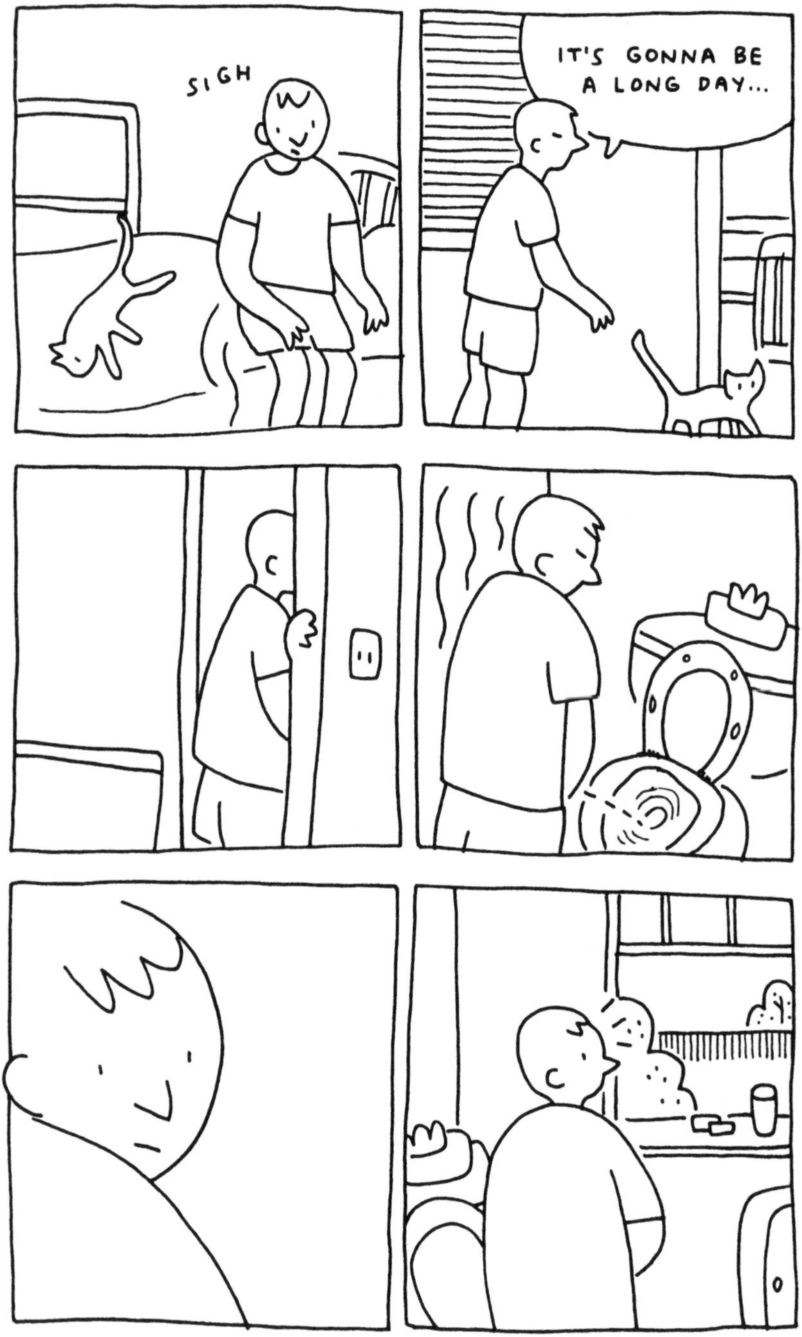
SIGH
IT'S GONNA BE A LONG DAY...

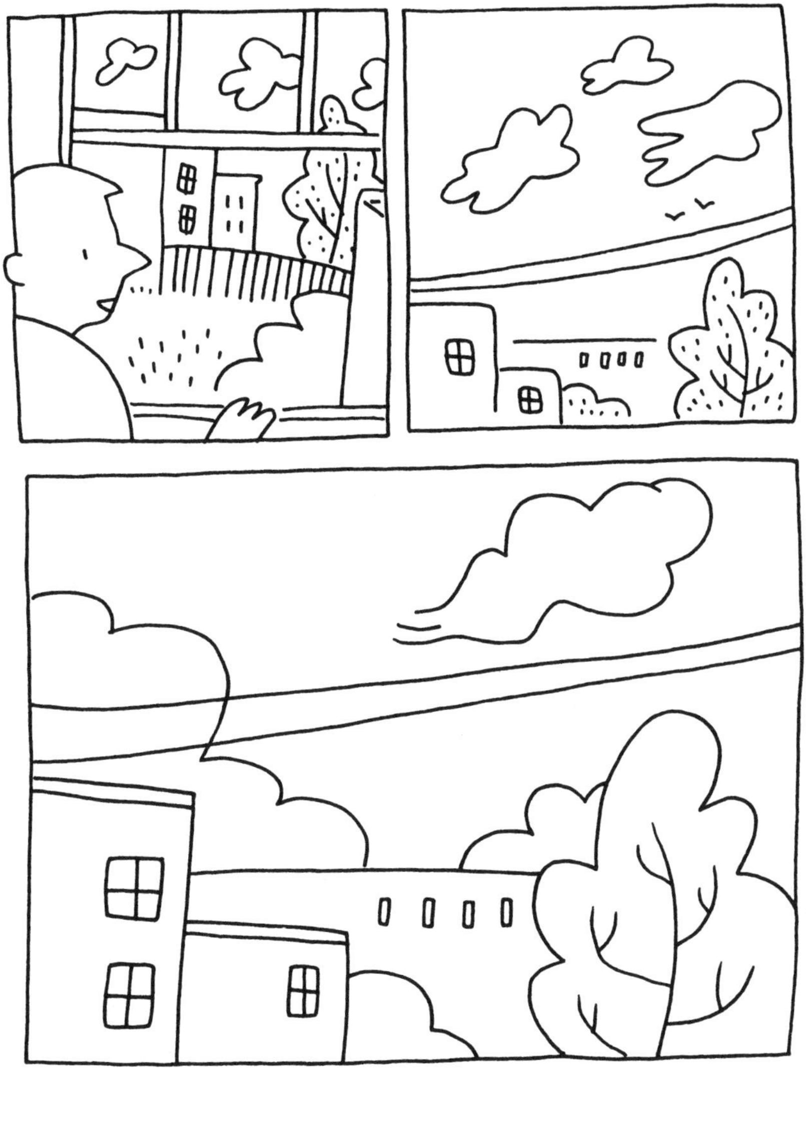

J.P. 2003

Fabyan Street Bridge

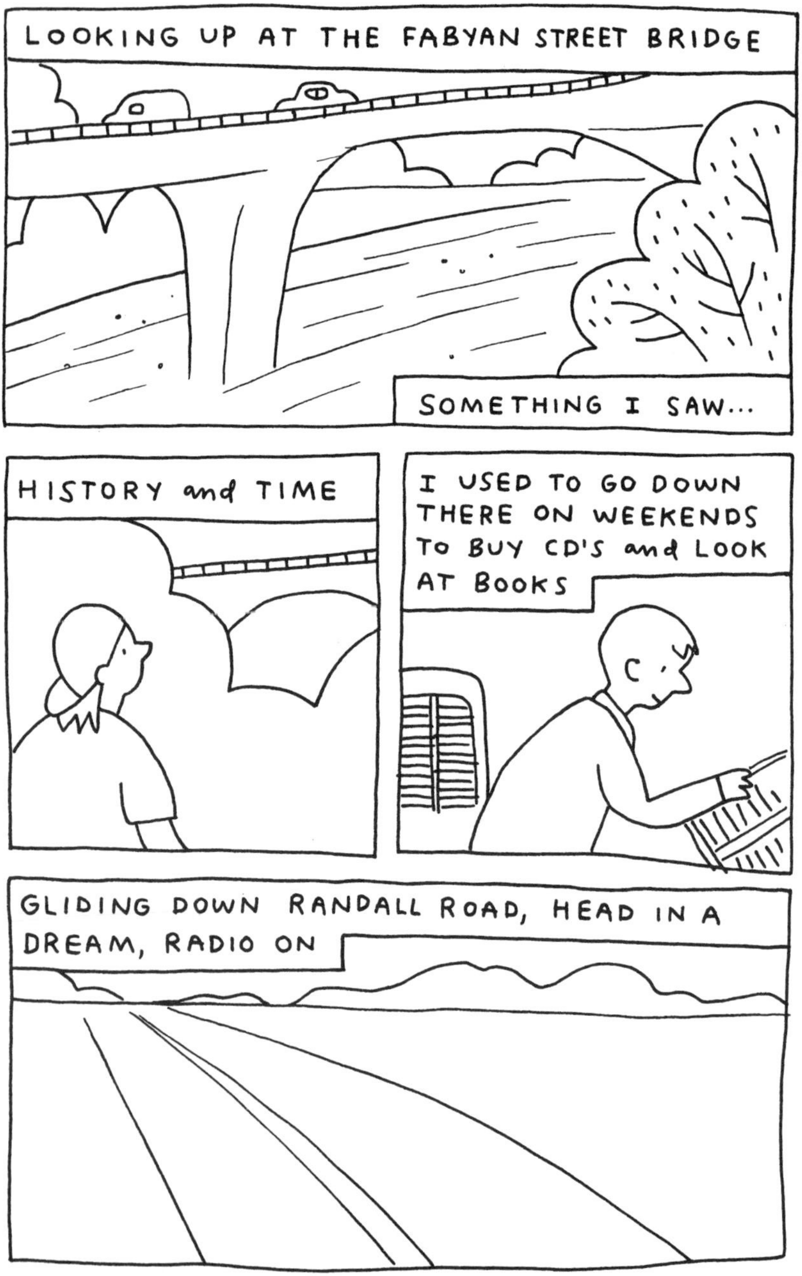
LOOKING UP AT THE FABYAN STREET BRIDGE
SOMETHING I SAW...
HISTORY and TIME
I USED TO GO DOWN THERE ON WEEKENDS TO BUY CD'S and LOOK AT BOOKS
GLIDING DOWN RANDALL ROAD, HEAD IN A DREAM, RADIO ON

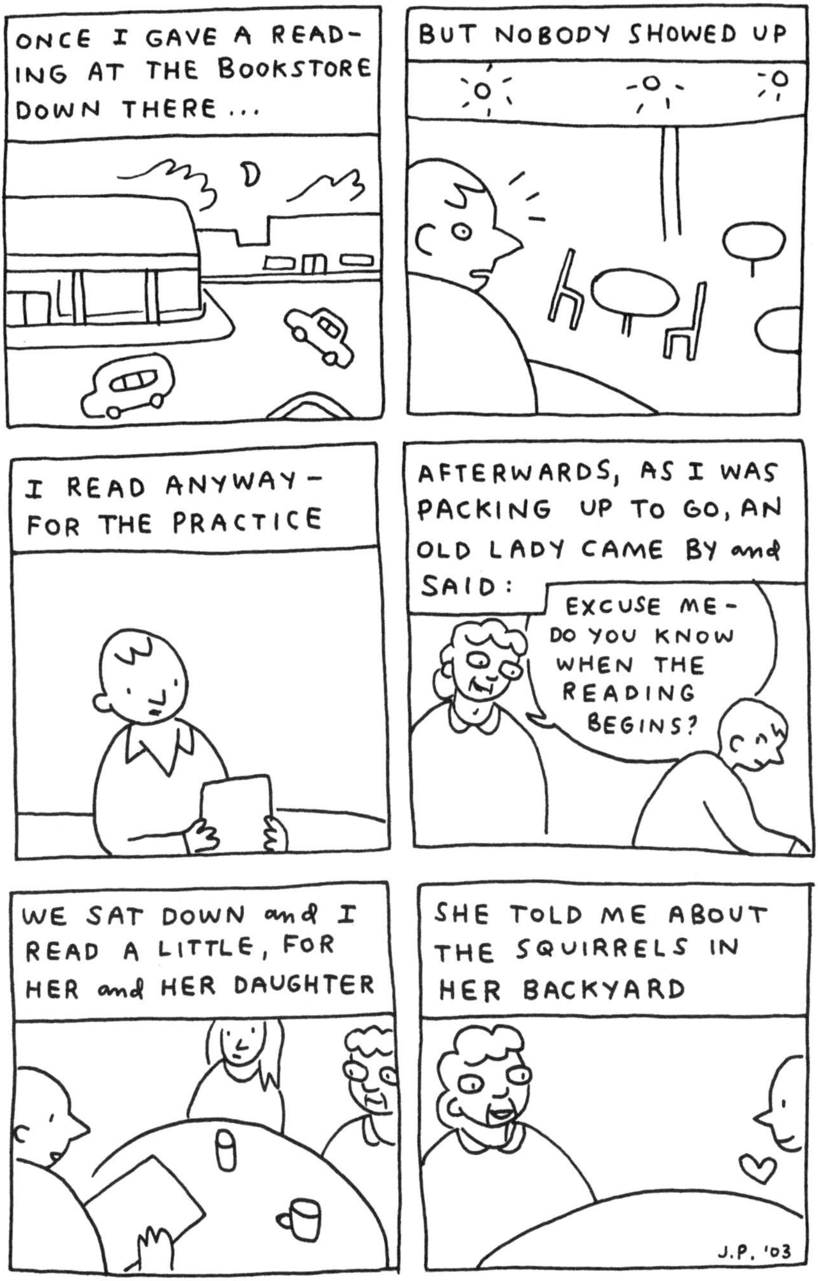
ONCE I GAVE A READING AT THE BOOKSTORE DOWN THERE...
BUT NOBODY SHOWED UP
I READ ANYWAY - FOR THE PRACTICE
AFTERWARDS, AS I WAS PACKING UP TO GO, AN OLD LADY CAME BY and SAID:
EXCUSE ME - DO YOU KNOW WHEN THE READING BEGINS?
WE SAT DOWN and I READ A LITTLE, FOR HER and HER DAUGHTER
SHE TOLD ME ABOUT THE SQUIRRELS IN HER BACKYARD
J.P. '03

A ZEN STORY Pai-Chang's "WILD DUCKS"

ONCE, PAI-CHANG WAS OUT WALKING WITH HIS MASTER, MA-TSU, WHEN A FLOCK OF WILD DUCKS FLEW PAST. MA-TSU SAID:

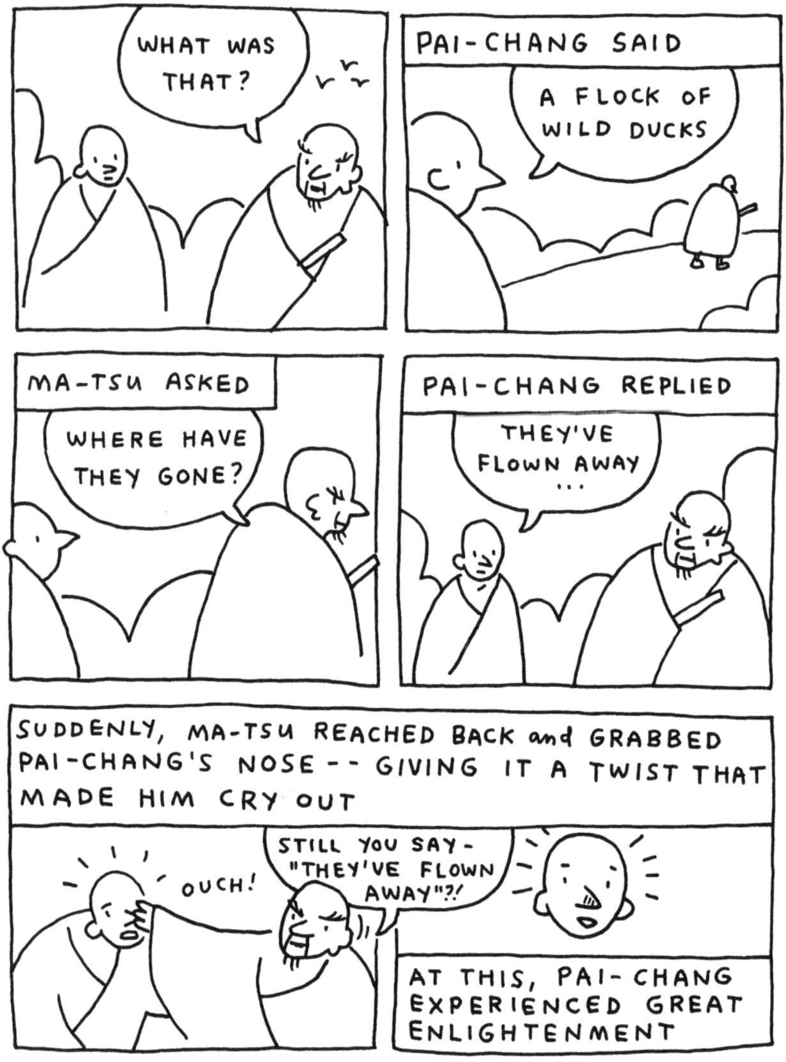

WHAT WAS THAT?
PAI-CHANG SAID
A FLOCK OF WILD DUCKS
MA-TSU ASKED
WHERE HAVE THEY GONE?
PAI-CHANG REPLIED
THEY'VE FLOWN AWAY ...
SUDDENLY, MA-TSU REACHED BACK and GRABBED PAI-CHANG'S NOSE -- GIVING IT A TWIST THAT MADE HIM CRY OUT
OUCH!
STILL YOU SAY - "THEY'VE FLOWN AWAY"?!
AT THIS, PAI-CHANG EXPERIENCED GREAT ENLIGHTENMENT

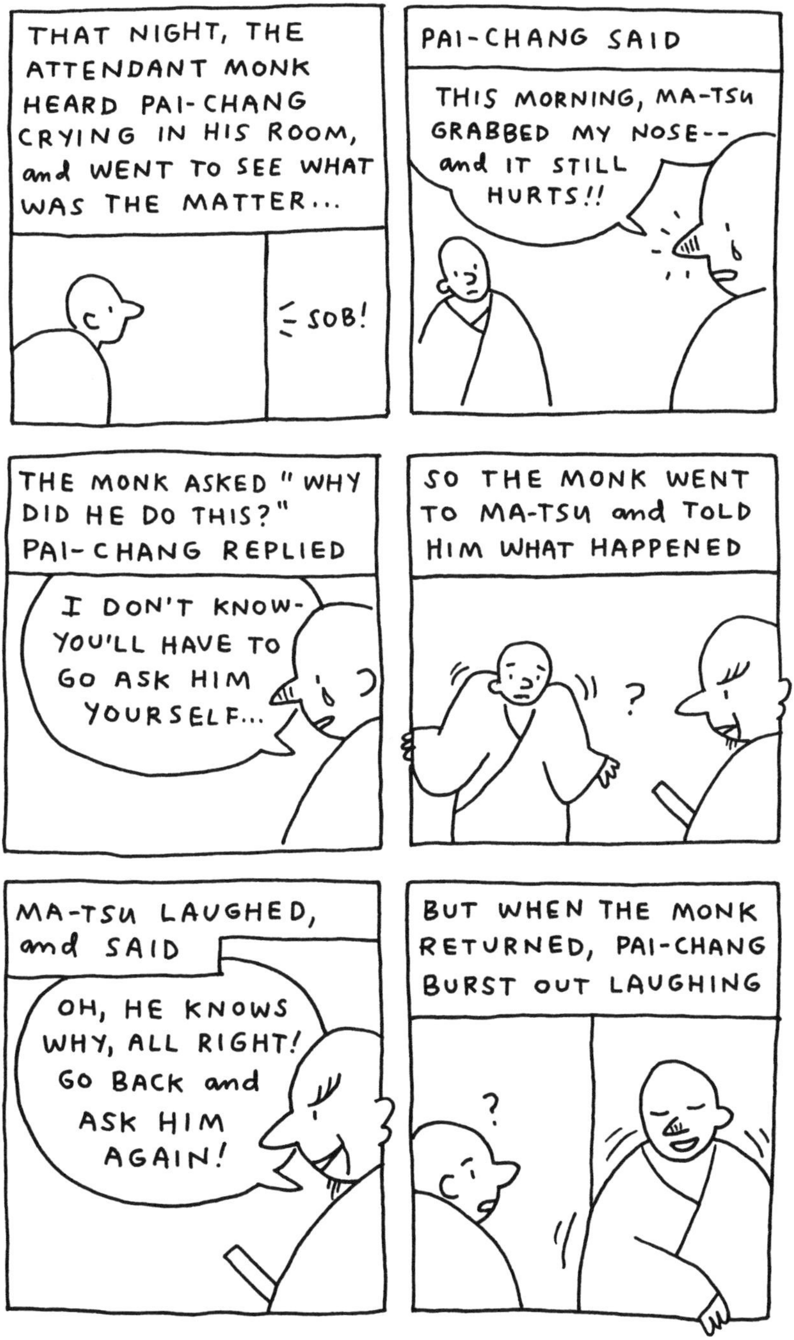
THAT NIGHT, THE ATTENDANT MONK HEARD PAI-CHANG CRYING IN HIS ROOM, and WENT TO SEE WHAT WAS THE MATTER...
SOB!
PAI-CHANG SAID
THIS MORNING, MA-TSU GRABBED MY NOSE-- and IT STILL HURTS!!
THE MONK ASKED "WHY DID HE DO THIS?" PAI-CHANG REPLIED
I DON'T KNOW- YOU'LL HAVE TO GO ASK HIM YOURSELF...
SO THE MONK WENT TO MA-TSU and TOLD HIM WHAT HAPPENED
?
MA-TSU LAUGHED, and SAID
OH, HE KNOWS WHY, ALL RIGHT! GO BACK and ASK HIM AGAIN!
BUT WHEN THE MONK RETURNED, PAI-CHANG BURST OUT LAUGHING
?

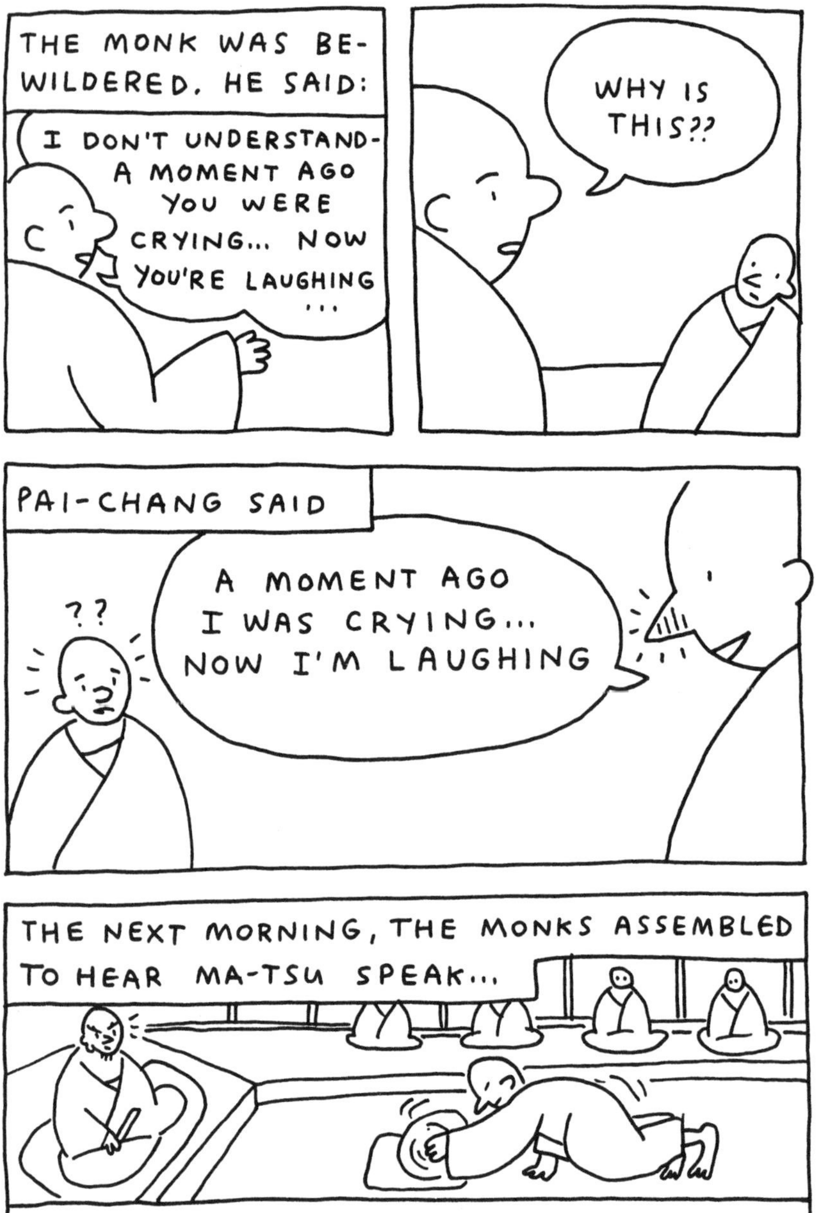

THE MONK WAS BE-WILDERED. HE SAID:
I DON'T UNDERSTAND- A MOMENT AGO YOU WERE CRYING... NOW YOU'RE LAUGHING ...
WHY IS THIS??
PAI-CHANG SAID
A MOMENT AGO I WAS CRYING... NOW I'M LAUGHING
??
THE NEXT MORNING, THE MONKS ASSEMBLED TO HEAR MA-TSU SPEAK...
BUT BEFORE HE HAD SPOKEN ONE WORD, PAI-CHANG CAME FORWARD and ROLLED UP THE BOWING MAT...

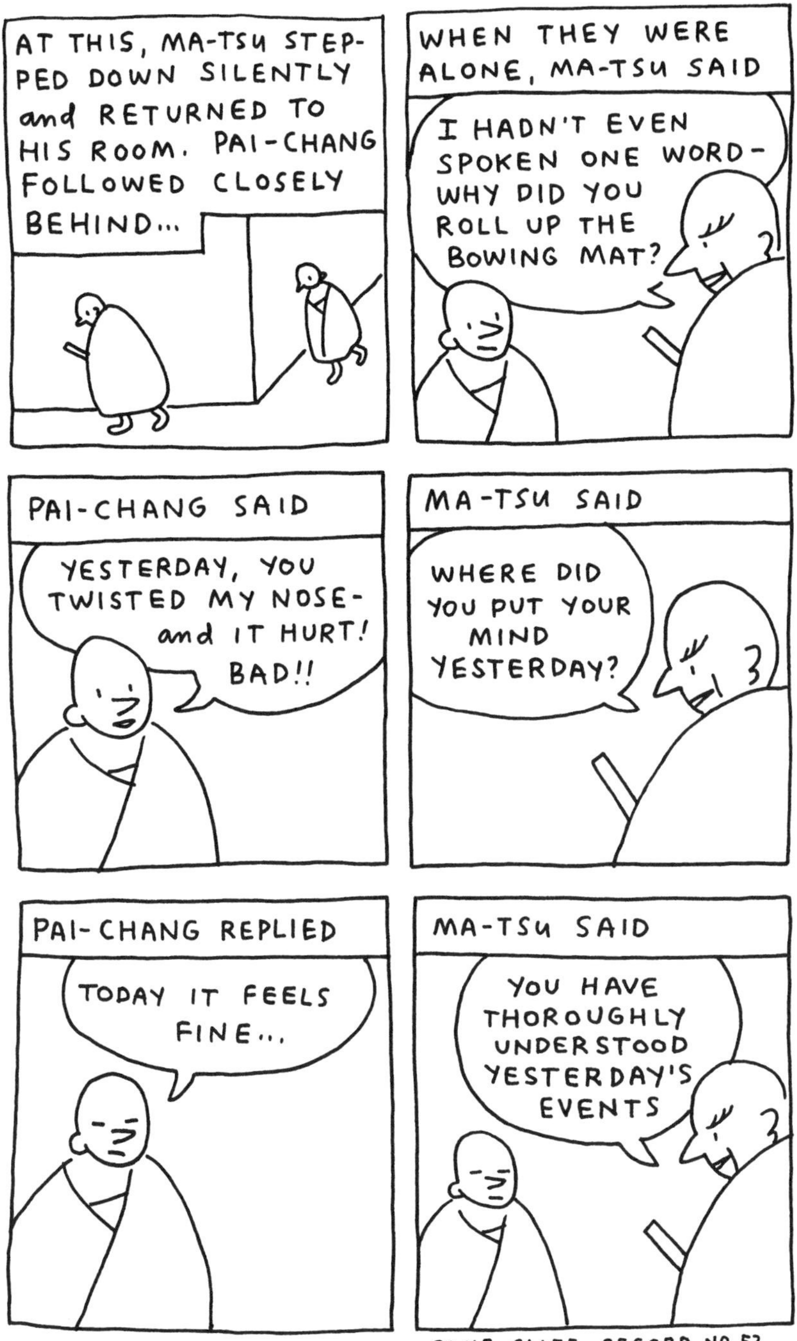
AT THIS, MA-TSU STEPPED DOWN SILENTLY and RETURNED TO HIS ROOM. PAI-CHANG FOLLOWED CLOSELY BEHIND...
WHEN THEY WERE ALONE, MA-TSU SAID
I HADN'T EVEN SPOKEN ONE WORD- WHY DID YOU ROLL UP THE BOWING MAT?
PAI-CHANG SAID
YESTERDAY, YOU TWISTED MY NOSE- and IT HURT! BAD!!
MA-TSU SAID
WHERE DID YOU PUT YOUR MIND YESTERDAY?
PAI-CHANG REPLIED
TODAY IT FEELS FINE...
MA-TSU SAID
YOU HAVE THOROUGHLY UNDERSTOOD YESTERDAY'S EVENTS

BLUE CLIFF RECORD NO. 53

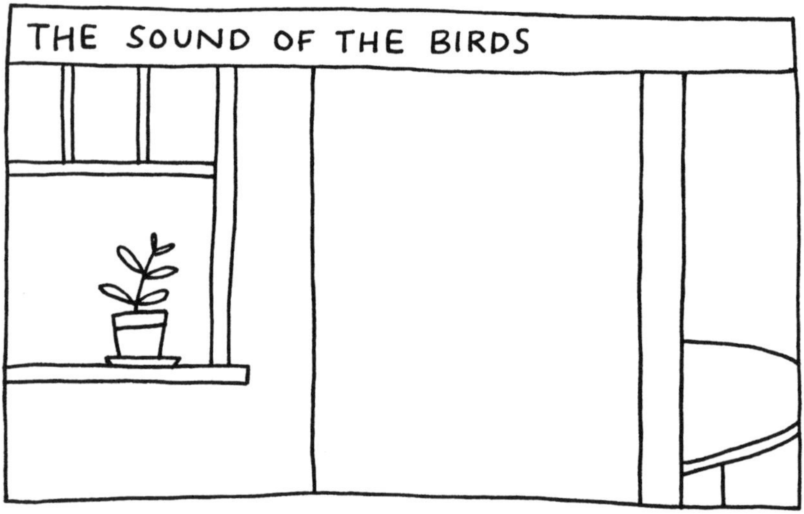
THE SOUND OF THE BIRDS

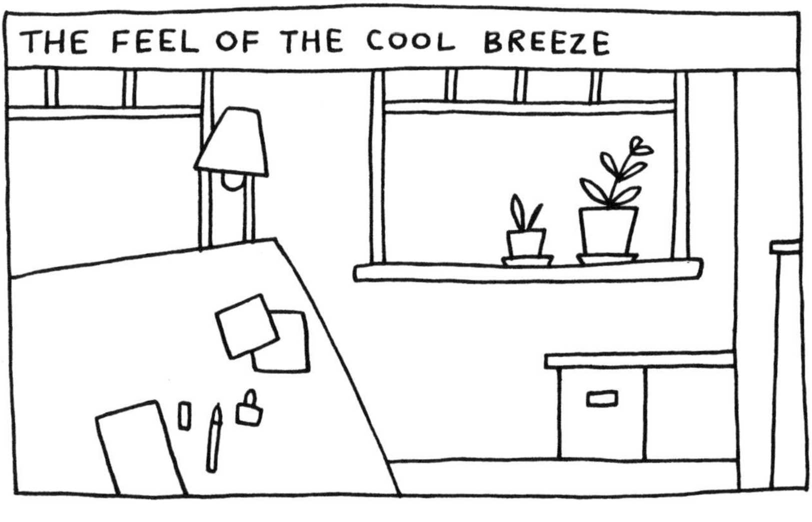
THE FEEL OF THE COOL BREEZE

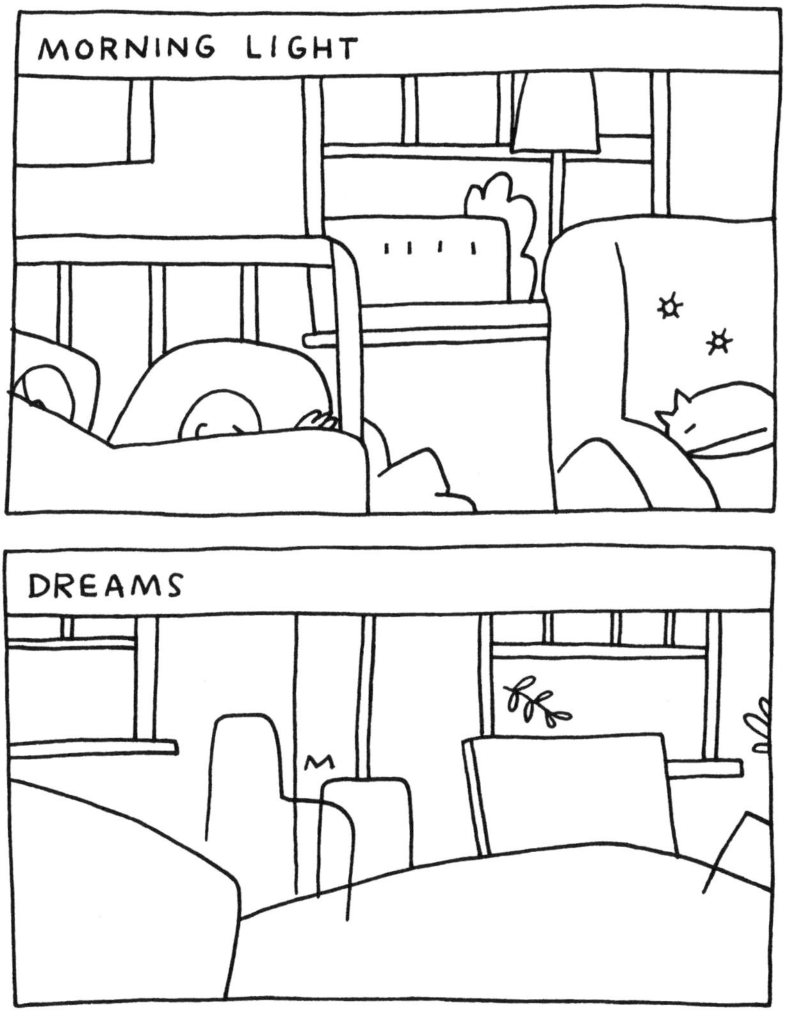
MORNING LIGHT
DREAMS
M

MAY 2003

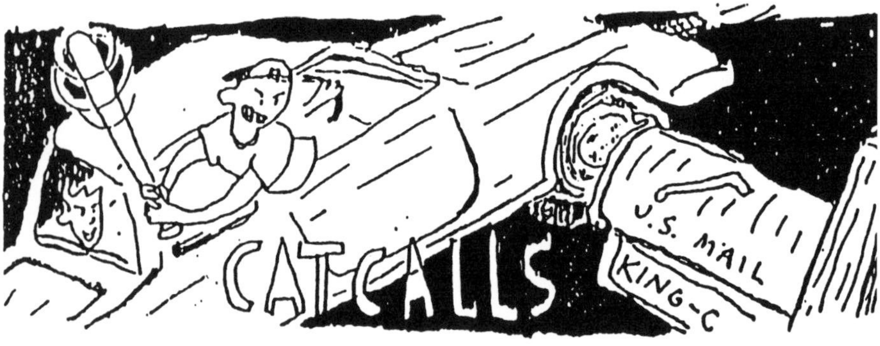
CATCALLS
U.S. MAIL
KING-C

Hey John

Just got done with the dishes. Went for a bike Ride and got called a "fucker" by someone in a Red Sports car... Also, saw a boy with his dog down by the River. He was this wiry ten year old out with this huge curly black dog. The boy was throwing sticks into the River for the dog to jump into the water and fetch. The dog wouldn't do it, though. It would just stand there completely still and stare intently at the stick as it floated away. The kid even tried pushing the dog in by its backside, but the dog wouldn't budge. →

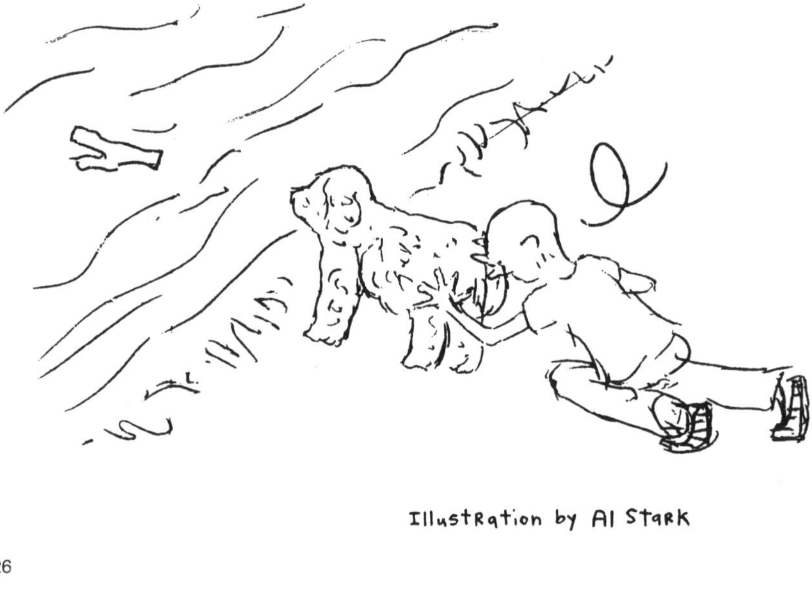

Illustration by Al Stark

Went out to Shabbona Park with Elinor yesterday. My dad said they'd built a new footbridge along one of the paths, and dug up a lot of dirt, so we went out to see if any arrowheads had been uncovered.

Anyhow, it was in the low 70's out yesterday but people were still out on the lake ice fishing, so we took a nervous shortcut across the ice. I found an old ice hole and stuck my arm down it to feel how thick the ice was... it was still a foot thick or so.

So we found the footbridge, but no arrowheads.

✳ ✳ ✳

One thing I like about the Hardware store [where he works-ed.] are all the undercurrents of life that are always going on. There's the patch of crabgrass growing out of the side of the building behind the dumpster that refuses to die, remaining bright green and lush, even in winter... there's the way customers are always seeming to run into each other after not seeing each other for years... there's the bag of grass seed in the backstock area that spilled onto a bag of potting soil ripped open on one end... wet from a leak in the foundation, that grew a patch of grass under the store lights... it grew for months and nobody cleaned it up... there's the way people are always coming in to have keys made all at the same time... there's the lonely old ladies bringing in their broken old lamps to have them fixed, or their husbands who cannot walk without a cane(s) who still want to buy two-hundred pounds of Sakrete or a snowshovel... there's the spider that lives below the caulk, catching Pill Bugs and Giant flies who is not there any longer because he was swept away on Saturday... There are so many people that seem like flawed characters in a perfect play, that come in and out of the store... I really love the place, but I don't get any dental insurance.
                                Love,

                    Al Stark - Dekalb, Ill.

27

THE KING-CAT TOP FORTY SUMMER 2002 TO SUMMER 2003

1. MISUN & MAISIE ♥
2. WEDDING BELLS! Sunday June 29, 2003
3. FROM ELVIS IN MEMPHIS - Elvis Presley (RCA Records, 1969) ★★★★★
4. Hank Mobley ROLL CALL (Blue Note / RVG Reissue)
5. OWL AT HOME by Norman Lobel ♥ (Harper Trophy) (As Read by Misun Oh)
6. Shunryu Suzuki Roshi: NOT ALWAYS SO and TO SHINE ONE CORNER OF THE WORLD (Harper Collins & Broadway Books)
7. KALE - why did I wait 34 years to try it??

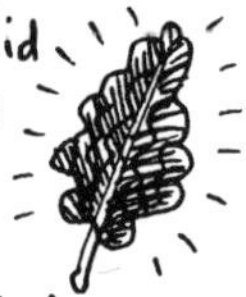

8. Thoreau: A Life of the Mind Excellent Biography by Robt. D. Richardson, JR. (U. of Calif. Press)
9. The Essential Charlie Rich Great, career spanning 2-CD set (Epic / Legacy) ★★★★★
10. DOING THE DISHES ♥
11. MARK TWAIN (PBS Home Video and Book)
12. DEPRESSION FREE NATURALLY by Joan Mathews-Larsen (Ballantine)
13. Saturday Night Fever Movie and Soundtrack

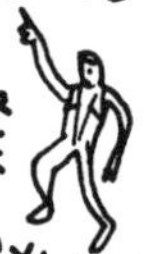

14. thinking about BOB DYLAN
15. the Beatles - "there's a Place" (Capitol / EMI) ★★★★★ AND: Revolution in the Head - The Beatles Records and the Sixties Ian MacDonald (Henry Holt)
16. Sonny Rollins - WAY OUT WEST (Contemporary)
17. The Young Ones T.V. Show (BBC Home Video) still cracks me up! ★★★★★
18. LEEKS
19. Nutrition & Mental Illness DR. Carl C. Pfeiffer, M.D. (Healing Arts Press)
20. Van Morrison - TUPELO HONEY (Polydor)
21. "Don't Say Nothin' Bad About My Baby" - the Cookies (Late Night Oldies Radio) ★★★★★
22. MAD Magazine! Yeah! (still funny!)
23. D.T. Suzuki the Awakening of Zen (Shambhala Books)
24. Toward a Psychology of Being - Abraham Maslowe (Van Nostrand Reinhold)
25. TAOIST MEDITATION and MINDING MIND - thos. Cleary, trans. (Shambhala)
26. MUNG BEAN NOODLES

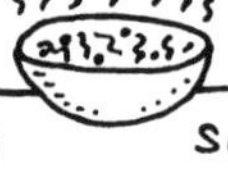

MAKE SOUP!

~ MORE TOP FORTY ~

27. CATALPA TREES
    ᗒ♥ᗕ

28. MORE ELVIS: the Memphis
    Record, Rhythm & Country,
    the Lost Album etc etc!!
    (RCA Records) ★★★★★

29. Denver Public Library!

30. COMICS ♡ 🎮 🐱 📚

31. Claude Monet - Water Lilies
    (paintings)

32. Staying up late to watch
    "Kiss me Kate" with Misun
    (T.V. Show - BBC/PBS)

33. FRANK SINATRA - More
    Reprise L.P.s: Moonlight
    Sinatra (thanx Jason!),
    the World we knew, Swingin'
    Brass, That's Life, Sinatra
    and Strings (Reprise Recs.)

34. Dainin Katagiri Roshi:
    You Have to Say Something
    (Shambhala)

35. SCARLET RUNNER ★
    Organic Canned Beans
    (Westbrae Natural Foods)
    ... never saw a Bean quite
    like it!! 🫘 🫘 🫘

36. Clouds, sky, Birds,
    Squirrels, leaves, Street-
    Lights, Everything!

37. Etc.   38. (LOVE)

FILLER™ PRESENTS:

TODAY FOR A MOMENT AT WORK—

I THOUGHT I HEARD "DON'T GO BACK TO ROCKVILLE" ON THE STORE RADIO

(NOPE.)

3/12/03 J.P.

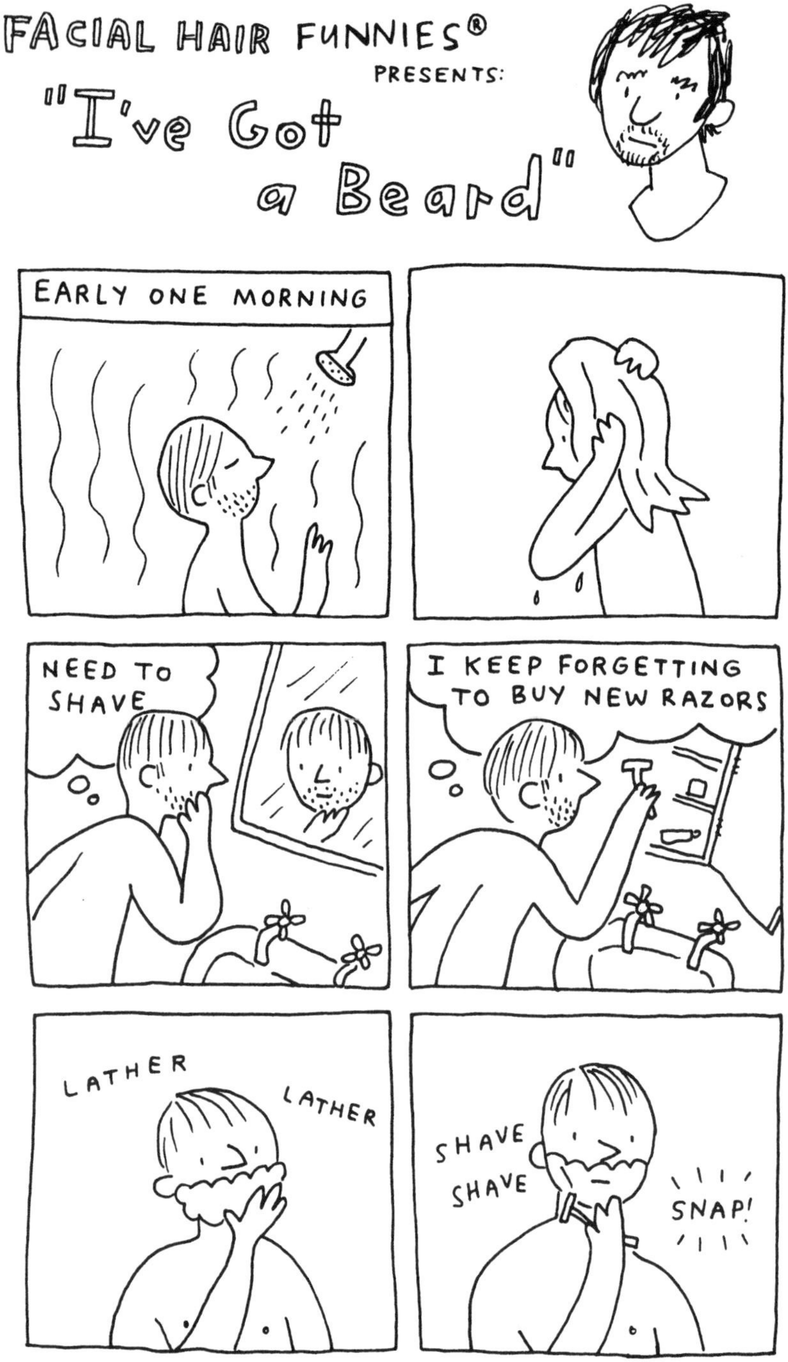
FACIAL HAIR FUNNIES®
PRESENTS:
"I've Got a Beard"
EARLY ONE MORNING
NEED TO SHAVE
I KEEP FORGETTING TO BUY NEW RAZORS
LATHER
LATHER
SHAVE
SHAVE
SNAP!

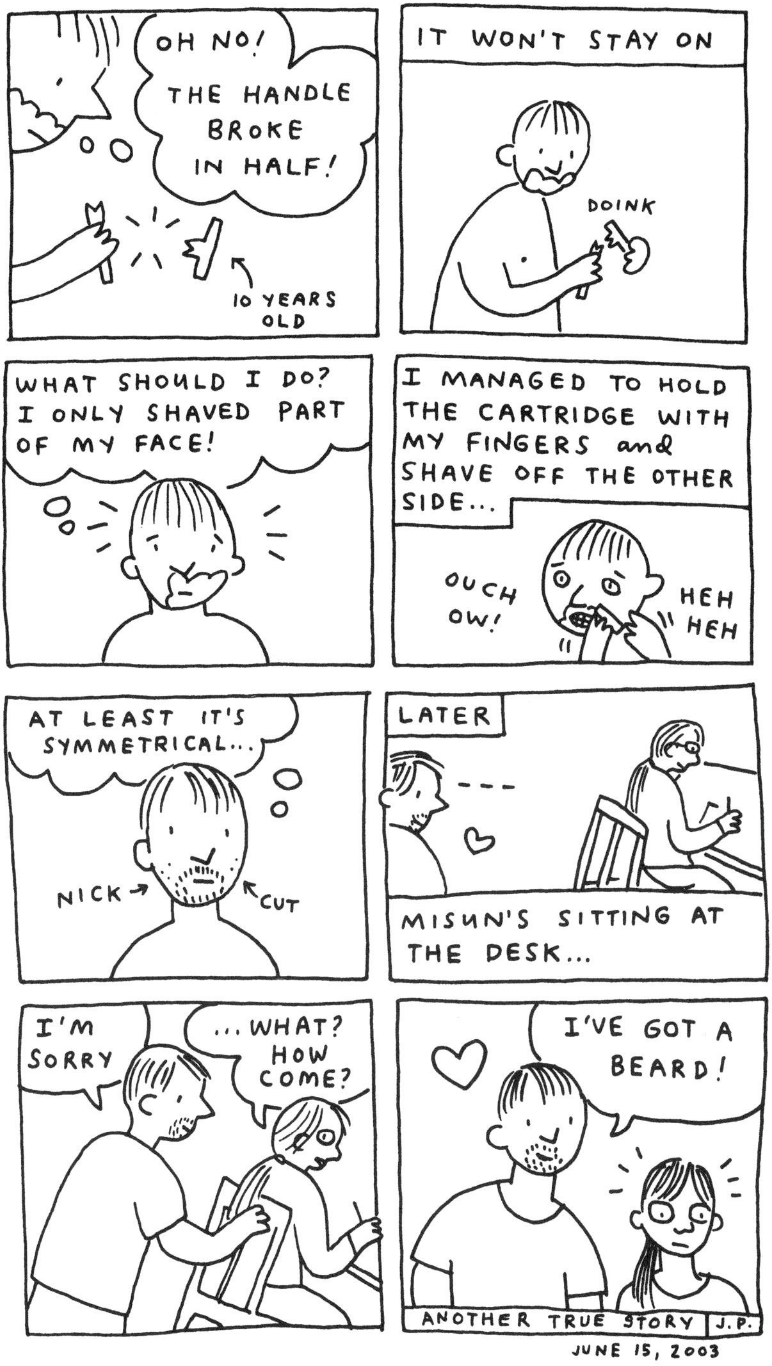
OH NO!
THE HANDLE BROKE IN HALF!
10 YEARS OLD
IT WON'T STAY ON
DOINK
WHAT SHOULD I DO? I ONLY SHAVED PART OF MY FACE!
I MANAGED TO HOLD THE CARTRIDGE WITH MY FINGERS and SHAVE OFF THE OTHER SIDE...
OUCH OW!
HEH HEH
AT LEAST IT'S SYMMETRICAL...
NICK
CUT
LATER

MISUN'S SITTING AT THE DESK...
I'M SORRY
...WHAT? HOW COME?
I'VE GOT A BEARD!
ANOTHER TRUE STORY
J.P.
JUNE 15, 2003

CATALPA TREES

Lately I fell in love with the Catalpa Trees;
you see - every Spring the air is filled with this
unusual odor, and I always wondered what it
was. Someone said it's unpleasant - Now, I
don't know, but Misun got it pretty close when
she said it smelled like the inside of a pumpkin.
It turns out this smell is the smell of the
Catalpa Tree in bloom.

We were walking down the street one day and
the Catalpa Trees were in bloom — Gorgeous
white billowing snowballs of flowers against
the huge, green, heart-shaped leaves. And the
smell: Catalpas, So I fell in love.

One day when I called my parents to say hello,
I asked my Dad about the Catalpa Tree. He said:

"I had a Catalpa Tree in the middle of the front
yard on Maypole Avenue — with the cigars - we
used to smoke them - didn't you know? We called
them Indian Cigars. I loved Catalpa Trees,
with the big flowers — and good branches for
climbing... Kids could put a swing on those
branches. You don't see them around much out
here, but in the old neighborhood... I loved
Catalpa Trees - but then, I love anything green-
all of it..."

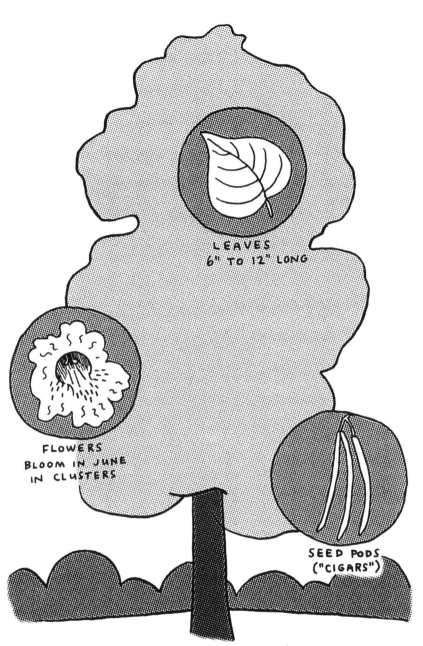

LEAVES
6" TO 12" LONG

FLOWERS
BLOOM IN JUNE
IN CLUSTERS

SEED PODS
("CIGARS")

CATALPA SPECIOSA
(FAMILY BIGNONIACEAE)

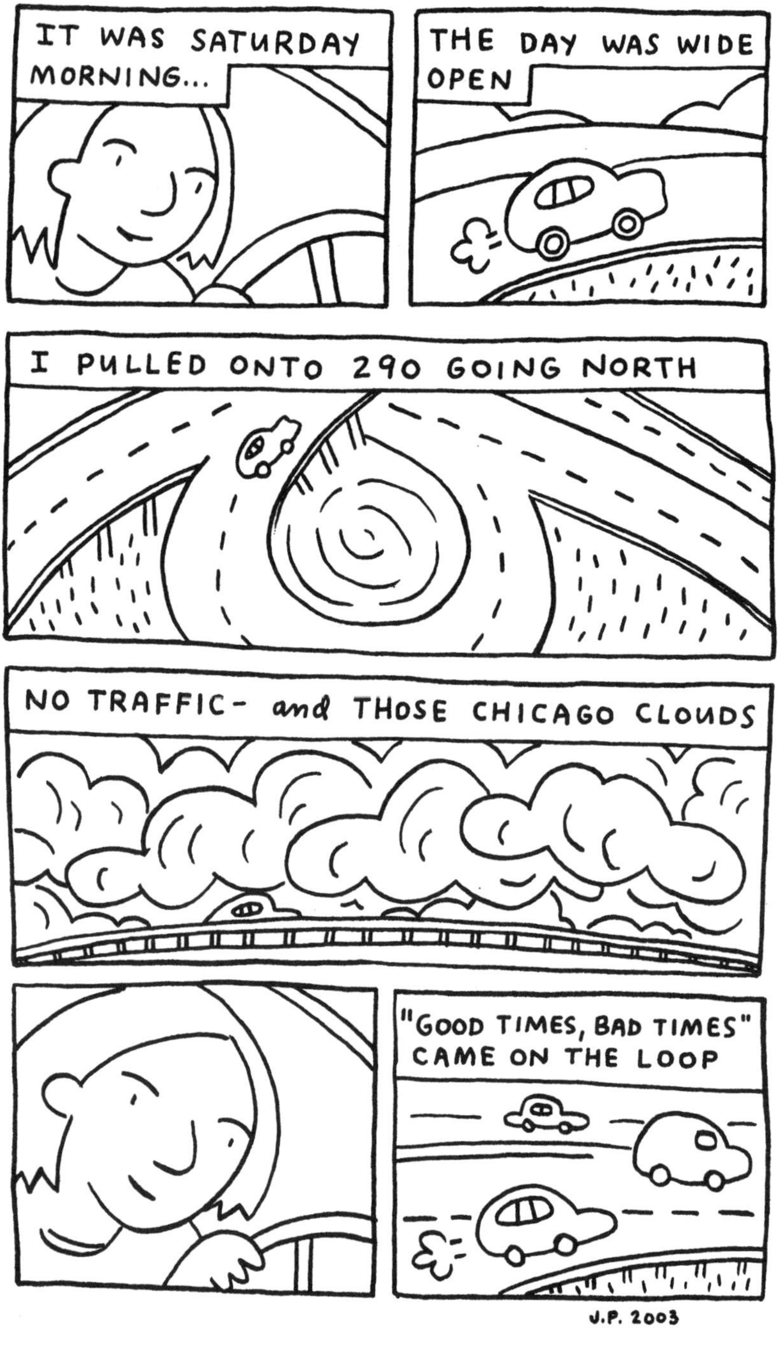
IT WAS SATURDAY MORNING...
THE DAY WAS WIDE OPEN
I PULLED ONTO 290 GOING NORTH
NO TRAFFIC- and THOSE CHICAGO CLOUDS
"GOOD TIMES, BAD TIMES" CAME ON THE LOOP
J.P. 2003

Trombones № 1

(please Read slowly)

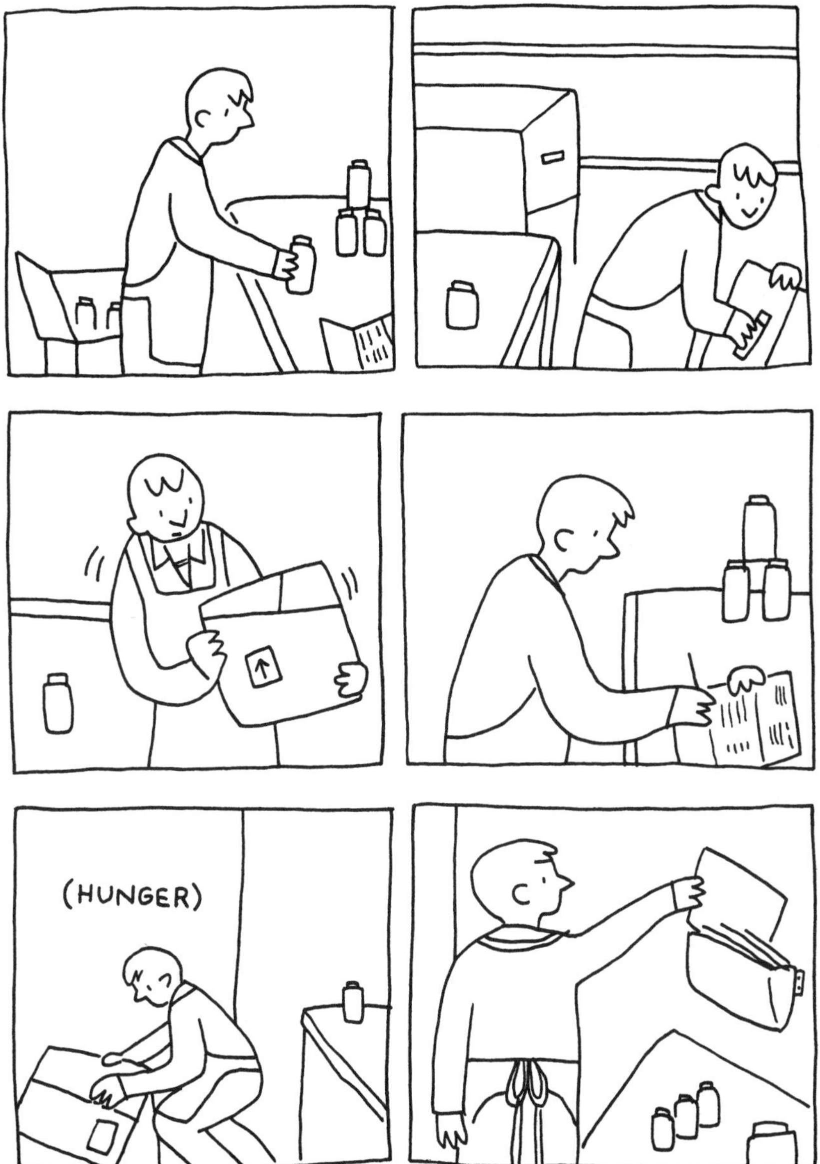
(HUNGER)

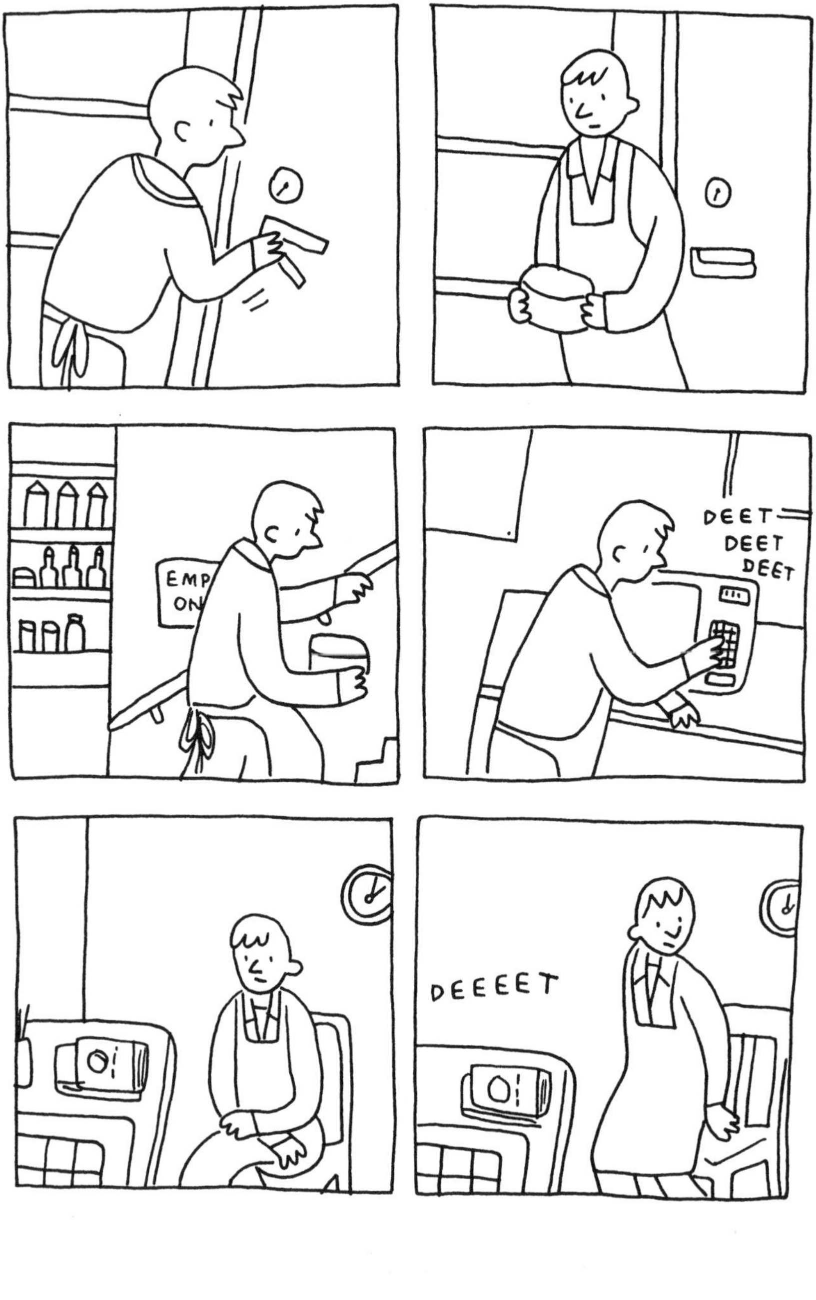
EMP
ON
DEET
DEET
DEET
DEEEET

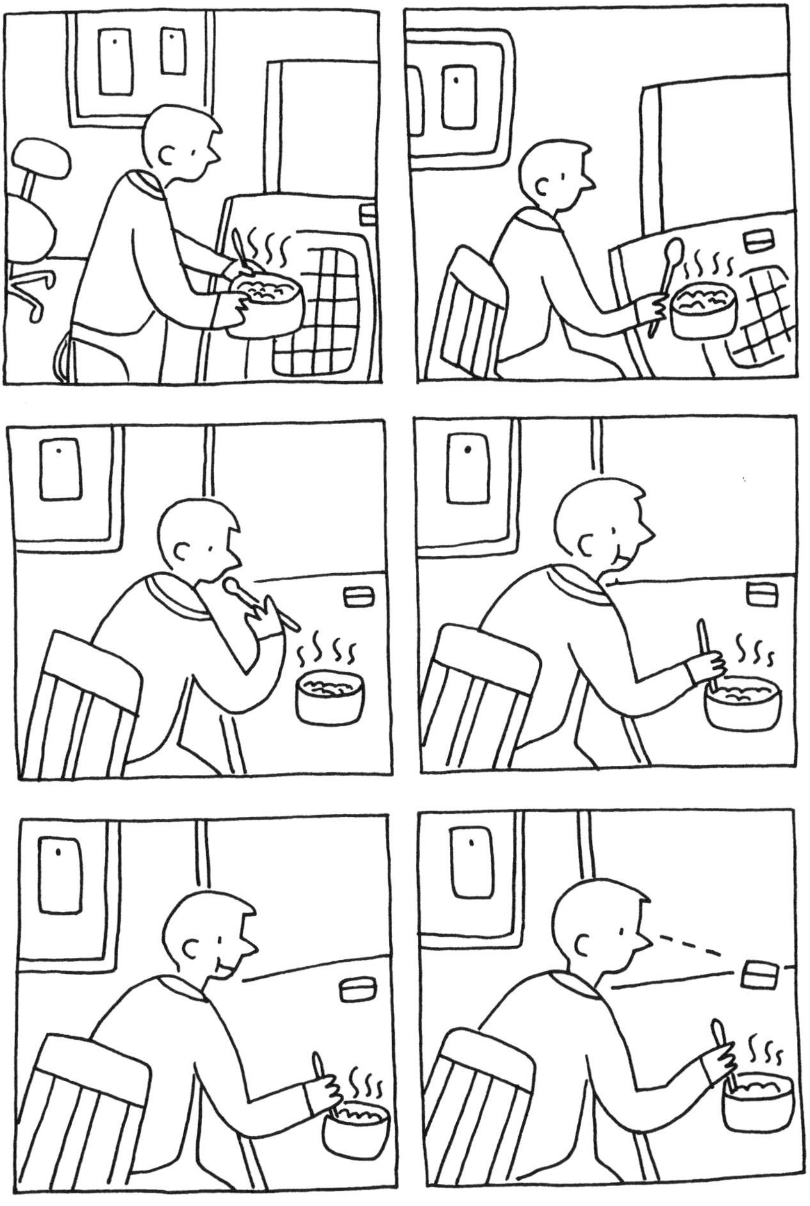

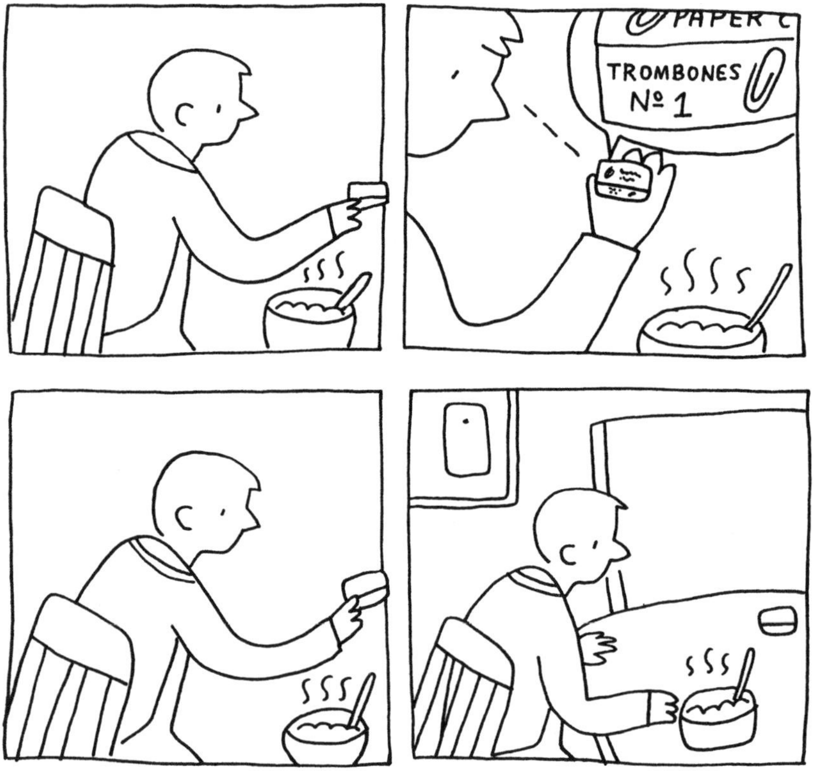
PAPER C
TROMBONES
Nº 1

JULY 12, 2003

Pingree Grove

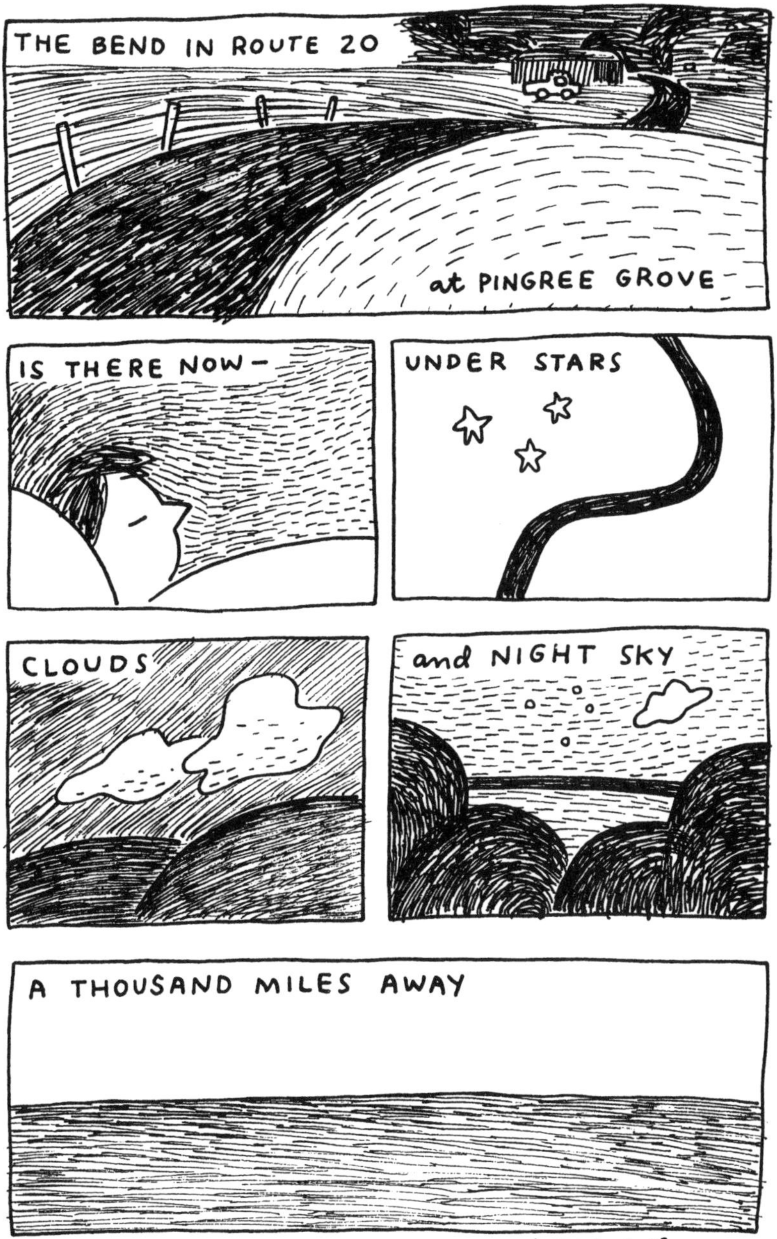
THE BEND IN ROUTE 20
at PINGREE GROVE
IS THERE NOW—
UNDER STARS
CLOUDS
and NIGHT SKY
A THOUSAND MILES AWAY
JOHN P. 6-03

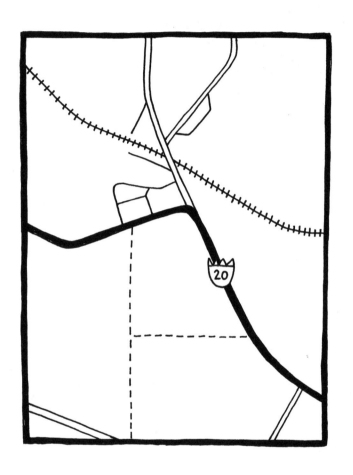

KING-CAT

COMICS & STORIES

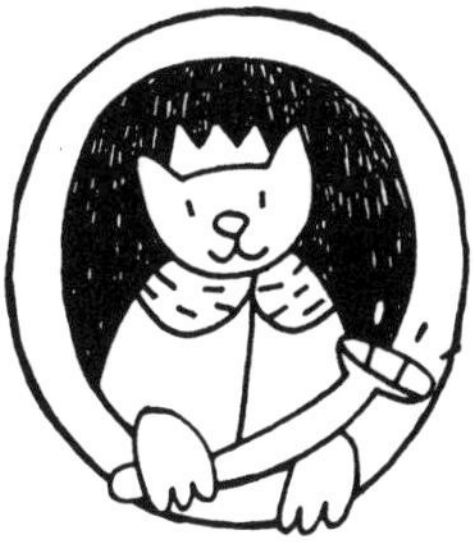

NUMBER 63 $2.50

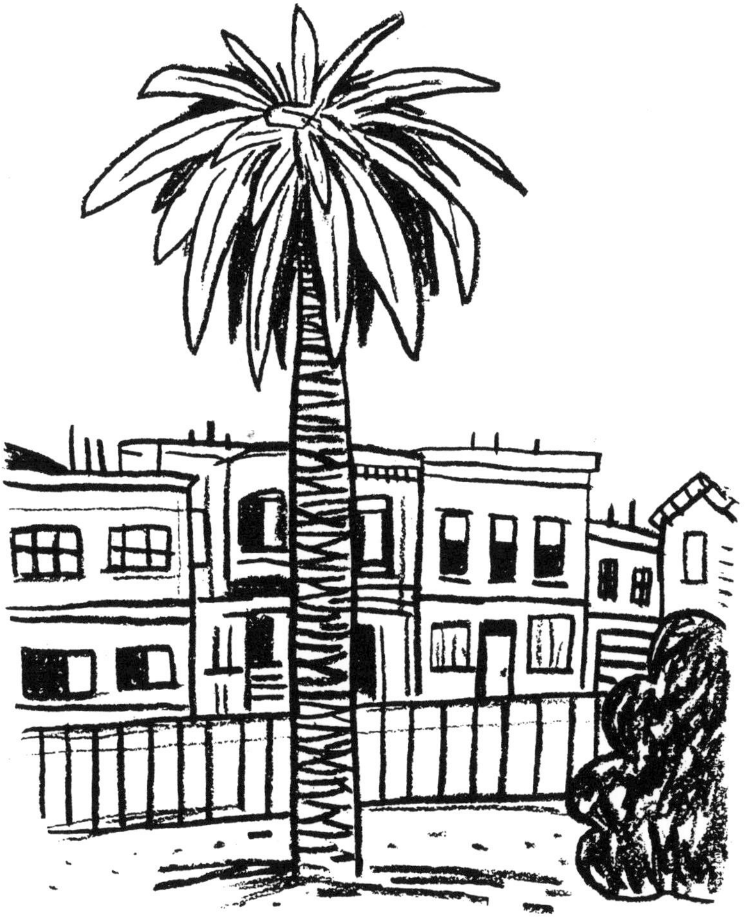

BY JOHN PORCELLINO

✳ KING-CAT SNORNOSE 63 ✳

WELL, MY FRIENDS — another issue, another city — After a lot of soul-searching, and much prose and conning, Misun and I made the decision: We packed up all our stuff again, and, after only one year in Denver, we moved to San Francisco.

I was of course really worried about it — about the expense, about being so far away from "home" (Chicago), about everything. But it was the way things were going, and when things are going a certain way I guess you can either go with them or you can resist them... we went with them, to California.

SO — one Saturday in late November, as they often do, our friends came over and helped us load the rental truck. We said goodbye, and climbed aboard, heading south down I-25 toward New Mexico. We took the desert route — through Albuquerque and Las Cruces, across Arizona and into L.A., then up the Central Valley of California.

The trip was grueling — and magnificent: we saw cactuses and crows, mountains, sky and pink hotels. Maisie sat on my lap the whole time and purred. Misun manned the radio. We drove and drove. By the time we got to San Francisco, five days later, we were baggy-eyed, sore, and thouroughly wasted... but we were home.

I'D BEEN TO SAN FRANCISCO a few times before, but I wasn't sure what it would be like to actually live there... As it turns out, I feel strangely at ease... the hills, the streets, the buildings and the sky all feel so right to me... and the beauty and creative spirit I've found here have been really inspiring — so there you go... In celebration, here's a short list of some of the things I love about our new city:

- the spice trees
- the bottle-brush trees
- All the trees
- Palm trees
- Flowers Everywhere
- Golden Gate Park
- Riding the bus
- the Mt. Sutro tower

- Bougainvillaeas
- St. Ignatius Church (lit up all beautiful at night)
- walking past the Jefferson Airplane House, and thinking to myself: "I'm walking past the Jefferson Airplane House"
- coming around a corner, and catching an unexpected glimpse of the ocean, or one of the bridges
- the ocean · the air · the fog

KING-CAT COMICS No. 63 -- PUBLISHED IN AUG. 2004 BY - S P I T and a HALF: ███████████

SAN FRANCISCO, CA ████ -- U.S.A.

www.king-cat.net

PLEASE NOTE OUR NEW ADDRESS!!

PLUM BLOSSOMS

AT THE END OF JANUARY OR SO, all the plum trees in our neighborhood started blooming. The air was fragrant and full of life, the sidewalks were littered with pink petals. I'd walk around at night, up and down my new streets, getting their feel — the funny houses stacked up on top of each other, the hills, the wide sky. Everything felt fresh and new.

Listen to your footsteps on the street-
Plum trees are all in bloom

OR coming home from the Post Office in a wild rainstorm that blew my umbrella inside out; huddled under a doorway while dollops of rain pounded the pavement, laughing...

February downpour-
Plum petals stuck to my shoe

ONE DAY Misun came home with some plum branches... A lady on the street had been pruning her yard, and had given them to her. The dark branches were covered in little buds, with pink petals just starting to show. We put them in a vase, on the speaker by the T.V.

The next day we looked up from the Reality show we were watching and were startled to see that overnight, when no one was looking, the branches had burst into brilliant pink popcorn flowers. We both noticed it at the same time, and we both gasped at the same time.

Meanwhile, here's the new King-Cat! Hope you enjoy it!

Love,

John P.
San Francisco, CA

"Officially, there's not enough room for a needle... Privately, carts and horses are able to pass through."

— Tao ch'uan

- FRONT COVER: Palm tree; Bernal Heights, SF CA
- BACK COVER: the Mt. Sutro tower, as seen from our Rooftop

This issue marks King-Cat's 15 year anniversary - so I just wanted to say thank you, to everyone... Thanks!

HARDY MUMS

YOU NEVER HEAR HER PLAY HER PIANO ANYMORE

(THE REFLECTION OF TREES ON THE ROOF OF THE CAR)

YELLOW LEAVES

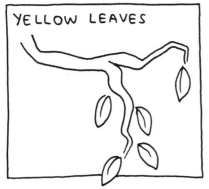

YELLOW FLOWERS

REMEMBER THE DAY YOU SAID I SAY THE WORD "ROOF" FUNNY and I ASKED MY DAD HOW TO SAY IT and HE SAID IT THE SAME WAY AS ME?

(HARDY MUMS).

NOV. 03/JAN. 04 – John P.

STUFF

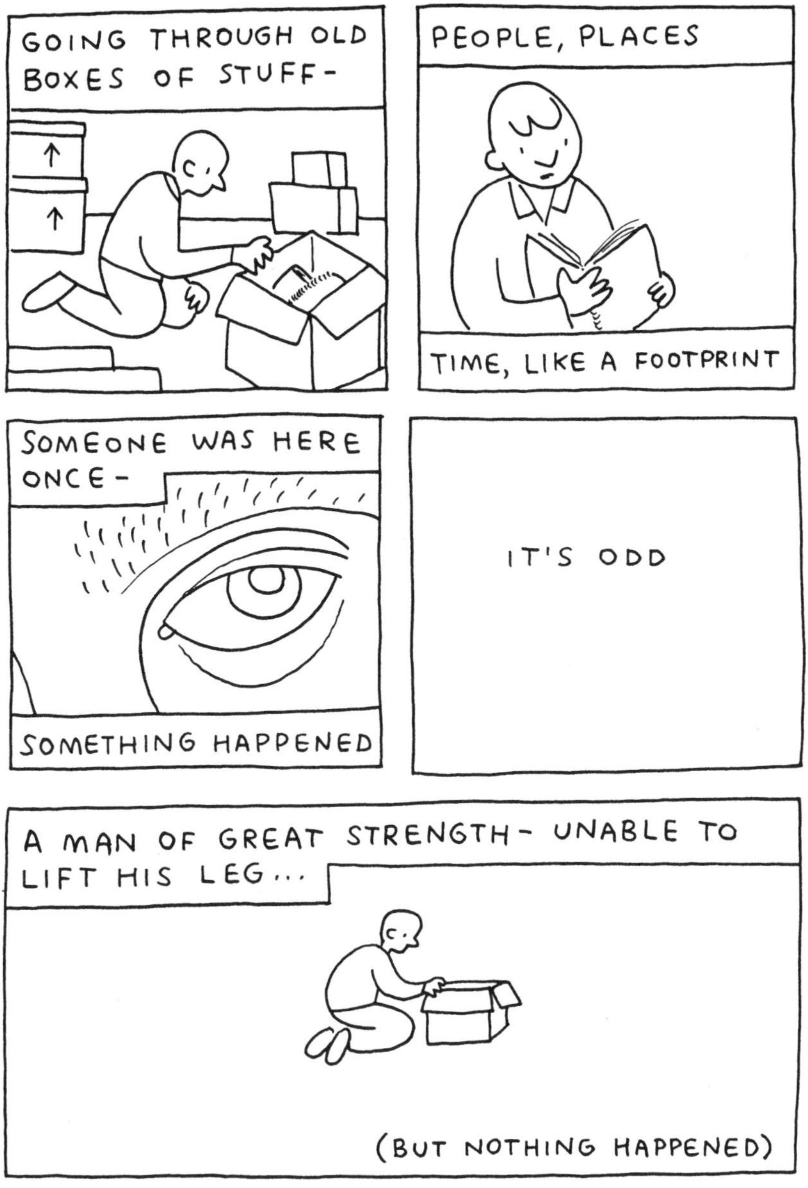

GOING THROUGH OLD BOXES OF STUFF-
PEOPLE, PLACES
TIME, LIKE A FOOTPRINT
SOMEONE WAS HERE ONCE-
SOMETHING HAPPENED
IT'S ODD
A MAN OF GREAT STRENGTH- UNABLE TO LIFT HIS LEG...
(BUT NOTHING HAPPENED)

DEC. 24 2003
JAN. 21 2004

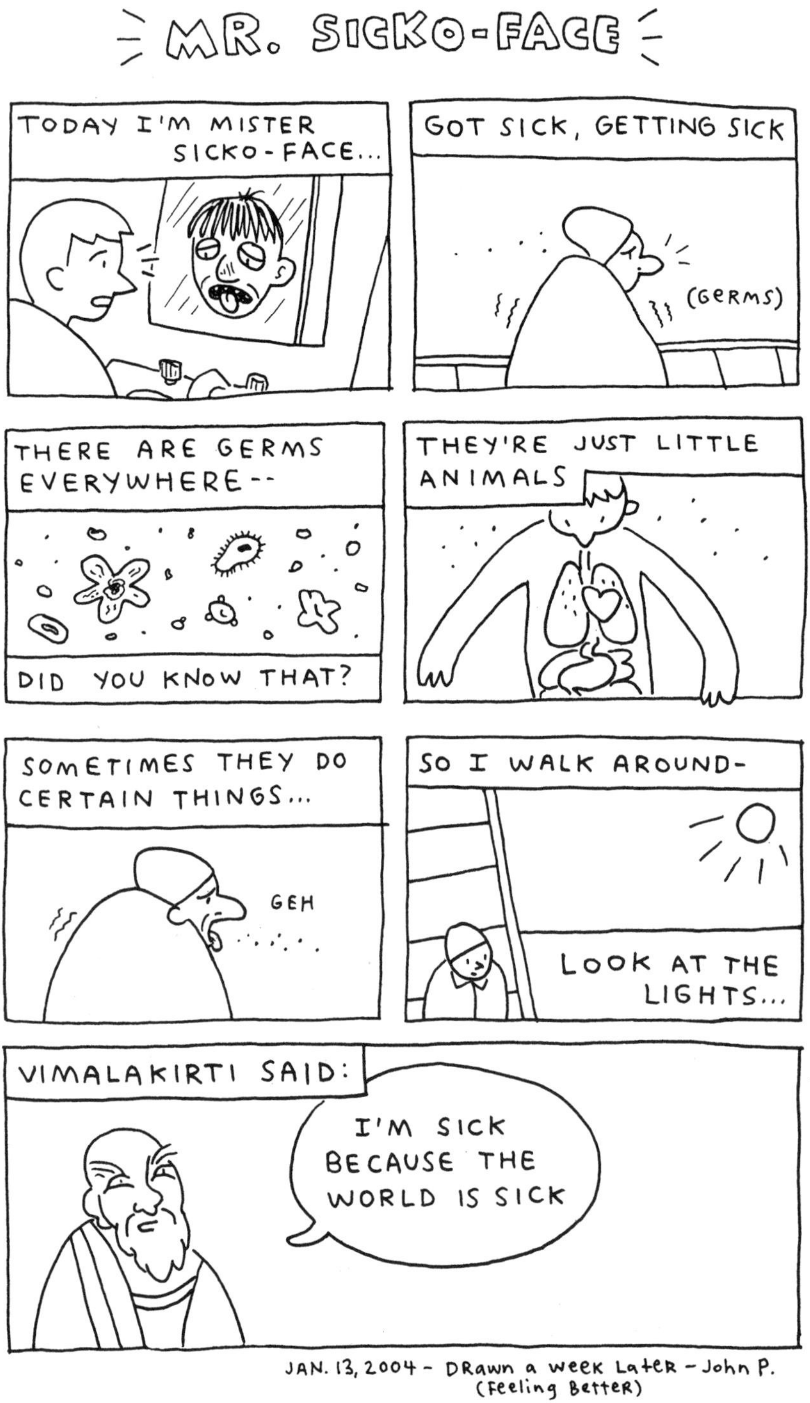
MR. SICKO-FACE
TODAY I'M MISTER SICKO-FACE...
GOT SICK, GETTING SICK
(GERMS)
THERE ARE GERMS EVERYWHERE--
DID YOU KNOW THAT?
THEY'RE JUST LITTLE ANIMALS
SOMETIMES THEY DO CERTAIN THINGS...
GEH
SO I WALK AROUND-
LOOK AT THE LIGHTS...
VIMALAKIRTI SAID:
I'M SICK BECAUSE THE WORLD IS SICK
JAN. 13, 2004 - DRAWN A WEEK LATER - John P.
(Feeling Better)

♪CALIFORNIA ROAD TRIP ♫
-ITINERARY and HIGHLIGHTS-

SUNDAY NOV. 30 – THURSDAY DEC. 4, 2003

- -

DAY ONE - Denver, CO – Las Vegas, NM (327 miles)
DAY TWO – Las Vegas, NM – Las Cruces, NM (342 mi.)
DAY THREE - Las Cruces, NM – Quartzsite, AZ (515 mi.)
DAY FOUR – Quartzsite, AZ – Lost Hills, CA (415 miles)
DAY FIVE – Lost Hills, CA – San Francisco, CA (238 mi.)

ALL MILEAGES ARE APPROXIMATE, and
SUBJECT TO CONSIDERABLE ERROR   **TOTAL: 1,837 mi.**

- -

SATURDAY EVENING we were running behind,
so we decided to stay one more night in Denver. That night
we walked out down Marion Street to the King Soopers
one last time. The air was cool and good, the Autumn
Moon shone down brightly between the branches. We
looked for Fast Charlie, but he wasn't around. That night
we slept on blankets on the floor.

Sunday we finished packing up the truck and cleaning the
apartment. We picked up Maisie and walked out, down
the steps where the bees lived, and into the truck,
heading South.

For the next five days we drove to California. It was
quite a trip. We had a cooler of food, water bottles,
trash bags and maps. We drove down through Colorado
Sagebrush hills at dusk, dusty red New Mexican plains,
Cactus, and the Arizona desert into California. The
Road stretched out before us, grey mountains on the
horizon. We listened to the radio.

One evening we were coming up the two-lane cutoff
north of Adelanto -- silence -- Maisie was asleep on my lap,
Misun was dozing beautifully in her seat. To the west
were Sunset Hills and the purple sky... to the east just
endless pink light fading into blue dust - and the
silhouettes of Joshua Trees standing quietly on the earth.

I sat in the truck, with my hands on the wheel. The
Road rolled away beneath us – it came forward to meet
us... I felt lucky to be alive.

o o o

KING-CAT TOP TEN

NOV. 30 – DEC. 4, 2003
CALIFORNIA ROAD TRIP

----

1. MY WIFE and MY CAT ♡
2. Moon over Raton Pass, 11/30
3. Barking dogs, cold wind, silence - 12/1 (A.M.)
   Las Vegas, NM
4. Neil Diamond - "Longfellow Serenade" (Radio
   Broadcast south of Los Lunas, NM)
5. Las Cruces, NM at night
6. Saguaros, ocotillos, chollas etc.
7. Sunset outside Phoenix, AZ 12/2
8. Crossing the River into California, morning
   of 12/3
9. Weird squirrels behind the IHOP,
   San Bernardino, CA
10. Joshua trees at dusk, Hwy 395
11. Fog over Tehachapi Pass
12. Coming down into Bakersfield and the
    air feels like a summer night in Illinois
13. Moss growing in the cracks between the
    lanes on Interstate 580
14. Crossing the Bay Bridge into SF in Rain
    and Fog
15. Pulling up next to Golden Gate Park and
    parking the truck - the scent of Eucalyptus,
    12/4/03

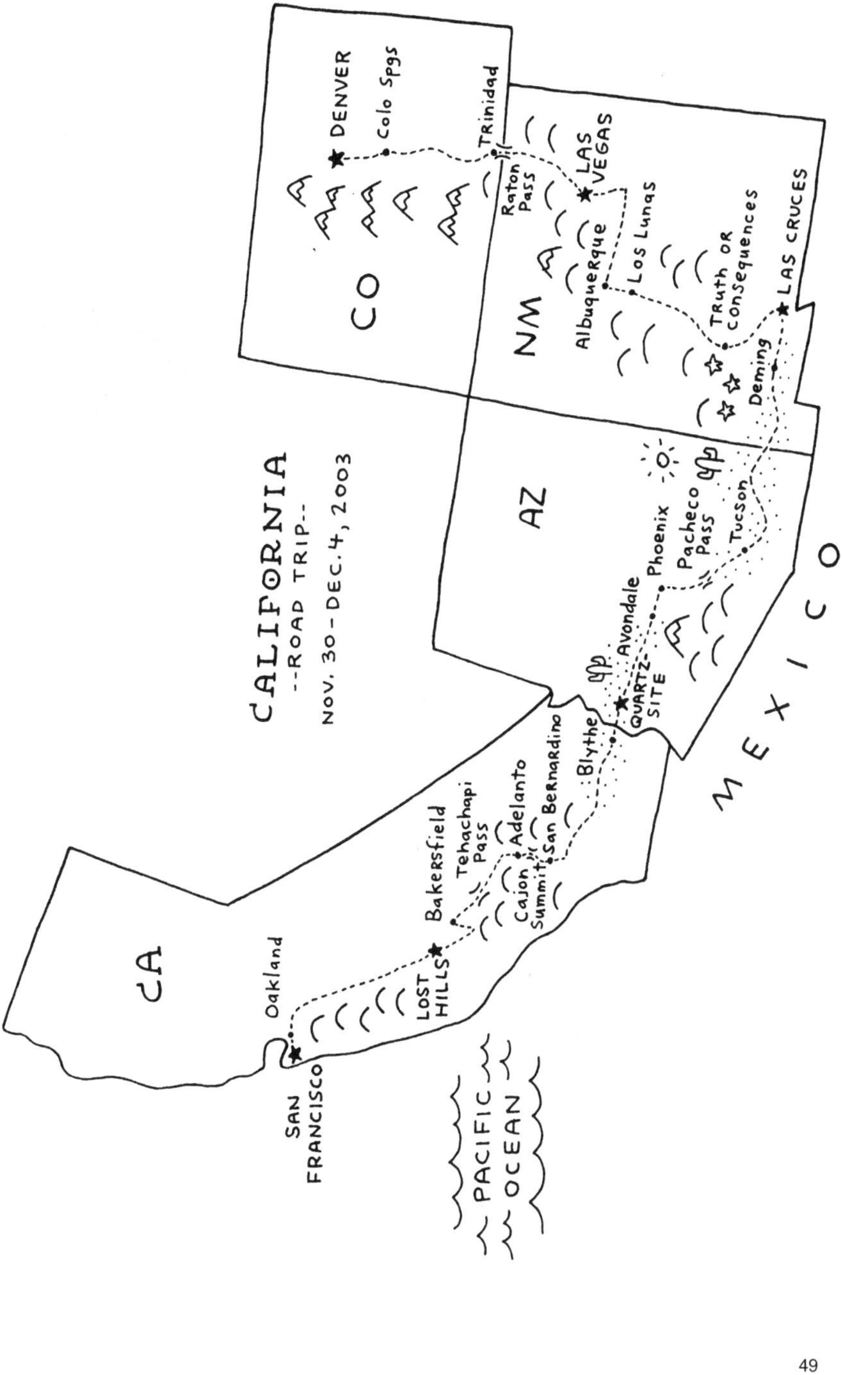
CALIFORNIA
--ROAD TRIP--
NOV. 30-DEC. 4, 2003
CO
DENVER
Colo Spgs
Trinidad
Raton Pass
NM
LAS VEGAS
Albuquerque
Los Lunas
Truth or Consequences
LAS CRUCES
Deming
AZ
Tucson
Pacheco Pass
Phoenix
Avondale
QUARTZSITE
CA
Blythe
San Bernardino
Adelanto
Cajon Summit
Tehachapi Pass
Bakersfield
LOST HILLS
Oakland
SAN FRANCISCO
PACIFIC OCEAN
MEXICO

Great Western Sky

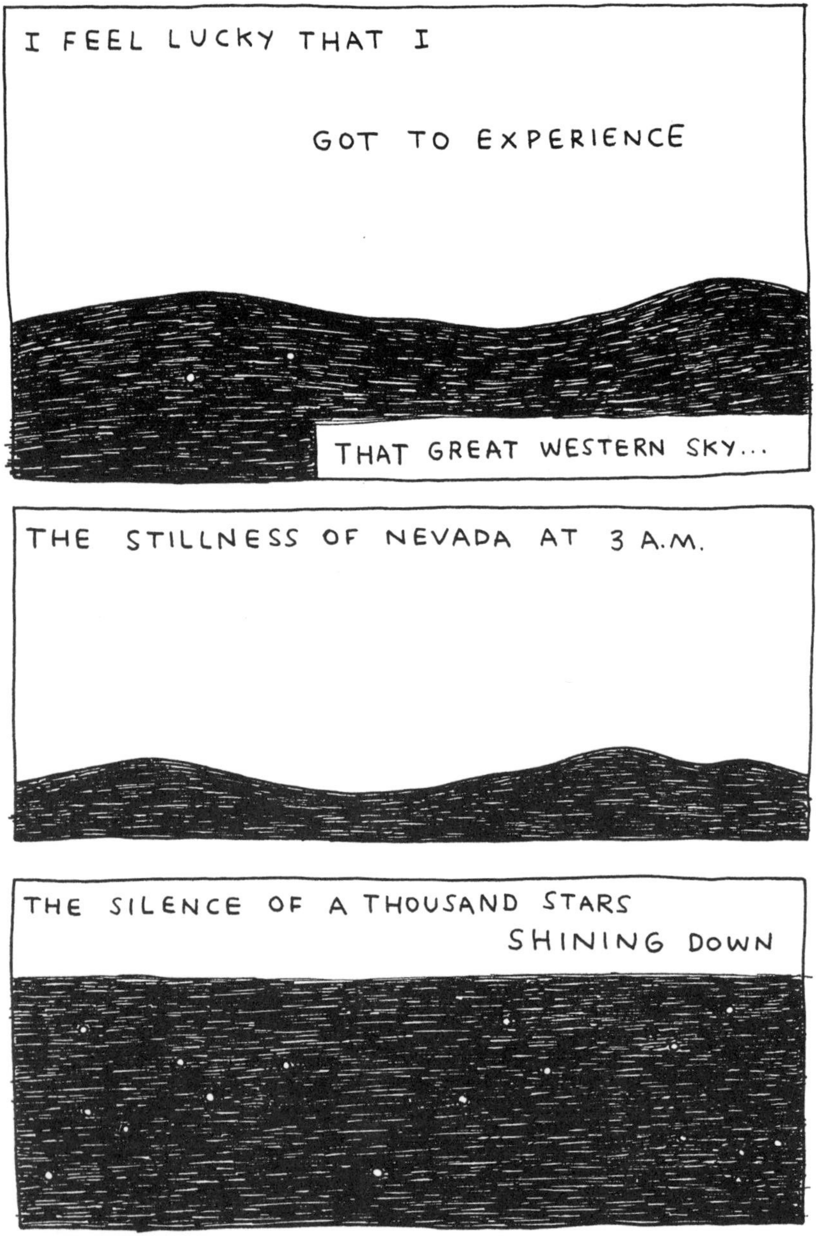
I FEEL LUCKY THAT I
GOT TO EXPERIENCE
THAT GREAT WESTERN SKY...
THE STILLNESS OF NEVADA AT 3 A.M.
THE SILENCE OF A THOUSAND STARS
SHINING DOWN

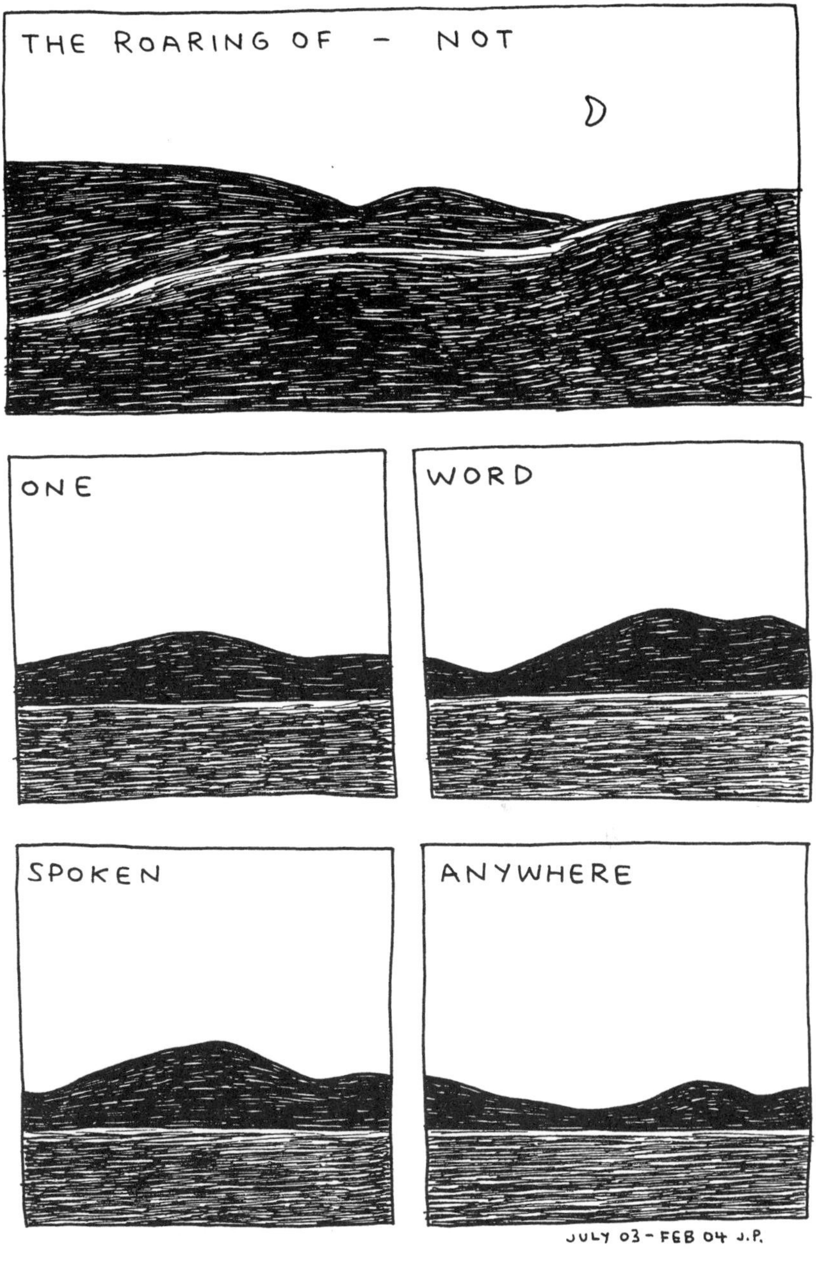
THE ROARING OF - NOT
ONE
WORD
SPOKEN
ANYWHERE
JULY 03 - FEB 04 J.P.

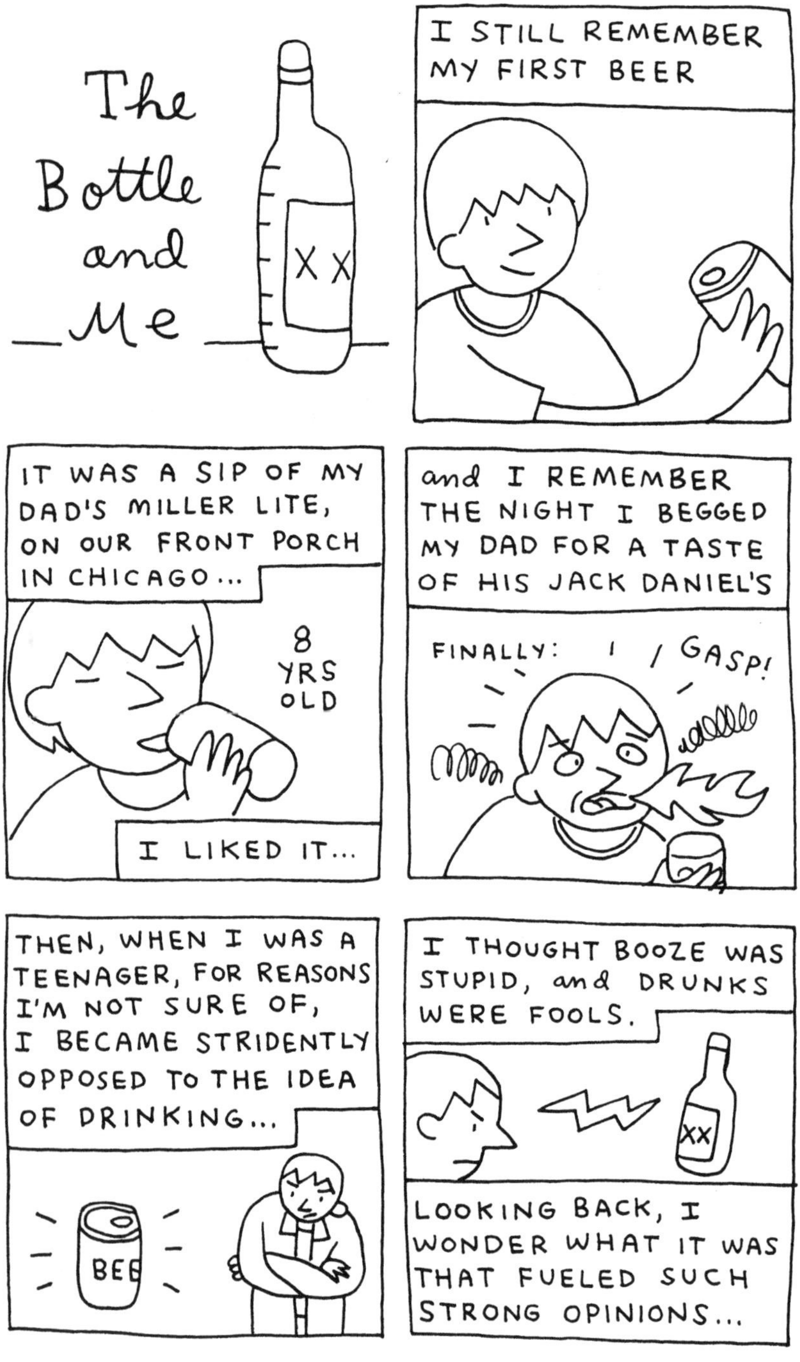
The Bottle and Me
XX
I STILL REMEMBER MY FIRST BEER
IT WAS A SIP OF MY DAD'S MILLER LITE, ON OUR FRONT PORCH IN CHICAGO...
8 YRS OLD
I LIKED IT...
and I REMEMBER THE NIGHT I BEGGED MY DAD FOR A TASTE OF HIS JACK DANIEL'S
FINALLY:
GASP!
THEN, WHEN I WAS A TEENAGER, FOR REASONS I'M NOT SURE OF, I BECAME STRIDENTLY OPPOSED TO THE IDEA OF DRINKING...
BEE
I THOUGHT BOOZE WAS STUPID, and DRUNKS WERE FOOLS.
XX
LOOKING BACK, I WONDER WHAT IT WAS THAT FUELED SUCH STRONG OPINIONS...

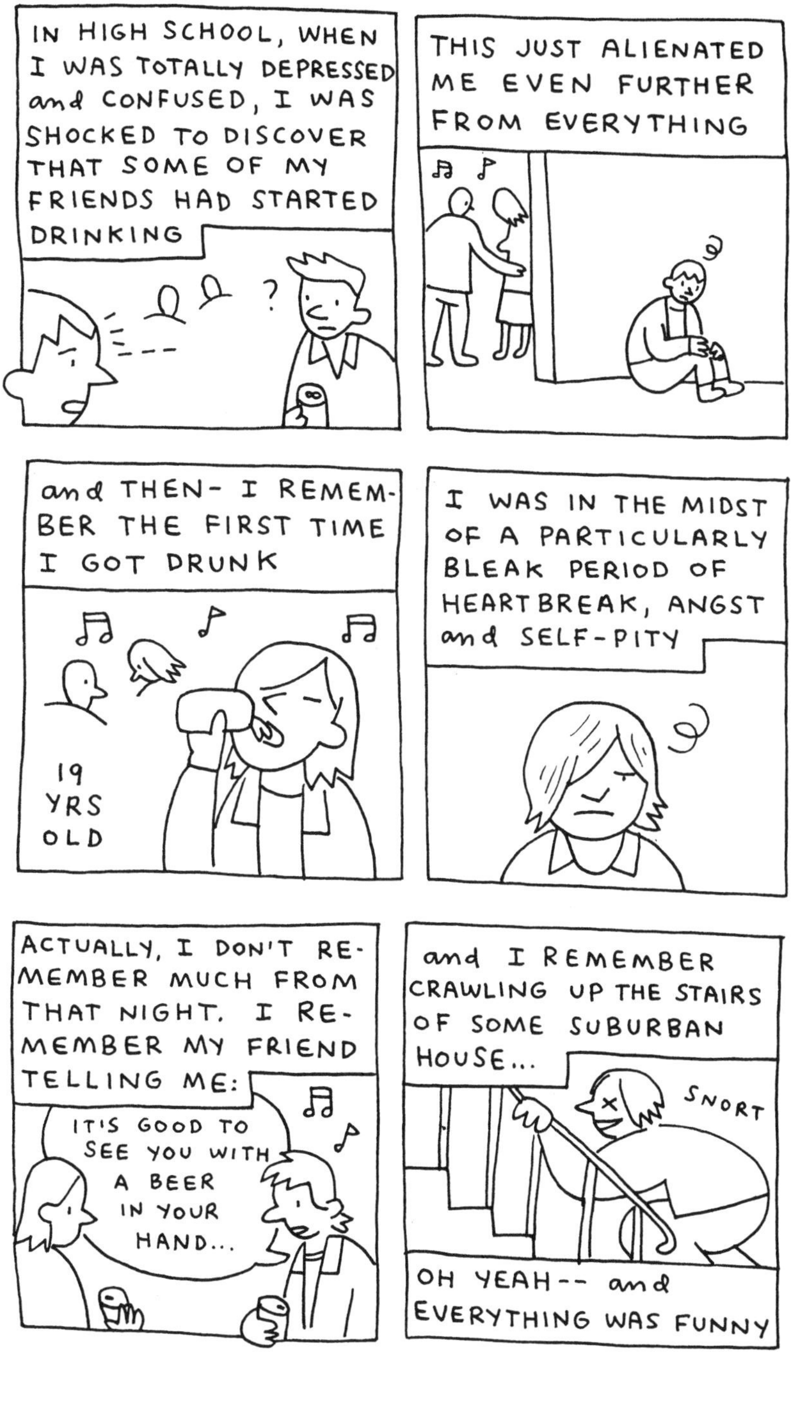
IN HIGH SCHOOL, WHEN I WAS TOTALLY DEPRESSED and CONFUSED, I WAS SHOCKED TO DISCOVER THAT SOME OF MY FRIENDS HAD STARTED DRINKING
?
THIS JUST ALIENATED ME EVEN FURTHER FROM EVERYTHING
and THEN- I REMEMBER THE FIRST TIME I GOT DRUNK
19 YRS OLD
I WAS IN THE MIDST OF A PARTICULARLY BLEAK PERIOD OF HEARTBREAK, ANGST and SELF-PITY
ACTUALLY, I DON'T REMEMBER MUCH FROM THAT NIGHT. I REMEMBER MY FRIEND TELLING ME:
IT'S GOOD TO SEE YOU WITH A BEER IN YOUR HAND...
and I REMEMBER CRAWLING UP THE STAIRS OF SOME SUBURBAN HOUSE...
SNORT
OH YEAH-- and EVERYTHING WAS FUNNY

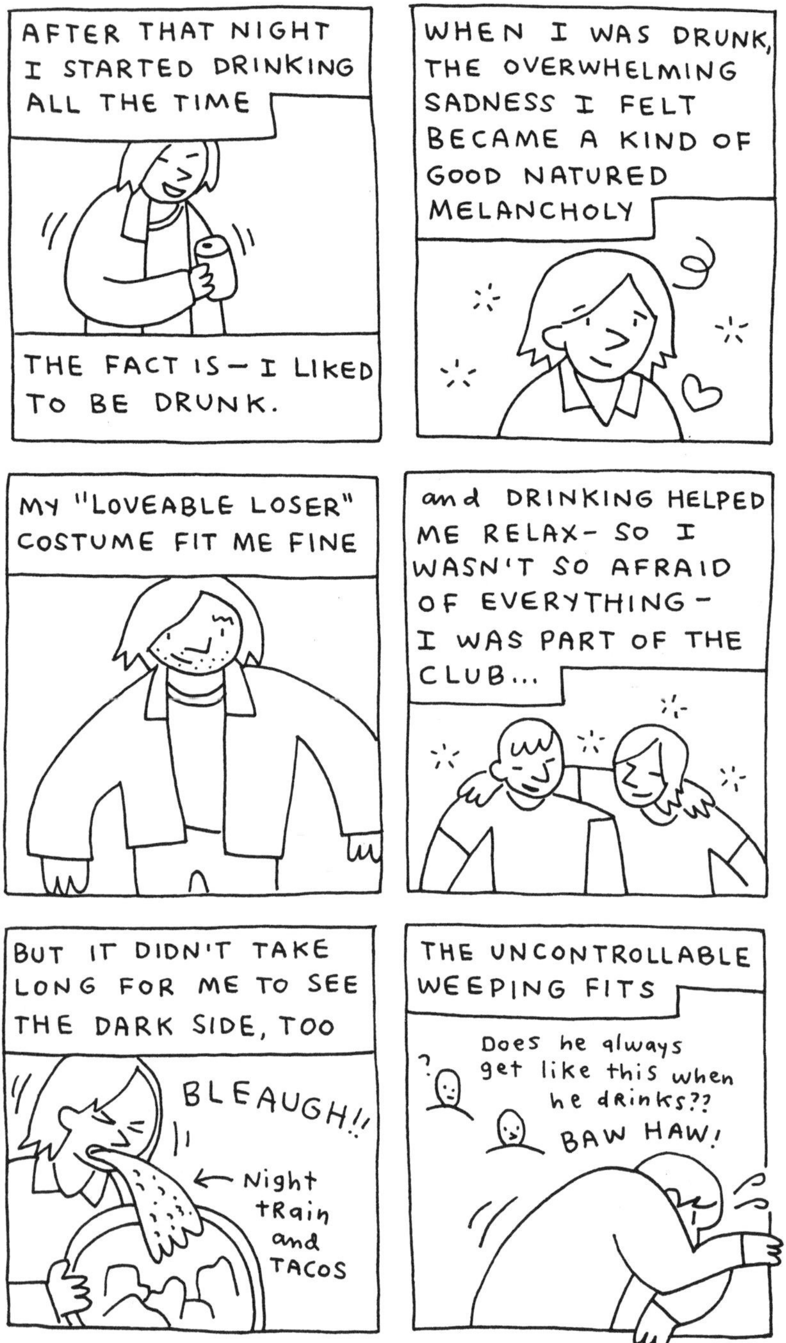
AFTER THAT NIGHT I STARTED DRINKING ALL THE TIME
THE FACT IS — I LIKED TO BE DRUNK.
WHEN I WAS DRUNK, THE OVERWHELMING SADNESS I FELT BECAME A KIND OF GOOD NATURED MELANCHOLY
MY "LOVEABLE LOSER" COSTUME FIT ME FINE
and DRINKING HELPED ME RELAX- SO I WASN'T SO AFRAID OF EVERYTHING - I WAS PART OF THE CLUB...
BUT IT DIDN'T TAKE LONG FOR ME TO SEE THE DARK SIDE, TOO
BLEAUGH!!
Night tRain and TACOS
THE UNCONTROLLABLE WEEPING FITS
?
Does he always get like this when he dRinks??
BAW HAW!

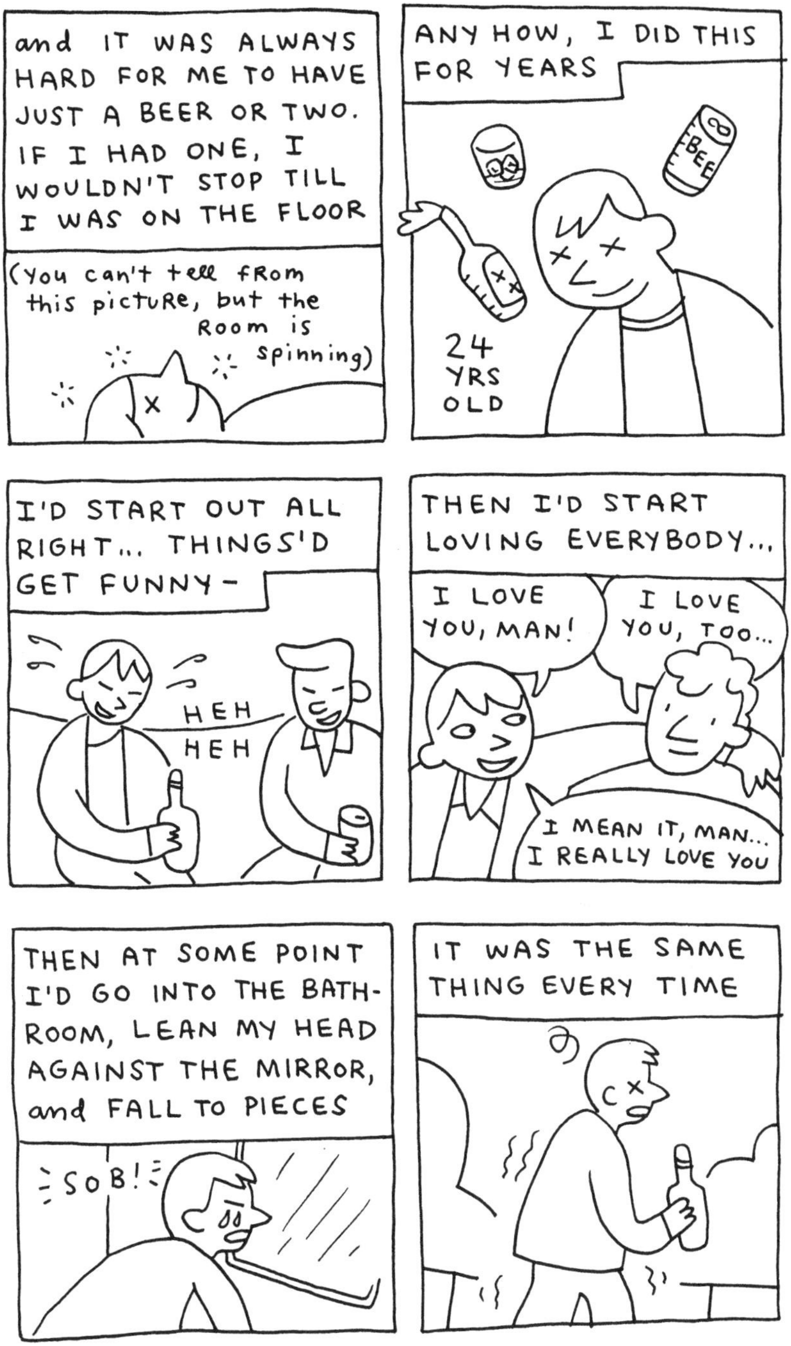
and IT WAS ALWAYS HARD FOR ME TO HAVE JUST A BEER OR TWO. IF I HAD ONE, I WOULDN'T STOP TILL I WAS ON THE FLOOR
(You can't tell from this picture, but the Room is spinning)
ANY HOW, I DID THIS FOR YEARS
BEE
24 YRS OLD
I'D START OUT ALL RIGHT... THINGS'D GET FUNNY-
HEH HEH
THEN I'D START LOVING EVERYBODY...
I LOVE YOU, MAN!
I LOVE YOU, TOO...
I MEAN IT, MAN... I REALLY LOVE YOU
THEN AT SOME POINT I'D GO INTO THE BATH-ROOM, LEAN MY HEAD AGAINST THE MIRROR, and FALL TO PIECES
SOB!
IT WAS THE SAME THING EVERY TIME

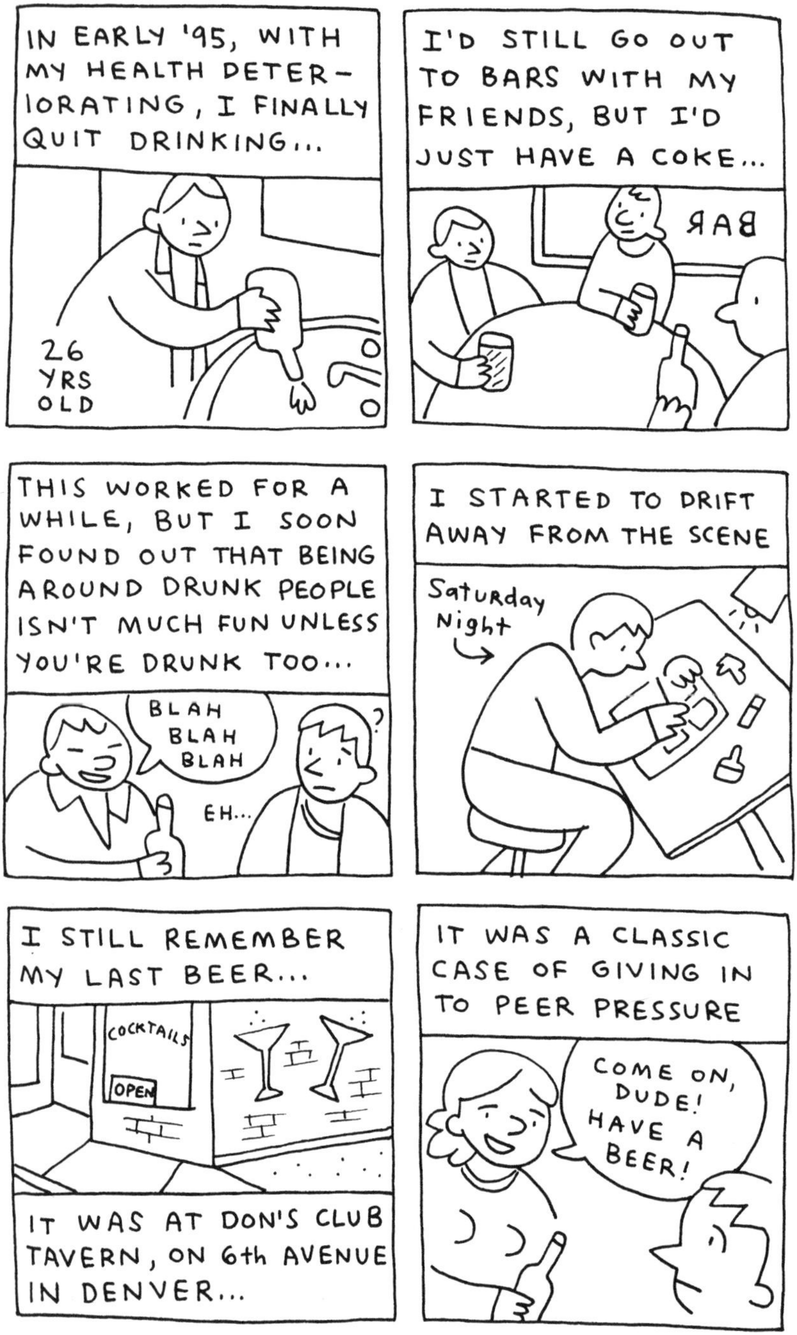
IN EARLY '95, WITH MY HEALTH DETER-IORATING, I FINALLY QUIT DRINKING...
26 YRS OLD
I'D STILL GO OUT TO BARS WITH MY FRIENDS, BUT I'D JUST HAVE A COKE...
BAR
THIS WORKED FOR A WHILE, BUT I SOON FOUND OUT THAT BEING AROUND DRUNK PEOPLE ISN'T MUCH FUN UNLESS YOU'RE DRUNK TOO...
BLAH BLAH BLAH
?
EH...
I STARTED TO DRIFT AWAY FROM THE SCENE
Saturday Night
I STILL REMEMBER MY LAST BEER...
COCKTAILS
OPEN
IT WAS AT DON'S CLUB TAVERN, ON 6th AVENUE IN DENVER...
IT WAS A CLASSIC CASE OF GIVING IN TO PEER PRESSURE
COME ON, DUDE! HAVE A BEER!

SO I HAD ONE—

IT WAS A PABST BLUE RIBBON

THAT NIGHT WE WERE WALKING HOME, and THE GIRL I WAS WITH HAD A BOTTLE IN A BAG

WHEN SHE FINISHED IT, SHE LAUGHED and HURLED IT INTO SOME BUSHES

EXCEPT IN THE DARKNESS, and IN HER DRUNKEN STATE, THE "BUSHES" WERE ACTUALLY A PARKED CAR

SMASH!

IT WAS AT THAT MOMENT I DECIDED NEVER TO DRINK AGAIN.

WITH
JOHN P. LOVE

FINISHED
JULY 2004

THE KING-CAT TOP FORTY

...SUMMER 2003 to SPRING 2004...

☆DENVER☆

1. MY WIFE and MY CAT ♡ ♡ ♡ ♡ ♡ ♡ ♡
2. Quadrophenia Movie (1979)
3. The Gateless Barrier - Zen Comments on the Mumonkan by Zenkei Shibayama (Shambala)
4. Watching the Breakfast Club on T.V., with misun ♡
5. the Katydid in the Hallway
6. MR. mouse
7. MR. SQUIRREL

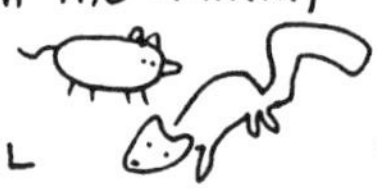

8. George Harrison "Stuck Inside A Cloud" (Capitol 2002) + ♡ ♡ ♡ ॐ
9. the swallows at the Intersection of Colorado and Evans
10. My friends ♡
11. Elvis Presley: Amazing Grace - His Greatest Sacred Recordings (2 CD Set - RCA)
12. Autumn
13. Brad Warner Hardcore Zen (wisdom Publications) (punk Rock - Zen Buddhism)
14. MR. Fast Charlie ♡
15. DENVER, COLORADO

☆SAN FRANCISCO☆

1. My wife and My Cat ♡ ♡ ♡ ♡ ♡ ♡ ♡
2. Mock Orange Victorian Box tree (pittosporum undulatum) et al
3. Flowers ♡
4. the Diamond Sutra translated with Commentary by Red Pine (Counterpoint, 2002) -Amazing- ★ ★ ★ ★ ★
5. Joni Mitchell Court and Spark (1974, Asylum Recs.)
6. Jeopardy (Game Show)
7. KABL ("Ding-Ding") - 960 AM, SF - "Playing the Great American Music"
8. Gophers ♡
9. the Zen teaching of Homeless Kodo - Kodo Sawaki Roshi & Kosho Uchiyama Roshi (Libri Books on Demand) ☆☆☆☆☆☆☆☆☆
10. Sly and the Family Stone Fresh (1973, Epic) ♡
11. Frank Sinatra "Silent Night" (Broadcast on Sid Mark's "Sounds of Sinatra" 12/21/03) ♡
12. Queen "Play the Game" ☆☆☆☆☆☆☆☆☆☆☆
13. Reluctant Saint: the Life of Francis of Assisi by Donald Spoto (Viking, '02) -Moving and inspirational ♡-
14. Van Morrison Moondance (Warner Brothers, 1970)
15. Spring!
16. SAN FRANCISCO, CALIFORNIA
17. EVERYTHING ELSE!!

WHO AM I KIDDING ??
MORE TOP-FORTY:

---

1. Joni Mitchell: <u>Blue</u>
   (Reprise Records, 1971)

2. Bats over Alamo Square

3. Alternative Press Expo-
   San Francisco, Feb. '04

4. Elvis Presley "Stranger
   in My Own Home Town"
   (RCA Records, 1969)

5. <u>Adaptation</u> movie
   (Spike Jonze, 2002)

6. Queen: <u>News of the World</u>
   (Elektra, 1977) ★ ★ ★ ★ ★

7. <u>The Beatles</u> (White Album)
   (1968 – EMI/Capitol Recs.)
   the first "post-modern" LP ??

8. Tara Jane O'Neil <u>In the
   Sun Lines</u> LP
   (Quarterstick, 2001)

9. Patrick Porter <u>Lisha Kill-
   Home Recordings</u> (2003)

10. Looking for mockingbirds
    in Noe Valley

11. MOCKINGBIRDS ♡

CAN'T STAND UP...

CAN'T SIT DOWN...

THE MYSTERIOUS WORKINGS OF OUR BODY

?

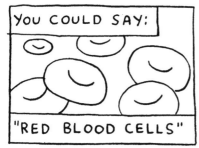

YOU COULD SAY:

"RED BLOOD CELLS"

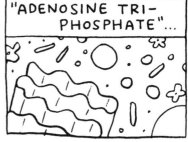

"ADENOSINE TRI-PHOSPHATE"...

BUT PART OF ME DOESN'T BELIEVE IT...

MERE WORDS TO DESCRIBE

THE FLOWERING OF BRANCHES

JOHN P. '03/'04

BARBERS I HAVE KNOWN

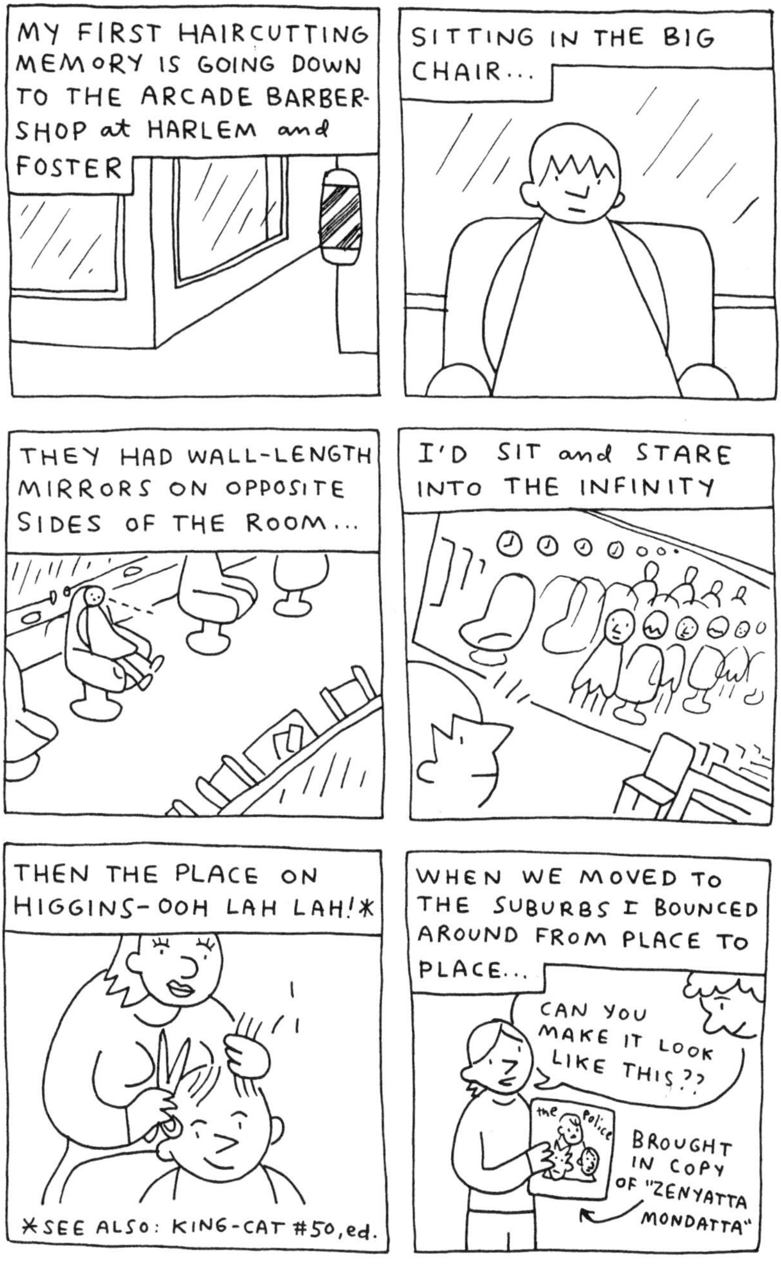
MY FIRST HAIRCUTTING MEMORY IS GOING DOWN TO THE ARCADE BARBER-SHOP at HARLEM and FOSTER
SITTING IN THE BIG CHAIR...
THEY HAD WALL-LENGTH MIRRORS ON OPPOSITE SIDES OF THE ROOM...
I'D SIT and STARE INTO THE INFINITY
THEN THE PLACE ON HIGGINS- OOH LAH LAH!*
*SEE ALSO: KING-CAT #50, ed.
WHEN WE MOVED TO THE SUBURBS I BOUNCED AROUND FROM PLACE TO PLACE...
CAN YOU MAKE IT LOOK LIKE THIS??
the Police
BROUGHT IN COPY OF "ZENYATTA MONDATTA"

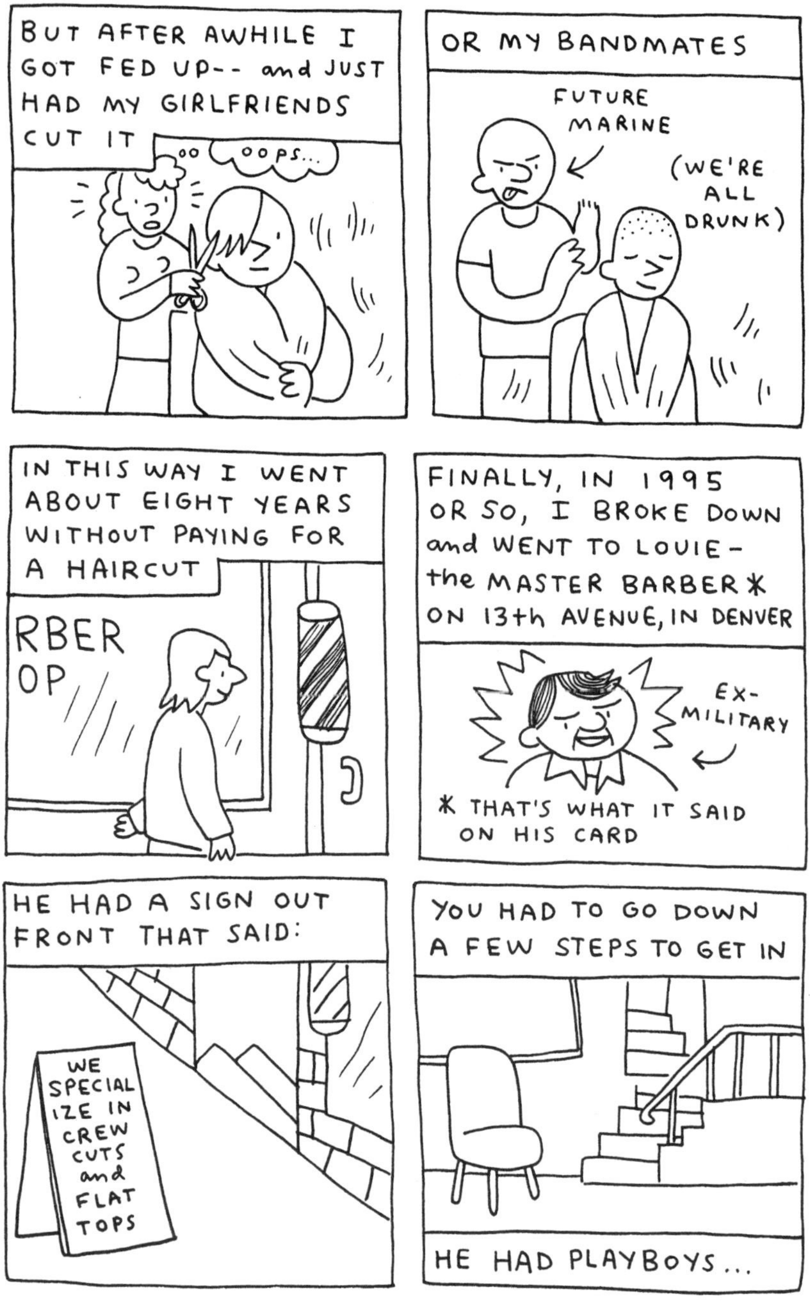
BUT AFTER AWHILE I GOT FED UP-- and JUST HAD MY GIRLFRIENDS CUT IT
OOPS...
OR MY BANDMATES
FUTURE MARINE
(WE'RE ALL DRUNK)
IN THIS WAY I WENT ABOUT EIGHT YEARS WITHOUT PAYING FOR A HAIRCUT
RBER
OP
FINALLY, IN 1995 OR SO, I BROKE DOWN and WENT TO LOUIE - the MASTER BARBER* ON 13th AVENUE, IN DENVER
EX-MILITARY
* THAT'S WHAT IT SAID ON HIS CARD
HE HAD A SIGN OUT FRONT THAT SAID:
WE SPECIALIZE IN CREW CUTS and FLAT TOPS
YOU HAD TO GO DOWN A FEW STEPS TO GET IN
HE HAD PLAYBOYS...

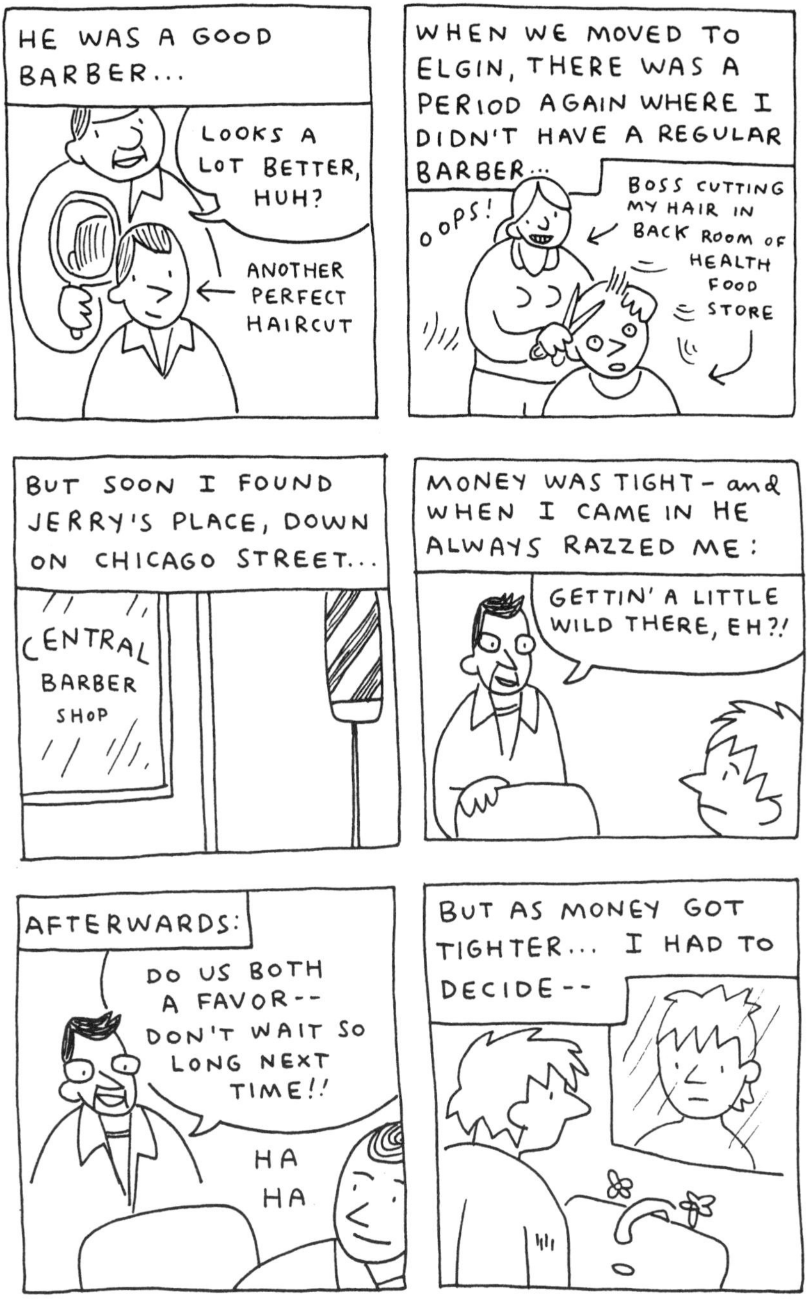

HE WAS A GOOD BARBER...
LOOKS A LOT BETTER, HUH?
ANOTHER PERFECT HAIRCUT
WHEN WE MOVED TO ELGIN, THERE WAS A PERIOD AGAIN WHERE I DIDN'T HAVE A REGULAR BARBER...
OOPS!
BOSS CUTTING MY HAIR IN BACK ROOM OF HEALTH FOOD STORE
BUT SOON I FOUND JERRY'S PLACE, DOWN ON CHICAGO STREET...
CENTRAL BARBER SHOP
MONEY WAS TIGHT - and WHEN I CAME IN HE ALWAYS RAZZED ME:
GETTIN' A LITTLE WILD THERE, EH?!
AFTERWARDS:
DO US BOTH A FAVOR-- DON'T WAIT SO LONG NEXT TIME!!
HA HA
BUT AS MONEY GOT TIGHTER... I HAD TO DECIDE--

ONE SUMMER'S DAY, I REACHED FOR THE CLIPPERS...

BUZZ!! ZZZTT!

IT WAS A TOTALLY LIBERATING EXPERIENCE!

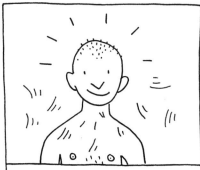

FOR THE NEXT THREE YEARS, I WAS MY OWN BARBER

ZZIT!

THEN, IN 2003, MISUN and I WERE LIVING IN DENVER, GETTING READY FOR OUR WEDDING...

I LET MY HAIR GROW OUT SO THEY'D HAVE SOMETHING TO WORK WITH...

BY THIS TIME, LOUIE'S WAS GONE, SO I WENT UP TO CHUCK'S, at 38th and TENNYSON

HE DID A GOOD JOB...

HE HAD THIS CRAZY OLD HANDHELD VIBRATING ELECTRICAL GIZMO...

CHROME ANCIENT
COVERED IN DUCT TAPE

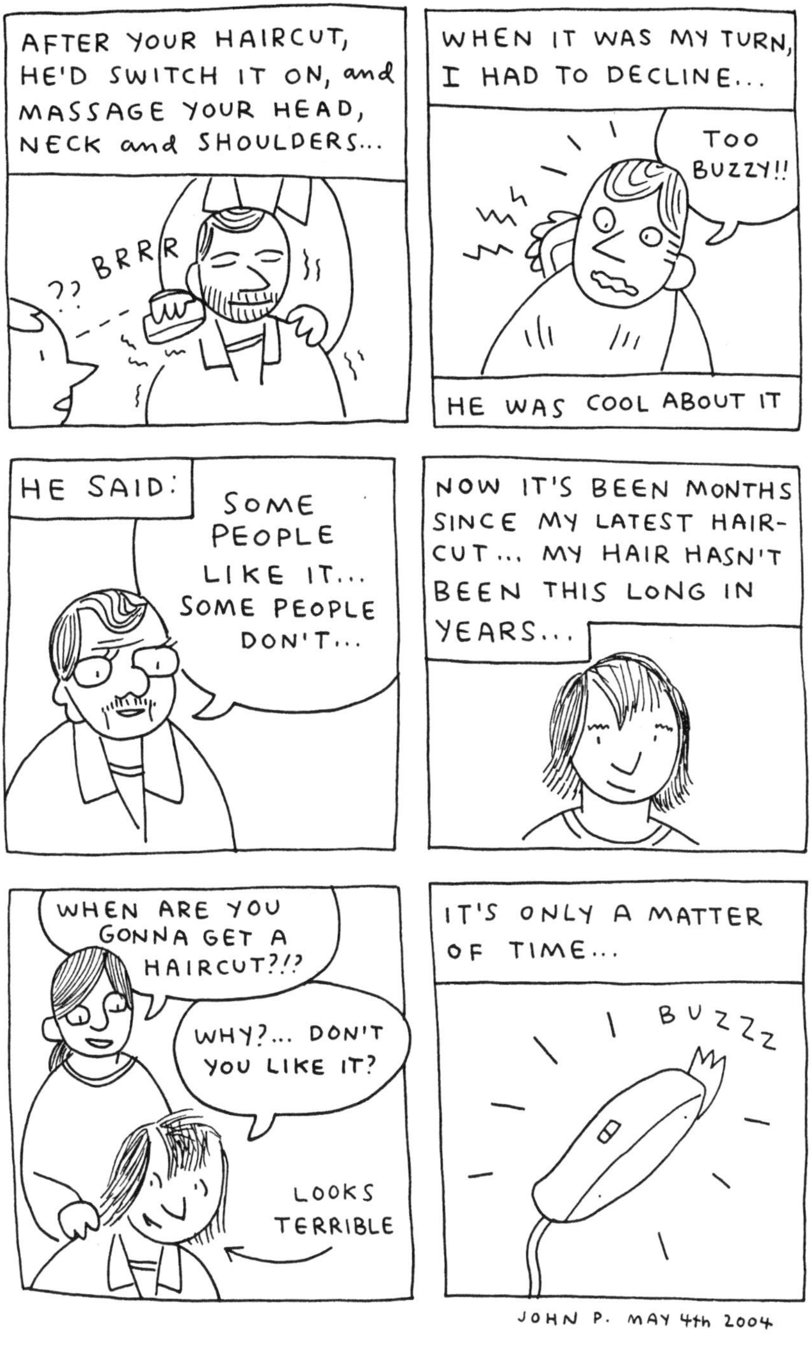
AFTER YOUR HAIRCUT, HE'D SWITCH IT ON, and MASSAGE YOUR HEAD, NECK and SHOULDERS...
BRRRR
??
WHEN IT WAS MY TURN, I HAD TO DECLINE...
TOO BUZZY!!
HE WAS COOL ABOUT IT
HE SAID:
SOME PEOPLE LIKE IT... SOME PEOPLE DON'T...
NOW IT'S BEEN MONTHS SINCE MY LATEST HAIR-CUT... MY HAIR HASN'T BEEN THIS LONG IN YEARS...
WHEN ARE YOU GONNA GET A HAIRCUT?!?
WHY?... DON'T YOU LIKE IT?
LOOKS TERRIBLE
IT'S ONLY A MATTER OF TIME...
BUZZZ
JOHN P. MAY 4th 2004

TRANSFERS

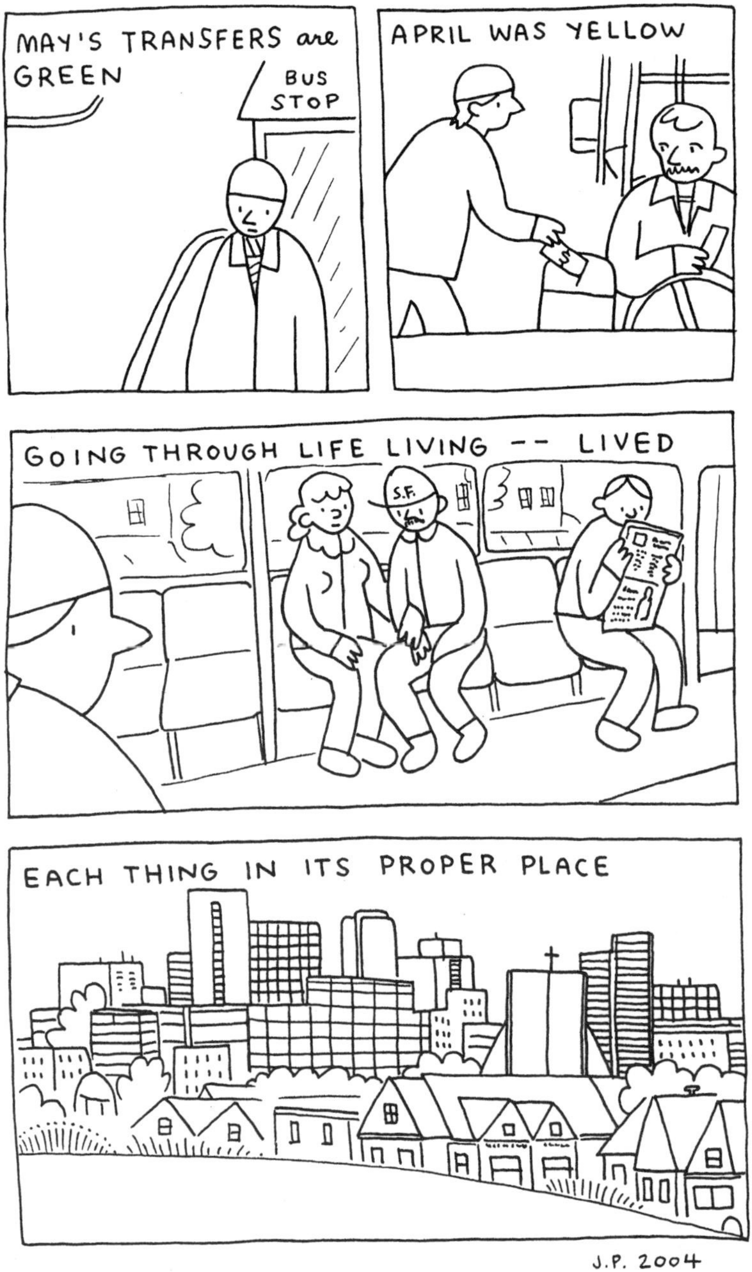
MAY'S TRANSFERS are GREEN
BUS STOP
APRIL WAS YELLOW
GOING THROUGH LIFE LIVING -- LIVED
S.F.
EACH THING IN ITS PROPER PLACE
J.P. 2004

LIKE A PIGEON

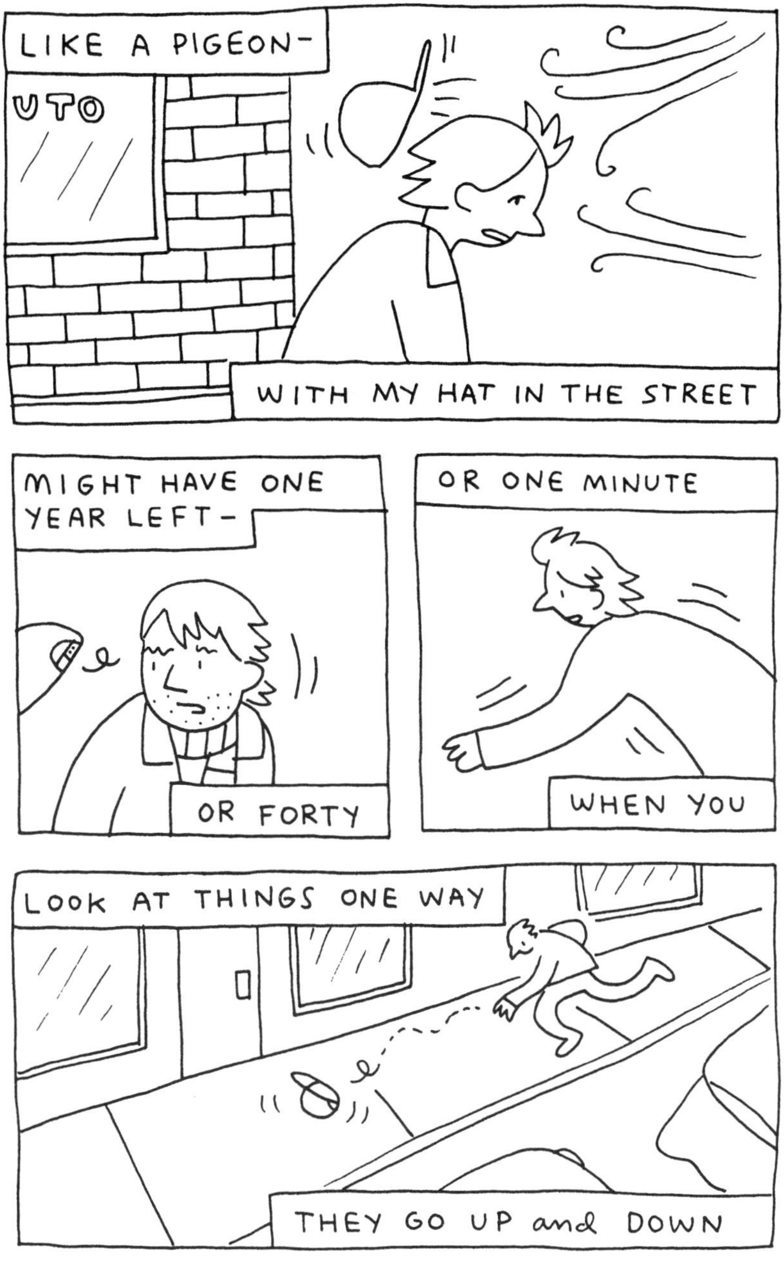

LIKE A PIGEON-
UTO
WITH MY HAT IN THE STREET
MIGHT HAVE ONE YEAR LEFT-
OR FORTY
OR ONE MINUTE
WHEN YOU
LOOK AT THINGS ONE WAY
THEY GO UP and DOWN

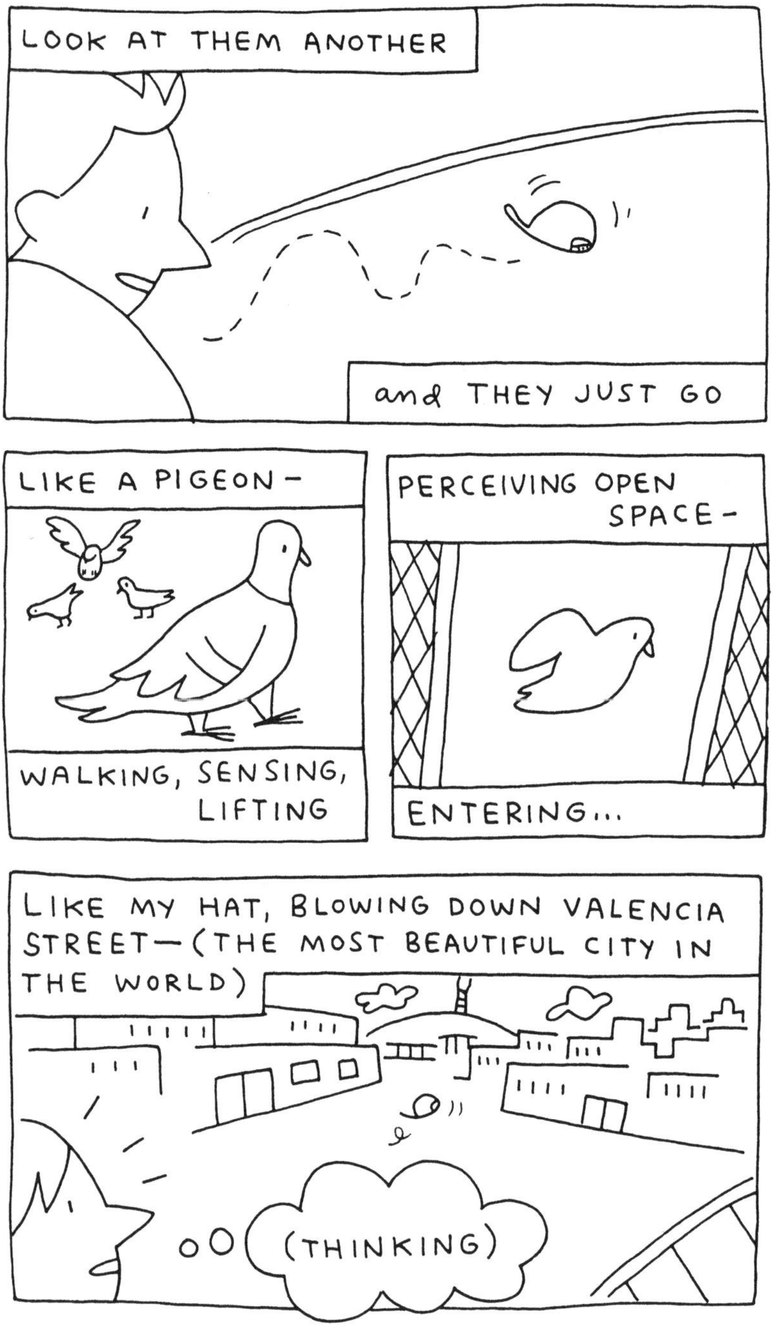
LOOK AT THEM ANOTHER
and THEY JUST GO
LIKE A PIGEON-
WALKING, SENSING, LIFTING
PERCEIVING OPEN SPACE-
ENTERING...
LIKE MY HAT, BLOWING DOWN VALENCIA STREET—(THE MOST BEAUTIFUL CITY IN THE WORLD)
(THINKING)

NO STREET NO ENTERING

LIFTING

WRITTEN TUES. MAY 18, 2004
DRAWN MAY 23RD – JOHN P.

"Mayfly" Incident

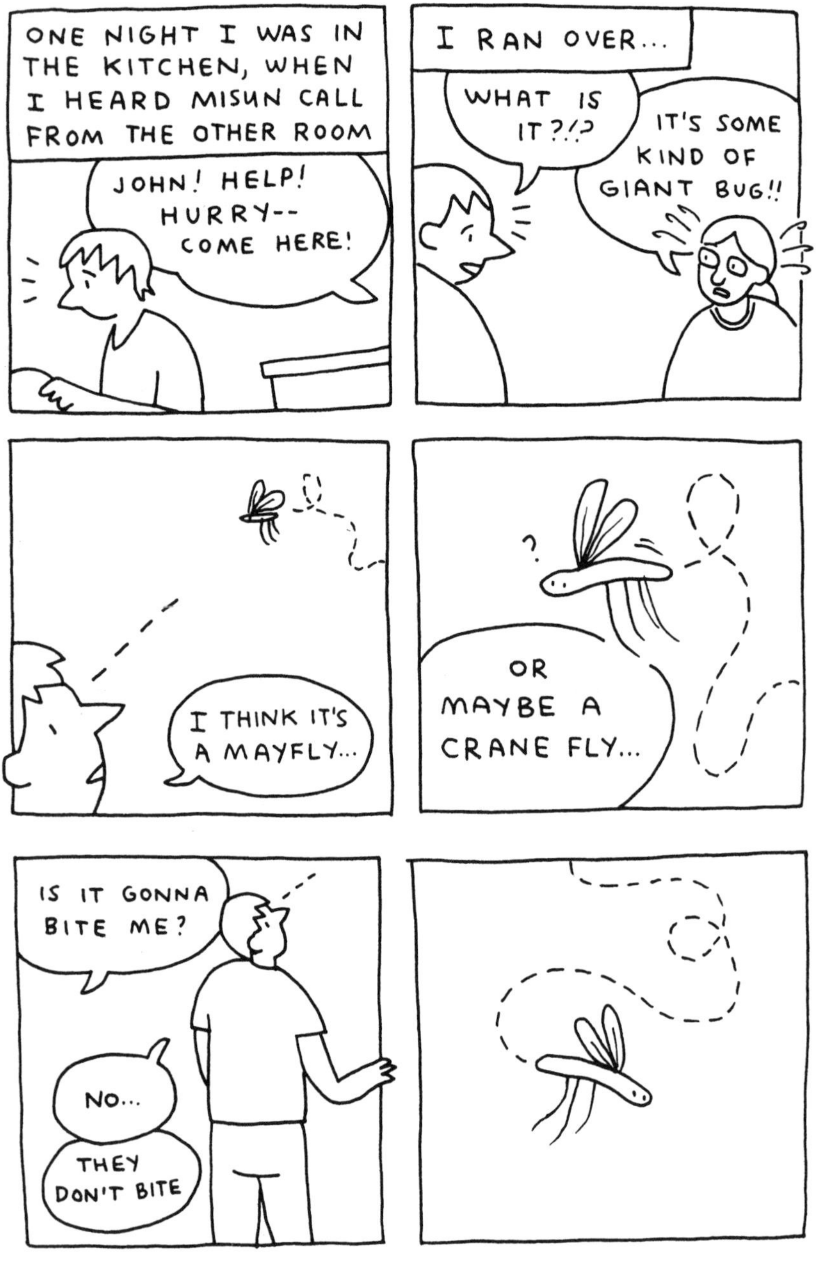

ONE NIGHT I WAS IN THE KITCHEN, WHEN I HEARD MISUN CALL FROM THE OTHER ROOM
JOHN! HELP! HURRY-- COME HERE!
I RAN OVER...
WHAT IS IT?!?
IT'S SOME KIND OF GIANT BUG!!
I THINK IT'S A MAYFLY...
OR MAYBE A CRANE FLY...
IS IT GONNA BITE ME?
NO...
THEY DON'T BITE

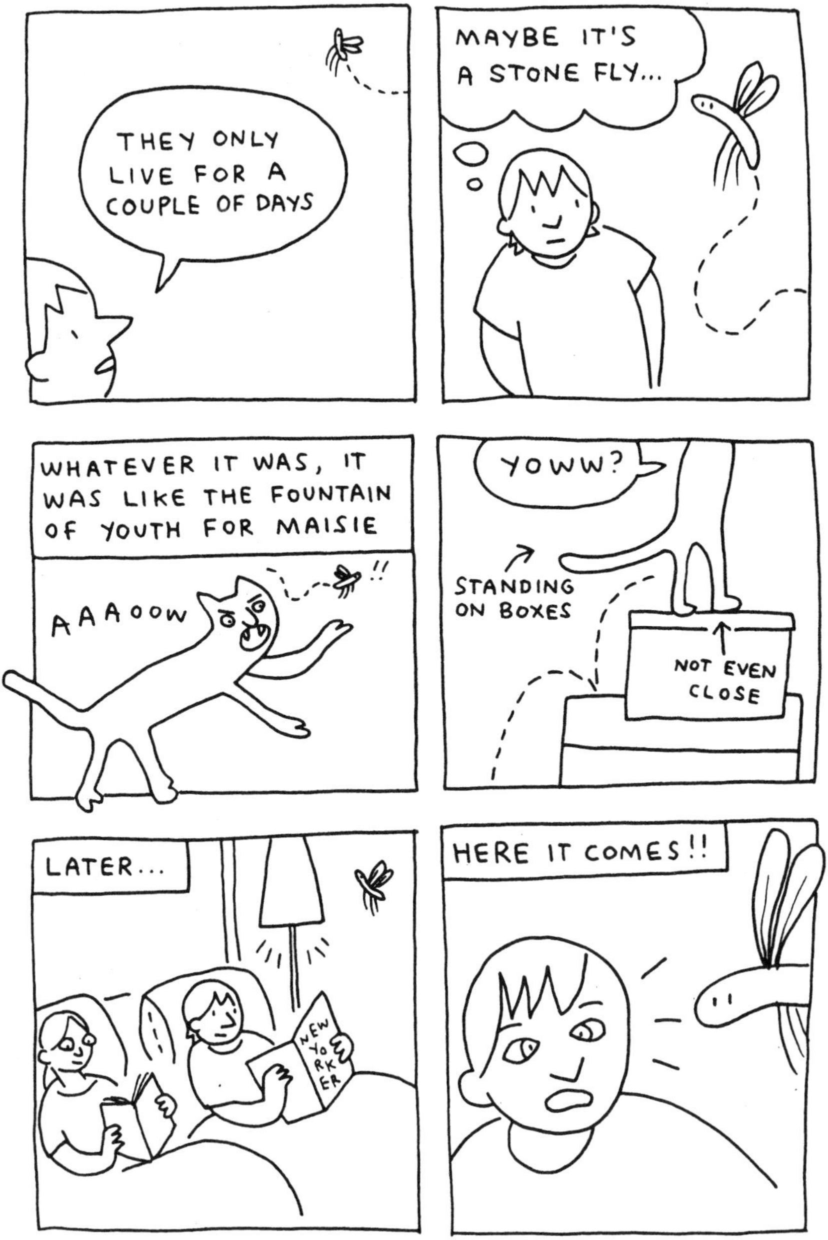
THEY ONLY LIVE FOR A COUPLE OF DAYS
MAYBE IT'S A STONE FLY...
WHATEVER IT WAS, IT WAS LIKE THE FOUNTAIN OF YOUTH FOR MAISIE
AAAOOW
!!
YOWW?
STANDING ON BOXES
NOT EVEN CLOSE
LATER...
NEW YORKER
HERE IT COMES!!

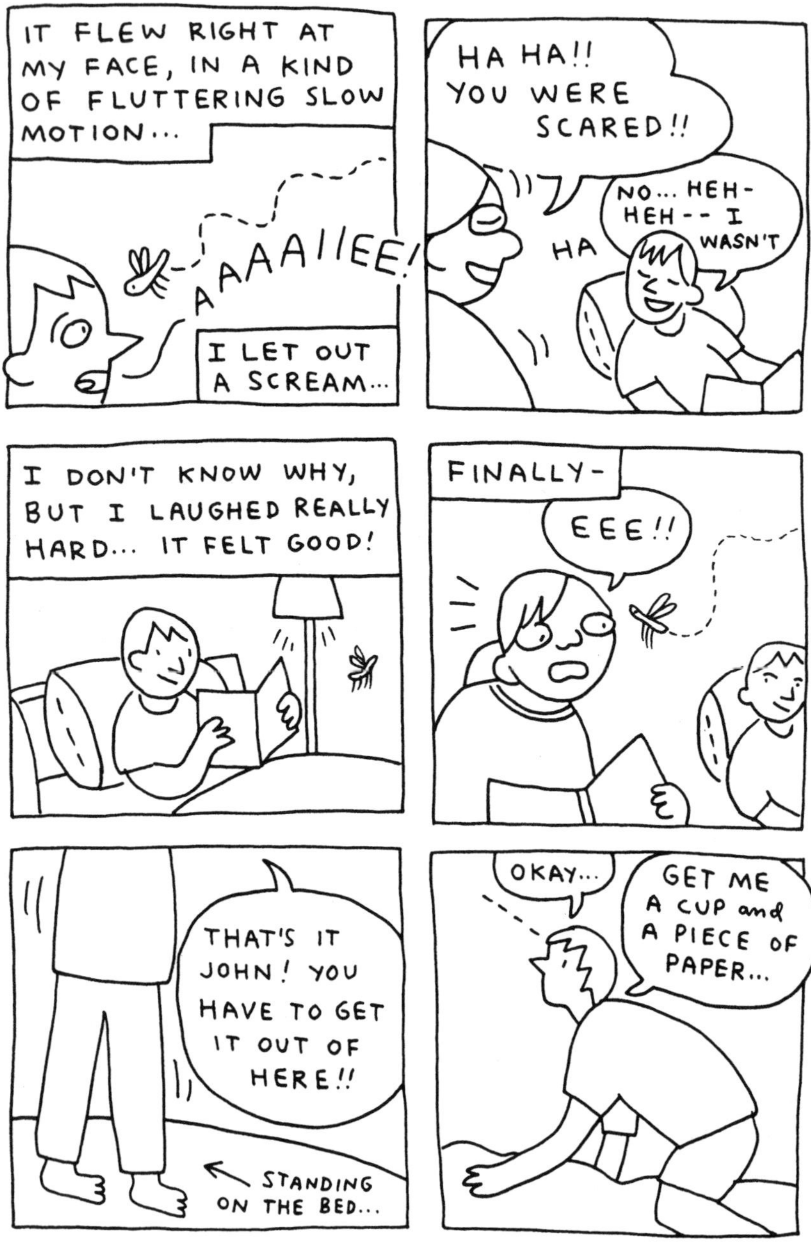
IT FLEW RIGHT AT MY FACE, IN A KIND OF FLUTTERING SLOW MOTION...
AAAAIIEE!
I LET OUT A SCREAM...
HA HA!! YOU WERE SCARED!!
HA
NO... HEH-HEH-- I WASN'T
I DON'T KNOW WHY, BUT I LAUGHED REALLY HARD... IT FELT GOOD!
FINALLY-
EEE!!
THAT'S IT JOHN! YOU HAVE TO GET IT OUT OF HERE!!
STANDING ON THE BED...
OKAY...
GET ME A CUP and A PIECE OF PAPER...

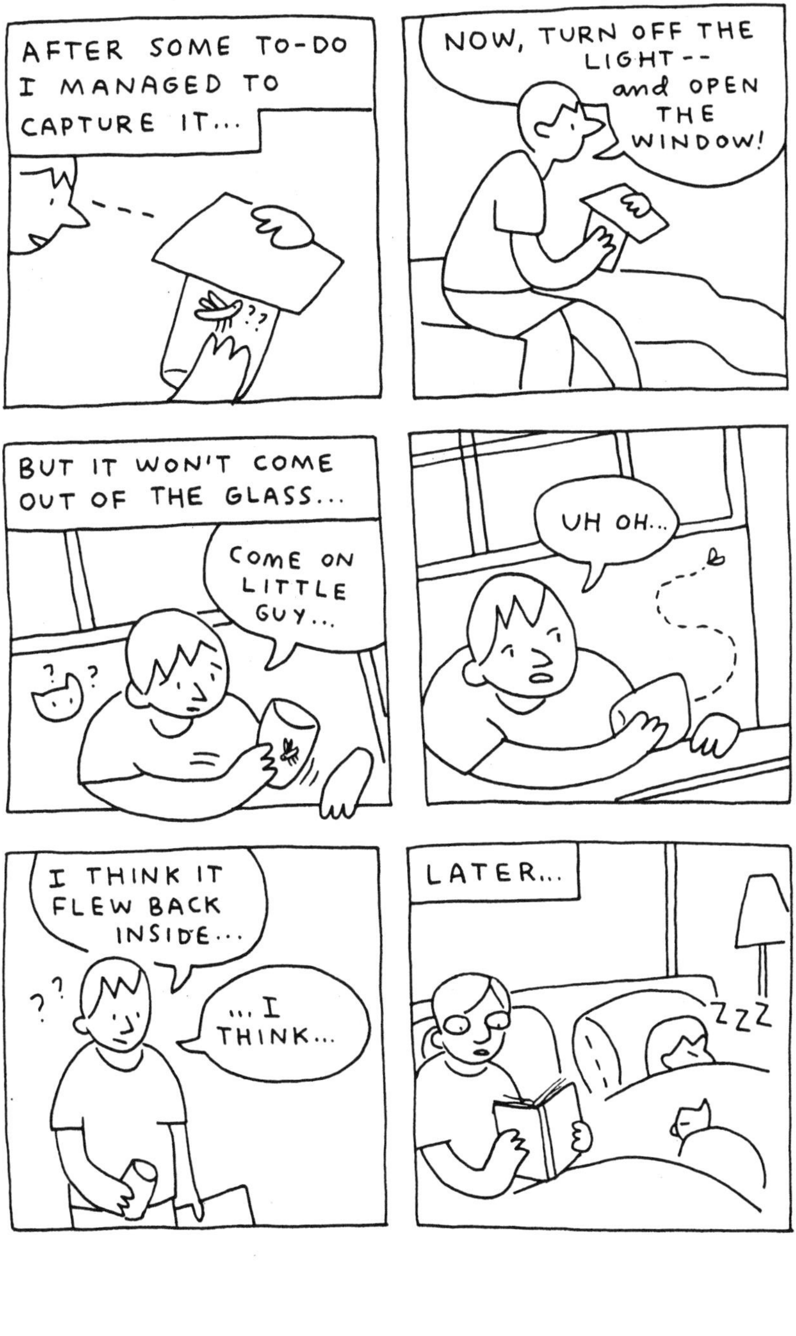
AFTER SOME TO-DO I MANAGED TO CAPTURE IT...
??
NOW, TURN OFF THE LIGHT-- and OPEN THE WINDOW!
BUT IT WON'T COME OUT OF THE GLASS...
COME ON LITTLE GUY...
??
UH OH...
I THINK IT FLEW BACK INSIDE...
??
...I THINK...
LATER...
ZZZ

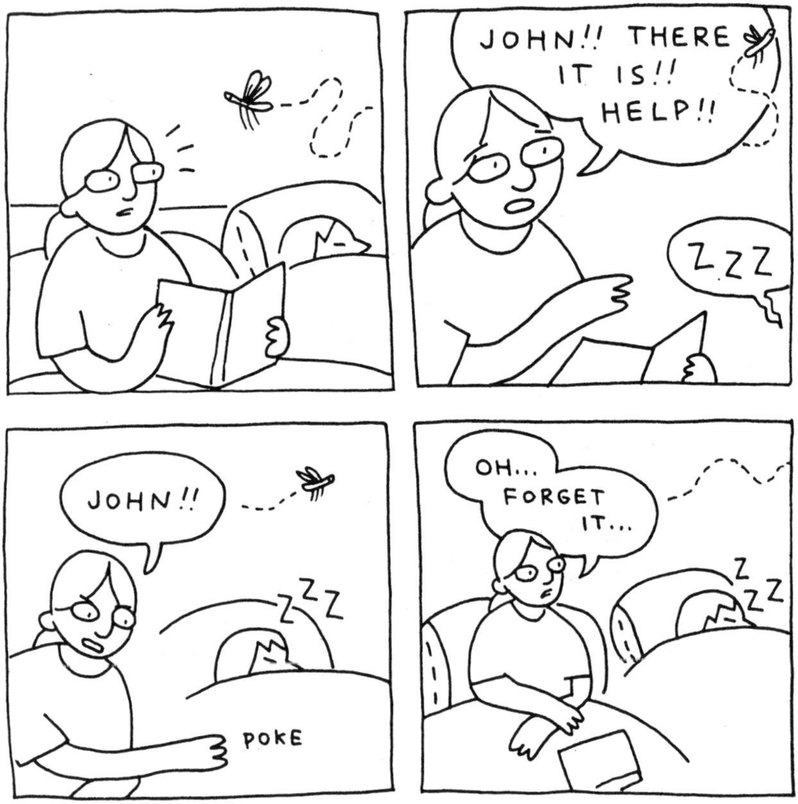
JOHN!! THERE IT IS!! HELP!!
ZZZ
JOHN!!
ZZZ
POKE
OH... FORGET IT...
ZZZ

HAPPENED MARCH 10TH
DRAWN 3/14/04 BY JOHN P.
"ANOTHER TRUE STORY"

P.S.: IT WAS A CRANE FLY...

SIZE, LOCATION and POSITION of the HEART

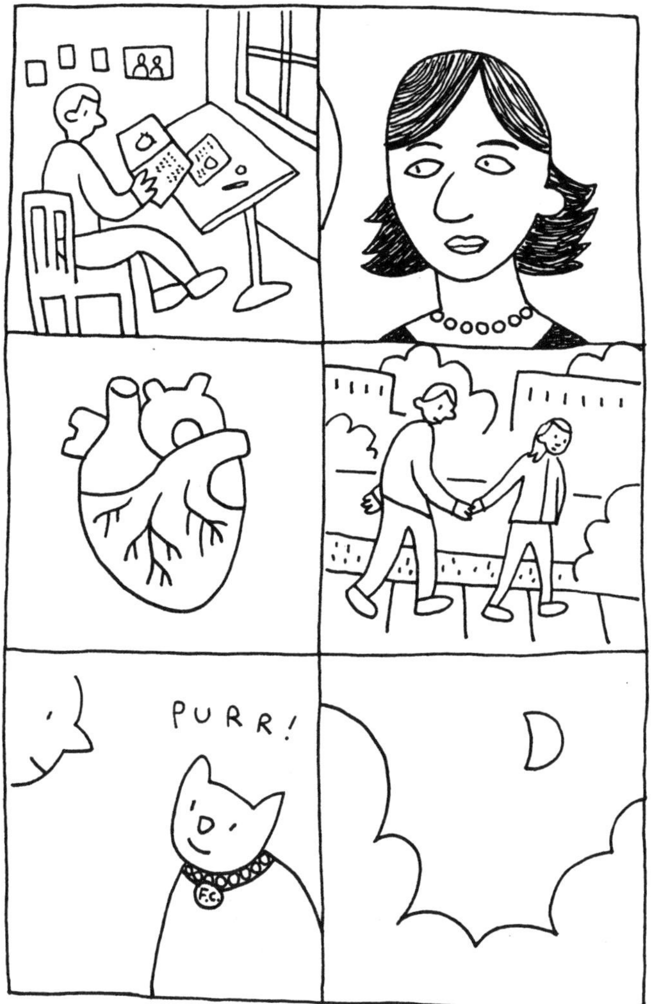

PURR!
F.C.

NOV 03

JUL-AUG 04

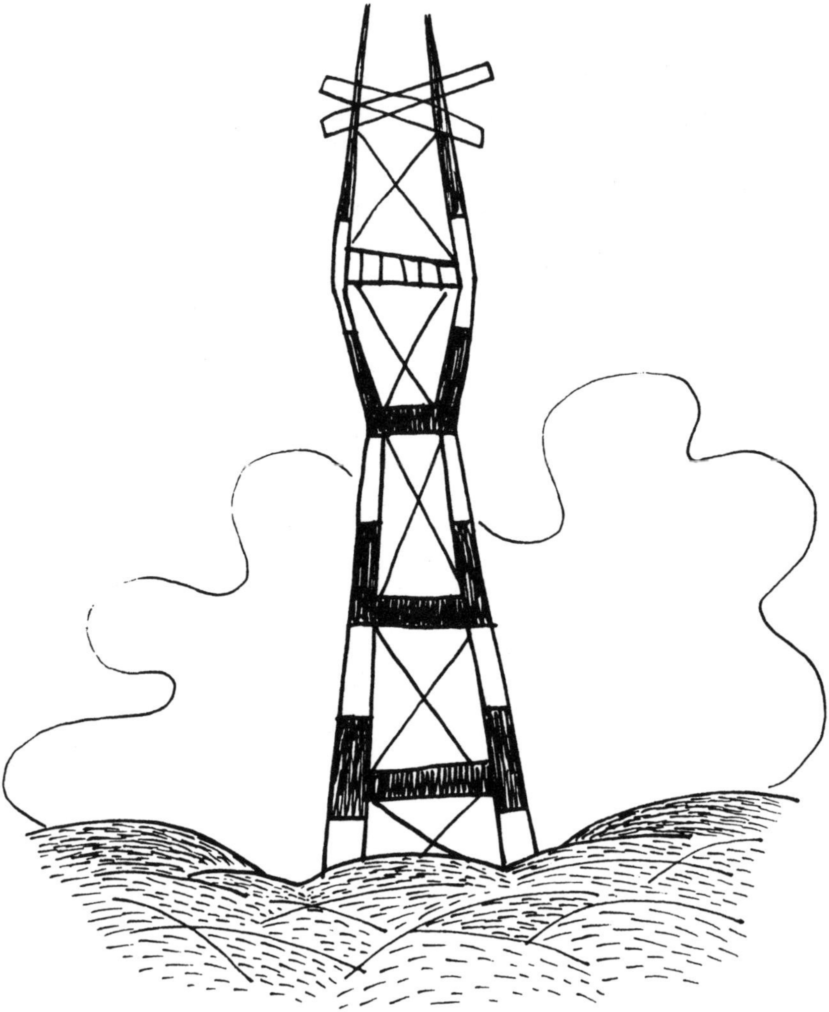

KING-CAT

COMICS and STORIES

NUMBER 64 $3.00

BY JOHN PORCELLINO   2005

Charles E. Porcellino
March 16, 1941 – April 6, 2005

My Father

This issue of King-Cat is for him.

King-Cat Comics and Stories No. 64; July 2005 ♡
Published by SPIT AND A HALF: ▮▮▮▮▮▮
San Francisco, CA ▮▮▮▮ USA • www.king-cat.net

©2005 John A. Porcellino--LOVE

"Renunciation is not giving
up the things of the world,
but accepting that they go
away."

    - ShunRyu Suzuki Roshi

Sometime in February, my Dad started having pain in his back-- his lower back-- and it would radiate at times down his legs and into his hips. The pain was terrible and nothing he tried seemed to relieve it. A couple of weeks earlier, he had fallen on the ice while taking the dogs out, and everyone seemed to think his pain had something to do with the fall. After a few weeks, though, it wasn't getting any better, so he went in to see the doctor.

They checked him out and thought maybe he had a prostate infection. He took the antibiotics they prescribed, but it didn't help the pain. Finally, at the beginning of March, he checked himself into the hospital-- the pain was unrelenting and he just wanted someone to figure out what was going on.

They ran all kinds of tests on him—(his prostate turned out to be fine). They found a small kidney stone, but it wasn't blocking anything, and they didn't think it could be causing the pain. They found an aneurysm in his belly, but it was too small to operate on, and anyway they said that it wasn't causing the pain either.

They thought maybe he was having small strokes, but CAT scans and MRIs all came back okay. A bone scan ruled out cancer, or any structural degeneration. Nothing seemed to explain the terrible pain he was in.

Finally, on March 16, his 64th birthday, they sent my Dad home. They'd run every test they could think of, and didn't know what else to do. They told him to have the aneurysm checked every six months, to make sure that it didn't get any bigger, but that otherwise he was in good health. That afternoon I called my Dad from work and sang Happy Birthday to him over the phone. (I live in San Francisco, my family lives in Illinois). It was very emotional, for the both of us.

He was still in bad pain, but we were so happy to have him home. We just figured that eventually they'd find out what was causing the problem and it'd get taken care of. At least it wasn't anything life threatening-- that had all been ruled out.

The Pain Specialist my Dad was seeing thought that there might be some deep bruising in my Dad's back, or maybe some inflammation… and maybe that was causing the pain.

The plan was to have him discontinue his blood thinning medication for ten days so the Pain Specialist could administer an epidural to his back. The hope was that it would reduce any swelling, and that would allow his back a chance to heal.

During that ten day wait, my Dad was in excruciating pain. He was on pain pills, but they didn't seem to help much. He couldn't sleep, and could barely eat. He had lost a lot of weight and was having a hard time walking.

My Dad and I have always been very close, and we talked on the phone a lot. But in those weeks we talked even more. We had long, meaningful conversations about the nature of pain... how it humbles you, and makes you aware of your connections to those who are trying to help you. We talked about how our pain enables other people to perform compassionate deeds—and how, in our humility, we become more acutely aware of our gratitude-- to God, and all those around us, to our whole life.

My Dad was always a spiritual person, but in those weeks he seemed to go even deeper-- into a point of clarity and sharpened awareness. His tears came easily then, not only because of the pain, but because of the beauty and absolute love he was sensing around him. Despite his suffering, he felt a profound sense of support and interconnection-- and that comforted him.

Finally, the ten days were up, and my Dad went in to have the epidural he had waited so long for. Afterwards, he said he thought it had helped, to a degree, but he had to be patient and see what happened.

Then, on Sunday, April 3rd, at about three o'clock in the morning, my Dad got up to use the bathroom, and collapsed. His dog Daisy, who stayed alongside him all the time, hurried off to wake my Mom, and she came running to help. When she got there, my Dad was lying on the floor, next to the bed. He was in terrible pain, and he couldn't stand up. So my Mom called my sister, who lives nearby, and she came over too. They helped him get back into bed, and stayed with him there for a little while, one on each side, holding his hands.

Finally, he asked them to help him get up to go to the bathroom, and they each put a shoulder under his arms and lifted him. When he stood up, though, his legs collapsed again, and he fell to the floor, unconscious.

By the time the paramedics arrived, he didn't have a pulse, but in the ambulance on the way to the hospital they managed to restore his heartbeat.

What had happened was the aneurysm in his belly had ruptured. The doctors prepared for emergency surgery, but the survival rate for that type of procedure is practically non-existent. We were told to prepare for the worst. Amazingly, my Dad made it through the surgery alive, but he was still unconscious and in critical condition. He had lost over four times his total blood volume during the surgery, and the potential for organ failure was very high. His blood pressure was weak and erratic, and his kidneys had shut down. To try to stabilize his condition, the doctors put him in a medically induced coma. If, after 24 – 48 hours he was still alive, they would begin looking for any signs of organ damage.

By Tuesday morning, though, my Dad's vital signs had not yet stabilized, and the doctors informed my mother that there was no chance of recovery. They withdrew the medication that was keeping his blood pressure up, and told us that most likely his heart would stop within an hour or two.

At the time, Misun, Maisie and I were heading east on I-80 in a rental car, trying to get to Illinois as fast as we could. (Because of my ear problems, I cannot fly).

We were in Park City, Utah, on the morning of Wednesday April 6th, when my sister called to tell me that our father had just died.

* * *

My Dad was a great man, and a wonderful human being. He was warm in spirit, kind, generous, loving and sincere. He was compassionate and sentimental-- always open with his boundless love and affection.

My Dad was also wise, and articulate (he was a great writer), down to earth and hard-working. He was always trying to help other people and he took great care with everything he did.

Despite all this, he was truly a humble man, and he never felt like he was doing enough.

My Dad was one of my best friends, and he really was my hero, my role model, and my mentor. I love him with all my heart, and I miss him more than words can say.

--John Porcellino, June 2005
   San Francisco

This is one of the last known photos of my Dad, taken at Christmas, 2004. They had decorated themselves with stickers and jewelry (he's wearing his Army dog tags). I apologize for the poor quality of the picture, it was the best I could do. JP

the Cat on the Sidewalk

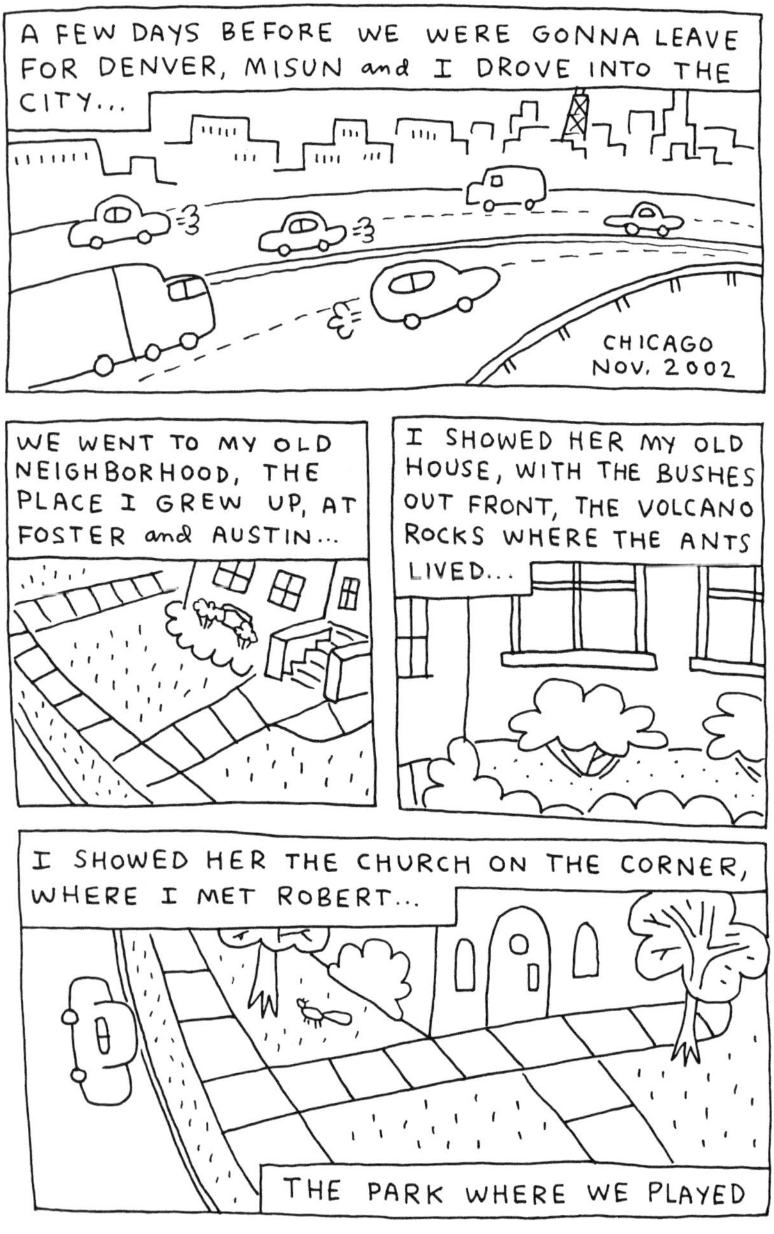

A FEW DAYS BEFORE WE WERE GONNA LEAVE FOR DENVER, MISUN and I DROVE INTO THE CITY...
CHICAGO NOV. 2002
WE WENT TO MY OLD NEIGHBORHOOD, THE PLACE I GREW UP, AT FOSTER and AUSTIN...
I SHOWED HER MY OLD HOUSE, WITH THE BUSHES OUT FRONT, THE VOLCANO ROCKS WHERE THE ANTS LIVED...
I SHOWED HER THE CHURCH ON THE CORNER, WHERE I MET ROBERT...
THE PARK WHERE WE PLAYED

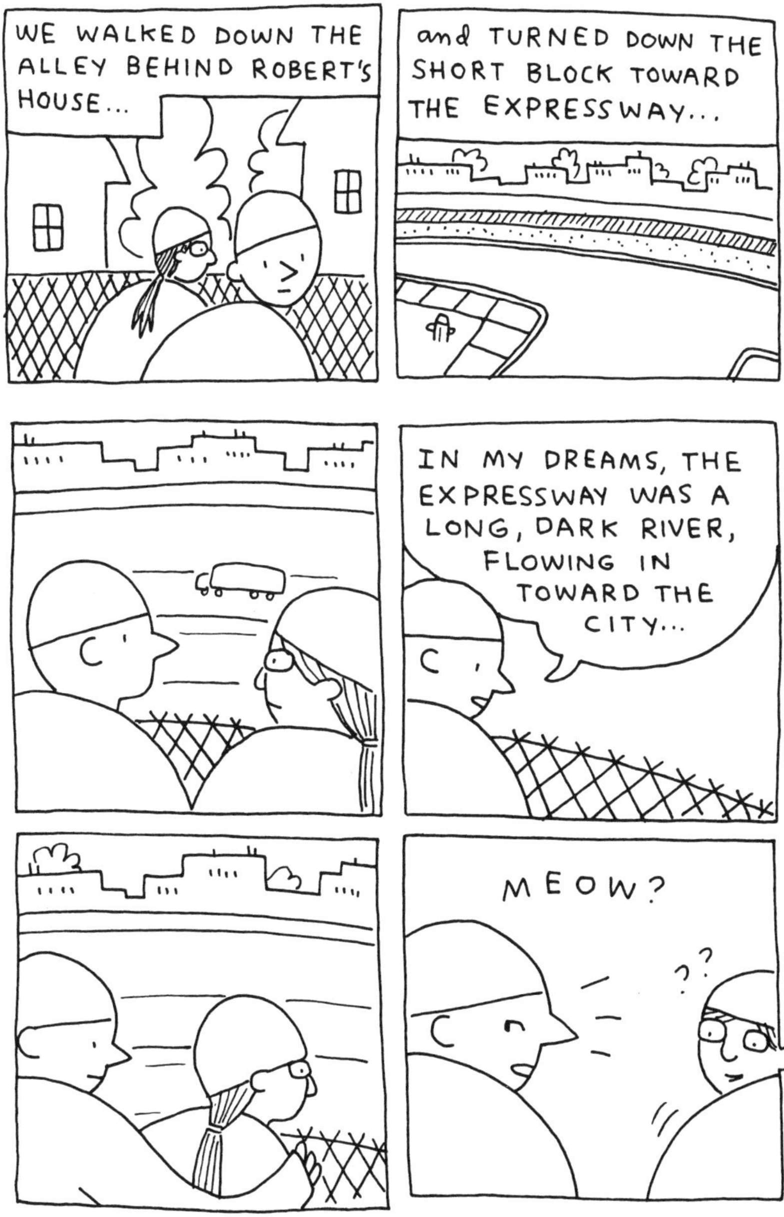
WE WALKED DOWN THE ALLEY BEHIND ROBERT'S HOUSE...
and TURNED DOWN THE SHORT BLOCK TOWARD THE EXPRESSWAY...
IN MY DREAMS, THE EXPRESSWAY WAS A LONG, DARK RIVER, FLOWING IN TOWARD THE CITY...
MEOW?
??

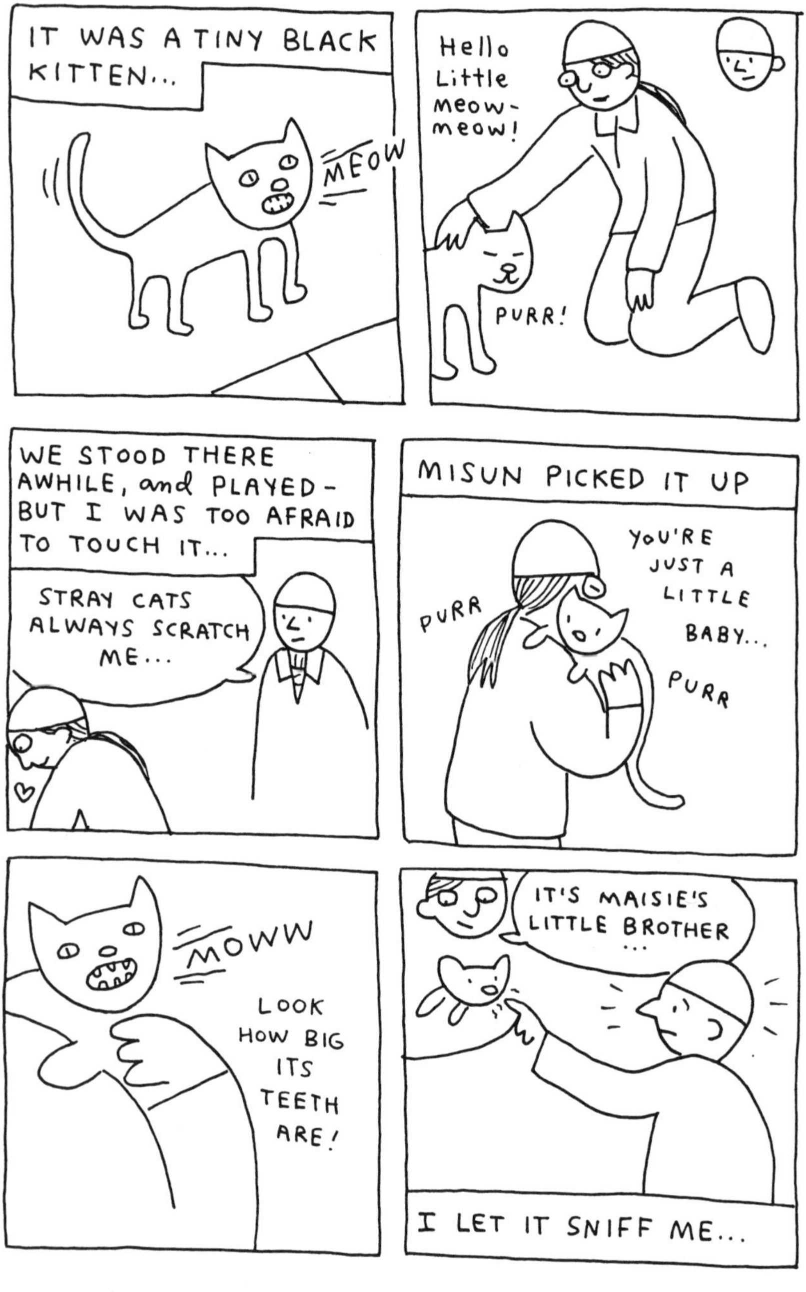
IT WAS A TINY BLACK KITTEN...
MEOW
Hello Little meow-meow!
PURR!
WE STOOD THERE AWHILE, and PLAYED-BUT I WAS TOO AFRAID TO TOUCH IT...
STRAY CATS ALWAYS SCRATCH ME...
MISUN PICKED IT UP
PURR
YOU'RE JUST A LITTLE BABY...
PURR
MOWW
LOOK HOW BIG ITS TEETH ARE!
IT'S MAISIE'S LITTLE BROTHER...
I LET IT SNIFF ME...

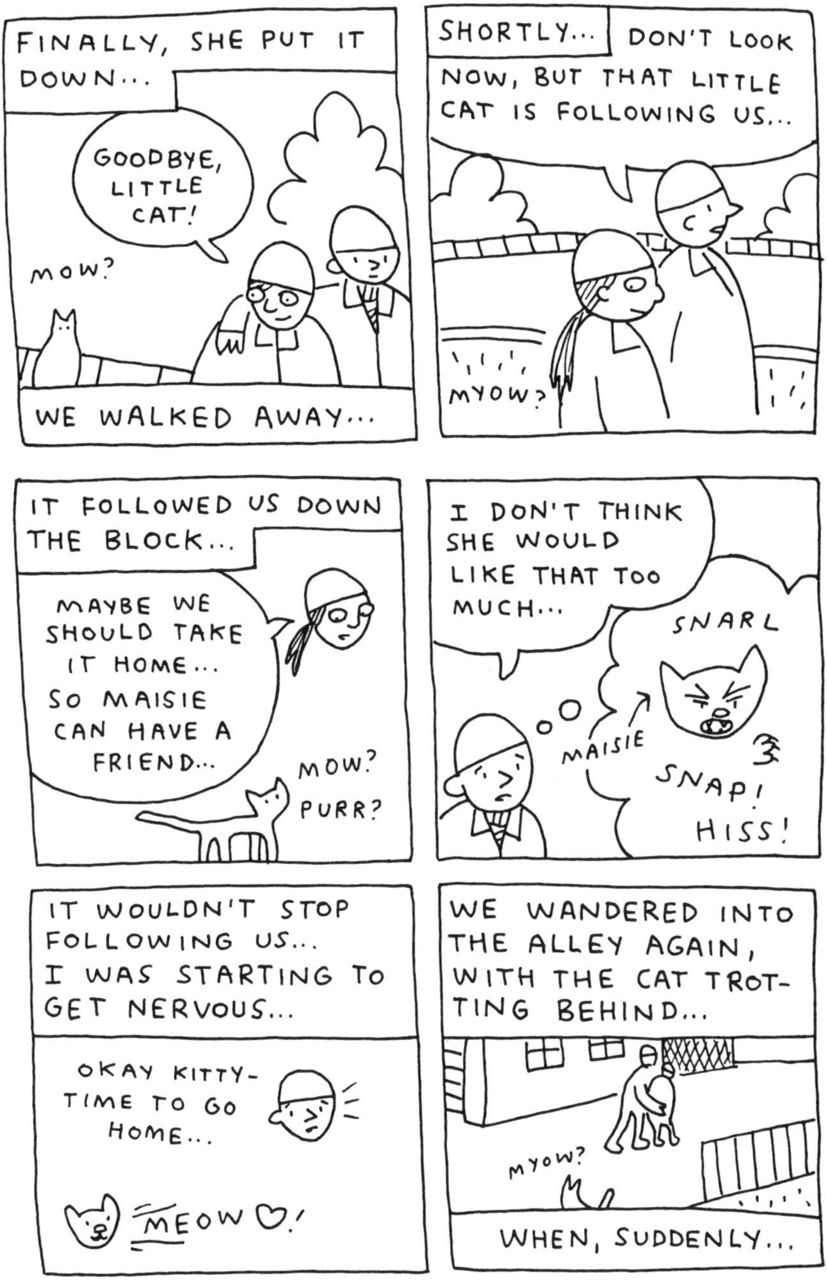
FINALLY, SHE PUT IT DOWN...
GOODBYE, LITTLE CAT!
MOW?
WE WALKED AWAY...
SHORTLY...
DON'T LOOK NOW, BUT THAT LITTLE CAT IS FOLLOWING US...
MYOW?
IT FOLLOWED US DOWN THE BLOCK...
MAYBE WE SHOULD TAKE IT HOME... SO MAISIE CAN HAVE A FRIEND...
MOW?
PURR?
I DON'T THINK SHE WOULD LIKE THAT TOO MUCH...
MAISIE
SNARL
SNAP!
HISS!
IT WOULDN'T STOP FOLLOWING US... I WAS STARTING TO GET NERVOUS...
OKAY KITTY- TIME TO GO HOME...
MEOW ♡!
WE WANDERED INTO THE ALLEY AGAIN, WITH THE CAT TROT- TING BEHIND...
MYOW?
WHEN, SUDDENLY...

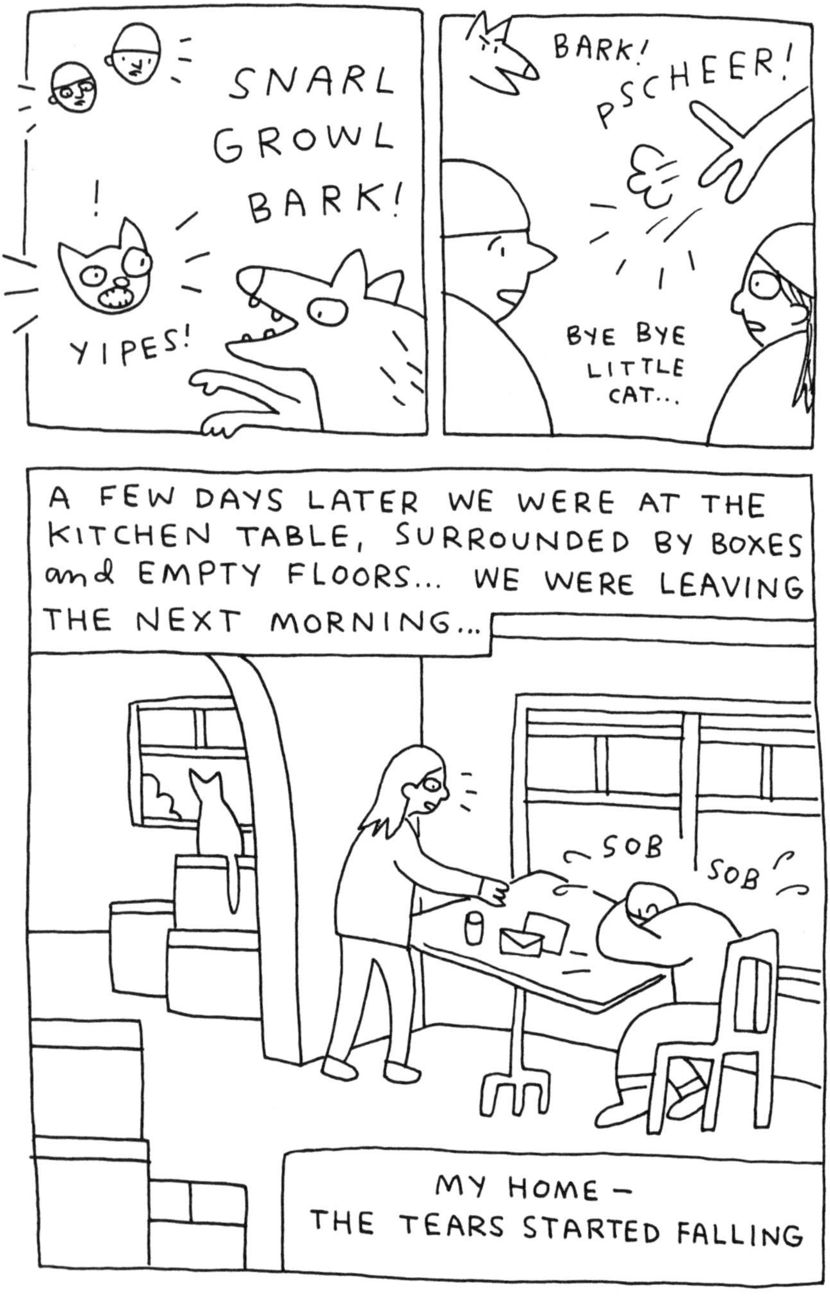
SNARL
GROWL
BARK!
YIPES!
BARK!
PSCHEER!
BYE BYE LITTLE CAT...
A FEW DAYS LATER WE WERE AT THE KITCHEN TABLE, SURROUNDED BY BOXES and EMPTY FLOORS... WE WERE LEAVING THE NEXT MORNING...
SOB
SOB
MY HOME – THE TEARS STARTED FALLING

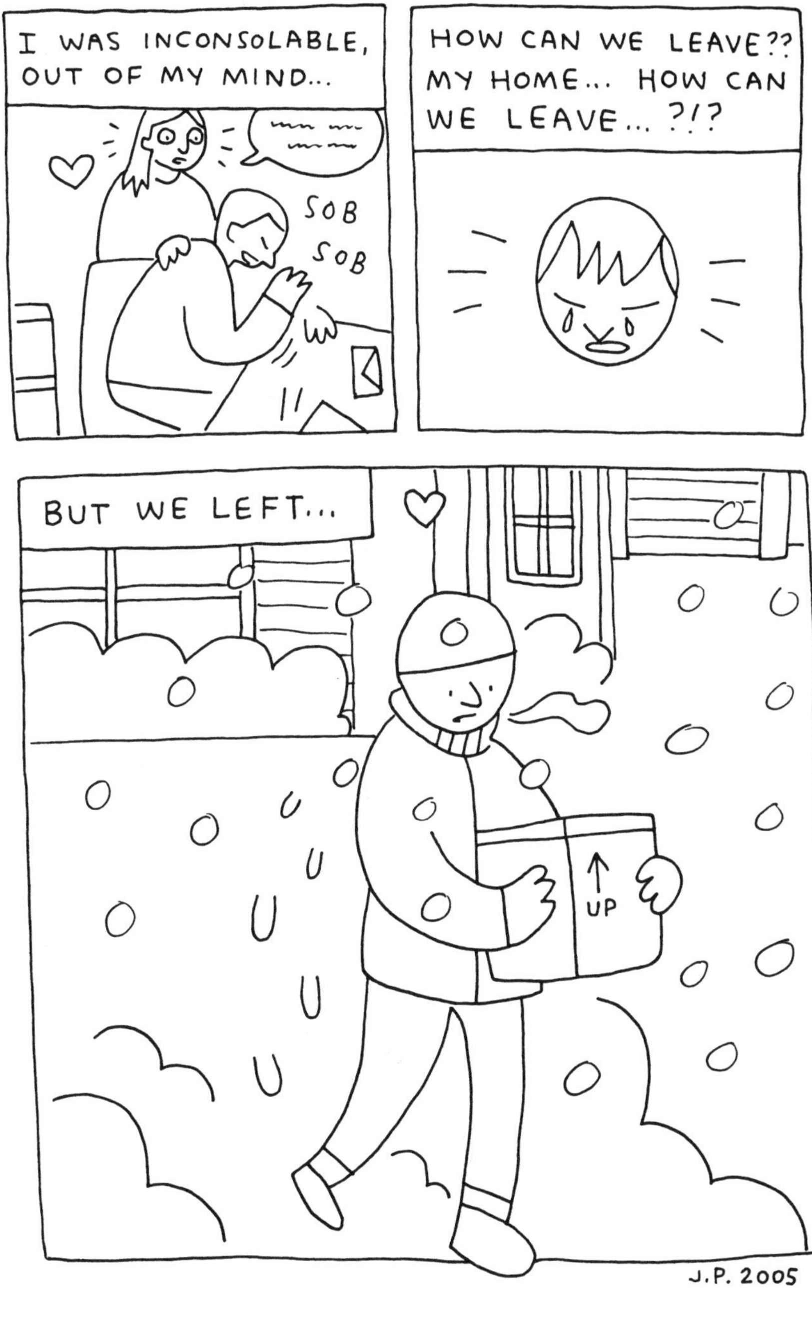
I WAS INCONSOLABLE, OUT OF MY MIND...
SOB
SOB
HOW CAN WE LEAVE?? MY HOME... HOW CAN WE LEAVE... ?!?
BUT WE LEFT...
UP
J.P. 2005

Baoche's

UNIVERSAL ACTION

A ZEN STORY

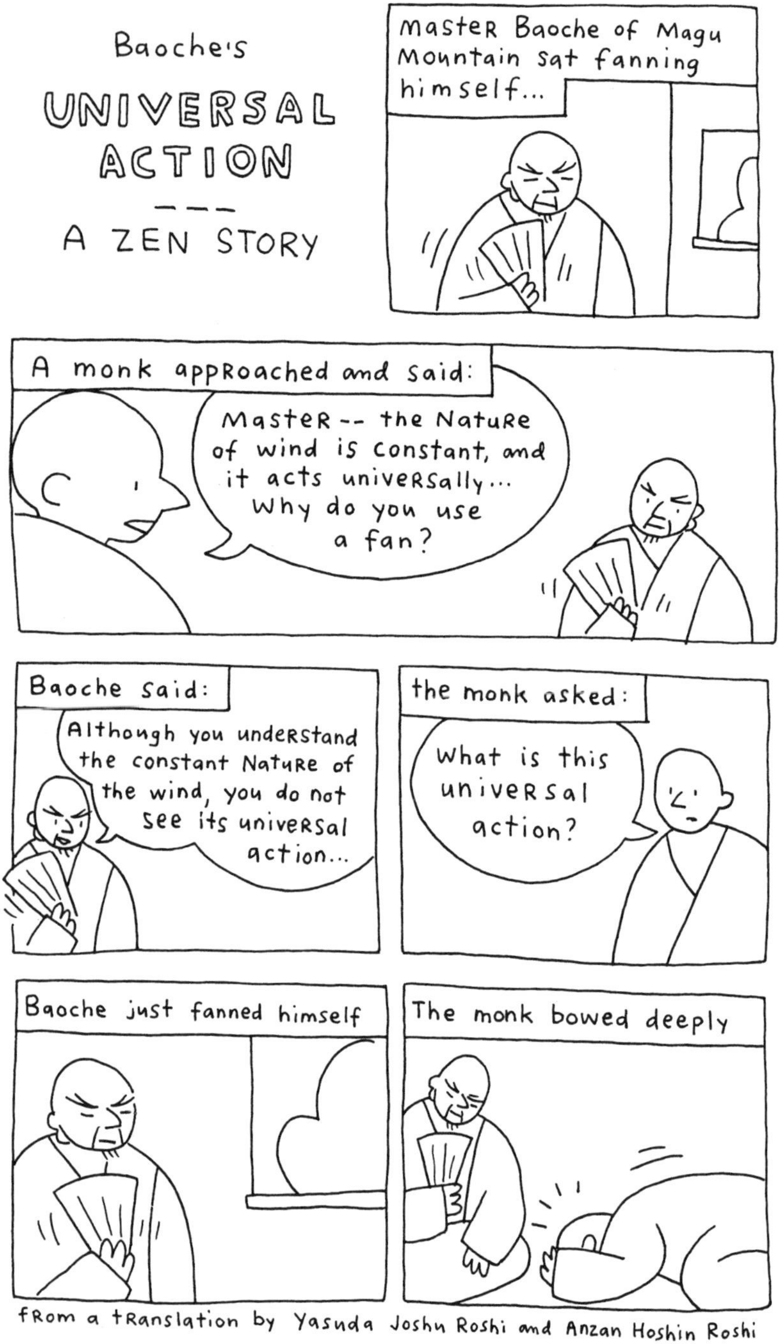

Master Baoche of Magu Mountain sat fanning himself...
A monk approached and said:
Master -- the Nature of wind is constant, and it acts universally... Why do you use a fan?
Baoche said:
Although you understand the constant Nature of the wind, you do not see its universal action...
the monk asked:
What is this universal action?
Baoche just fanned himself
The monk bowed deeply

from a translation by Yasuda Joshu Roshi and Anzan Hoshin Roshi

THE TOPS OF THE TREES

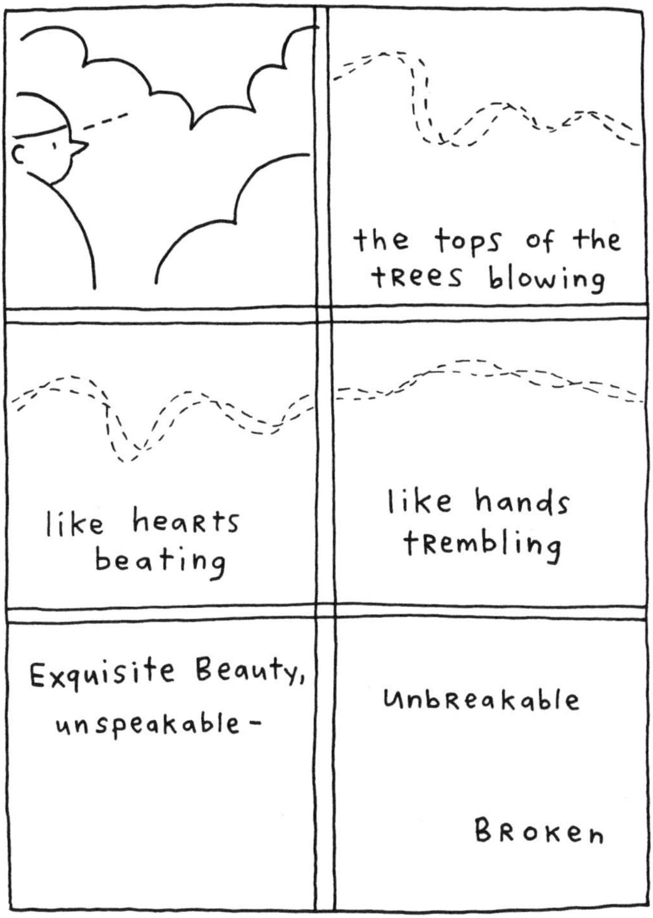

the tops of the trees blowing
like hearts beating
like hands trembling
Exquisite Beauty, unspeakable -
Unbreakable
Broken

MARCH 2005

Fifty-eight

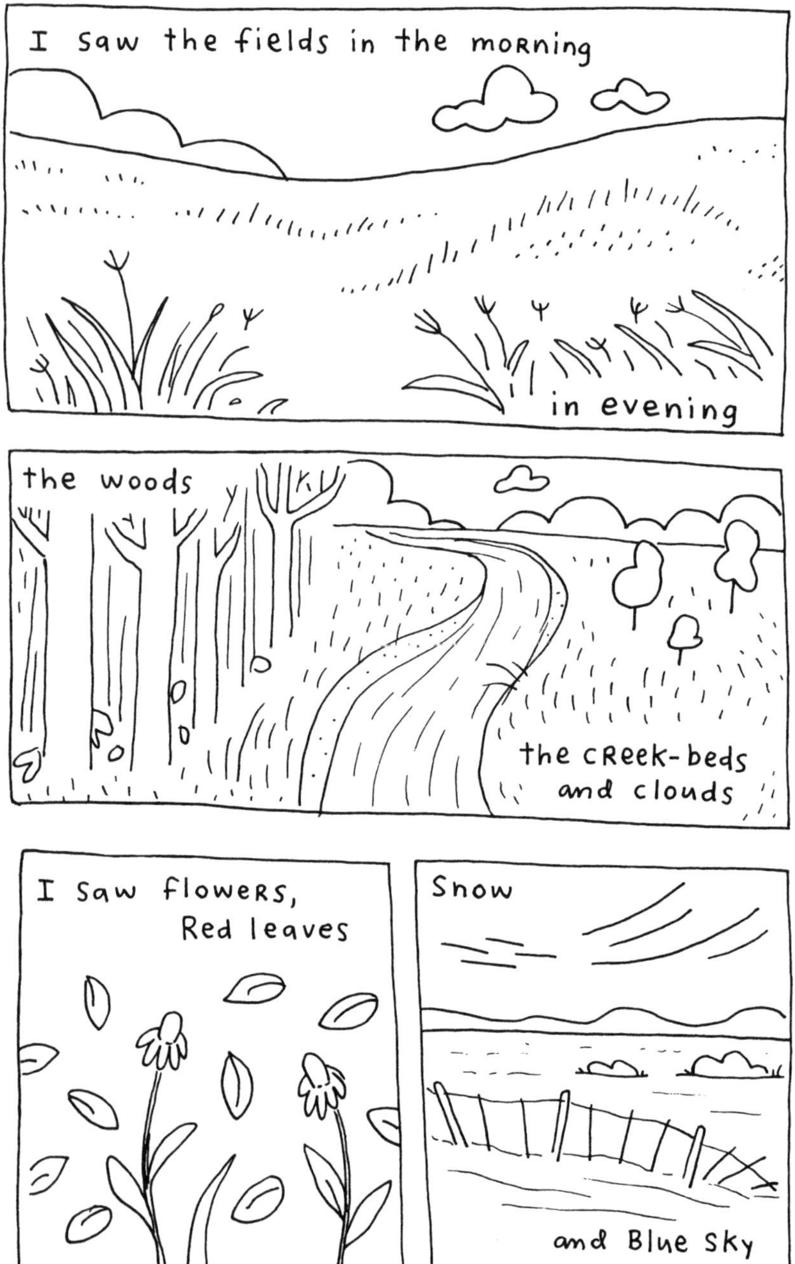
I saw the fields in the morning
in evening
the woods
the creek-beds
and clouds
I saw flowers,
Red leaves
Snow
and Blue Sky

In my heart, in my mind, I'm there now —

the buzzing of insects

the gentle breeze

written June 13, 2004
Drawn June 20, 2005

MEMORIES OF MY DAD

I think the earliest memory I have of my Dad is one of my earliest
memories of all-- it was the day he graduated from Law School, in 1972,
and I ran next door to ask our neighbor to take a picture of our family --
my Mom, my sister and I, and my Dad in his cap and gown. I guess
I was three years old.

My Dad didn't talk too much about his younger days-- I knew he was
somewhat of a shiftless, juvenile delinquent-type, hanging out on street
corners in his West Side neighborhood, getting into trouble and avoiding
responsibility (He told me he had to get his first job in order to pay for
damage he did by driving a car into a neighbor's garage wall).

He graduated from Austin High School in Chicago in 1959, near the
bottom of his class-- a fact he always remembered and always reminded
people of.

From 1961 – 62 he served in the US Army, stationed in South Korea.
He was a radio operator, overlooking the 38th Parallel, the border
between North and South Korea. He used to sit on his side of the valley,
looking through binoculars at the North Koreans, who were looking right
back at him through theirs. That's where he was during the Cuban
Missile Crisis, and as you can imagine, that was pretty intense.

(When I was a kid, I used to sit and stare at his photo album of
pictures from the Army, and Korea: My Dad, skinny in a tee-shirt and
sunglasses with a military haircut, his friends, cute Korean girls in mod
dresses, mountains, and pyramids of empty beer cans four feet tall...)

After the Army, he got a job at Commonwealth Edison, the local
Chicago electrical utility, and began working his way through college,
and then Law School.

After graduation, he started working as a lawyer downtown, and I'd
sit every evening on our front porch on Foster Avenue, waiting for his
bus to come by. As each bus went past, I'd scan the windows for his
face, and when I'd finally see him I'd run down to the corner in my
stocking feet as fast as I could. I'd meet him as he stepped off the bus
and we'd walk back home together.

In those days my Mom was still working as a nurse, and my Dad would take care of my sister and I when she had to work a Saturday shift. We'd sit around all day and watch monster movies on Channel 32. My Dad would make us lunch-- it was the same thing every time-- a baloney sandwich on white bread with Swiss cheese and mustard. He'd take the squeezable mustard bottle and draw a smiley-face for us on each sandwich, or write out our names. The sandwiches tasted good. We ate them with Fritos.

(Later my Dad always signed his letters to me with a smiley-face-- well, really a mumbley-face-- a squiggly self-portrait with glasses and kooky hair, a crooked smile... always so beautiful, my Dad...).

Sometimes, on Saturdays, I'd go along with him when he went into his office to work a few extra hours. We'd wake up early, get in the car and head downtown on the expressway, past the Magikist sign and the Morton Salt factory ("When it rains, it pours..."), pull off at Washington and into the parking garage off Wells Street.

The Parking Garage was a great mystery to me-- we'd leave our car there, give the keys to the guy who knew my Dad by name. He'd drive it up the strange spiral ramp and out of sight, blowing his horn as he went.

We'd stop next at the Three Coins Restaurant for breakfast. I'd get scrambled eggs with bacon and hash browns... searching through the little tubs of jelly for the Raspberry jam... (always too many Mixed Fruit). Then over to 33 North LaSalle, where my Dad's office was. Through the dark wooden lobby, the giant elevators, and up to the 25th floor.

My Dad's office was a never-ending source of fascination for me. I'd spin in the office chairs, sit at the desk and draw, Xerox my drawings, my face, my hands... hunt through the coffee cabinet for the box of sugar cubes... sugar cubes-- what an amazing idea.

I'd look through the Law Library, trying in vain to find something interesting to read, sit and stare out the big windows at the beautiful city, the skyscrapers, the rooftops, the lake in the distance, blue with boats and sky.

Sometimes I'd sneak into the stairwell and drop paperclips between the stairs, watching them fall 25 stories to the ground below.

When we were done we'd head back to the garage. The car keys hung on a board behind the glass window. I'd get to pick out some kind of candy from the machine-- "Boston Baked Beans"? I never figured that one out-- but I never quit trying.

When I think of those early years with my Dad, I inevitably think of the Chicago Bears. He was a fanatic about the Bears, and we watched every season on TV religiously. One time he finally relented and took me to see them play the Oilers at Soldier Field. Yeah-- they lost.

No matter how bad the Bears were (and they were pretty bad) we watched them every Sunday. My most vivid memory is the day the Bears beat the Giants, in 1978, with a field goal in the last few seconds of overtime, to make it into the playoffs for the first time in fourteen years. As the kick sailed through, and the Bears won, we both leapt off our couch in the basement TV room, and jumped around like maniacs. I was so proud and happy, and so was he...

And who could forget the 1985 – 86 season, when the Bears rolled through the NFL on the way to their Super Bowl destiny? I remember sitting on the couch with my Dad, watching the game. I don't think either of us could quite believe it-- after years of watching them lose, the Bears were actually in the Super Bowl, and not only that-- they were actually gonna win it... It seemed impossible, but it really happened.

For years afterward, the license plates on my Dad's car read, simply: "XX4610" – the final score in the Bears triumphant Super Bowl XX.

Later, when I was a morose teenager, there was a distance between me and my Dad, between me and everyone. My Dad really tried to figure me out, but that was quite a project.

One day in High School, I borrowed a pair of clip-on earrings from my friend's sister. I put one in my left ear and sat down at the kitchen table, waiting for my Dad to come home from work. Finally, he came in and sat down at the table next to me. When he saw the earring he didn't say a word. He just stood up, walked calmly down into the basement, and started kicking boxes around with all his might. I had to run down and show him it was fake, the poor guy...

Later, he would do favors for me. When I started drawing comics he would take my originals with him into work and Xerox copies of my books for me to give to my friends. And he'd bring home the Chicago Reader for me every week. They ran *Ernie Pook* by Lynda Barry, and *Life in Hell* by Matt Groening. These were my two biggest inspirations when I started to draw comics again, as a teenager. The Reader was also my introduction to the world of underground music and art, creative weirdness. It was just what I needed.

When I got into punk rock there were no good record stores out in the suburbs where we lived, so I'd make lists for my Dad, and he'd stop at Rolling Stones Records on his way home from work and pick up the albums I'd requested. I always wondered what those record store clerks thought of the middle-aged guy in the suit who'd stop in regularly to buy LPs by Black Flag and the Replacements.

Inexplicably, as he got older, my Dad came to grow fonder and fonder of hard rock and heavy metal. So many times he'd pull up into the driveway blasting Judas Priest in the car super loud. He loved Creedence too, and he'd put his fists out like a boxer, and punch the air, saying "Heavy bass... Heavy drums..." His favorite song was "Renegade" by Styx.

Somehow, when I went away to college, I got to take a bunch of my Dad's records with me. One day, heartbroken, I pulled out "Only the Lonely" by Frank Sinatra. My Dad loved Sinatra, but to me it was just an abstract concept, old and curious. But I put the record on, and listened... and the music settled right down into my heart and soul.

After that, Sinatra became one of the hinges around which my relationship with my Dad revolved. Like the guy said in those liner notes: "Frank Sinatra wasn't just singing *to* me-- Frank Sinatra *was* me..." Frank Sinatra was my Dad, and he was me, too. So my Dad and I were one.

In later years we took a couple of road trips together. I always hoped that the long miles would let us open up to each other and really talk, but mostly we just listened to the radio. Still, it was just a blessing to be in his presence. When I moved to Denver in '92, he drove with me in the U-Haul out there. We had one day in Denver together, then I took him to the airport.

Coming back to the apartment after dropping him off, it was one of those Denver afternoons in summer, where the rain pours out of a sunny blue sky. I was driving slow, down unknown new streets, through the smeary, glaring windshield and tears that wouldn't stop. I realized suddenly how far away I was, how alone I felt. I was suddenly in my future, and there was no going back.

I'd call home every week from Denver and talking to my Dad was always a joy. He was so full of love and encouragement. I could turn to him with any problem and he always had such good advice. Somehow, the physical distance between us brought us closer, kept our love and connection at the forefront of our minds constantly.

When I moved back home to Illinois, in 1998, it was a momentous occasion. It was such a relief to be back there on those streets, under that sky, in those arms.

My Dad and my sister and her kids would come over to my place to watch the Bears again every Sunday. It made me feel so happy, so connected, and alive. We'd eat, and joke around; jump up off the couch and yell at the TV. Remember when they blocked that last minute field goal and finally beat the Packers? We fell all over the room.

Then they changed my schedule at work and I had to start working on Sundays. And that was the end of that. Looking back now, I see what a rip-off it was. I should've quit right then and there.

The last time I saw my Dad was the day before we moved again, back to Denver, in 2002. I was beside myself. I didn't wanna go, I didn't wanna leave, but I knew that's where my life was taking me.

We stood there in the empty, boxy house, in each other's arms. My Dad dispensed some words of wisdom… probably "Be good to each other" and "Know that we love you" and then he stepped out the door with tears in his eyes, down the driveway, and into his car. He drove away.

Ever since I got sick I've been acutely aware of the fleeting nature of our lives. As he walked away, I knew, in the back of my mind, that there was the possibility I'd never see him again. I'd force the thought away, again and again, but it'd creep up into my head nearly every day for the next few years.

When he was struggling with his pain, at what was to be the end of his life, we talked on the phone practically every day... good, honest, real conversations, heart to heart. In those moments we were so close, our love was right there-- so deep, so open, and alive. I take consolation in knowing that when he went, there was not a shred of doubt in our minds about how much we meant to each other, how much we loved each other. It was an honor for me to be his son.

After he died, I was back in Illinois, everything touched by his presence. I sat in his office room and cried: the photos, the little notes, his books and records, his Bears stuff-- my Dad's life.

I was going through old papers, and I found this poem he had kept up on his office wall for years, a Xerox tucked into the corner of his bulletin board, surrounded by photos of family and friends, some gone, some still here. This is what the poem said:

"Do not stand at my grave and weep:
I am not there; I do not sleep.
I am a thousand winds that blow,
I am the diamond glints of snow.
I am the sunlight on ripened grain,
I am the gentle Autumn's rain.

When you awaken in the morning's hush,
I am the swift uplifting rush
Of quiet birds in circled flight.
I am the soft stars that shine at night.
Do not stand at my grave and cry;
I am not there, I did not die."

I don't know what happens to us after we die-- the great mystery-- but I do feel in my heart that death is not the end. I loved my Dad his whole life, and I love my Dad now, in ways that words can't adequately express. He was the best man I ever knew.

--John Porcellino, May-June 2005
San Francisco

BIDING TIME

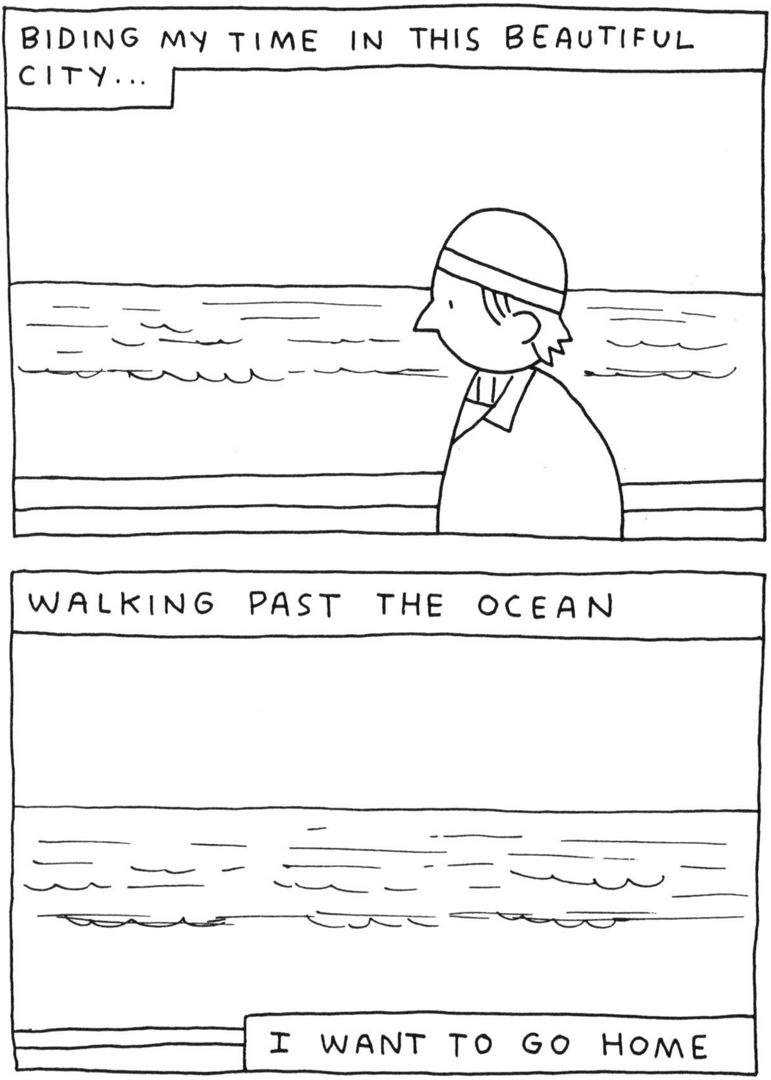
BIDING MY TIME IN THIS BEAUTIFUL CITY...
WALKING PAST THE OCEAN
I WANT TO GO HOME

APRIL / JUNE 2005

APRIL 5th – PARK CITY

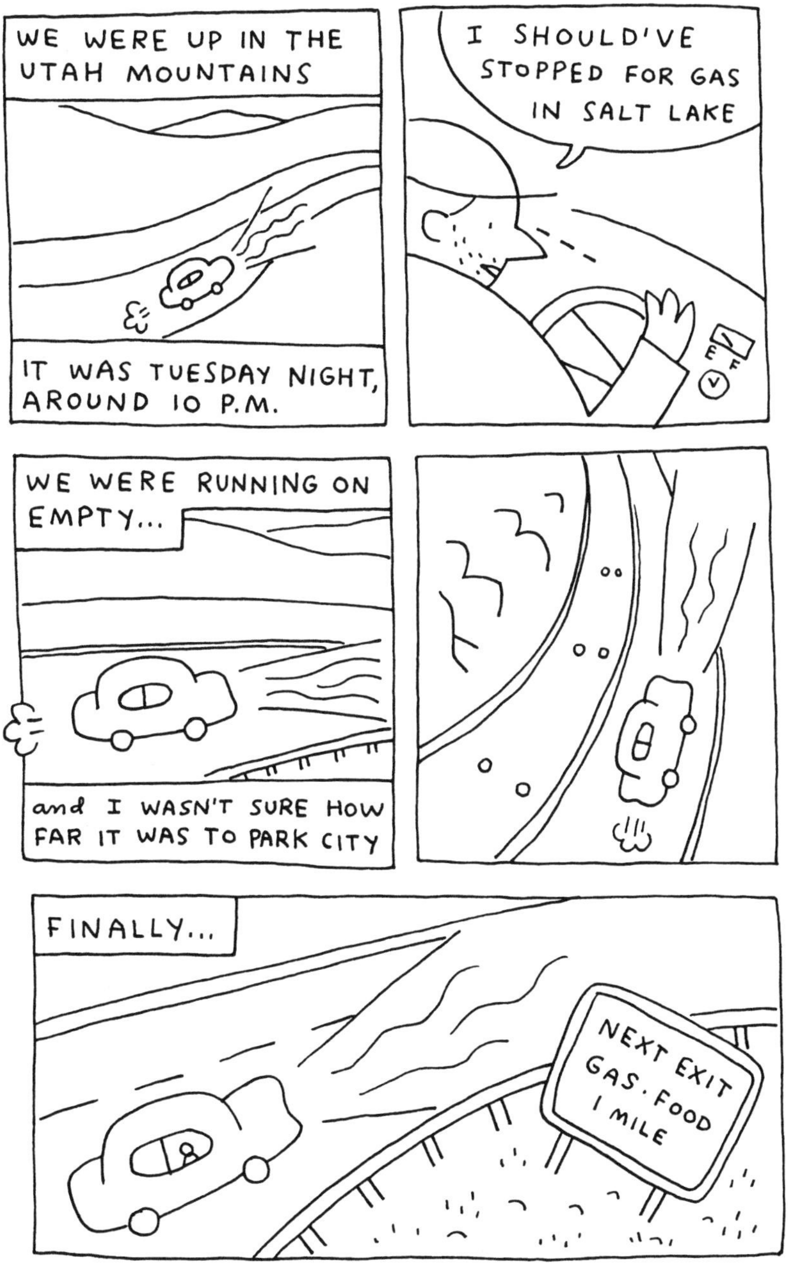

WE WERE UP IN THE UTAH MOUNTAINS
IT WAS TUESDAY NIGHT, AROUND 10 P.M.
I SHOULD'VE STOPPED FOR GAS IN SALT LAKE
WE WERE RUNNING ON EMPTY...
and I WASN'T SURE HOW FAR IT WAS TO PARK CITY
FINALLY...
NEXT EXIT GAS · FOOD 1 MILE

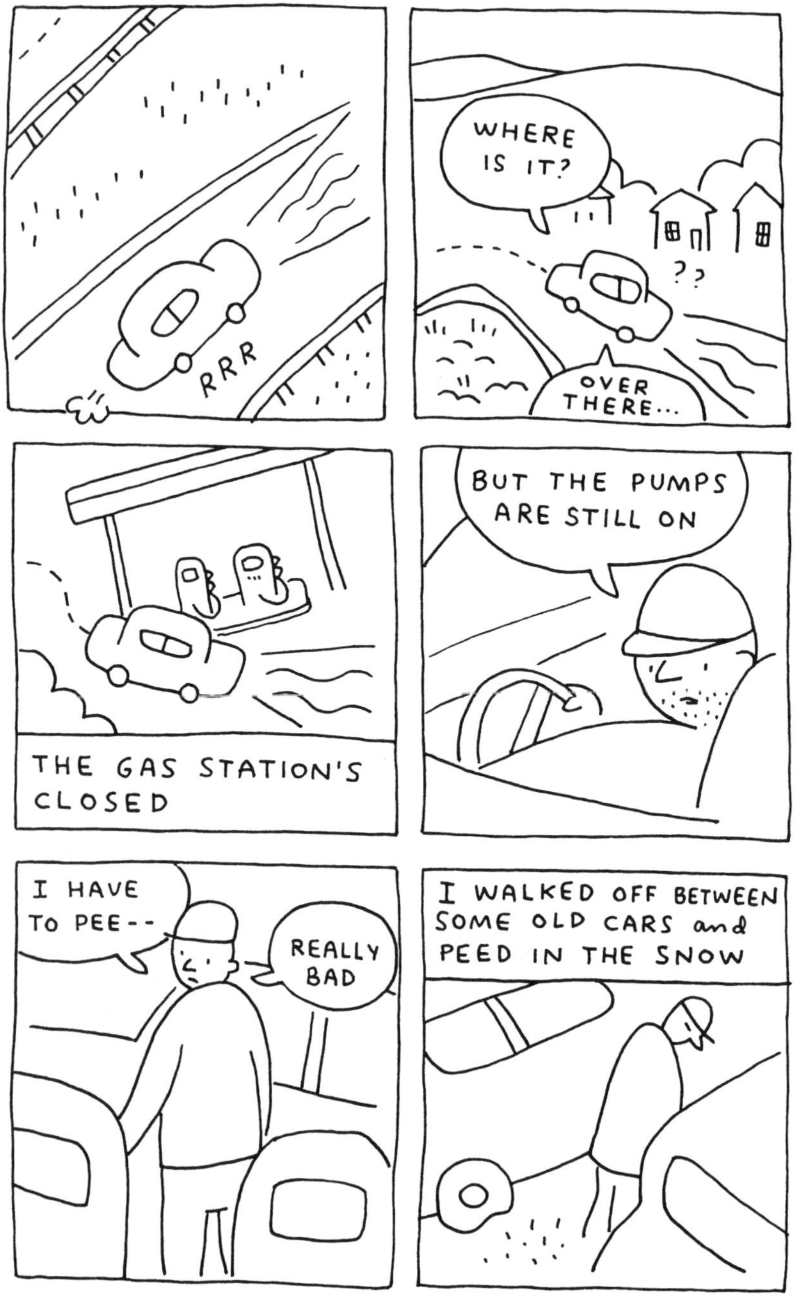
RRR
WHERE IS IT?
??
OVER THERE...
THE GAS STATION'S CLOSED
BUT THE PUMPS ARE STILL ON
I HAVE TO PEE--
REALLY BAD
I WALKED OFF BETWEEN SOME OLD CARS and PEED IN THE SNOW

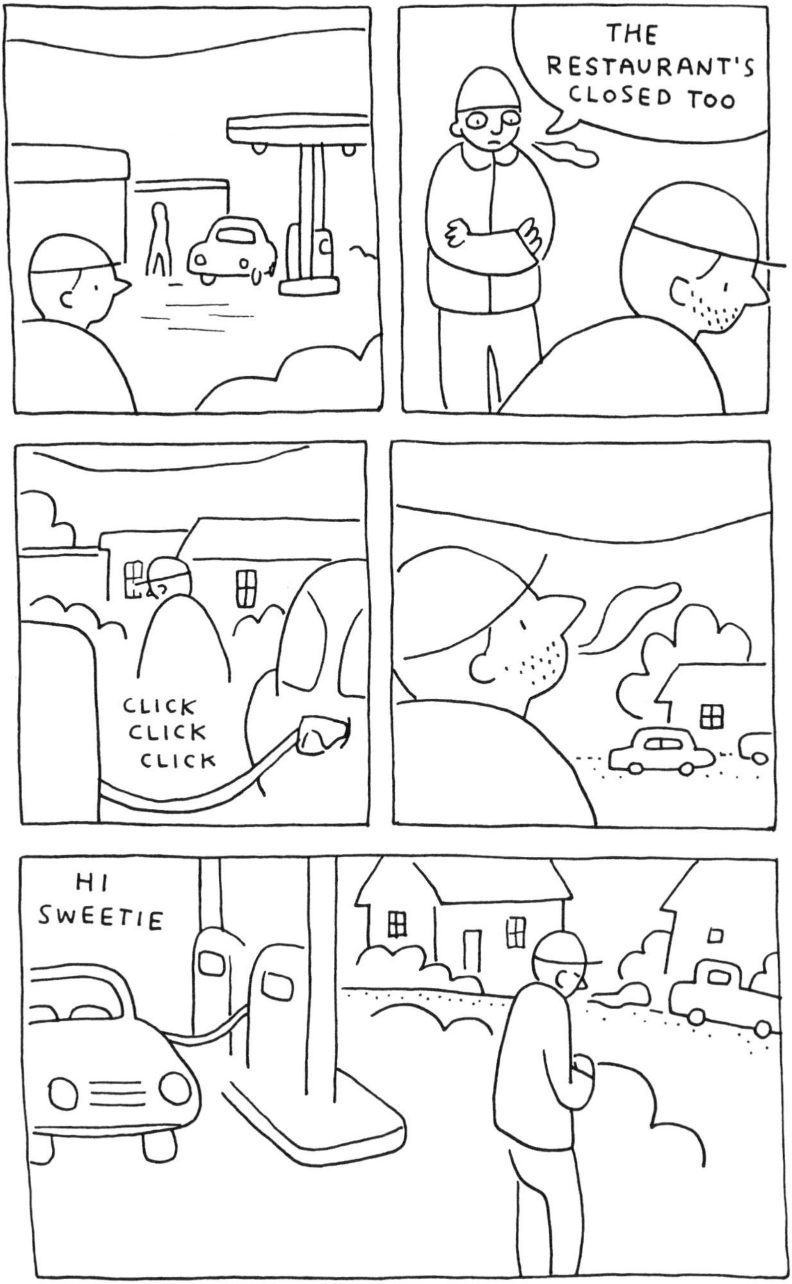
THE RESTAURANT'S CLOSED TOO
CLICK CLICK CLICK
HI SWEETIE

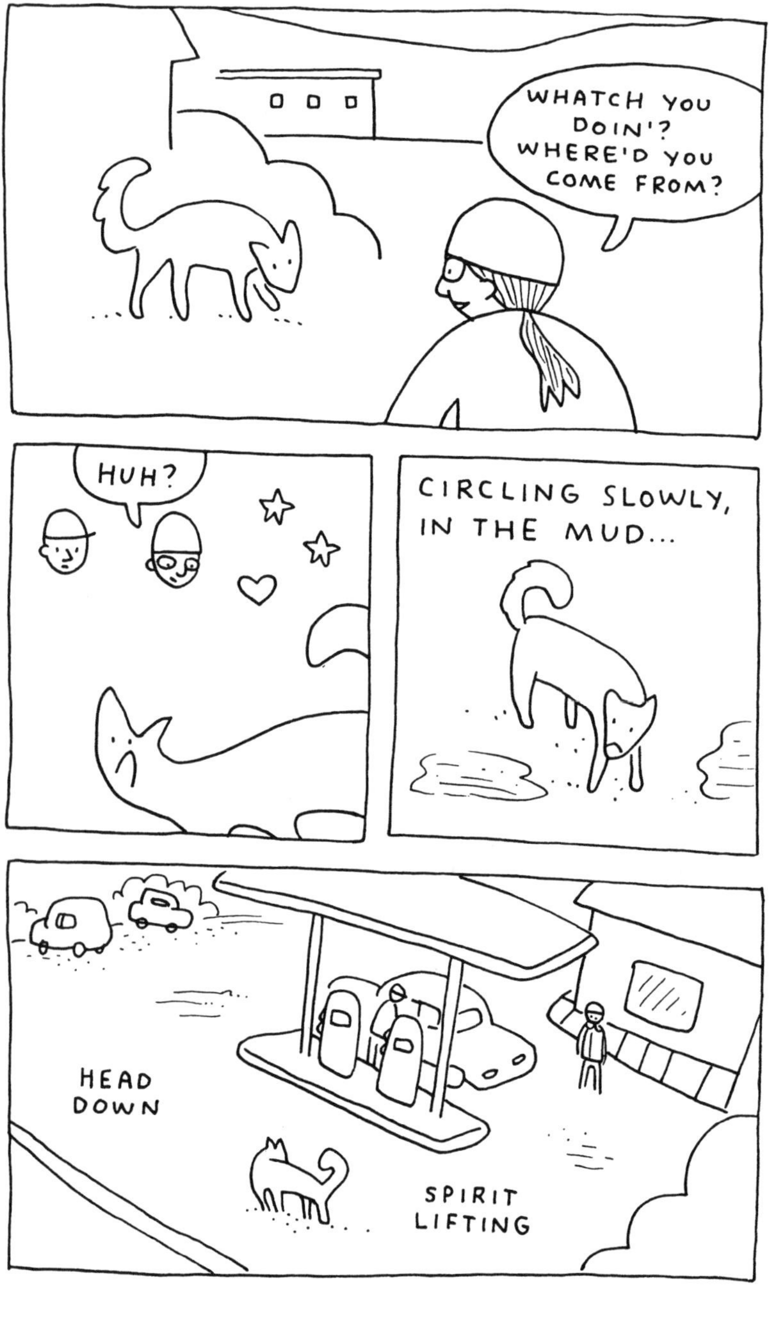
WHATCH YOU DOIN'? WHERE'D YOU COME FROM?
HUH?
CIRCLING SLOWLY, IN THE MUD...
HEAD DOWN
SPIRIT LIFTING

LOOKING OUT
THROUGH TIRED,
QUIET EYES...

IT'S ALL RIGHT,
NOW — IT'S
OKAY

... and INTO THE NIGHT

JOHN P. JUNE 2005 ♡

ENDLESS BRIGHT WORLD

We're driving across Nebraska at night, driving, driving, through the dark. The images come to mind, again and again— the feelings. The last moments my Dad was here, his pain. I feel him going, again and again, but it makes no sense — it can't be real— touching the void, looking into the void— in a Rental Car in Nebraska, at night, against the bed— My Dad's spirit Rising up, the tears — my heart— cold fear, and wordless, mindless dark.

I'm standing in my Dad's bedroom— that's where he lay, that's where he stood, that's where he fell— he called out in the night. I can see the paramedic's feet, my Dad, my family, this world. The endless bright world, the darkness. The coming and going, again and again and again.

I stand up— that's where he stood, I look out— that's what he saw... My father...

A week ago he was here, brushing his teeth, watching TV. Now he's gone and it doesn't make any sense.

I got home, I finally got home, but somehow he's not here. Where did my Dad go? I got home, but I was a week late. A week ago he was here, in this bed. I could have touched him, talked to him— I could have held him, felt him, heard him. My Dad's eyes, his tears, his heart. His head on his pillow, now it's my pillow, but where's my Dad?

> tiny birds, the size of a thumb
> Fragrant flowers and evening sky—
> Where's my Dad?

John Porcellino
APRIL 24, 2005

The Monk

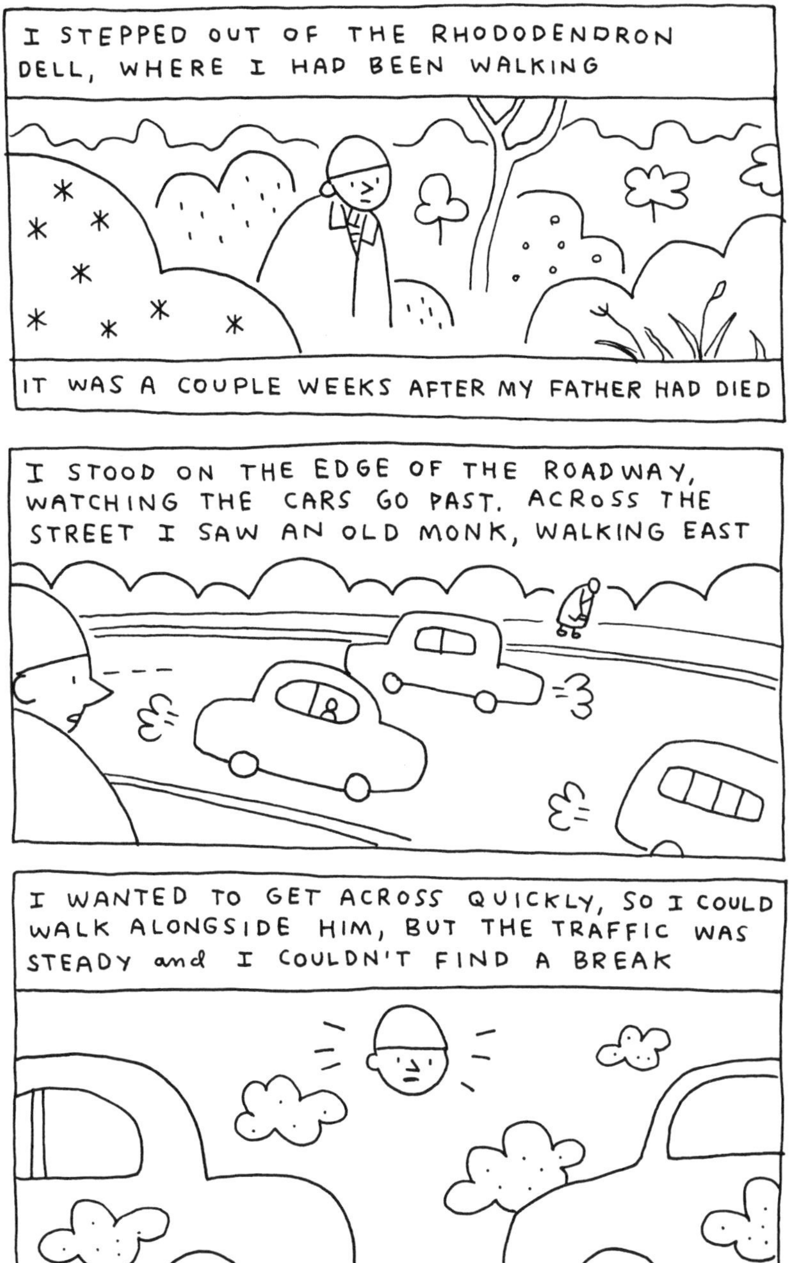
I STEPPED OUT OF THE RHODODENDRON DELL, WHERE I HAD BEEN WALKING
IT WAS A COUPLE WEEKS AFTER MY FATHER HAD DIED
I STOOD ON THE EDGE OF THE ROADWAY, WATCHING THE CARS GO PAST. ACROSS THE STREET I SAW AN OLD MONK, WALKING EAST
I WANTED TO GET ACROSS QUICKLY, SO I COULD WALK ALONGSIDE HIM, BUT THE TRAFFIC WAS STEADY and I COULDN'T FIND A BREAK

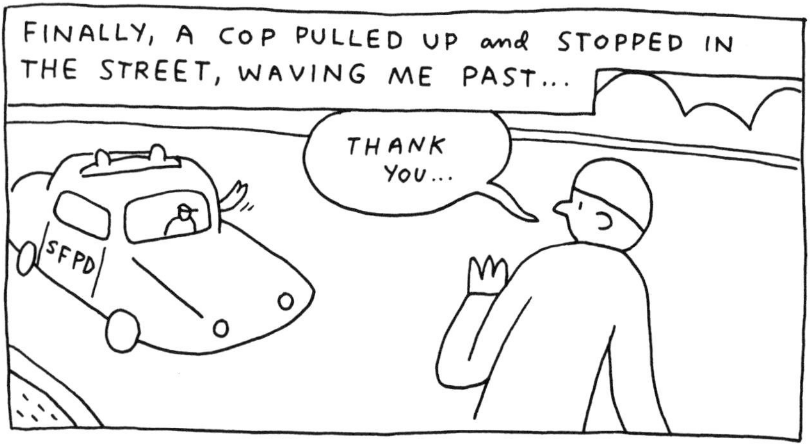
FINALLY, A COP PULLED UP and STOPPED IN THE STREET, WAVING ME PAST...
SFPD
THANK YOU...

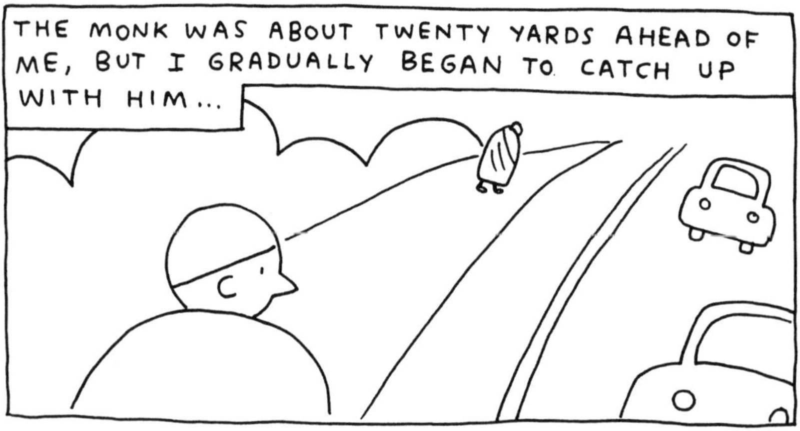
THE MONK WAS ABOUT TWENTY YARDS AHEAD OF ME, BUT I GRADUALLY BEGAN TO CATCH UP WITH HIM...

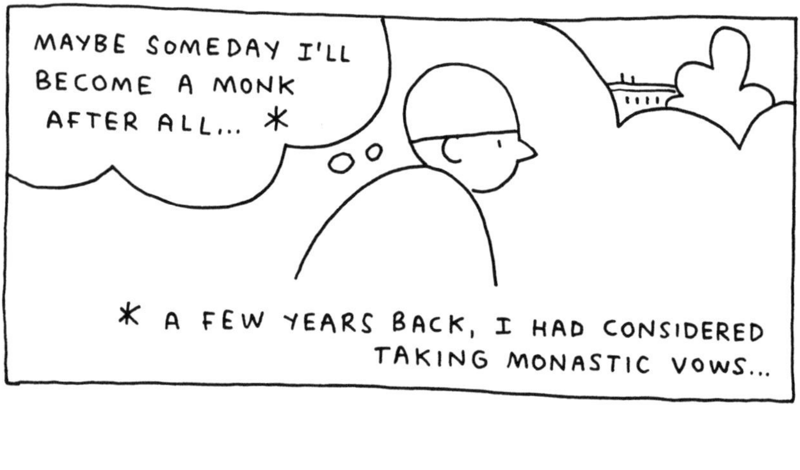
MAYBE SOMEDAY I'LL BECOME A MONK AFTER ALL... *
* A FEW YEARS BACK, I HAD CONSIDERED TAKING MONASTIC VOWS...

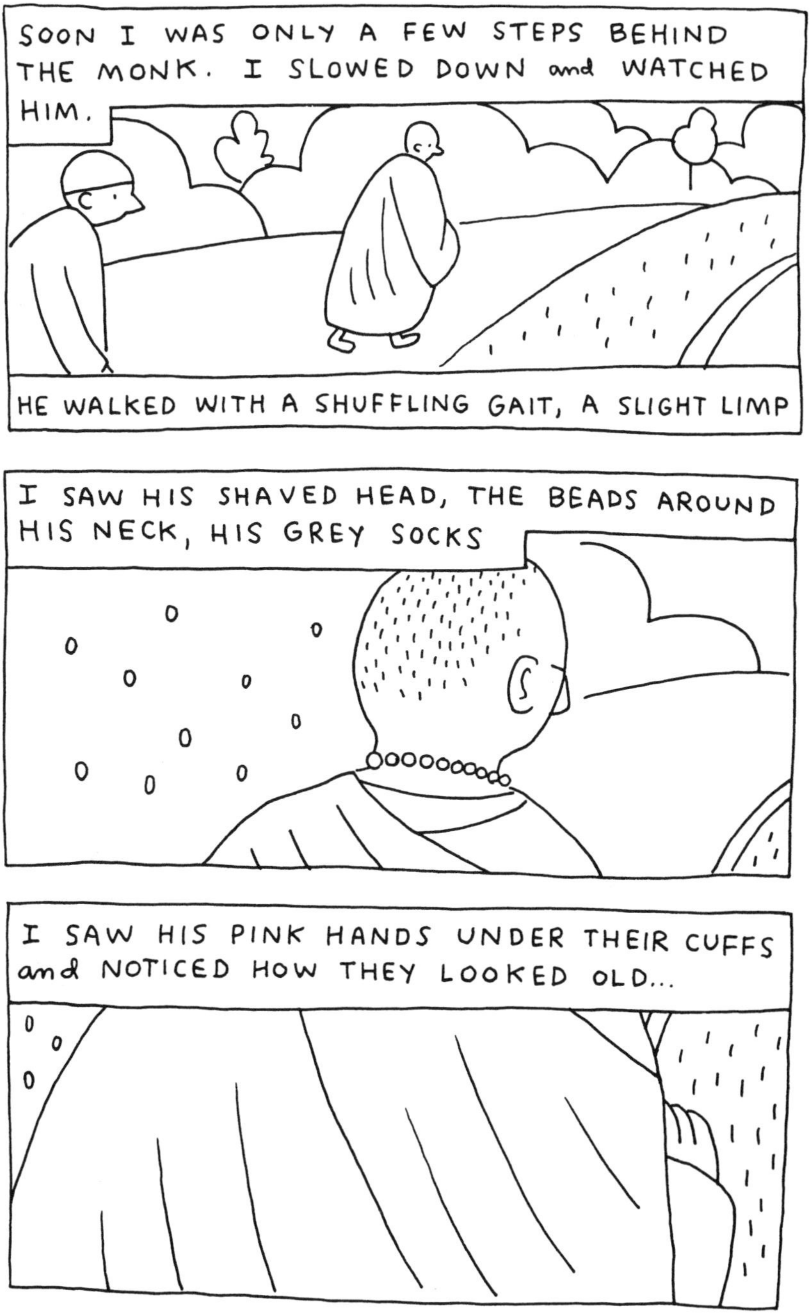
SOON I WAS ONLY A FEW STEPS BEHIND THE MONK. I SLOWED DOWN and WATCHED HIM.
HE WALKED WITH A SHUFFLING GAIT, A SLIGHT LIMP
I SAW HIS SHAVED HEAD, THE BEADS AROUND HIS NECK, HIS GREY SOCKS
I SAW HIS PINK HANDS UNDER THEIR CUFFS and NOTICED HOW THEY LOOKED OLD...

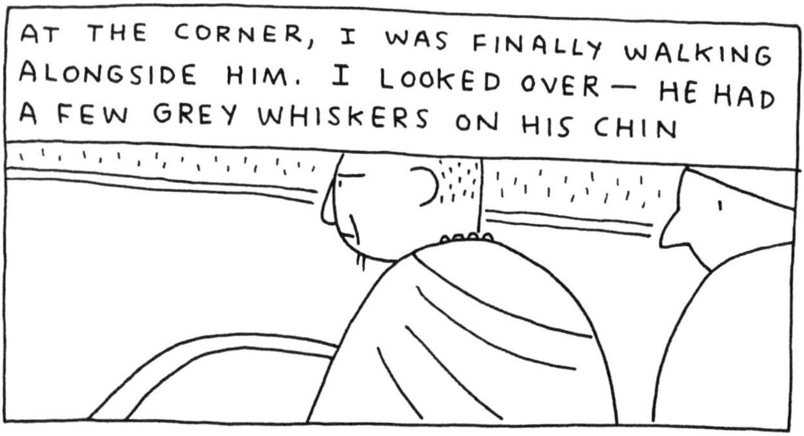
AT THE CORNER, I WAS FINALLY WALKING ALONGSIDE HIM. I LOOKED OVER — HE HAD A FEW GREY WHISKERS ON HIS CHIN

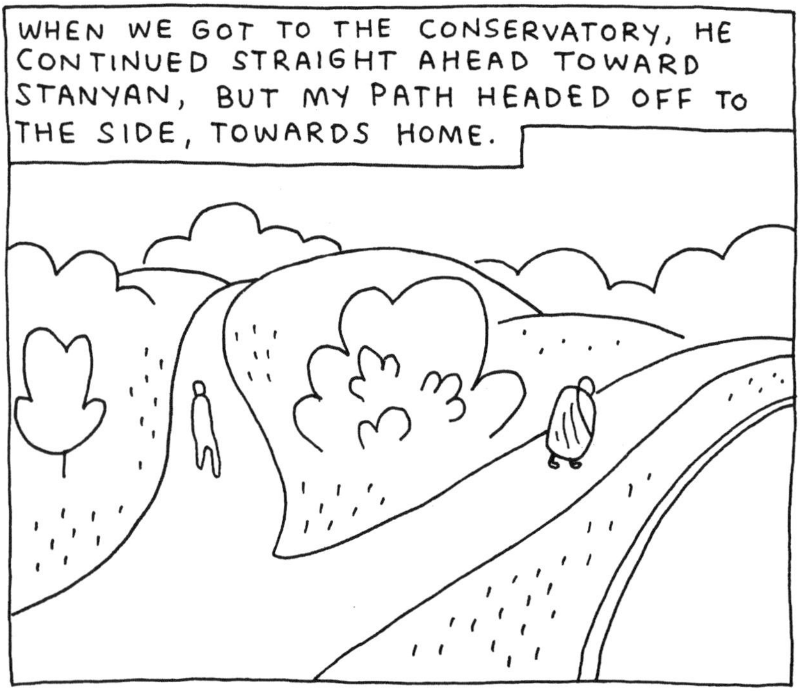
WHEN WE GOT TO THE CONSERVATORY, HE CONTINUED STRAIGHT AHEAD TOWARD STANYAN, BUT MY PATH HEADED OFF TO THE SIDE, TOWARDS HOME.

4/19/05 - DRAWN JUNE 12, 2005

Sunlight slips through
cRacks in the buildings...

you can't take a single thing
with you.

2003   2005
DENVER   S.F.   J.P.

APRIL 7th–WESTERN ILLINOIS

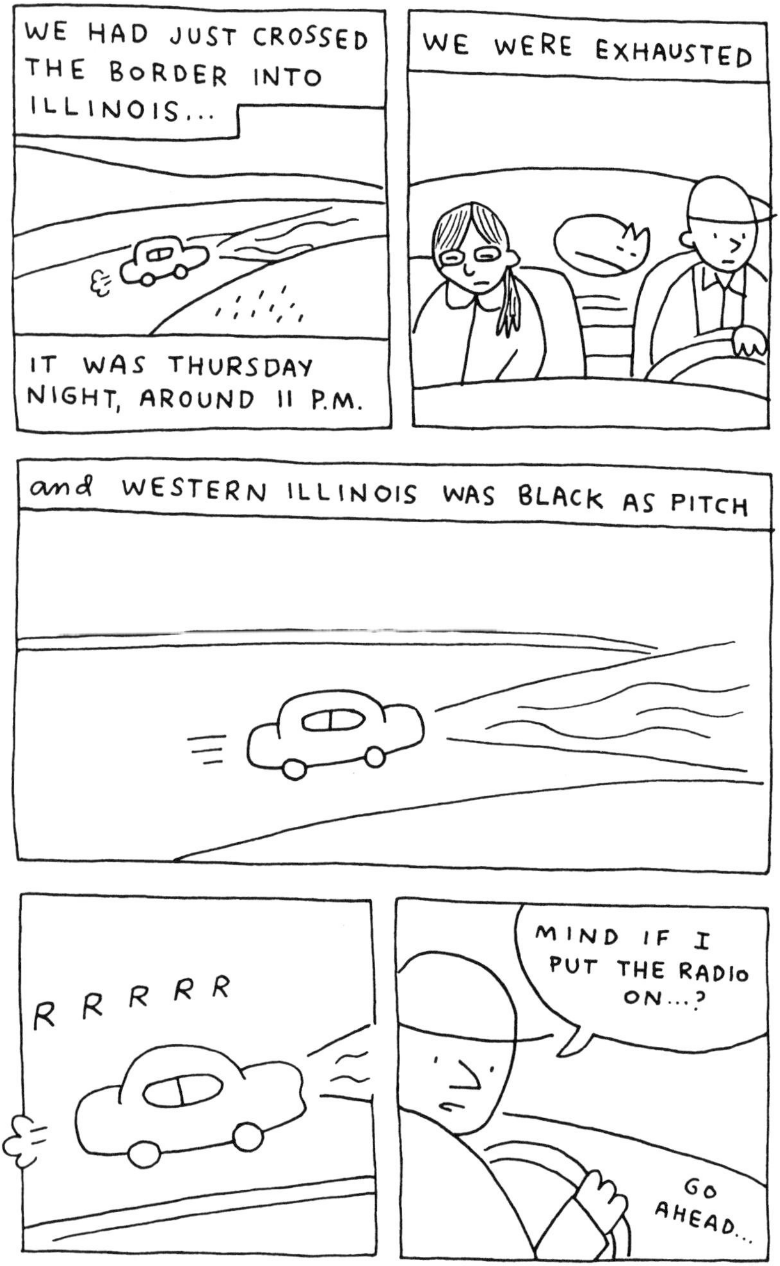
WE HAD JUST CROSSED THE BORDER INTO ILLINOIS...
IT WAS THURSDAY NIGHT, AROUND 11 P.M.
WE WERE EXHAUSTED
and WESTERN ILLINOIS WAS BLACK AS PITCH
R R R R R
MIND IF I PUT THE RADIO ON...?
GO AHEAD...

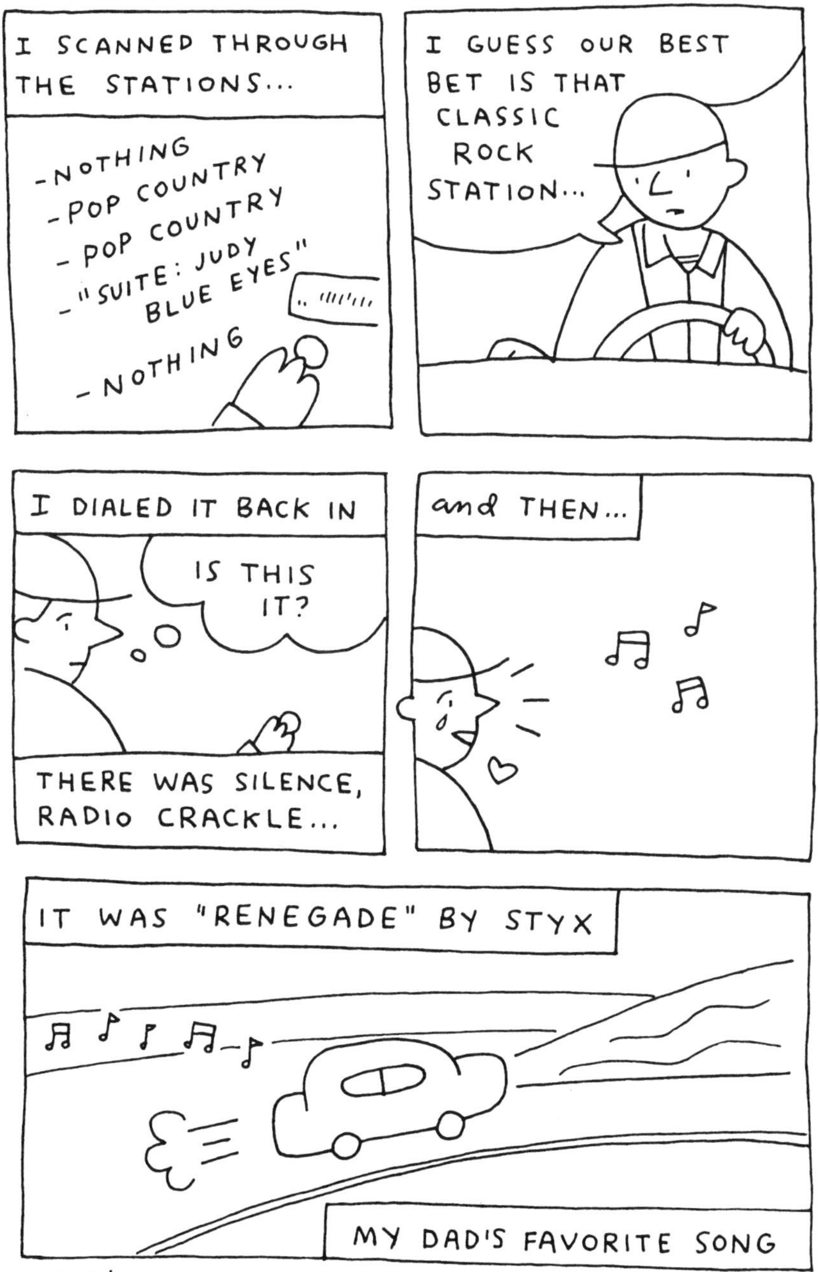
I SCANNED THROUGH THE STATIONS...
-NOTHING
-POP COUNTRY
-POP COUNTRY
-"SUITE: JUDY BLUE EYES"
-NOTHING
I GUESS OUR BEST BET IS THAT CLASSIC ROCK STATION...
I DIALED IT BACK IN
IS THIS IT?
THERE WAS SILENCE, RADIO CRACKLE...
and THEN...
IT WAS "RENEGADE" BY STYX
MY DAD'S FAVORITE SONG

J.P. 6/05 - ANOTHER TRUE STORY

DREAM

Last night I had a wonderful dream. Misun and I were walking on a dirt road out in the country. We came to a creek, where the road forded across. My Dad was there, standing in the water. He reached out to us, to lead us into the stream, then we crossed together.

When we got to the other side, we continued down the dirt road into a charming little town. People were outside on the streets, and everyone knew my Dad, waving and saying Hello. We ended up at a country club-type building and went inside. People were sitting around at tables, eating or reading the paper etc. My Dad was happily taking us around to meet all his friends...

dreamt May 3rd, 2005
in the morning

John P.

(the countryside was beautiful, bright sunshine, blue skies, sunlight filtering through green leaves, warm and summery with a nice breeze. The water was cool and clean, tumbling over round stones, sparkling in the light. The houses were like little cottages, with fences etc. It was very peaceful, serene...)

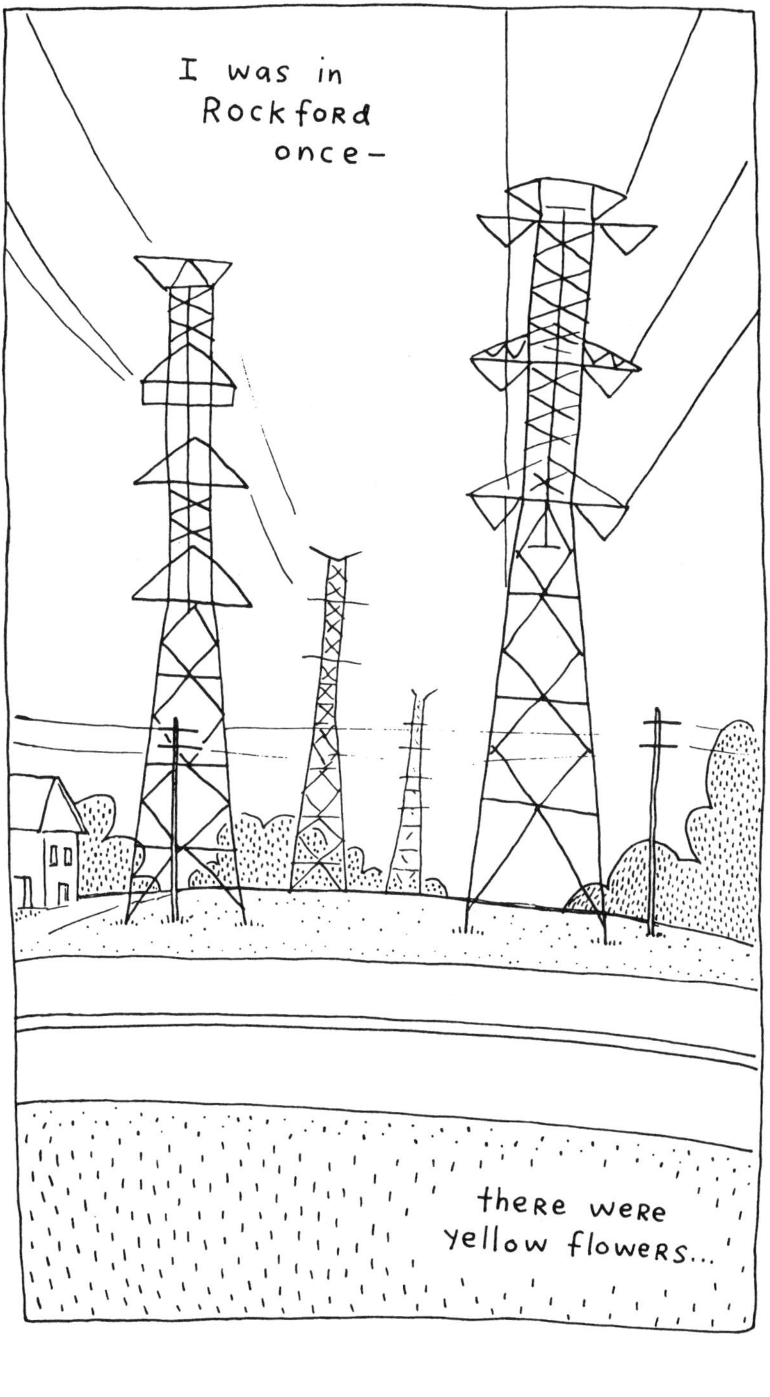
I was in Rockford once-
there were yellow flowers...

KING-CAT
COMICS & STORIES

No. 65 $3.00

BY JOHN PORCELLINO

✳ PLACES. ✳

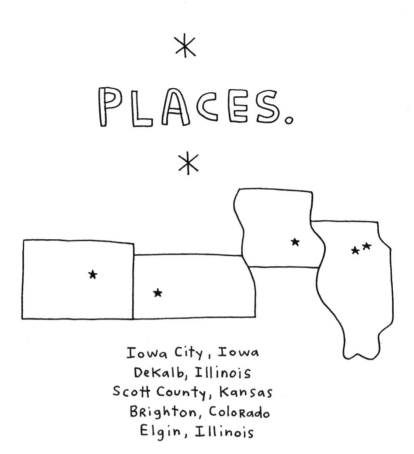

Iowa City, Iowa
DeKalb, Illinois
Scott County, Kansas
Brighton, Colorado
Elgin, Illinois

KING-CAT COMICS and STORIES, Number 65.
Dedicated to Mark Simpson (thank you)
Published in October, 2005 by: SPIT and A HALF

please write!   ♡   ███████████
www. king-cat.net   San Francisco, CA
                         ██████ - USA

★★ K.C. SNORNOSE '65 ★★

I WAS coming down Lone Mountain one day, on a bright sunshiny evening in September. I looked to the east and saw vast patterns of clouds spread out over the city, in an egg-shell blue sky, and I thought: "Somewhere out there is home." Home is Illinois.

Somewhere out there, after mile upon mile of Mountains, Deserts, Great Salt Lakes and Plains, you round the bend once more and cross the River bridge, at last, into Illinois.

I would like to think I could just be at home anywhere, to make any place my home, and to a certain extent maybe that's true. But maybe it's also true that Illinois is my home sweet home. Maybe those fields are where I belong. I don't know; I just know this longing inside when I think of it — standing out on the hillside, looking down across the grass, and the train tracks, and tree line after tree line across the fields, to the hazy edge of the sky.

I was thinking about it the other day, and I thought: "I wanna live some place where there's woodchucks" and that sounded about right to me.

✳ ✳ ✳

IN JULY we drove down to L.A. for Misun's sister's wedding. I was excited to see Los Angeles again (the last time I was there I was one years old!)... And I loved it — the heat, the wide boulevards, the palm trees dark against the evening sky... we walked on hot sidewalks, looked at strange plants, went to the ocean and saw two people get married. While the partygoers danced, I sat in the car, in the dark, and read Rolling Stone under the parking lot light; I stood out on the beach, watching waves roll in, and I thought about Neil Young.

(continued →)

In the mornings we walked in cool desert light, in the alley, behind the gas station. The local mockingbird stood up on the highest tree branch and called out to us. The palm trees leaned over along the Roadside. Everything felt okay.

✳ ✳ ✳

THIS ISSUE is all about PLACES — places I've lived, places I've been, places I wanted to be. We've been on the Road now for almost three years, and I'm tired. I'm waiting for home.

One day, not long ago, I was in bed reading. Misun was at her TV tray, exhausted, studying for her nine hour exam. She looked up and said "Sometimes life is hard." I said, "Yeah — sometimes it is..." and she said, "But even when it's hard, it still feels good somehow, doesn't it? Like now..."

Here's King-Cat 65... I hope you enjoy it.

LOVE,
John P.
San Francisco, CA
Oct. 17, 2005

M.K.
♡

IOWA CITY

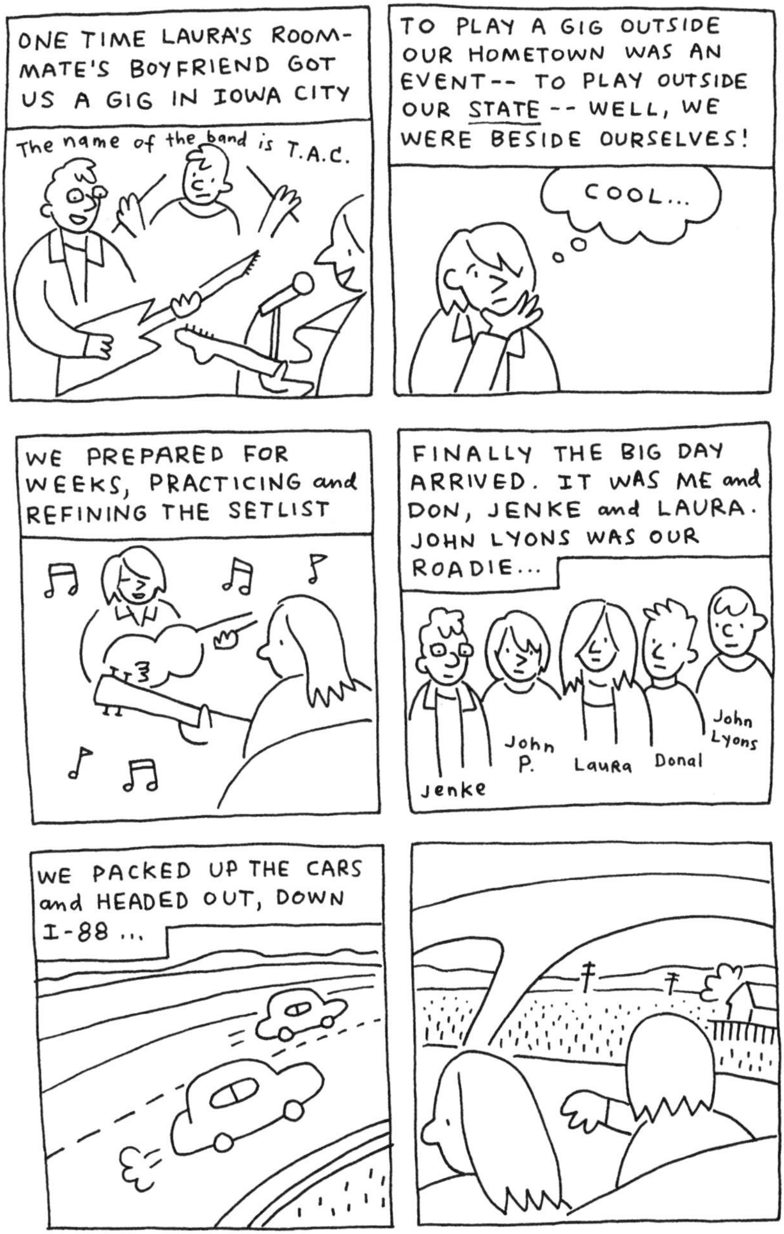
ONE TIME LAURA'S ROOM-MATE'S BOYFRIEND GOT US A GIG IN IOWA CITY
The name of the band is T.A.C.
TO PLAY A GIG OUTSIDE OUR HOMETOWN WAS AN EVENT-- TO PLAY OUTSIDE OUR STATE -- WELL, WE WERE BESIDE OURSELVES!
COOL...
WE PREPARED FOR WEEKS, PRACTICING and REFINING THE SETLIST
FINALLY THE BIG DAY ARRIVED. IT WAS ME and DON, JENKE and LAURA. JOHN LYONS WAS OUR ROADIE...
Jenke
John P.
Laura
Donal
John Lyons
WE PACKED UP THE CARS and HEADED OUT, DOWN I-88 ...

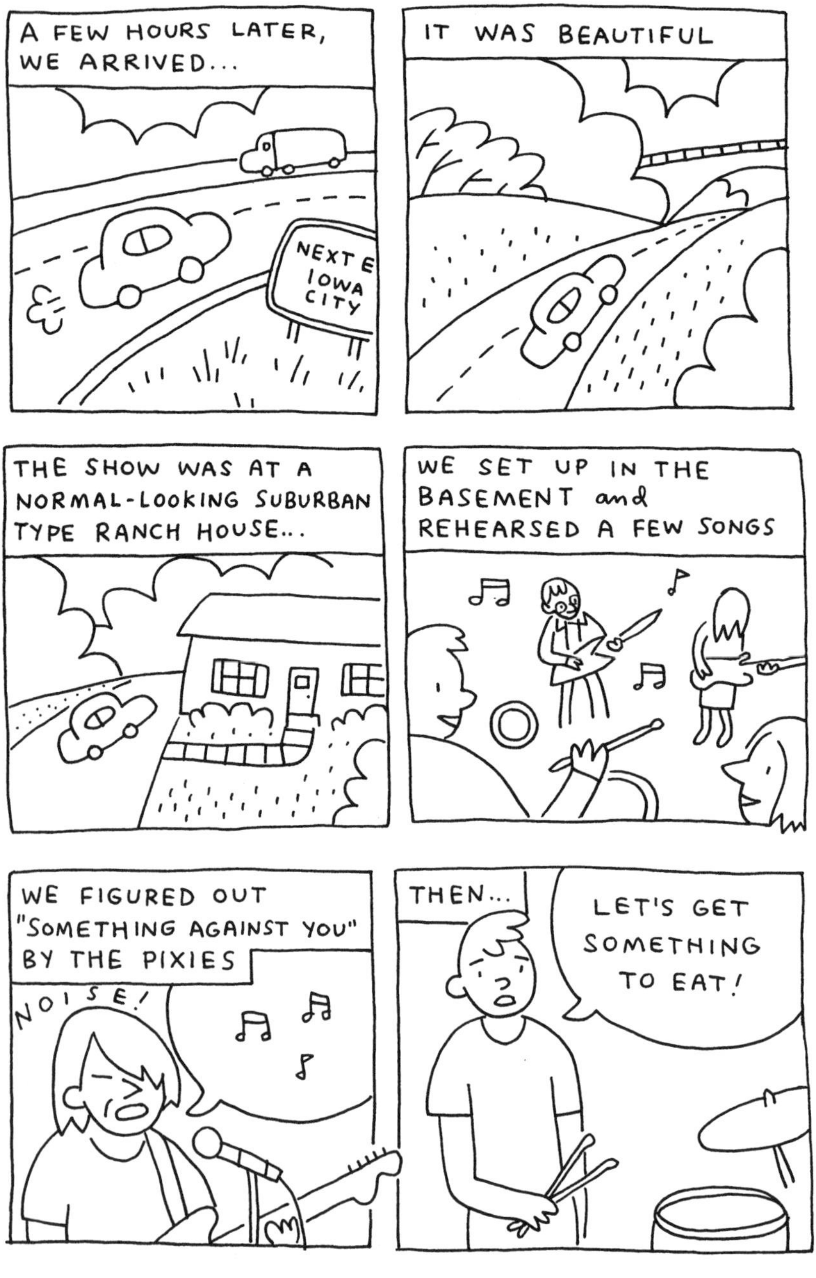
A FEW HOURS LATER, WE ARRIVED...
NEXT E IOWA CITY
IT WAS BEAUTIFUL
THE SHOW WAS AT A NORMAL-LOOKING SUBURBAN TYPE RANCH HOUSE...
WE SET UP IN THE BASEMENT and REHEARSED A FEW SONGS
WE FIGURED OUT "SOMETHING AGAINST YOU" BY THE PIXIES
NOISE!
THEN...
LET'S GET SOMETHING TO EAT!

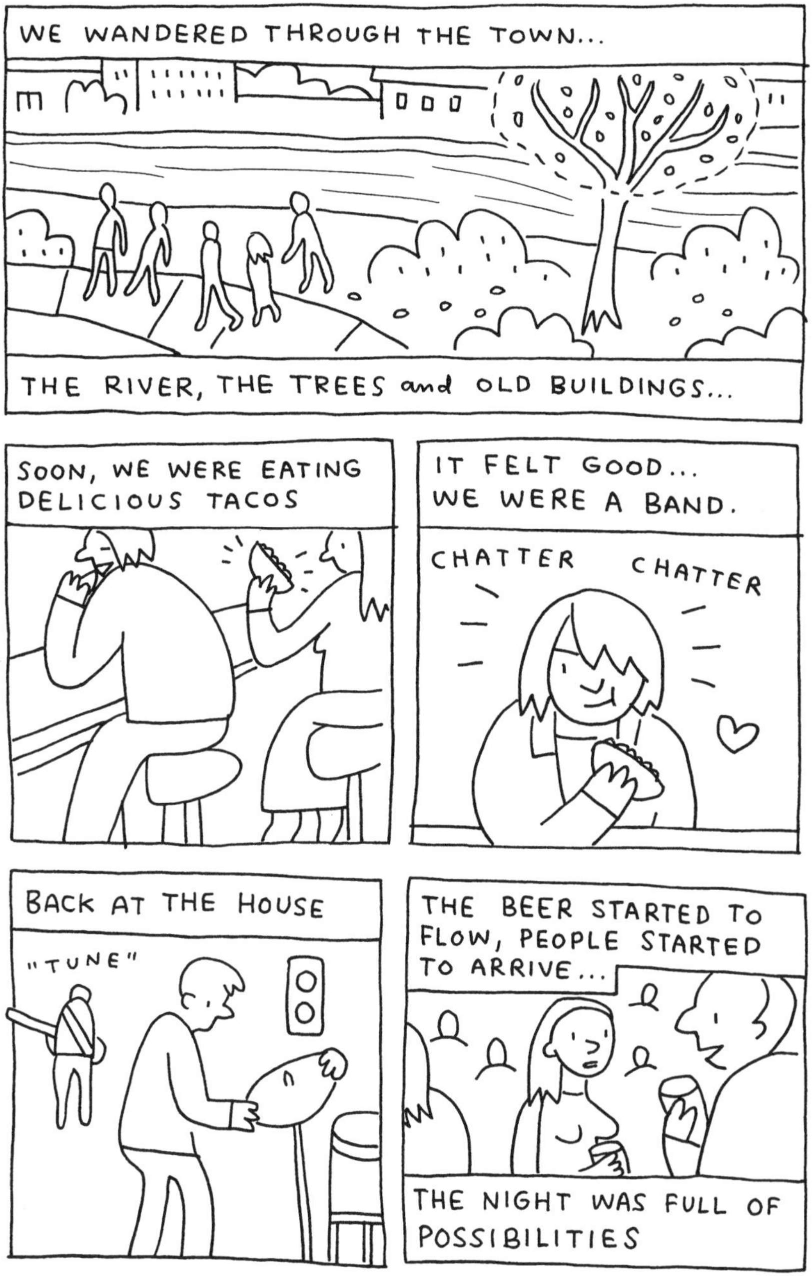
WE WANDERED THROUGH THE TOWN...
THE RIVER, THE TREES and OLD BUILDINGS...
SOON, WE WERE EATING DELICIOUS TACOS
IT FELT GOOD... WE WERE A BAND.
CHATTER
CHATTER
BACK AT THE HOUSE
"TUNE"
THE BEER STARTED TO FLOW, PEOPLE STARTED TO ARRIVE...
THE NIGHT WAS FULL OF POSSIBILITIES

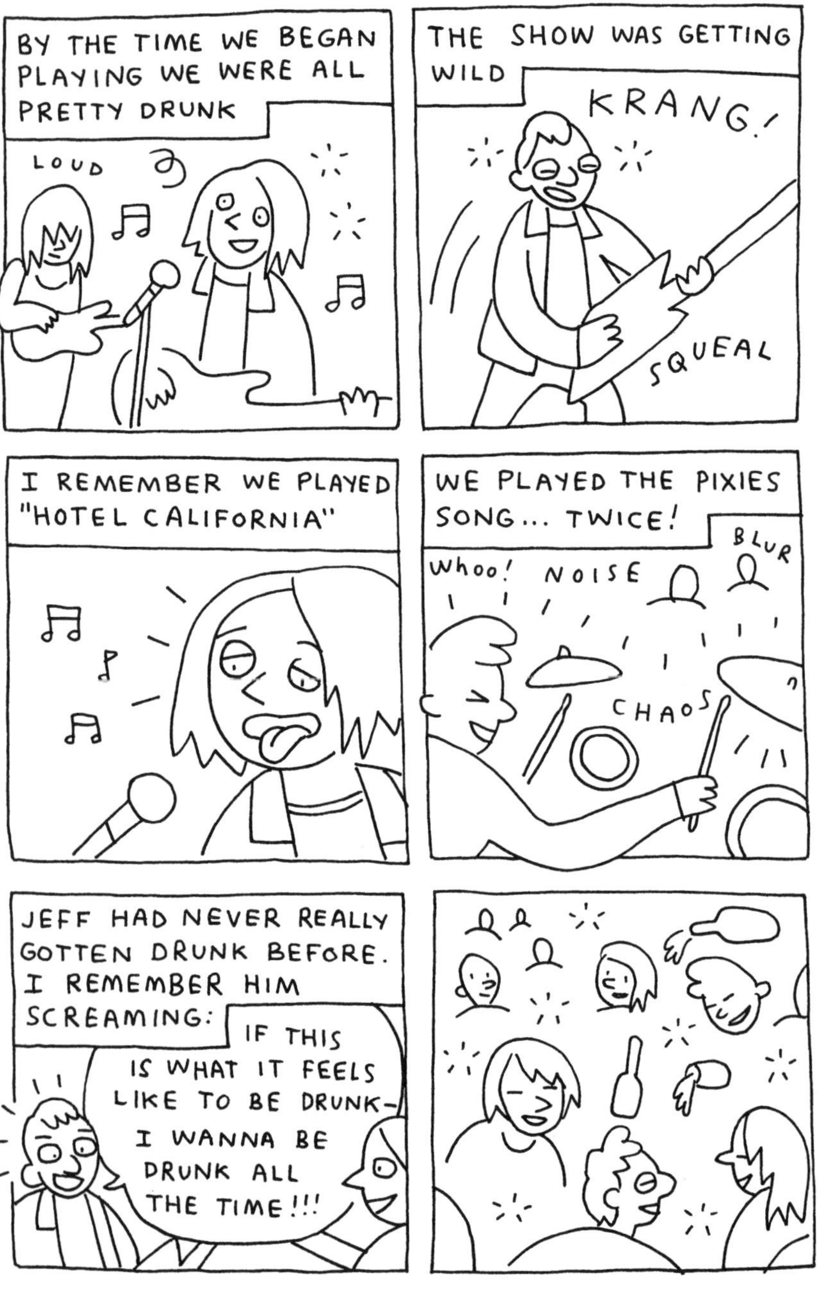
BY THE TIME WE BEGAN PLAYING WE WERE ALL PRETTY DRUNK
LOUD
THE SHOW WAS GETTING WILD
KRANG!
SQUEAL
I REMEMBER WE PLAYED "HOTEL CALIFORNIA"
WE PLAYED THE PIXIES SONG... TWICE!
Whoo!
NOISE
BLUR
CHAOS
JEFF HAD NEVER REALLY GOTTEN DRUNK BEFORE. I REMEMBER HIM SCREAMING:
IF THIS IS WHAT IT FEELS LIKE TO BE DRUNK- I WANNA BE DRUNK ALL THE TIME!!!

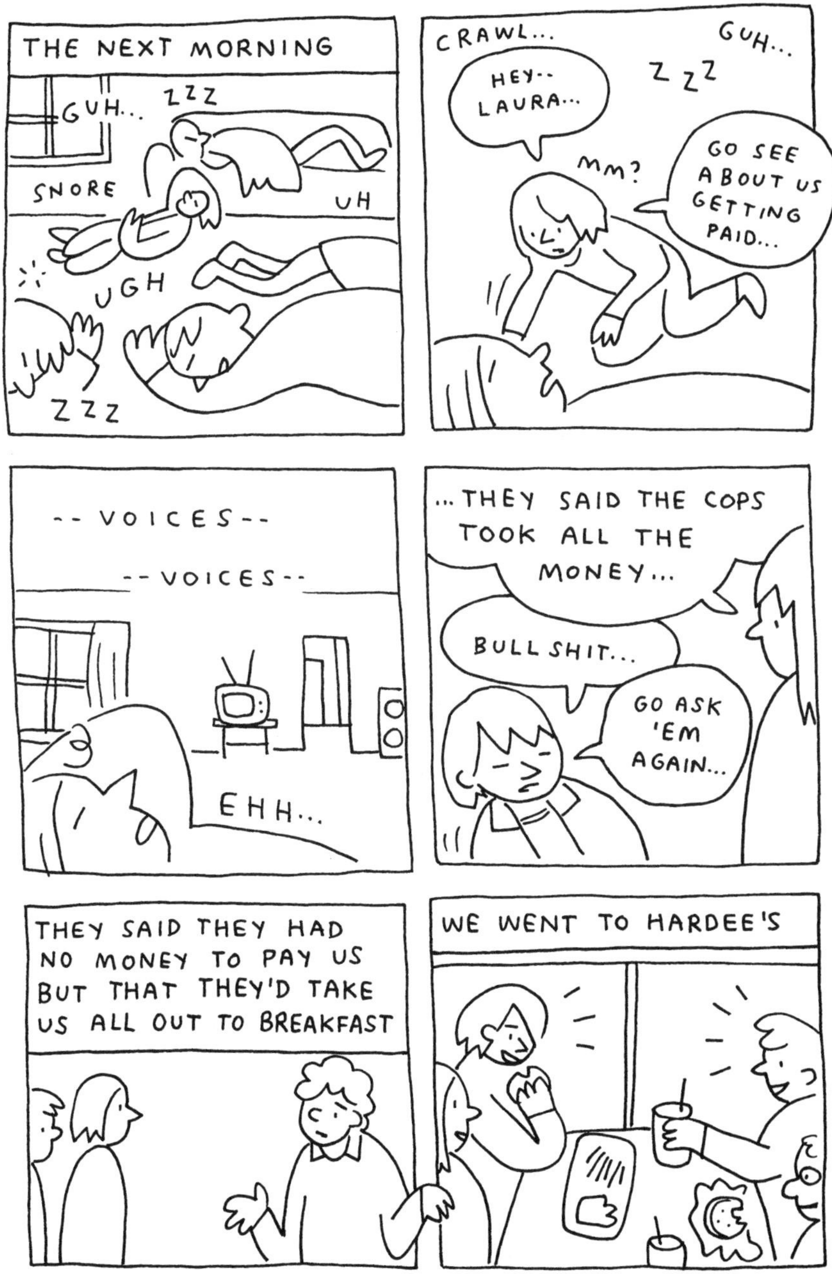
THE NEXT MORNING
GUH... ZZZ
SNORE
UH
UGH
ZZZ
CRAWL...
GUH...
ZZZ
HEY.. LAURA...
MM?
GO SEE ABOUT US GETTING PAID...
-- VOICES --
-- VOICES --
EHH...
...THEY SAID THE COPS TOOK ALL THE MONEY...
BULLSHIT...
GO ASK 'EM AGAIN...
THEY SAID THEY HAD NO MONEY TO PAY US BUT THAT THEY'D TAKE US ALL OUT TO BREAKFAST
WE WENT TO HARDEE'S

HAPPENED SPRING 1989(?) • DRAWN 2005 • JOHN P.

EPILOGUE

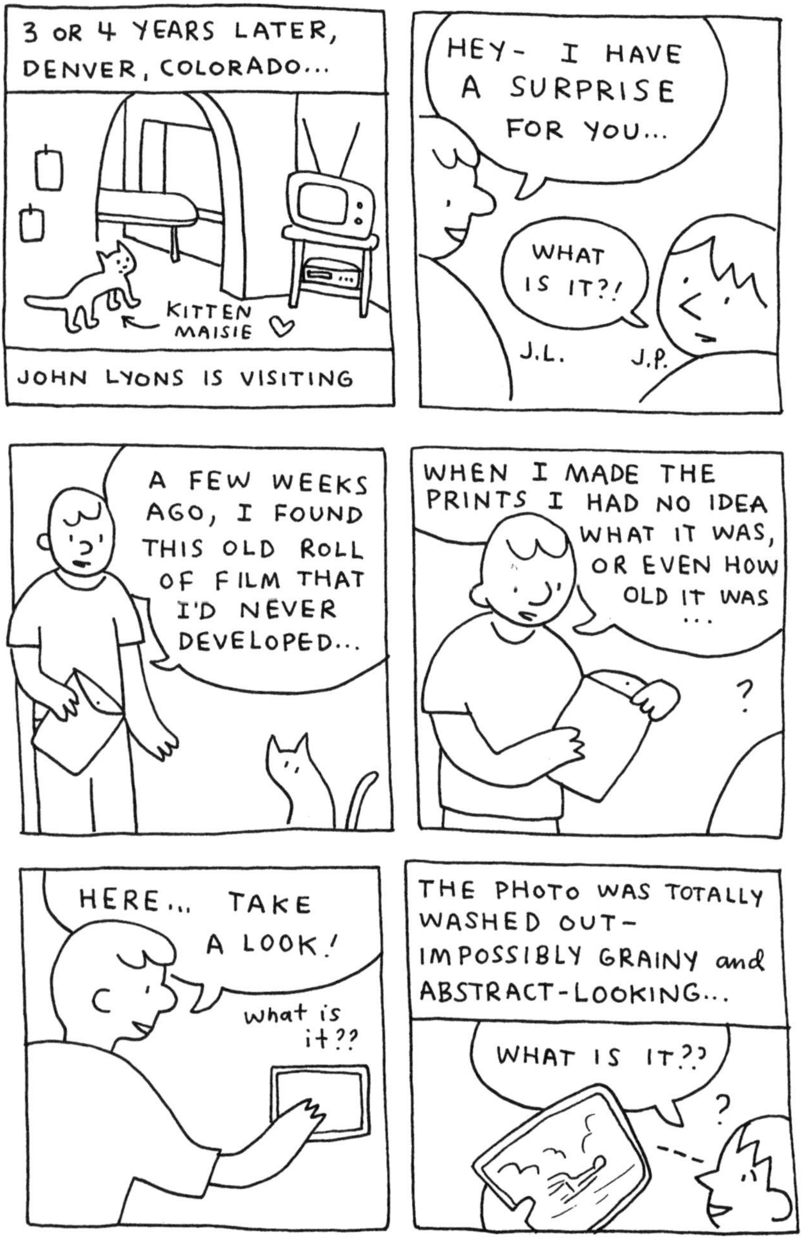
3 OR 4 YEARS LATER, DENVER, COLORADO...
KITTEN MAISIE
JOHN LYONS IS VISITING
HEY- I HAVE A SURPRISE FOR YOU...
WHAT IS IT?!
J.L.
J.P.
A FEW WEEKS AGO, I FOUND THIS OLD ROLL OF FILM THAT I'D NEVER DEVELOPED...
WHEN I MADE THE PRINTS I HAD NO IDEA WHAT IT WAS, OR EVEN HOW OLD IT WAS...
?
HERE... TAKE A LOOK!
what is it??
THE PHOTO WAS TOTALLY WASHED OUT- IMPOSSIBLY GRAINY and ABSTRACT-LOOKING...
WHAT IS IT??
?

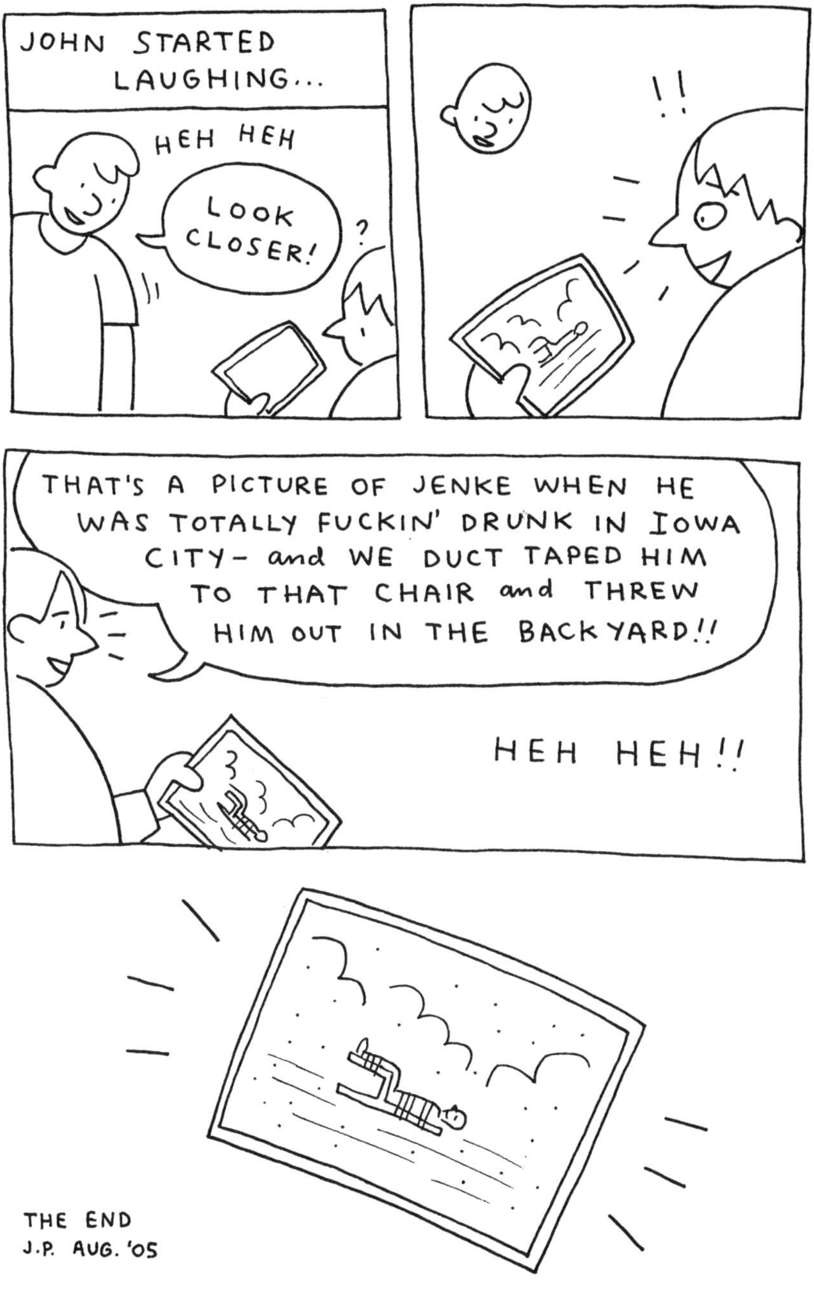
JOHN STARTED LAUGHING...
HEH HEH
LOOK CLOSER!
?
!!
THAT'S A PICTURE OF JENKE WHEN HE WAS TOTALLY FUCKIN' DRUNK IN IOWA CITY- and WE DUCT TAPED HIM TO THAT CHAIR and THREW HIM OUT IN THE BACKYARD!!
HEH HEH!!
THE END
J.P. AUG. '05

DEKALB, '91-'92

In the fall of 1991, I moved into my new place on Eleventh Street, in DeKalb. I lived alone on the second floor of an old blue house near Pleasant Street, out by the railroad yards and the water tower, on the edge of town.

I was working at the time at a place called Creative Calligraphy. C.C. was an operation that manufactured those "Country Craft" type gewgaws and whatsits that were so popular in the Midwest back then. Their bestselling items were framed calligraphic prints of sayings like "A House Is Not a Home Without a Meow" and "Bless This Mess." I worked in the warehouse, unloading trucks and running the glass machine, which was a machine that cleaned the glass used to make the framed pictures. One guy stood on one side of the machine and fed in dusty plates of glass, and another guy pulled them, clean, out of the other, and placed them in empty picture frames of various sizes. It was maddening, repetitive work. To keep our sanity we blasted rock music over the incessant blare of the machine, and "sang" along at the top of our lungs. *Van Halen I*, the first Traveling Wilburys album, *News of the World* by Queen.

When we weren't unloading trucks or running the glass machine, we were assembling frames. The frames came to us in big square boxes from Colorado Springs, and we'd use air-compressor powered staple guns to blow staples into the inside edges of them. The frames would stack up in towering piles on our tables and occasionally, "accidentally", fall over. This job was maddening too. We'd listen to music as we worked and bullshit around.

After the frames were all stapled we had to bend back the steel staples by hand, to allow us to fit the glass in later. After awhile our thumbs became mangled and raw from the constant bending. Then, one day, we invented THUM-GARD® by cutting the fingertips off a pair of old leather gloves and placing the tips over our sore thumbs, to protect them from the ravages of our dumb job. Still later, one of us came up with the bright idea of using a metal spoon to bend the staples. After that things got a lot better.

I liked the people I worked with. There was Gary Whitehair, a crazy brilliant writer/madman who hoped someday to complete his great novel "Brain Fever"; Josh, the owner's son who overcame that stigma to become "one of the guys"; Al, a gentle spirited and quiet spoken ex-National Guardsman; Ed, the hard drinking, always smiling body builder; Joe G., who got laid off from his job making screwdrivers across the street, and brought to the warehouse his love of Bart Simpson and Hair Metal; Billy Bob the country boy who loved his girlfriend and his flatbed pick-up; and Jim Mack, the psychedelic local guitar hero and general lunatic. We were a sorry bunch of suckers, a ragtag band of misfits and losers (as the story goes), but I think we knew from the start that we were all brothers, connected by the madness of our mind-numbing manual labor, by the dead ends we all woke up each morning looking down. We ate Toaster Pastries all day long and debated our sorry lives, this sorry world.

And then there was old John Abbott: a quiet, big-hearted WWII veteran who worked with us younger kids and who gradually opened up to us. He regaled us with stories of France after the liberation, and provided us with soul-searching gems of his age-wizened advice and commentary. One day we were listening to *Double Nickels on the Dime* by the Minutemen. John sat silently throughout it all, patiently bending back staple after staple. Finally, I asked him what he thought of the music. He said, simply, in his quiet gravelly drawl: "Tell it like it is."

As I mentioned, John gradually opened up to us—but it wasn't until after I had left C.C. and moved on a few years that I found out that the whole time I worked with him he would have preferred to have been called "Jack".

So I worked this crazy job and tried to get by. I was making my comics at night and on weekends, trying to figure out my life.

I'd come home from work, park in the alley, and come up the back stairs to my apartment. The apartment was huge and cheap, windows everywhere and wide open dusty floors.

Cooking dinner meant opening a can of refried beans onto a tortilla and microwaving them one after the other. I put pre-shredded cheddar cheese on them and when I was fancy some lettuce. I ate them with tortilla chips and generic cola. They were damn good.

Once a week I'd pull out the little old 9" TV my parents had given me, balance it on a chair, and watch *Roseanne* in grainy black and white. When it was over I'd unplug it and put it back in the closet. I was in a weird state of mind. I'd listen to Brasil '66 records or the Tijuana Brass and draw comics all evening. The comics just came out of me. I'd stack them up and when I had enough pages I'd go down to the copy shop and put out a new issue of King-Cat.

At eleven each night I'd go to bed on an old springy mattress. Outside, the night sky went past, full of stars, the moon, luminous clouds. The world was a magical place.

Anyhow, I'd work all week and on Fridays it was like letting out a long held-in breath. Sometimes I'd drive in to Chicago to see friends or hang out with my girlfriend, but increasingly I just stayed at home; I stayed put. I enjoyed my solitude and the quiet apartment. I enjoyed making comics.

On Saturday mornings I'd go downtown to the Salvation Army and look for new Tijuana Brass albums, or Captain and

Tennille. There was no shortage of these things. I'd buy strange objects for a dollar and bring them home. Life was good.

In the afternoons, in Fall, in the evening, I'd wander through my neighborhood: the weird little houses, the Church, children's bikes knocked over on front lawns, pick-up trucks on gravel driveways. Who were these people, ...my neighbors? Above me the sky rolled mysterious, the Midwestern sky in Fall. The world crackled with energy, and the energy was in me, the energy and the world and me were one.

Sometimes after work we'd go down to the Twin Tap, the Twin Tavern, and drink beer, order onion rings, and wait for our sausage sandwiches. Men in flannel jackets and baseball caps sat at the darkened counter, a silent TV set flickered in the corner, unwatched. This was like a dream come true. We'd laugh and eat and step outside into the nighttime air, say so long with our bellies full of beer and good food, the moonlight shining bright through cold backlit white clouds.

The Twin Tavern had pinwheels in the urinals that spun when you peed on them. It just didn't get better than that.

Still, I wasn't totally satisfied. I thought I could be more free. My job made me increasingly numb—I could laugh about it, but inside I knew it wasn't for me. What I wanted was to *feel* each day, to really live each day. It was an abstract concept in my head, but it was pulling me along toward something.

I remember waking up one workday morning and just wishing somehow that the day could be over. If I could have one wish it would be that somehow the next eight hours of my life would just disappear. And I thought how sad that was—to just want your life to go away. I didn't wanna live like that. I wanted to wake up each day and feel glad I was alive. And for the first time that didn't seem like too much to ask for.

My old friend Donal had moved to Denver a few months earlier and he entreated me with tales of blue sunshine skies and mind-blowingly cheap rent. If I moved out there and lived with him it would be even cheaper. I was ready to go. I made plans to leave for Denver in June.

Before I left, I threw a big party at my apartment—for friends and near-friends, all the people I had grown to know and love. I threw a party for six years in DeKalb, that little blank lovely little Midwestern college town; for the bars and bands, the girlfriends, the train tracks, the old brick buildings and the river. I threw a party for the town in which I entered a confused and frightened, excited little kid, and from which I emerged, six years later, full of possibility and hope. I was not yet an adult but I knew I wasn't a child anymore.

So everyone came to my party. We drank sickeningly sweet alcoholic concoctions I had invented myself. John R. showed movies on a sheet hung in the doorway. I filled one room with mylar clouds suspended from the ceiling. I got very drunk.

At 3 AM only a few guests remained. I was standing in the doorway waving goodbye to people, when I saw my estranged friend Fred. We hadn't really spoken in a couple years and we didn't speak a word this time either, but just automatically fell into each other's arms and started sobbing.

We cried and shook, holding on for dear life, for love...
I remember his leather jacket, heavy and wet with my tears running down. I was leaving DeKalb. I was leaving my home.

Scott County Memories

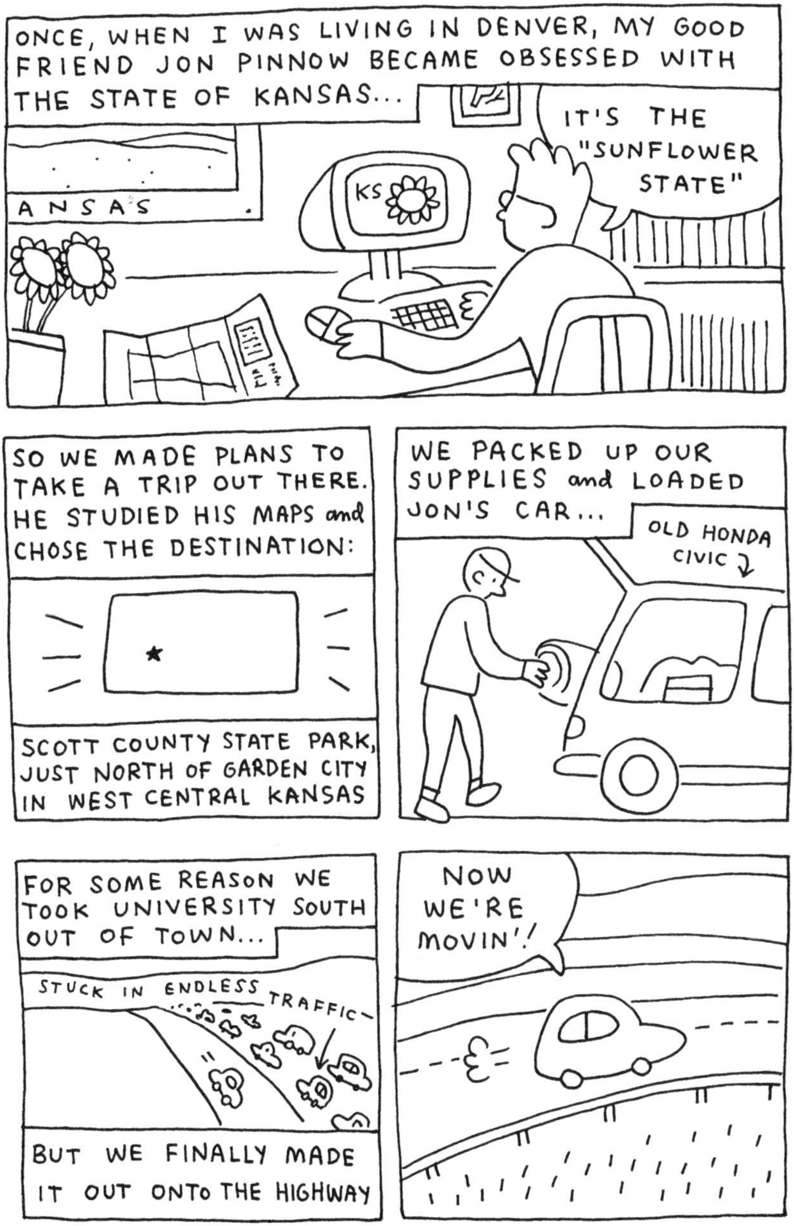

ONCE, WHEN I WAS LIVING IN DENVER, MY GOOD FRIEND JON PINNOW BECAME OBSESSED WITH THE STATE OF KANSAS...
ANSAS
KS
IT'S THE "SUNFLOWER STATE"
SO WE MADE PLANS TO TAKE A TRIP OUT THERE. HE STUDIED HIS MAPS and CHOSE THE DESTINATION:
SCOTT COUNTY STATE PARK, JUST NORTH OF GARDEN CITY IN WEST CENTRAL KANSAS
WE PACKED UP OUR SUPPLIES and LOADED JON'S CAR...
OLD HONDA CIVIC
FOR SOME REASON WE TOOK UNIVERSITY SOUTH OUT OF TOWN...
STUCK IN ENDLESS TRAFFIC
BUT WE FINALLY MADE IT OUT ONTO THE HIGHWAY
NOW WE'RE MOVIN'!

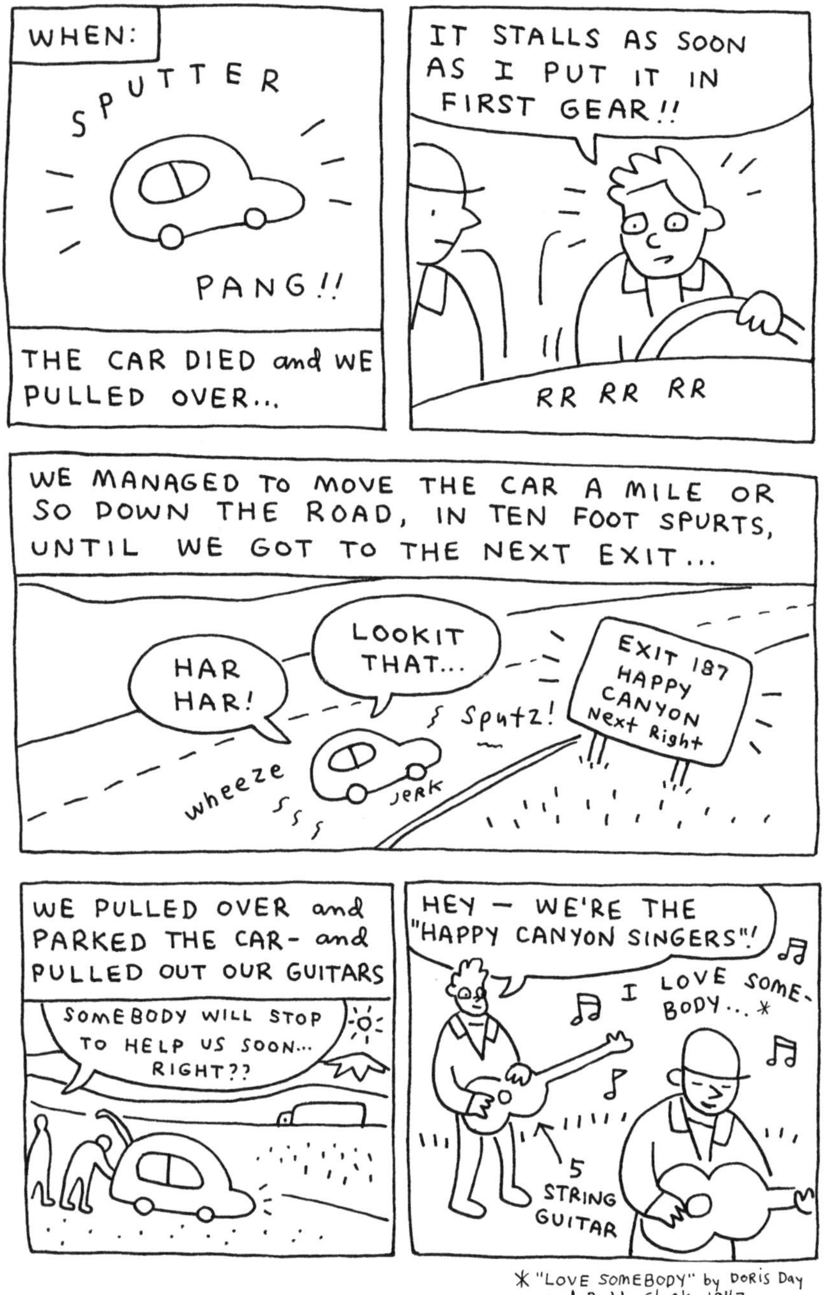
WHEN:
SPUTTER
PANG!!
THE CAR DIED and WE PULLED OVER...
IT STALLS AS SOON AS I PUT IT IN FIRST GEAR!!
RR RR RR
WE MANAGED TO MOVE THE CAR A MILE OR SO DOWN THE ROAD, IN TEN FOOT SPURTS, UNTIL WE GOT TO THE NEXT EXIT...
HAR HAR!
LOOKIT THAT...
Sputz!
EXIT 187 HAPPY CANYON Next Right
wheeze
JERK
WE PULLED OVER and PARKED THE CAR- and PULLED OUT OUR GUITARS
SOMEBODY WILL STOP TO HELP US SOON... RIGHT??
HEY — WE'RE THE "HAPPY CANYON SINGERS"!
I LOVE SOME-BODY... *
5 STRING GUITAR

* "LOVE SOMEBODY" by DORIS Day and Buddy Clark, 1947.

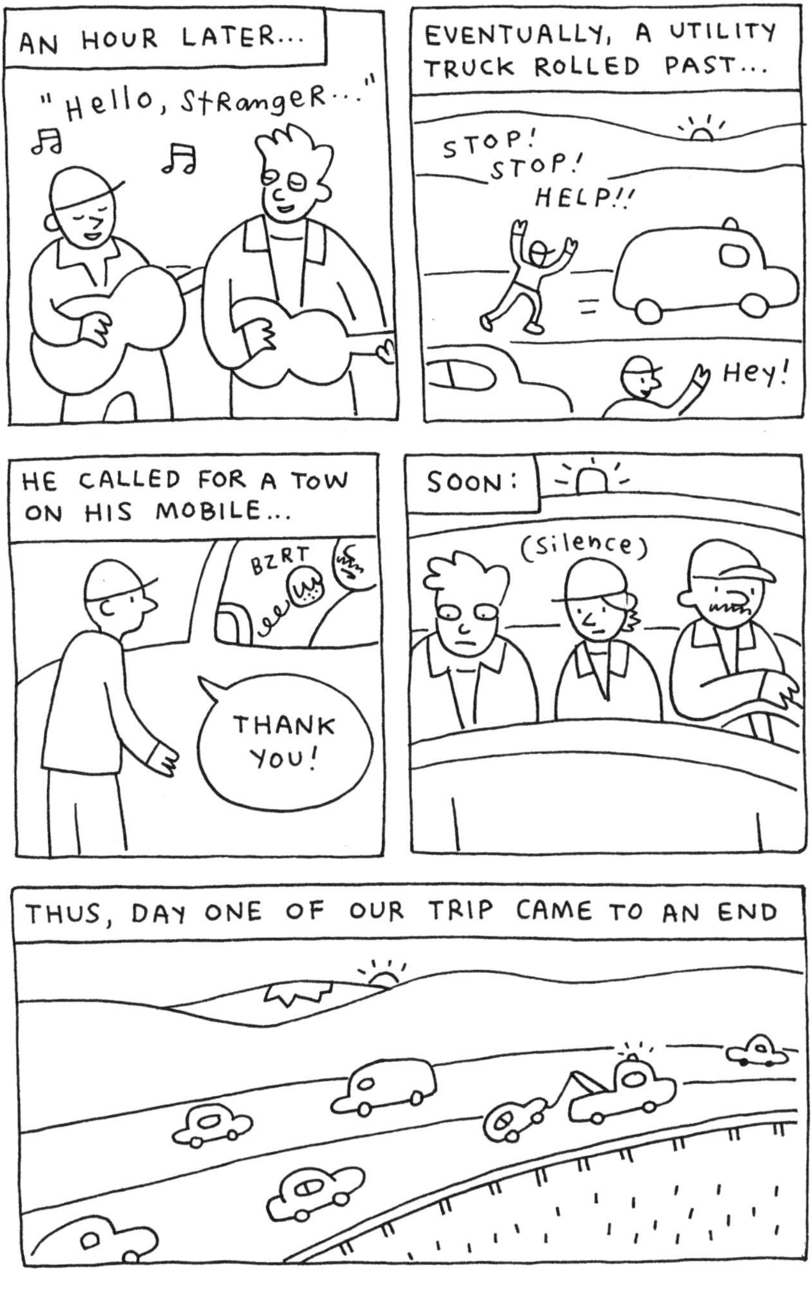
AN HOUR LATER...
"Hello, StRanger..."
EVENTUALLY, A UTILITY TRUCK ROLLED PAST...
STOP!
STOP!
HELP!!
Hey!
HE CALLED FOR A TOW ON HIS MOBILE...
BZRT
THANK YOU!
SOON:
(silence)
THUS, DAY ONE OF OUR TRIP CAME TO AN END

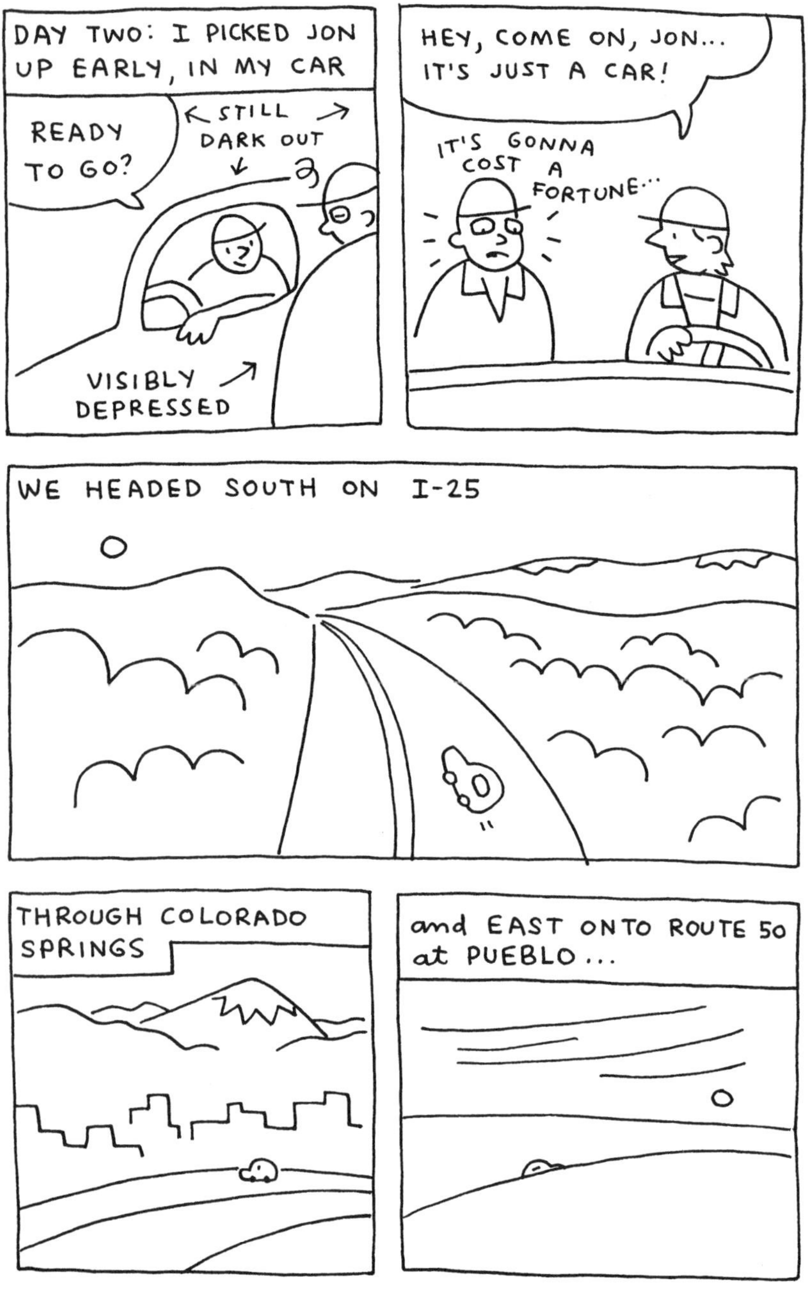

DAY TWO: I PICKED JON UP EARLY, IN MY CAR
READY TO GO?
STILL DARK OUT
VISIBLY DEPRESSED
HEY, COME ON, JON... IT'S JUST A CAR!
IT'S GONNA COST A FORTUNE...
WE HEADED SOUTH ON I-25
THROUGH COLORADO SPRINGS
and EAST ONTO ROUTE 50 at PUEBLO...

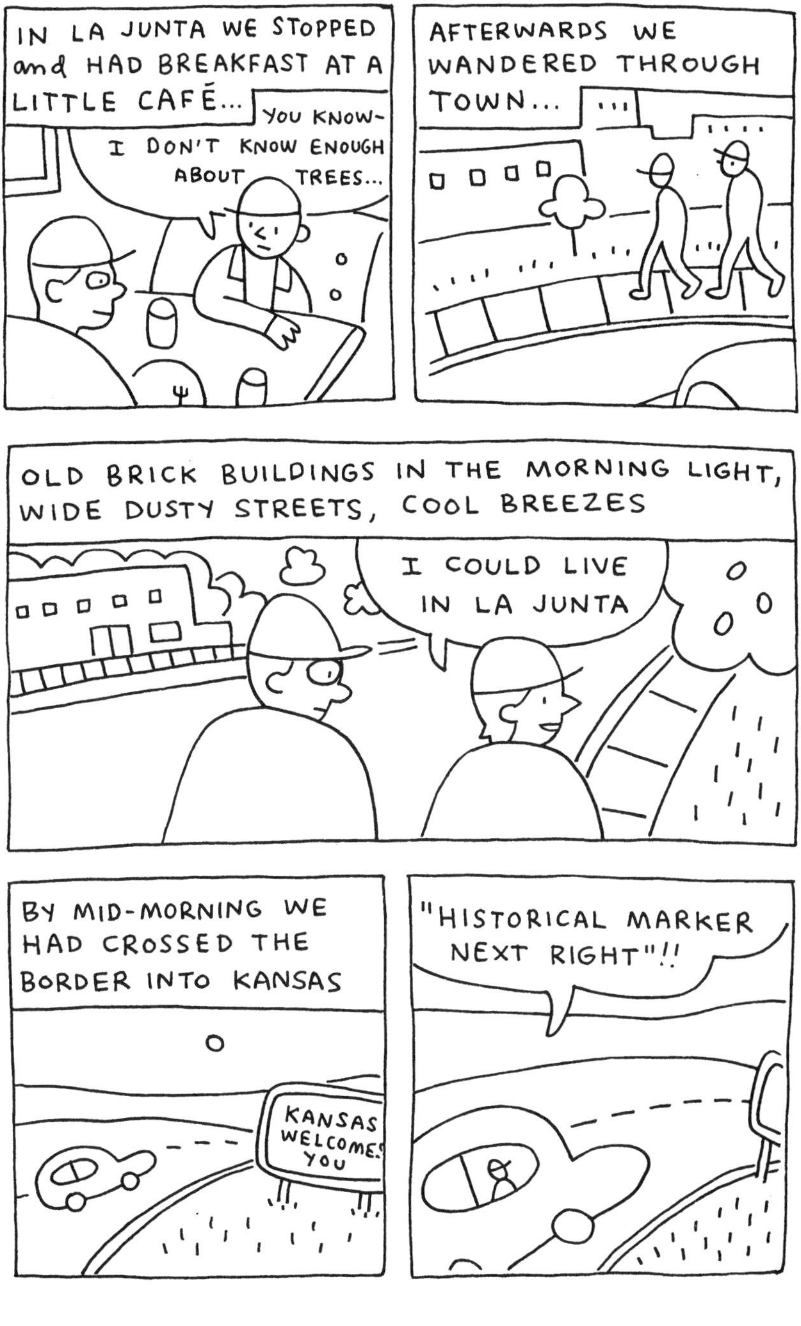
IN LA JUNTA WE STOPPED and HAD BREAKFAST AT A LITTLE CAFÉ...
YOU KNOW- I DON'T KNOW ENOUGH ABOUT TREES...
AFTERWARDS WE WANDERED THROUGH TOWN...
OLD BRICK BUILDINGS IN THE MORNING LIGHT, WIDE DUSTY STREETS, COOL BREEZES
I COULD LIVE IN LA JUNTA
BY MID-MORNING WE HAD CROSSED THE BORDER INTO KANSAS
KANSAS WELCOMES YOU
"HISTORICAL MARKER NEXT RIGHT"!!

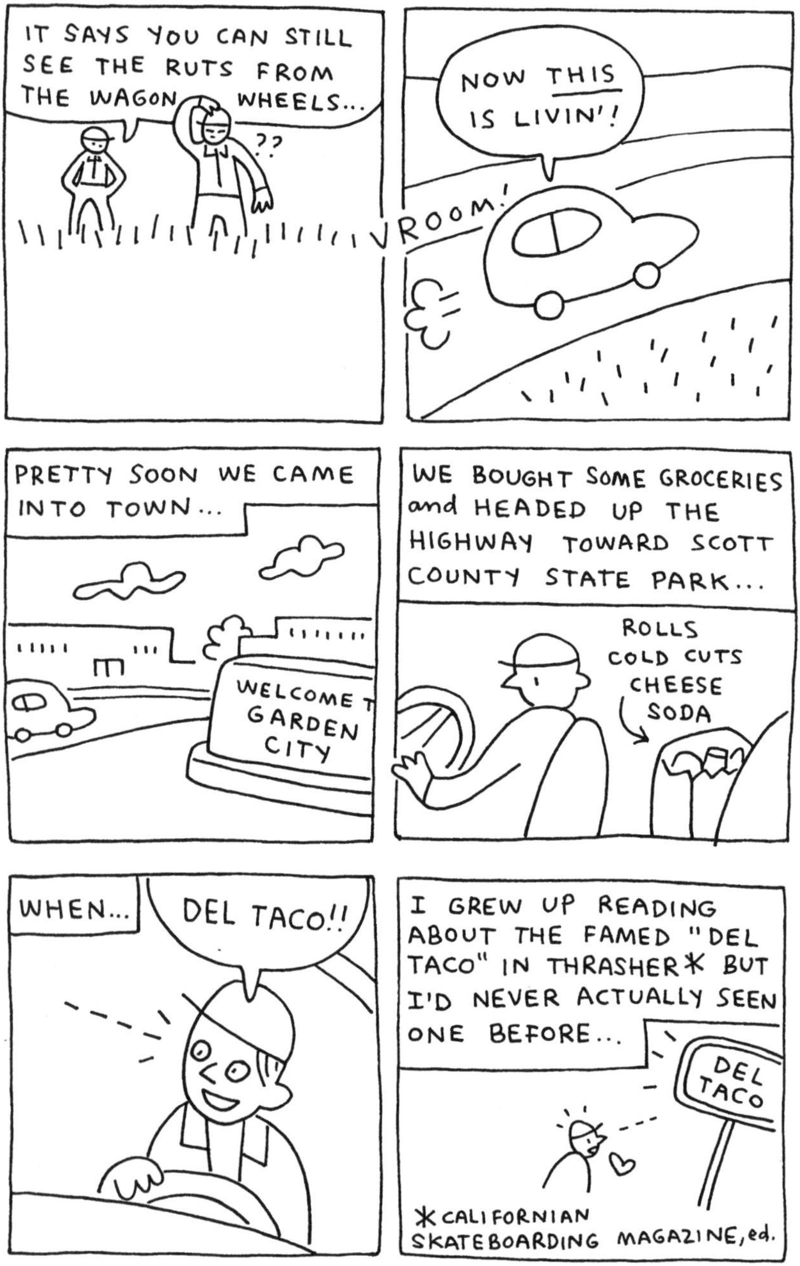
IT SAYS YOU CAN STILL SEE THE RUTS FROM THE WAGON WHEELS...
??
VROOM!
NOW THIS IS LIVIN'!
PRETTY SOON WE CAME INTO TOWN...
WELCOME T
GARDEN CITY
WE BOUGHT SOME GROCERIES and HEADED UP THE HIGHWAY TOWARD SCOTT COUNTY STATE PARK...
ROLLS
COLD CUTS
CHEESE
SODA
WHEN...
DEL TACO!!
I GREW UP READING ABOUT THE FAMED "DEL TACO" IN THRASHER* BUT I'D NEVER ACTUALLY SEEN ONE BEFORE...
DEL TACO
*CALIFORNIAN SKATEBOARDING MAGAZINE, ed.

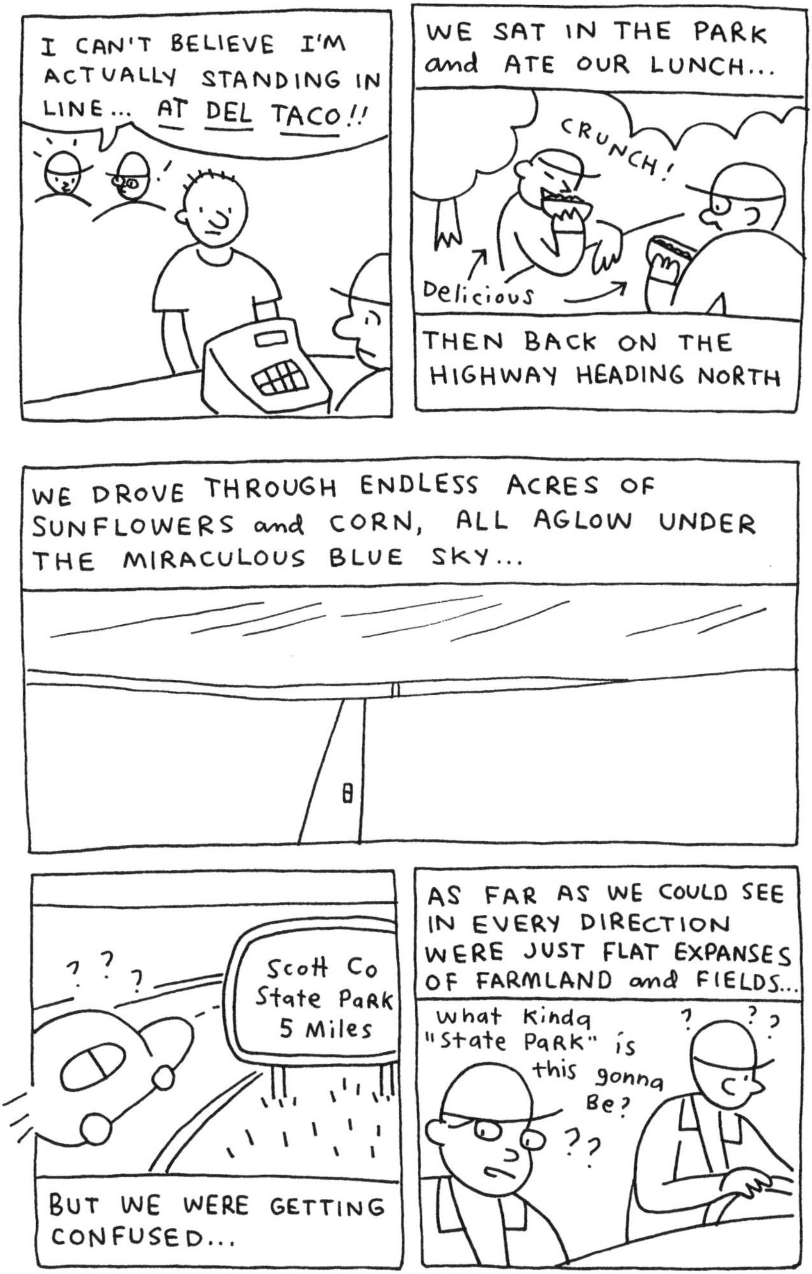
I CAN'T BELIEVE I'M ACTUALLY STANDING IN LINE... AT DEL TACO!!
WE SAT IN THE PARK and ATE OUR LUNCH...
CRUNCH!
Delicious
THEN BACK ON THE HIGHWAY HEADING NORTH
WE DROVE THROUGH ENDLESS ACRES OF SUNFLOWERS and CORN, ALL AGLOW UNDER THE MIRACULOUS BLUE SKY...
Scott Co State Park 5 Miles
BUT WE WERE GETTING CONFUSED...
AS FAR AS WE COULD SEE IN EVERY DIRECTION WERE JUST FLAT EXPANSES OF FARMLAND and FIELDS...
What kinda "State Park" is this gonna Be?

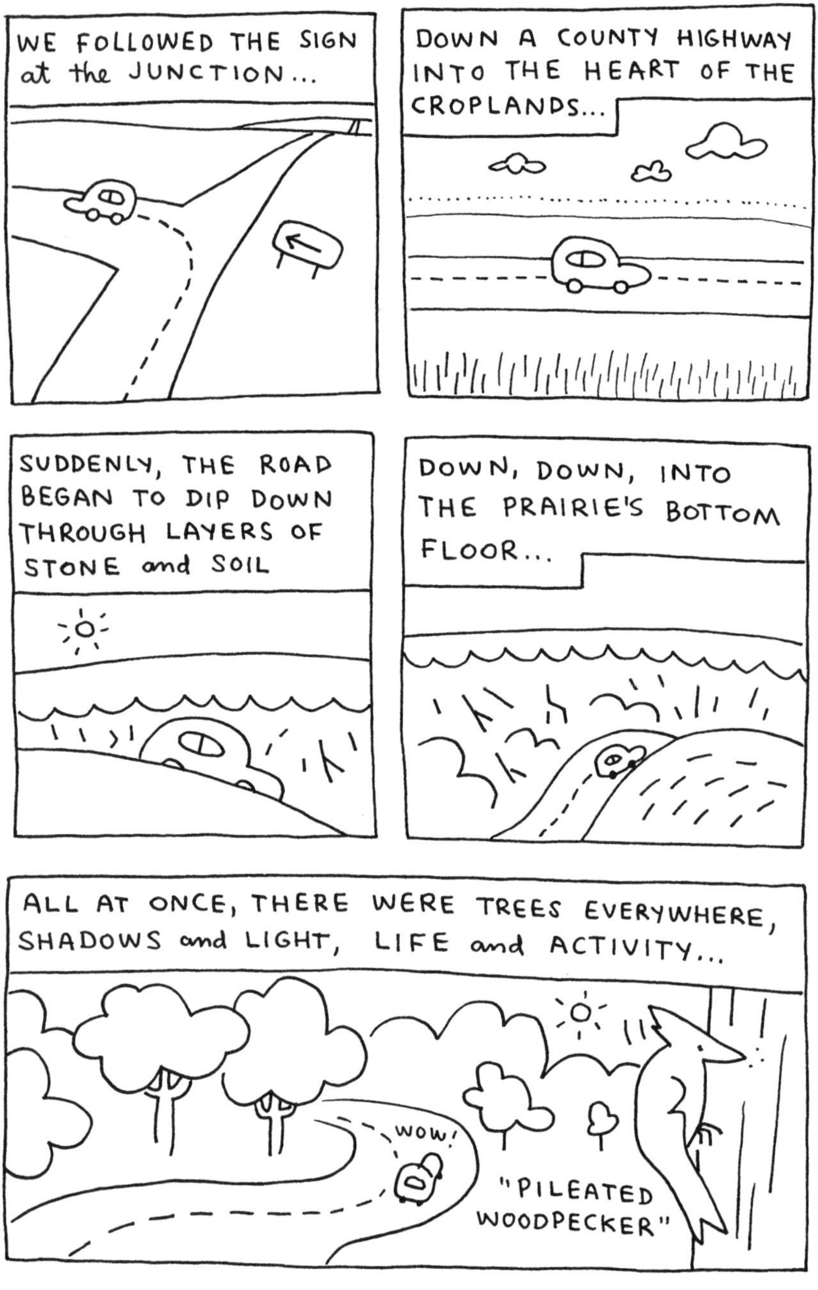
WE FOLLOWED THE SIGN at the JUNCTION...
DOWN A COUNTY HIGHWAY INTO THE HEART OF THE CROPLANDS...
SUDDENLY, THE ROAD BEGAN TO DIP DOWN THROUGH LAYERS OF STONE and SOIL
DOWN, DOWN, INTO THE PRAIRIE'S BOTTOM FLOOR...
ALL AT ONCE, THERE WERE TREES EVERYWHERE, SHADOWS and LIGHT, LIFE and ACTIVITY...
WOW!
"PILEATED WOODPECKER"

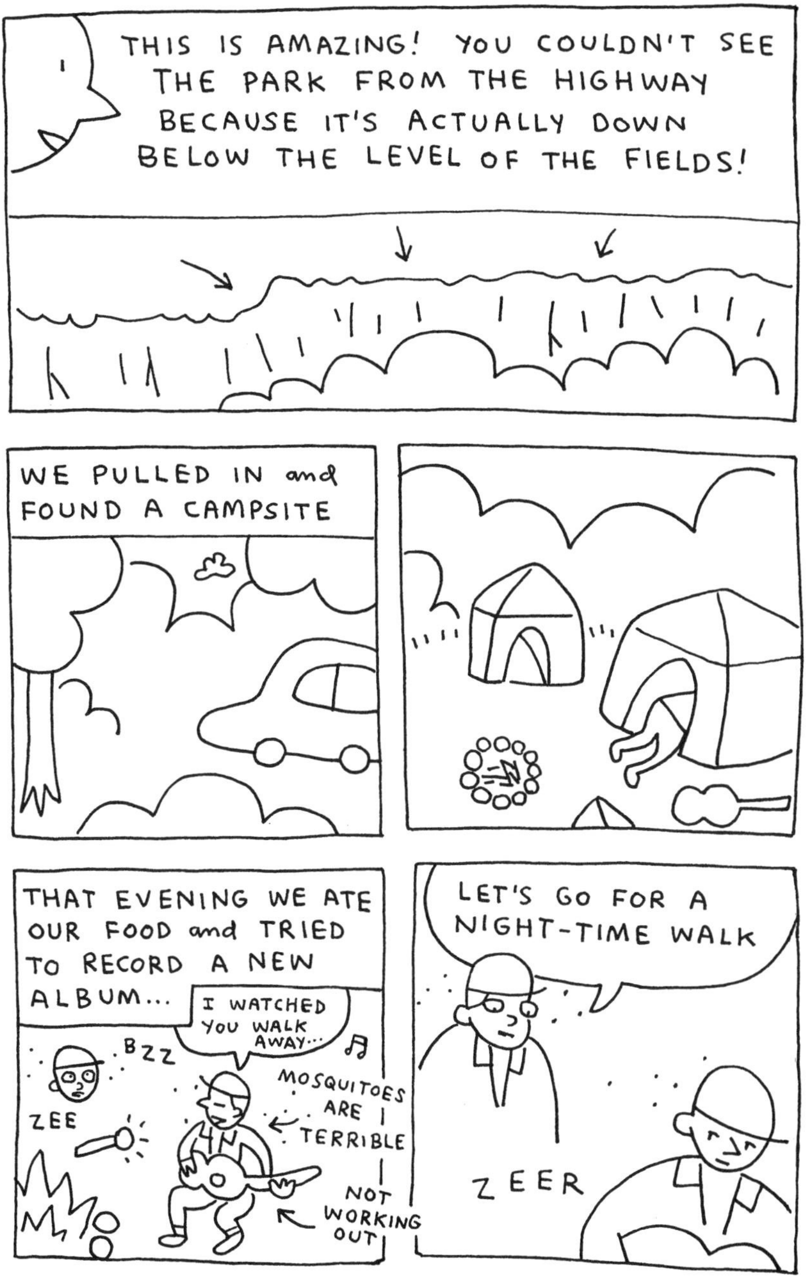
THIS IS AMAZING! YOU COULDN'T SEE THE PARK FROM THE HIGHWAY BECAUSE IT'S ACTUALLY DOWN BELOW THE LEVEL OF THE FIELDS!
WE PULLED IN and FOUND A CAMPSITE
THAT EVENING WE ATE OUR FOOD and TRIED TO RECORD A NEW ALBUM...
I WATCHED YOU WALK AWAY...
BZZ
ZEE
MOSQUITOES ARE TERRIBLE
NOT WORKING OUT
LET'S GO FOR A NIGHT-TIME WALK
ZEER

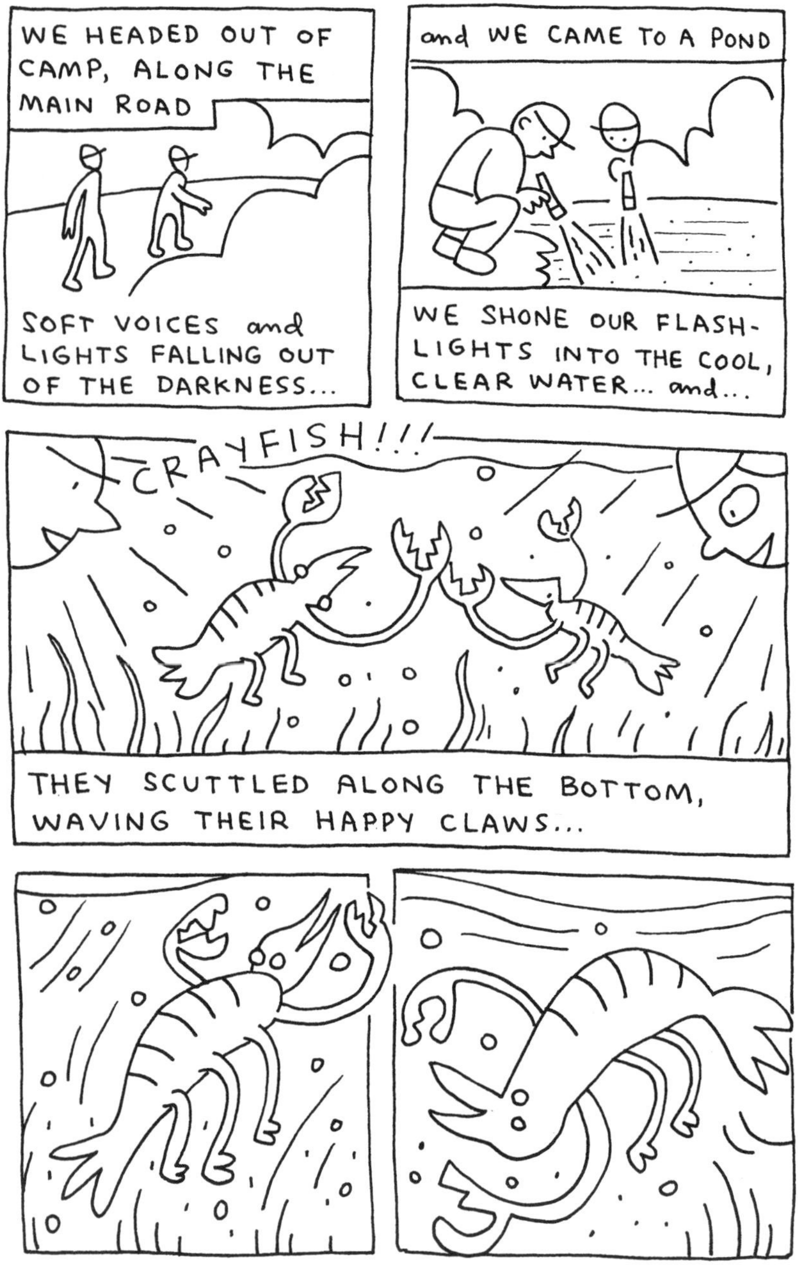
WE HEADED OUT OF CAMP, ALONG THE MAIN ROAD
SOFT VOICES and LIGHTS FALLING OUT OF THE DARKNESS...
and WE CAME TO A POND
WE SHONE OUR FLASH-LIGHTS INTO THE COOL, CLEAR WATER... and...
CRAYFISH!!!
THEY SCUTTLED ALONG THE BOTTOM, WAVING THEIR HAPPY CLAWS...

THEN FURTHER DOWN THE ROAD...

LOOKING AWAY FROM THE HEADLIGHTS OF CARS WHEN THEY APPROACHED

WALKING IN THE NIGHT AIR, OUR EYES ADJUSTING TO THE DARK...

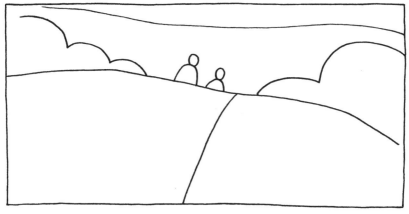

THEN SUDDENLY, WE CAME AROUND A BEND—

and THE WORLD UNFOLDED BEFORE US

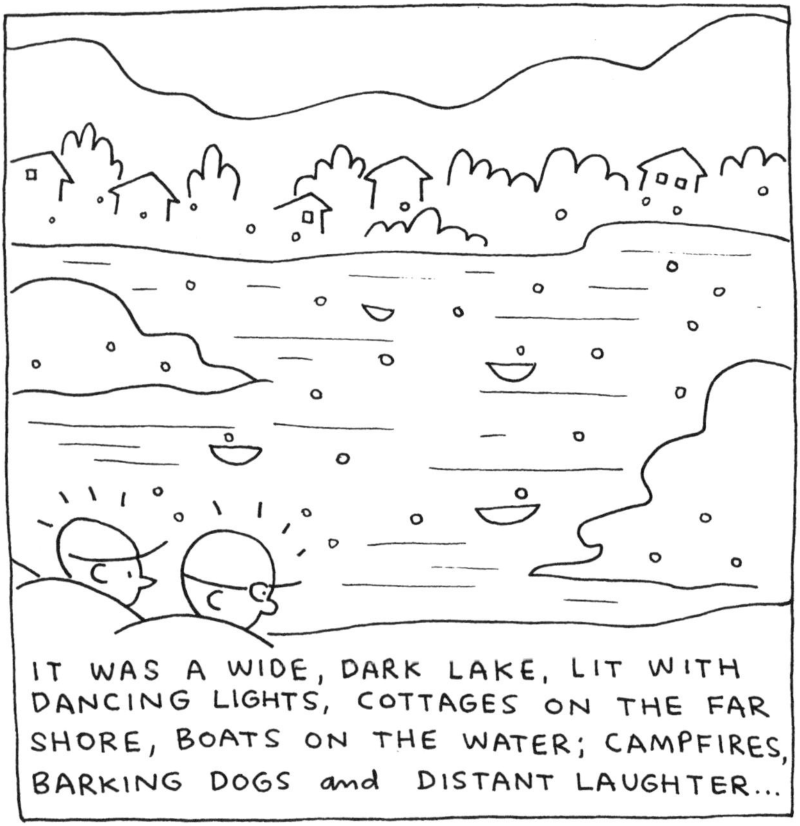
IT WAS A WIDE, DARK LAKE, LIT WITH DANCING LIGHTS, COTTAGES ON THE FAR SHORE, BOATS ON THE WATER; CAMPFIRES, BARKING DOGS and DISTANT LAUGHTER...

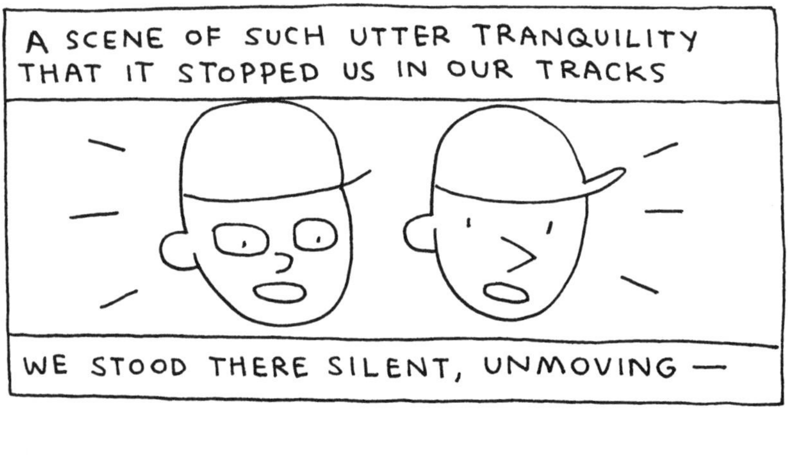
A SCENE OF SUCH UTTER TRANQUILITY THAT IT STOPPED US IN OUR TRACKS
WE STOOD THERE SILENT, UNMOVING —

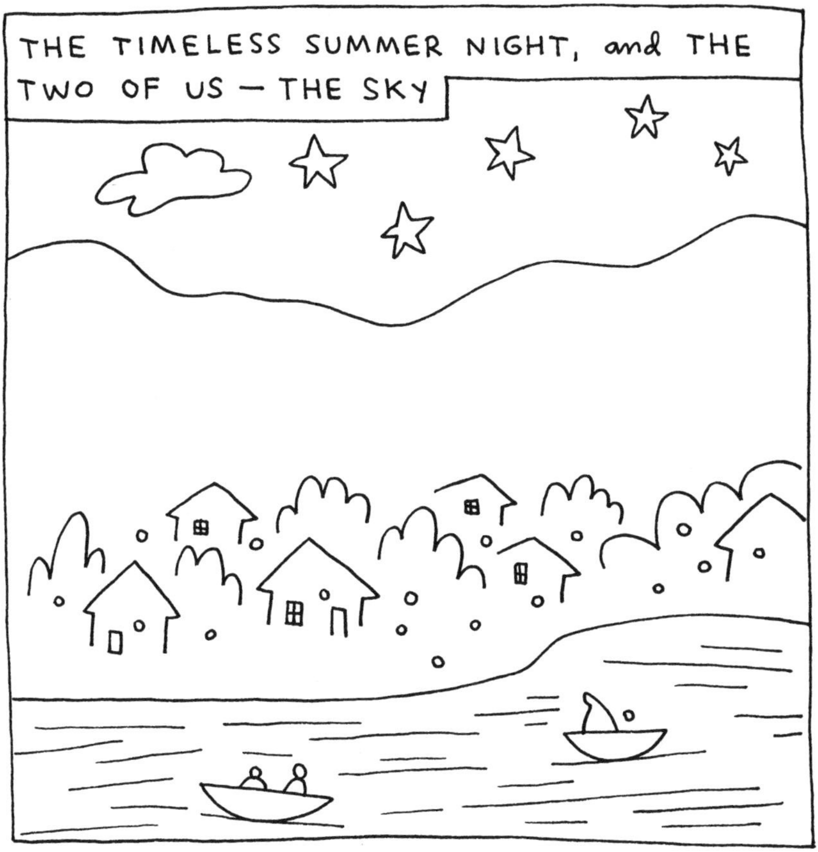
THE TIMELESS SUMMER NIGHT, and THE TWO OF US — THE SKY

HAPPENED JUNE 23-24, 1995
WRITTEN DOWN DEC. 14, 2004 —
TO OCT. 16, 2005

John Porcellino

SOOPER SIZE KING-CAT TOP FORTY

FALL '04 TO FALL '05

1. MY WIFE and MY CAT ♡
2. Joni Mitchell Ladies of the Canyon (Reprise, 1970)
3. BOB DYLAN: Self Portrait, Bootleg Series, Love & Theft, Time Out of Mind, and THINKING ABOUT BOB DYLAN
4. BOB DYLAN Chronicles, Volume One · Reading this book changed my Life!
5. THANK YOU! FOR RIDING MUNI!
6. Monty Python's FLYING CIRCUS
7. SONNY ROLLINS Work Time (Prestige Records, 1955)
8. Ed Wood movie starring Johnny Depp (dir. Tim Burton) ★★★★★
9. Led Zeppelin "Down By The Seaside"
10. Elvis Presley "If I Can Dream" from '68 Comeback Special (T.V. Performance)
11. thinking about THOREAU
12. Beck Sea Change (Interscope Records, 2002)
13. KEEPING UP APPEARANCES and AS TIME GOES BY (T.V. shows – BBC/PBS) ♡♡♡
14. MATISSE AND PICASSO by Jack Flam (Westview, 2003)
15. Steely Dan "FM"
16. Brian Wilson SMiLE (Nonesuch, 2004) Gave me Hope.
17. The Doo Wop Box (Rhino Records Box Set) ♡
18. SOFT BOYS "Where Are The Prawns?" (Rykodisc) ★★★★★
19. Thinking about ADAM and the ANTS
20. Paul McCartney Wingspan (2 CD set, Capitol Records) (Lotta Good Songs on there)
21. BEARS 27, DOLPHINS 24 (NFL Hall of Fame Game, Canton OHIO – August 8, 2005) ♡
22. ELVIS PRESLEY · Aloha Live from Hawaii Via Satellite and Moody Blue Albums (RCA) ★★★★★★★★
23. Ramones: End of the Century (DVD, 2004) ♡ (Movie)
24. LOVE and ROCKETS "No New Tale to Tell"
25. Duran Duran – Rio album (Capitol, 1982) still one of the best records I ever heard!
26. HERB ALPERT and the TIJUANA BRASS: Lost Treasures CD (Shout! Factory) THANK YOU!
27. The Who "Eminence Front"
28. ZZ Top: "Waitin' for the Bus" and "Jesus Just Left Chicago" (Medley) Warner Bros. Records
29. ROYAL TENENBAUMS Motion Picture Soundtrack
30. Night Train to Nashville: Amazing 2-CD set of Nashville R&B, 1940's – 1970's (Country Music Hall of Fame Records)
31. The Who Who's Next (MCA, 1971) ★★★★★
32. LAURA NYRO "Desiree" --WOW--
33. talkin' to Zak ♡

· TOP FORTY CONTINUED ·

34. Complete FREAKS and GEEKS DVD Set (Shout! Factory) ♡

35. Neil Young "Cinnamon Girl" (Reprise) - soundin' pretty good right about now...

36. Sleepin' in the car in L.A. (Thursday Night - July 14, 2005) ♡

37. Los Angeles, CA 8/14 - 8/19

38. 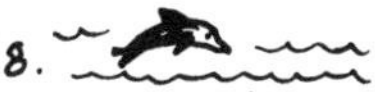 DOLPHINS JUMPING in the OCEAN

39. LOW in EUROPE DVD

Inspirational . . .

40. The Beatles "And Your Bird Can Sing" (Capitol Records)

41. L.A. Sunsets / Palm Trees

42. Getting my watch fixed for two dollars in L.A.

43. Ebert and Roeper At the Movies T.V. Show (Comforting)

44. Aaron Cometbus: CHICAGO STORIES book (cover by Megan Kelso!)

45. FRANK SINATRA - Complete Reprise Studio Recordings and SINATRA IN HOLLYWOOD (Reprise Records) ★★★★★

and LOTS LOTS MORE!!

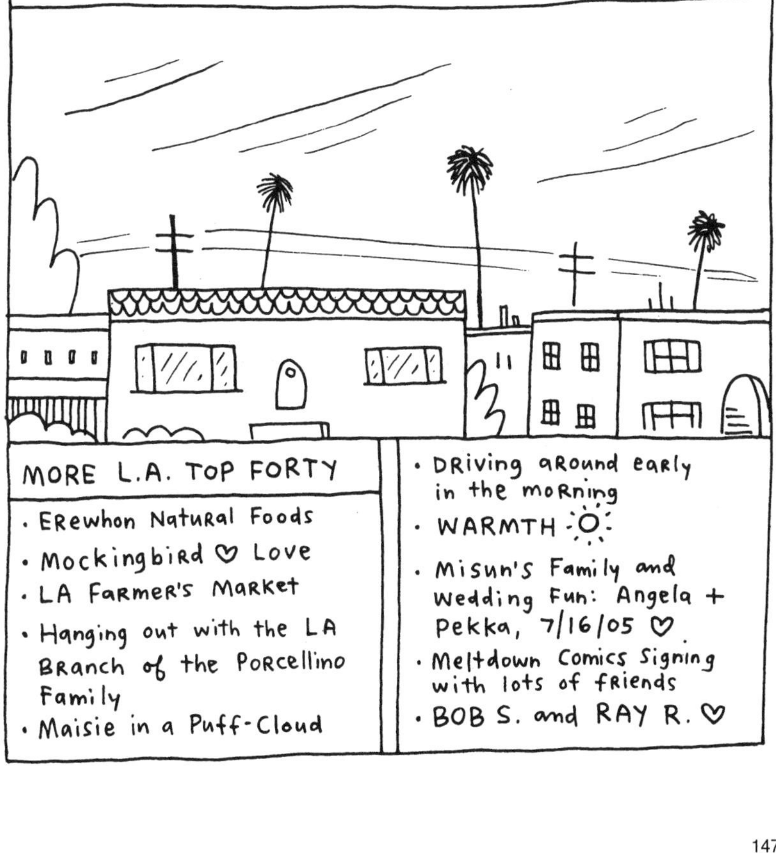

MORE L.A. TOP FORTY

- Erewhon Natural Foods
- Mockingbird ♡ Love
- LA Farmer's Market
- Hanging out with the LA Branch of the Porcellino Family
- Maisie in a Puff-Cloud
- Driving around early in the morning
- WARMTH ☼
- Misun's Family and Wedding Fun: Angela + Pekka, 7/16/05 ♡
- Meltdown Comics Signing with lots of friends
- BOB S. and RAY R. ♡

COUNTRY ROADS – BRIGHTON

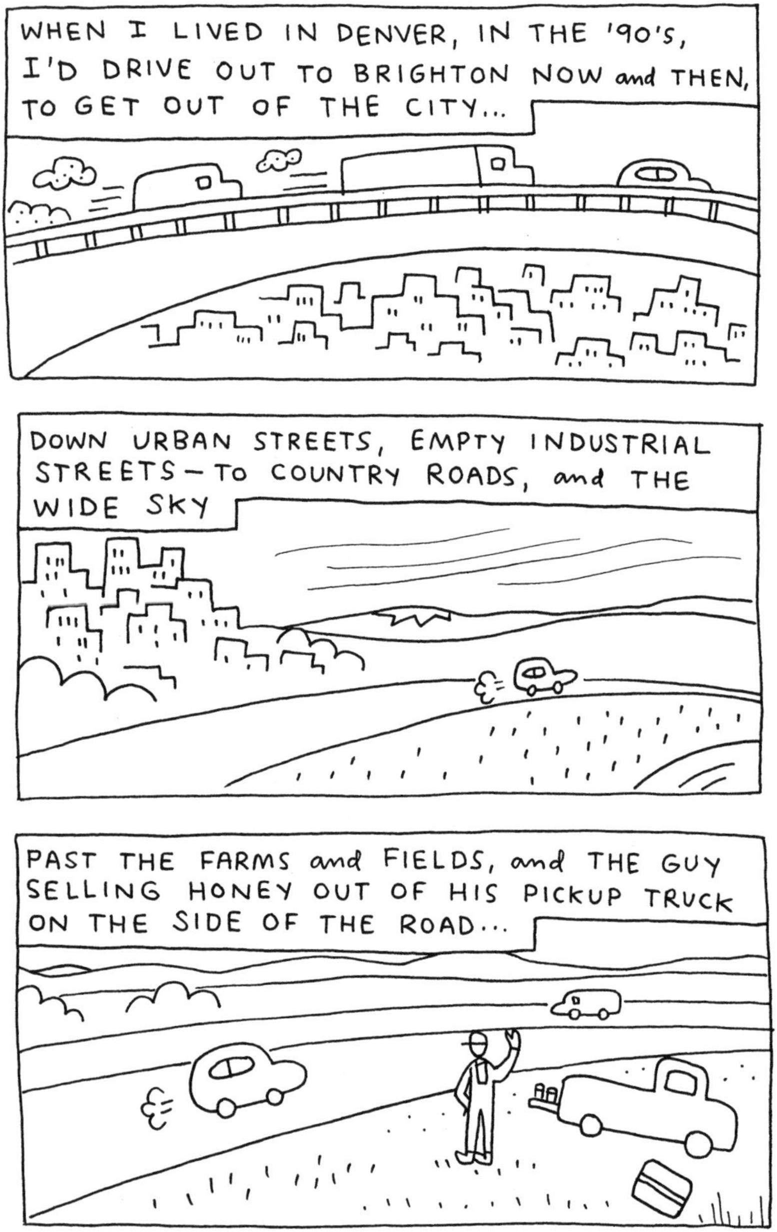
WHEN I LIVED IN DENVER, IN THE '90'S, I'D DRIVE OUT TO BRIGHTON NOW and THEN, TO GET OUT OF THE CITY...
DOWN URBAN STREETS, EMPTY INDUSTRIAL STREETS – TO COUNTRY ROADS, and THE WIDE SKY
PAST THE FARMS and FIELDS, and THE GUY SELLING HONEY OUT OF HIS PICKUP TRUCK ON THE SIDE OF THE ROAD...

WHEN YOU GOT TO THE GRAIN ELEVATORS YOU WERE ALMOST THERE--

BRIGHTON and HER DUSTY STREETS

THE THRIFT STORE

SALV
AR
THR

THE MEXICAN RESTAURANT...

La Estrellita

OUT WEST OF TOWN, PAST THE TRACKS and THE HIGHWAY, THE RIVER FLOWED ALONG, and I'D SIT ON ITS BANKS and EAT LUNCH, WATCH THE WATER ROLL BY, THE FIELDS and TREES, THE MOUNTAINS IN THE DISTANCE

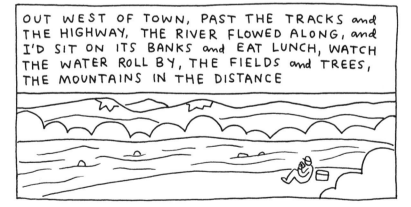

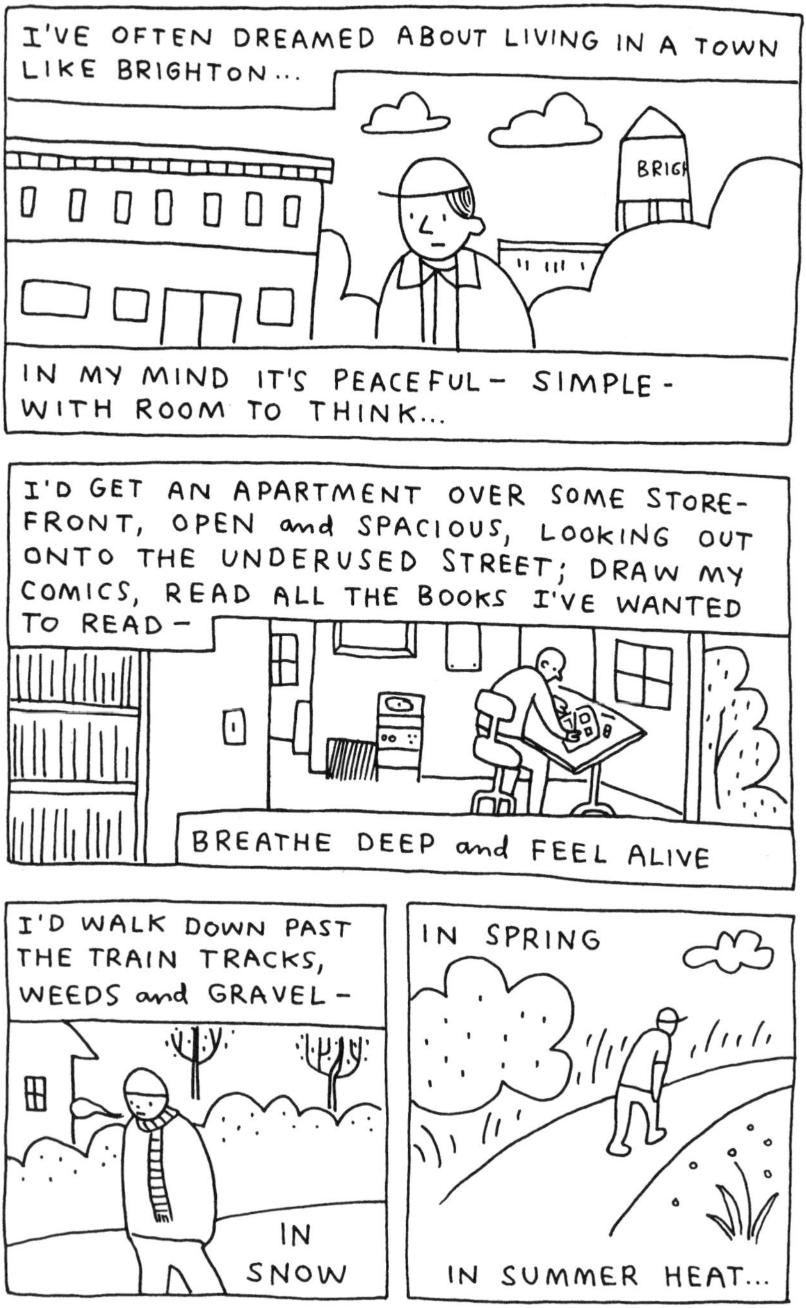
I'VE OFTEN DREAMED ABOUT LIVING IN A TOWN LIKE BRIGHTON...
BRIGH
IN MY MIND IT'S PEACEFUL- SIMPLE- WITH ROOM TO THINK...
I'D GET AN APARTMENT OVER SOME STORE-FRONT, OPEN and SPACIOUS, LOOKING OUT ONTO THE UNDERUSED STREET; DRAW MY COMICS, READ ALL THE BOOKS I'VE WANTED TO READ-
BREATHE DEEP and FEEL ALIVE
I'D WALK DOWN PAST THE TRAIN TRACKS, WEEDS and GRAVEL-
IN SNOW
IN SPRING
IN SUMMER HEAT...

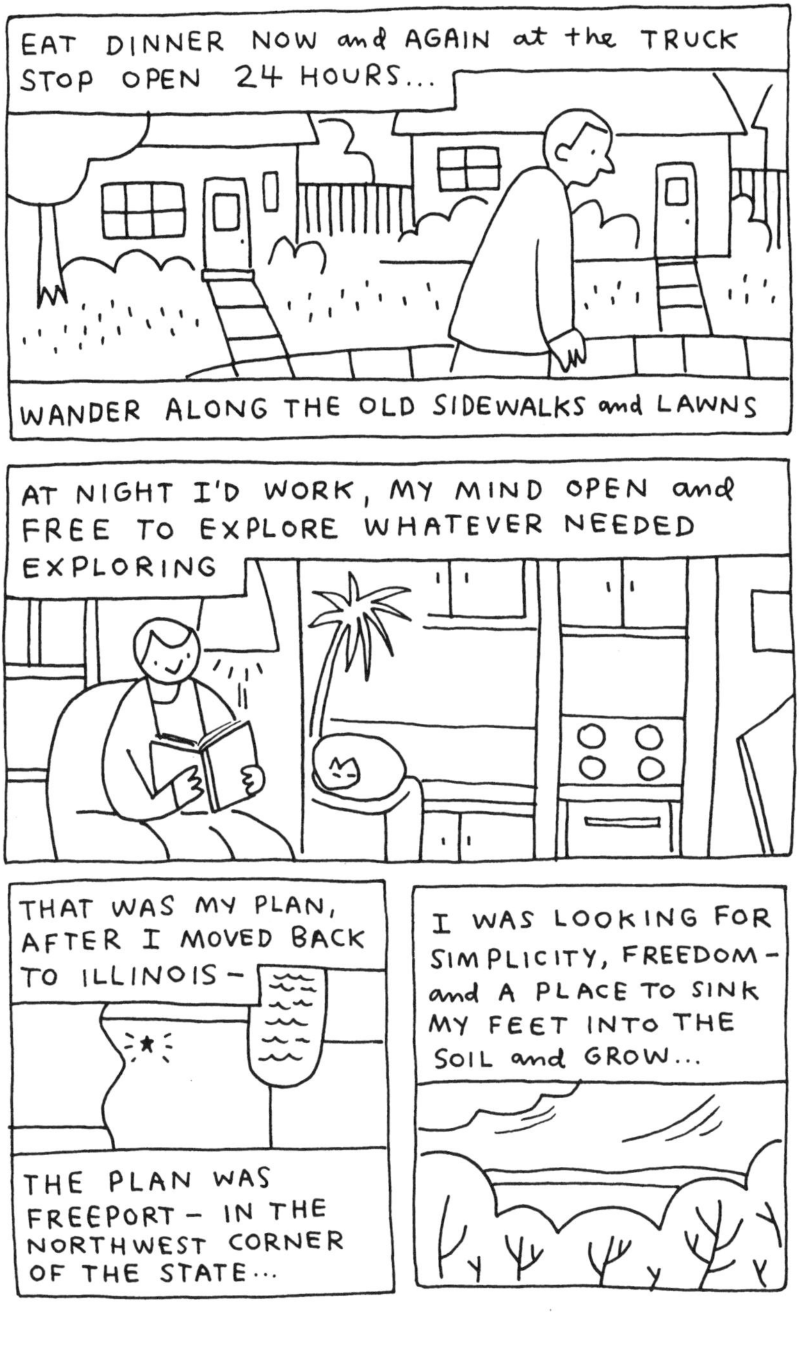

EAT DINNER NOW and AGAIN at the TRUCK STOP OPEN 24 HOURS...
WANDER ALONG THE OLD SIDEWALKS and LAWNS
AT NIGHT I'D WORK, MY MIND OPEN and FREE TO EXPLORE WHATEVER NEEDED EXPLORING
THAT WAS MY PLAN, AFTER I MOVED BACK TO ILLINOIS -
THE PLAN WAS FREEPORT - IN THE NORTHWEST CORNER OF THE STATE...
I WAS LOOKING FOR SIMPLICITY, FREEDOM - and A PLACE TO SINK MY FEET INTO THE SOIL and GROW...

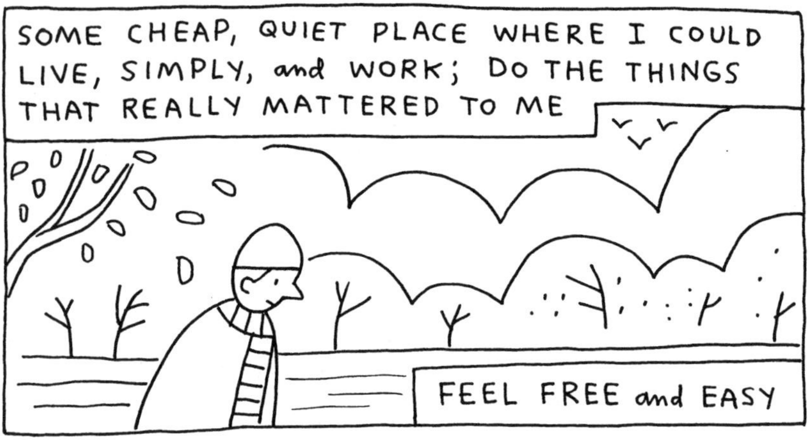
SOME CHEAP, QUIET PLACE WHERE I COULD LIVE, SIMPLY, and WORK; DO THE THINGS THAT REALLY MATTERED TO ME
FEEL FREE and EASY

IT DIDN'T WORK OUT THAT WAY...

2/25/05
8/7/05 J.P.

NORTH ALFRED STREET

When I lived in Elgin, alone, one of my main sources of amusement was walking around. I'd walk to the library and the Post Office, to the video store; to buy groceries or just around the neighborhood.

One of my favorite walks was what I called "North Alfred Street". I'd go outside, at night, after dinner, and head up Melrose (the street where I lived), across Lawrence, past the house where dogs always barked at me, past the house with the chainsaw sculpture of a bear on the front lawn.

Then, the empty schoolyard—vast, under wide open sky and streetlights. At Demmond, Melrose jogged right and I'd head over a few blocks to Aldine. There were pine trees there, and I'd always stop to breathe deep, looking for their scent. It reminded me of Colorado.

A few blocks on, I'd come to the "Peace" House—which was like a beacon of hope for me in my loneliness and despair.

The Peace House was just an average looking brown suburban ranch house, set back from the street on an oversized lot, but it was surrounded by beauty and love... plastic deer grazed on the lawn alongside pinwheels and wild landscaped mounds covered in crazy bushes; a little wooden bridge crossed between trees from one spot to another.

On the corner, under the streetlight, was a hand-painted sign that read:

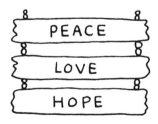

It shone out in the night like magic.

Next to the driveway, laid out in bricks on a carefully crafted earthen berm, was the word PEACE.

In the empty lot next door their handiwork continued—a wild, semi-overgrown patch of earth, birdbaths, snaggly bushes, and shrubberies. An old iron gateway stood in the brush—crowned with steel letters painted white:

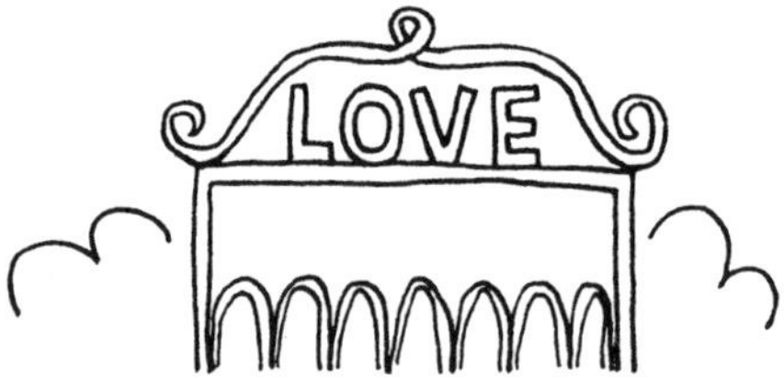
LOVE

From the Peace House I'd walk up the last block of Alfred Street, to Wing, where it ended at the park. This long block reminded me of Denver—there were a few Southwestern-style stucco houses, but something of the spirit there reminded me of Denver too… the sense of peace, and possibilities… the wide-open sky cradling the city below. At Wing Street I reversed my path, and headed back down Alfred again.

South of Demmond, the road curved and opened up into a wide expansive boulevard lined with wide expensive houses. The sidewalks ran right up against the street, endless green lawns sprawled off toward ritzy front doors. Rich kids were always having late night parties on this stretch of North Alfred Street. I'd shuffle past the lights and laughter, feeling alone but happy.

Here you walk under the beckoning sky, look up: maybe the white clouds, the moon. The stars, kicking stones, and idly garbage-picking your way along, looking for something good…

Down past the evergreen trees, the quiet night; the lovely old houses with green glass windows. Then around the corner and back on home to Melrose.

In the four years I lived in Elgin, I walked that route countless times. In Elgin I felt the oddest confliction of emotions. On the one hand, real peace—the sense that I was here, at last, in the right place, on the right street, in the right town. That I was finally home.

On the other hand there was the relentless doubt and longing. I felt alone, trapped, inescapable, hopeless.

One night I felt particularly bad, and I ended up walking downtown, across the bridges, beneath the warehouse walls and factories, along by the river. I crossed the railroad tracks and came to the little shack that served coffee and newspapers to commuters bound each morning for Chicago. A Greyhound Bus sign hung beside the door. I shaded my hands against my face and peered through the dark window: magazines, a counter, candy and gum. A signboard on the wall listed the daily Greyhound departures: Rockford, Madison Wis., and Laredo Texas.

For some reason, seeing those words—Laredo, Texas—struck me with a force that stunned me. I stepped back and stood on the pavement, blinking in the night, on the empty street. In that instant, I realized I was free... absolutely free. In this moment, and in any moment at all, I was completely and boundlessly free.

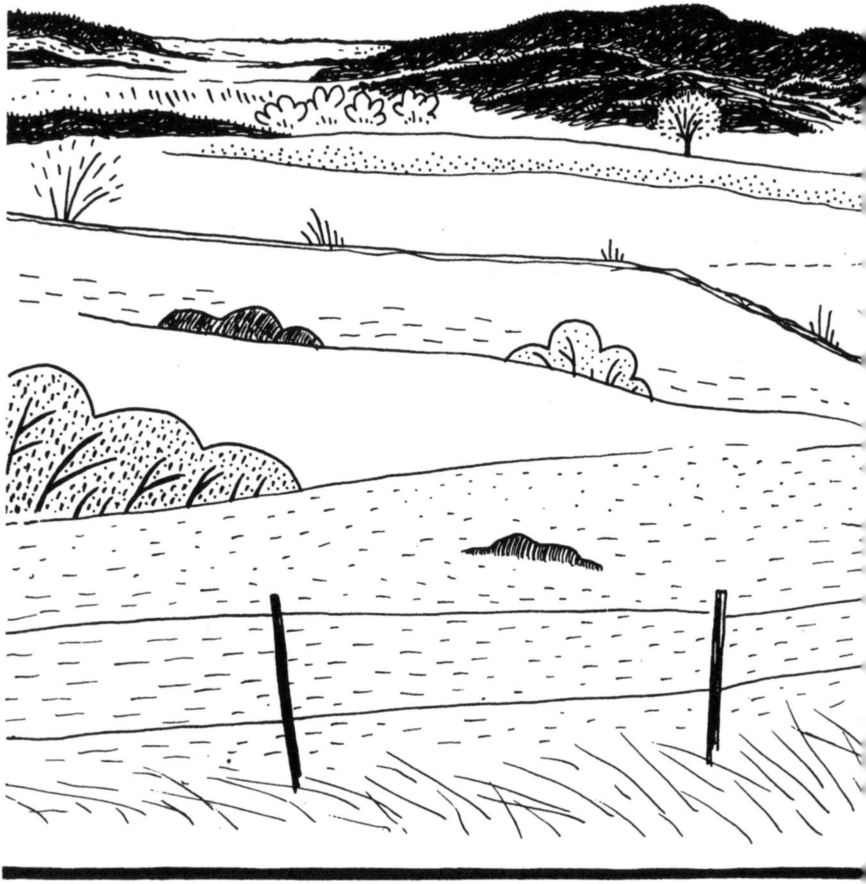

KING-CAT

COMICS & STORIES

No. 66 $3.00

BY JOHN PORCELLINO

ONE MORNING I woke up early, and couldn't get back to sleep. I laid there in the dark and thought about Route 47, and the Plank Road Cutoff; the church on the corner; how the road goes under the train tracks there, past the mysterious stairway leading up the hillside into the woods.

I thought about the color of the grass, greyish-green after the spring thaw, the red brambles, and the color of the sky.

I laid there and wondered about this feeling I have, what I was going to do with it, where it was going to take me.

✳ ✳ ✳

KING-CAT COMICS & STORIES #66
Published 12/05 by: SPIT and a HALF
▓▓▓▓▓▓▓▓▓▓▓▓▓▓
please write!   San Francisco, CA
www.king-cat.net   ▓▓▓▓▓ - U.S.A.

© 2005 John A. Porcellino, LOVE. ♡   Forge.

Las Hojas

CAST OF CHARACTERS

JOHN P. NATHAN KELSEY LUPE ALVARO

ANGEL LOUIE JACOB JOSH SEAN

LATE NOVEMBER 2001... ELGIN, ILLINOIS

BETTER GET OUT and RAKE THE LEAVES... BEFORE IT STARTS TO RAIN

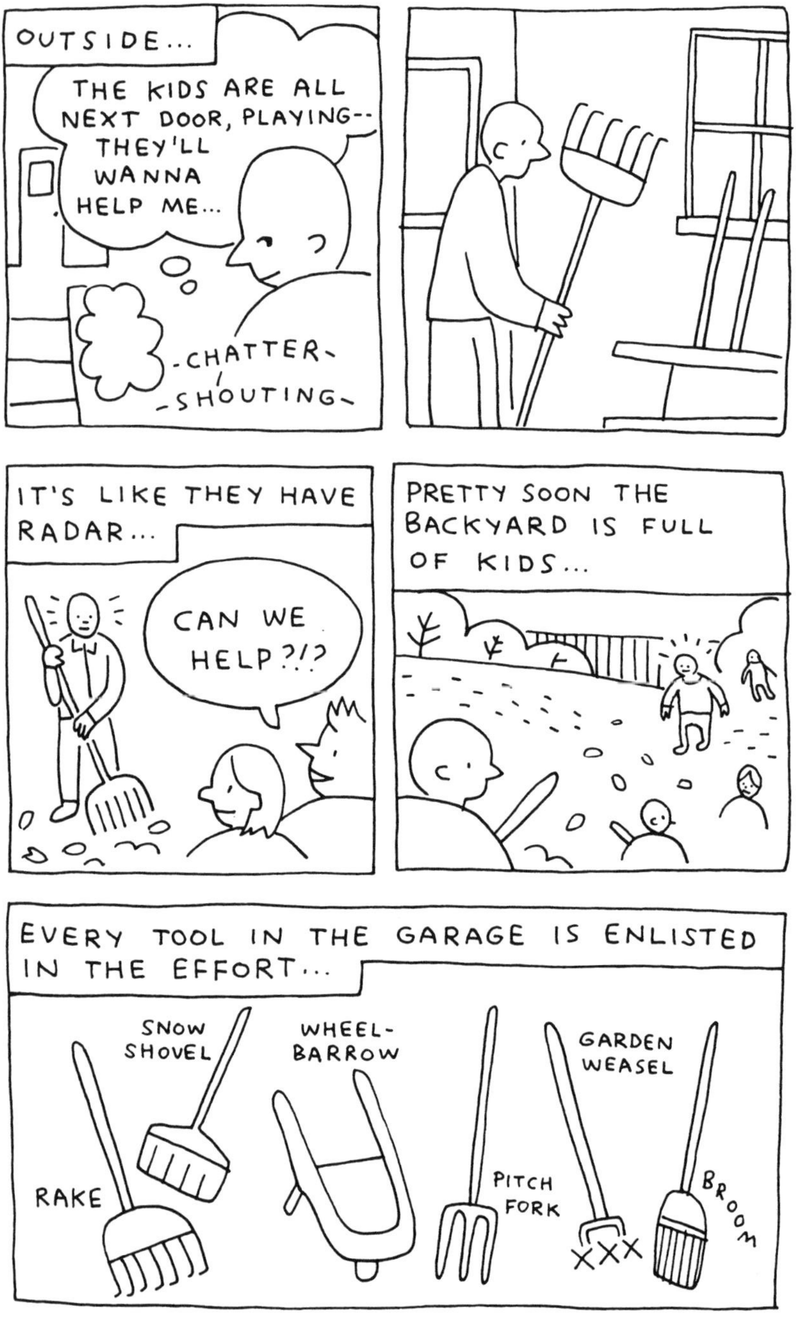
OUTSIDE...
THE KIDS ARE ALL NEXT DOOR, PLAYING-- THEY'LL WANNA HELP ME...
-CHATTER-
-SHOUTING-
IT'S LIKE THEY HAVE RADAR...
CAN WE HELP?!?
PRETTY SOON THE BACKYARD IS FULL OF KIDS...
EVERY TOOL IN THE GARAGE IS ENLISTED IN THE EFFORT...
SNOW SHOVEL
WHEEL-BARROW
GARDEN WEASEL
RAKE
PITCH FORK
BROOM

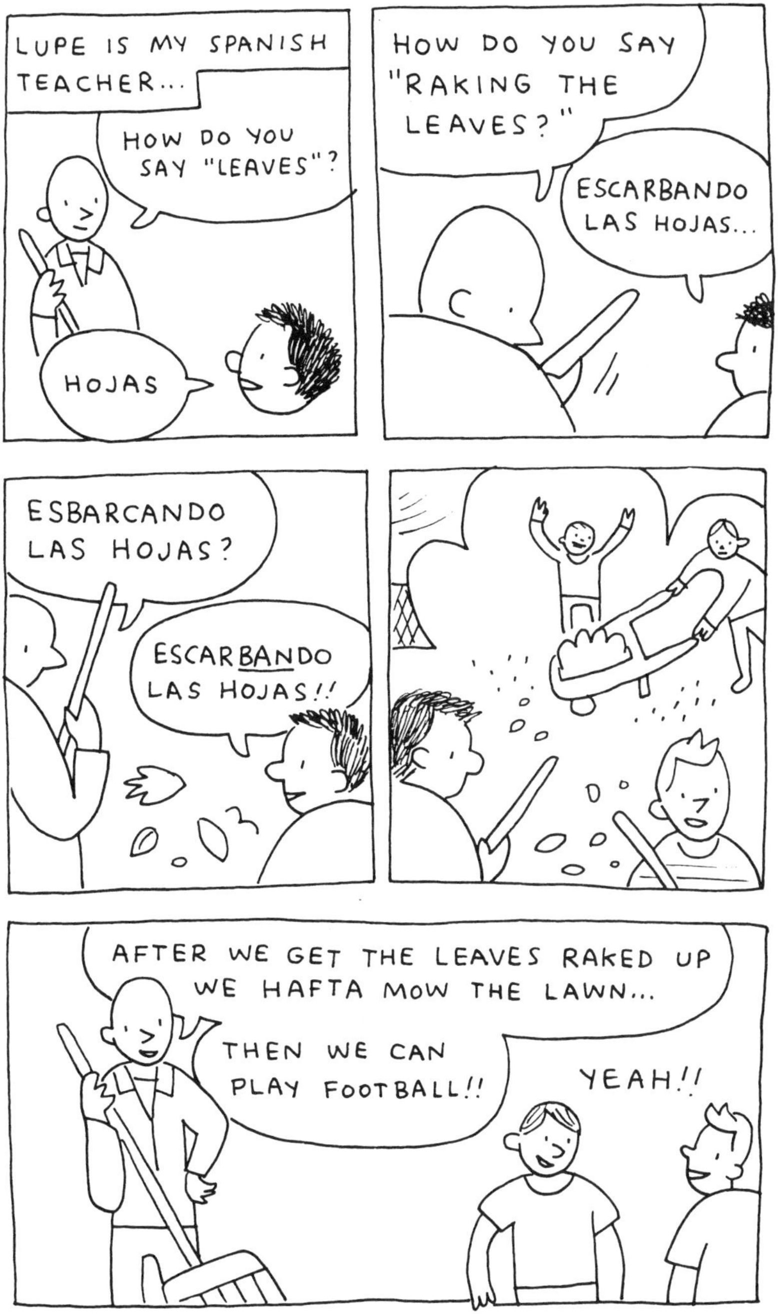
LUPE IS MY SPANISH TEACHER...
HOW DO YOU SAY "LEAVES"?
HOJAS
HOW DO YOU SAY "RAKING THE LEAVES?"
ESCARBANDO LAS HOJAS...
ESBARCANDO LAS HOJAS?
ESCARBANDO LAS HOJAS!!
AFTER WE GET THE LEAVES RAKED UP WE HAFTA MOW THE LAWN...
THEN WE CAN PLAY FOOTBALL!!
YEAH!!

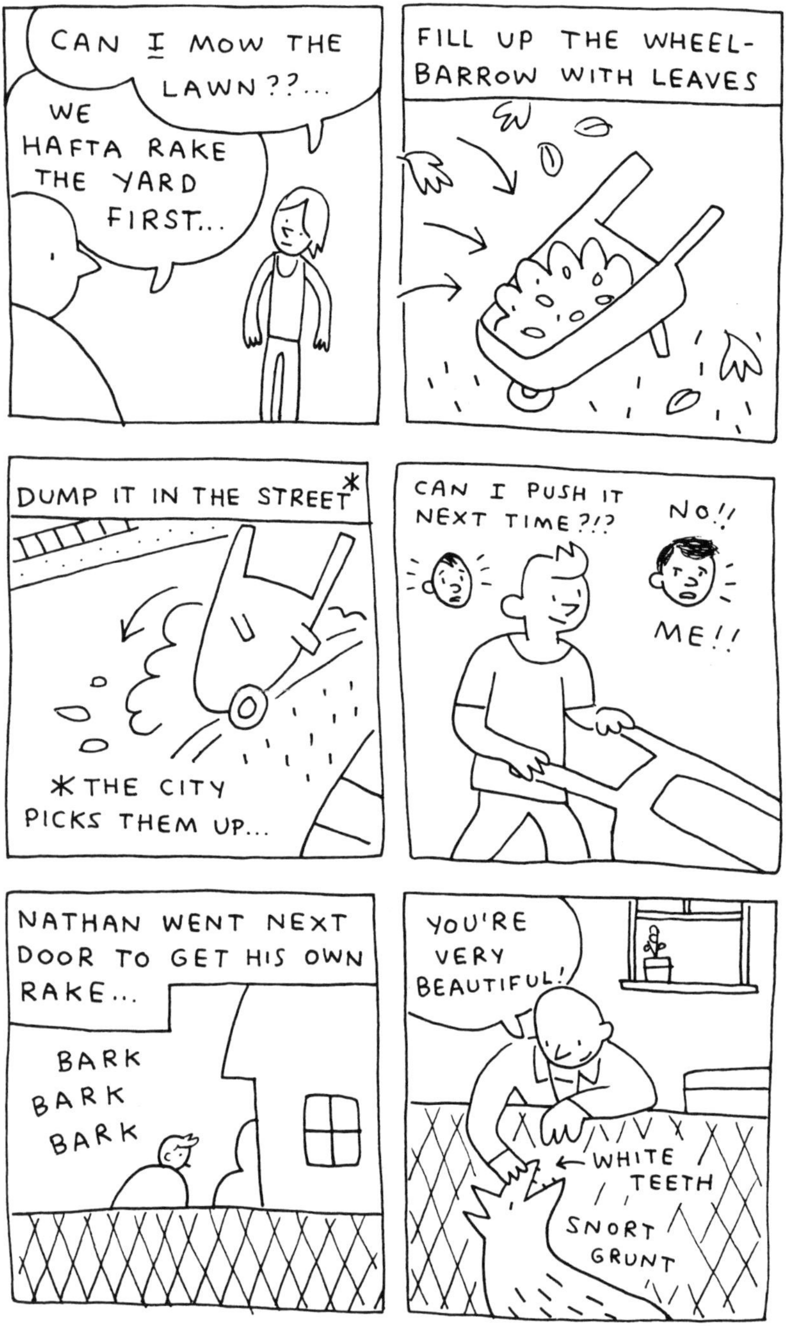
CAN I MOW THE LAWN??...
WE HAFTA RAKE THE YARD FIRST...
FILL UP THE WHEEL-BARROW WITH LEAVES
DUMP IT IN THE STREET*
*THE CITY PICKS THEM UP...
CAN I PUSH IT NEXT TIME?!?
NO!!
ME!!
NATHAN WENT NEXT DOOR TO GET HIS OWN RAKE...
BARK
BARK
BARK
YOU'RE VERY BEAUTIFUL!
WHITE TEETH
SNORT
GRUNT

PUSH MOWER
RUHR
FINALLY, WE THREW THE BALL AROUND A LITTLE...
BUT THEN...
NATHAN! KELSEY!! IT'S TIME TO EAT!!
WE'LL PLAY MORE AFTER LUNCH!!
PSHEER

INTERMISSION

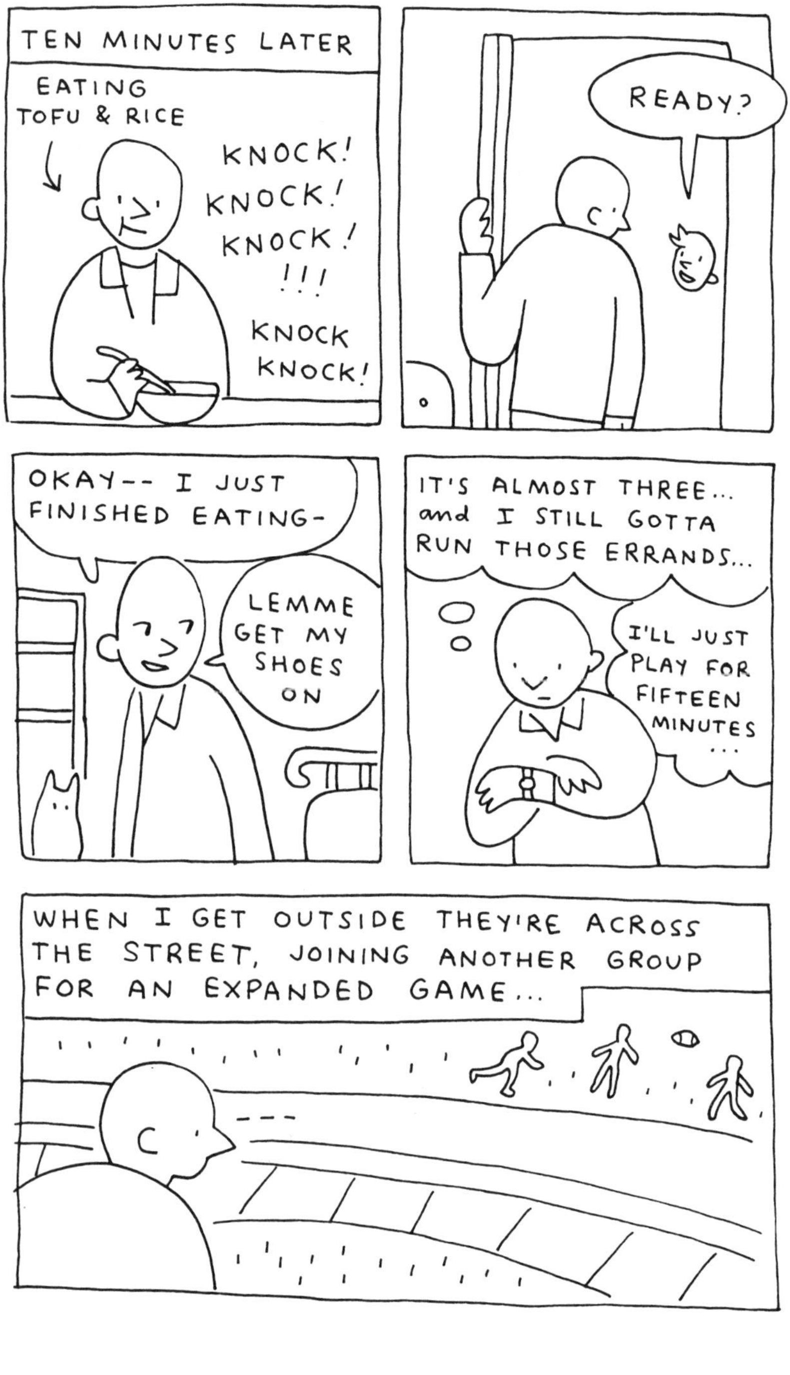
TEN MINUTES LATER
EATING TOFU & RICE
KNOCK! KNOCK! KNOCK! !!!
KNOCK KNOCK!
READY?
OKAY-- I JUST FINISHED EATING-
LEMME GET MY SHOES ON
IT'S ALMOST THREE... and I STILL GOTTA RUN THOSE ERRANDS...
I'LL JUST PLAY FOR FIFTEEN MINUTES ...
WHEN I GET OUTSIDE THEY'RE ACROSS THE STREET, JOINING ANOTHER GROUP FOR AN EXPANDED GAME...

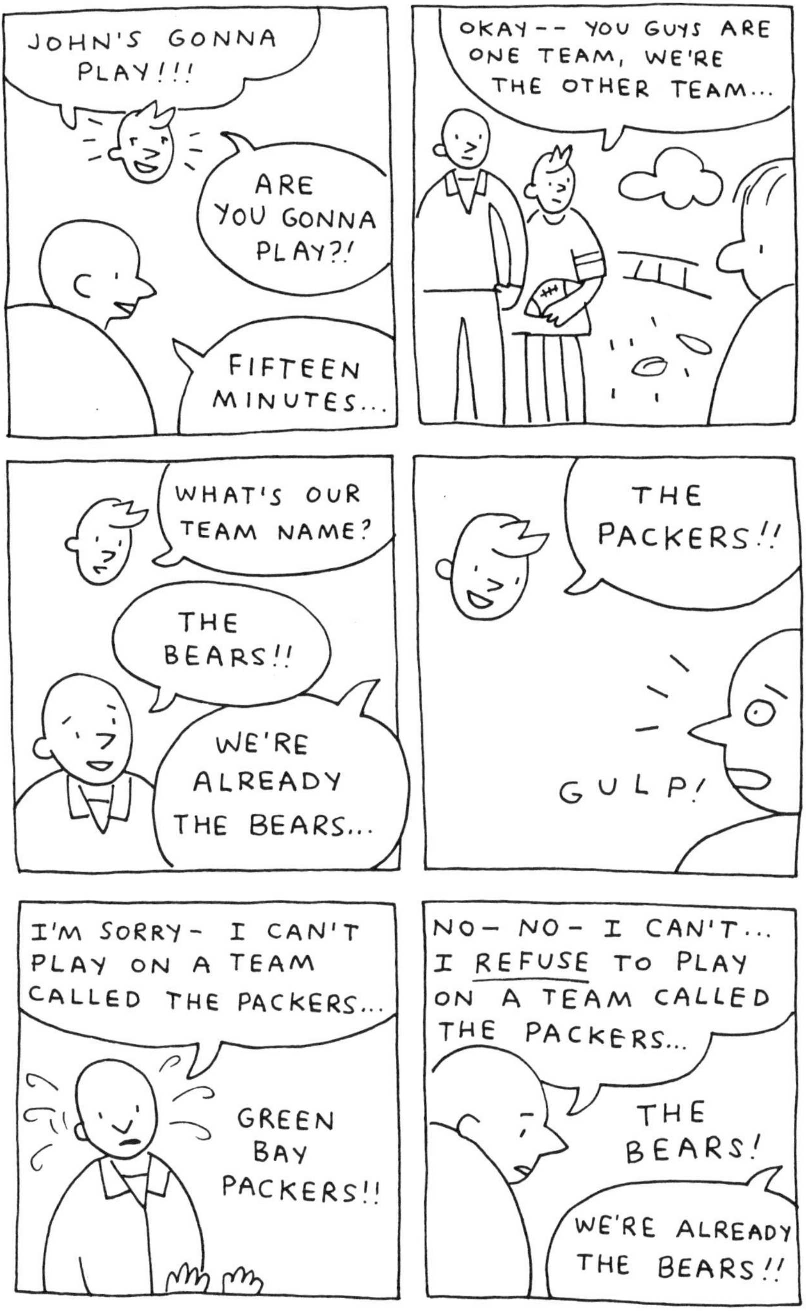
JOHN'S GONNA PLAY!!!
ARE YOU GONNA PLAY?!
FIFTEEN MINUTES...
OKAY-- YOU GUYS ARE ONE TEAM, WE'RE THE OTHER TEAM...
WHAT'S OUR TEAM NAME?
THE BEARS!!
WE'RE ALREADY THE BEARS...
THE PACKERS!!
GULP!
I'M SORRY- I CAN'T PLAY ON A TEAM CALLED THE PACKERS...
GREEN BAY PACKERS!!
NO- NO- I CAN'T... I REFUSE TO PLAY ON A TEAM CALLED THE PACKERS...
THE BEARS!
WE'RE ALREADY THE BEARS!!

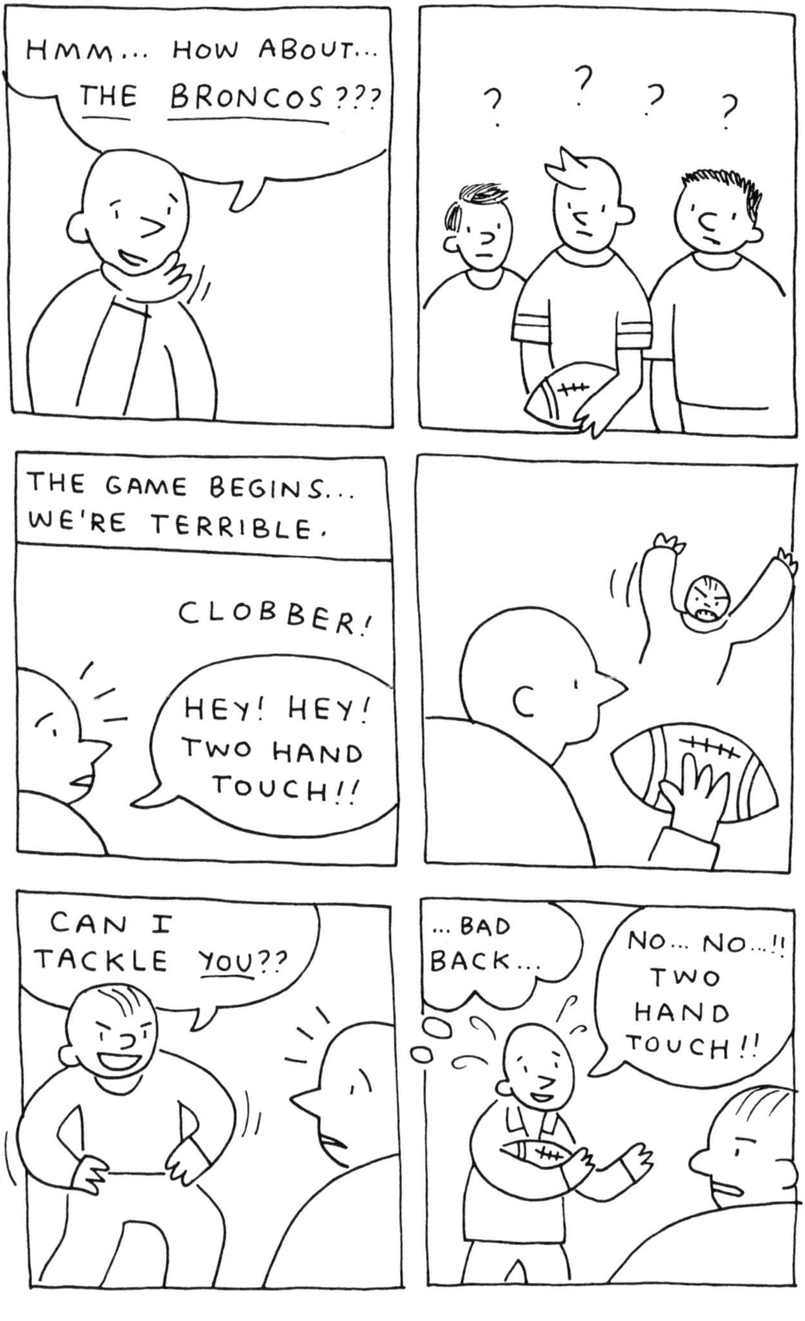
HMM... HOW ABOUT... THE BRONCOS???
? ? ? ?
THE GAME BEGINS... WE'RE TERRIBLE.
CLOBBER!
HEY! HEY! TWO HAND TOUCH!!
CAN I TACKLE YOU??
...BAD BACK...
NO... NO...!! TWO HAND TOUCH!!

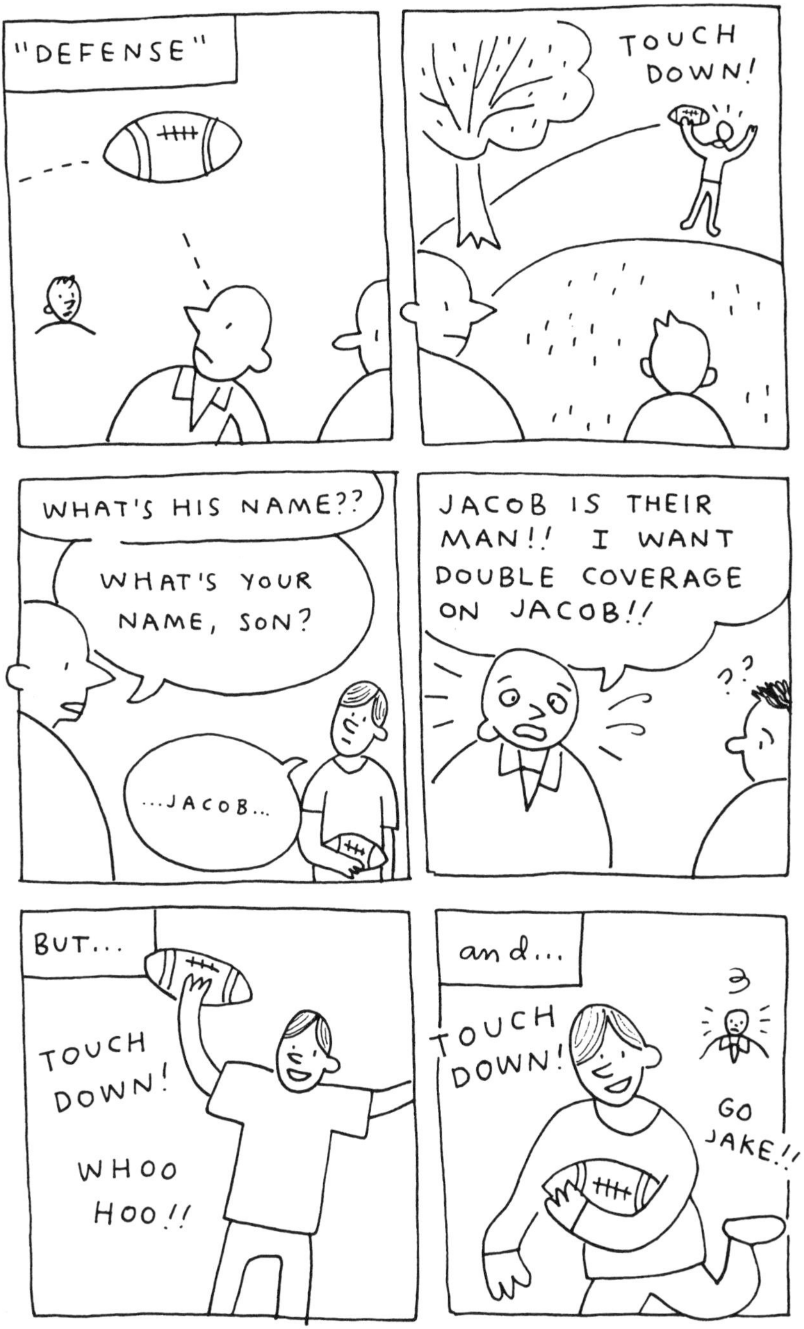
"DEFENSE"
TOUCH DOWN!
WHAT'S HIS NAME??
WHAT'S YOUR NAME, SON?
...JACOB...
JACOB IS THEIR MAN!! I WANT DOUBLE COVERAGE ON JACOB!!
??
BUT...
TOUCH DOWN!
WHOO HOO!!
and...
TOUCH DOWN!
GO JAKE!!

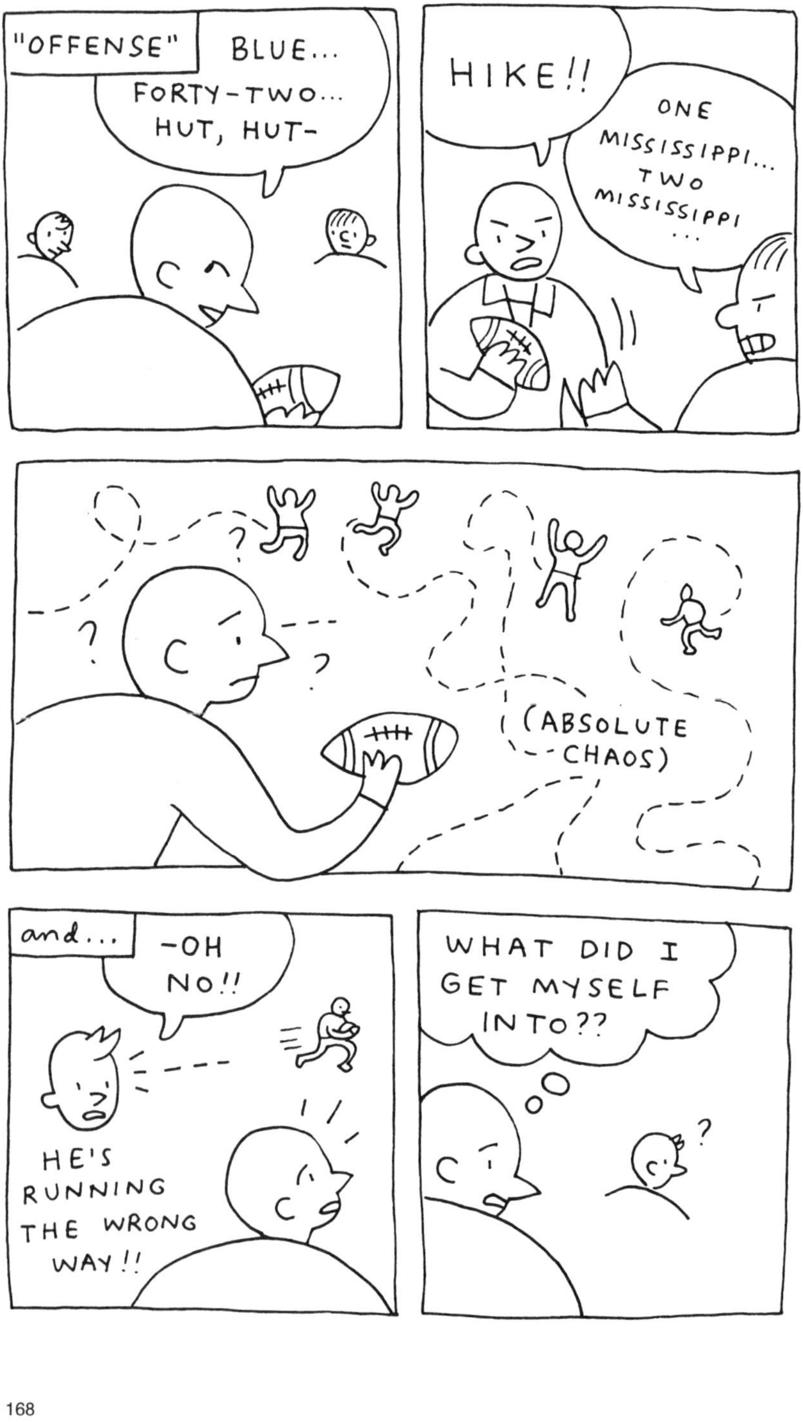

"OFFENSE"
BLUE... FORTY-TWO... HUT, HUT-
HIKE!!
ONE MISSISSIPPI... TWO MISSISSIPPI ...
(ABSOLUTE CHAOS)
and...
-OH NO!!
HE'S RUNNING THE WRONG WAY!!
WHAT DID I GET MYSELF INTO??

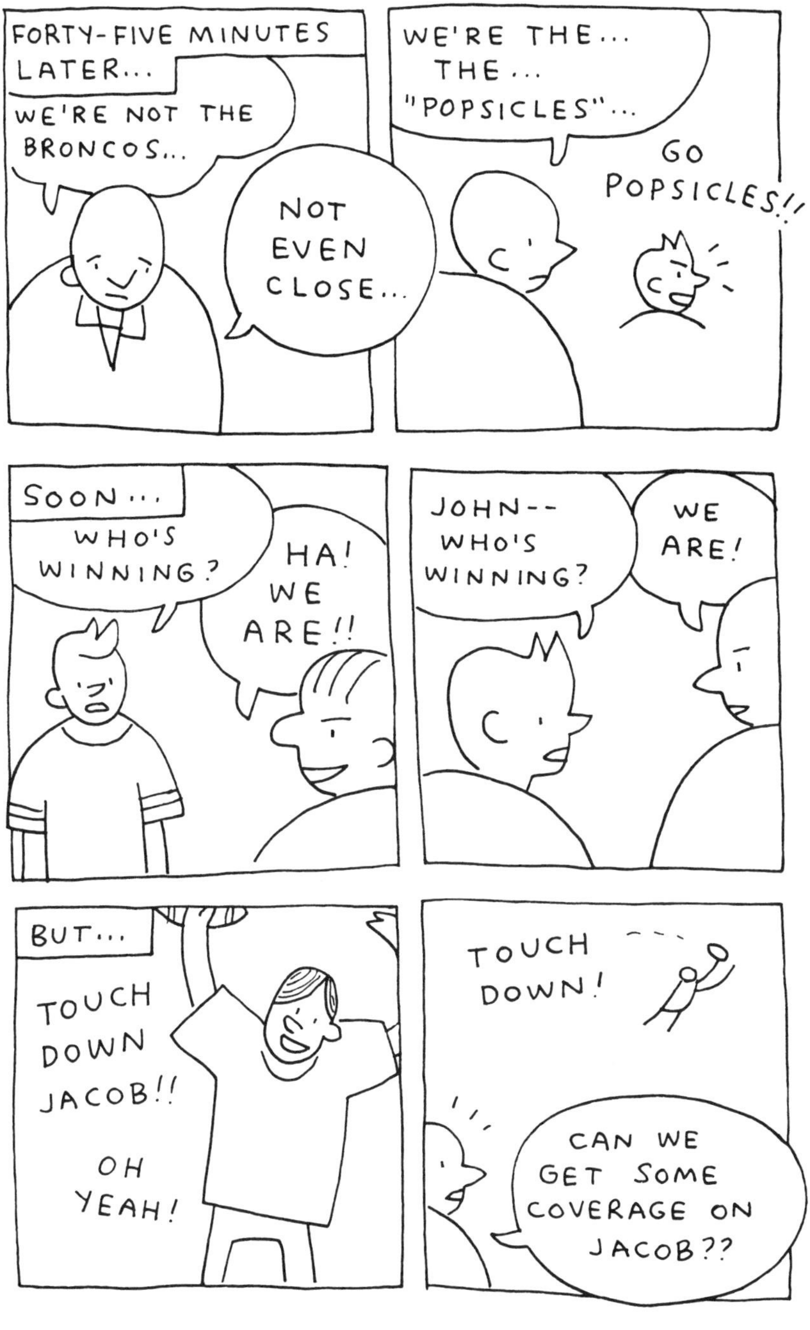
FORTY-FIVE MINUTES LATER...
WE'RE NOT THE BRONCOS...
NOT EVEN CLOSE...
WE'RE THE... THE... "POPSICLES"...
GO POPSICLES!!
SOON...
WHO'S WINNING?
HA! WE ARE!!
JOHN-- WHO'S WINNING?
WE ARE!
BUT...
TOUCH DOWN JACOB!!
OH YEAH!
TOUCH DOWN!
CAN WE GET SOME COVERAGE ON JACOB??

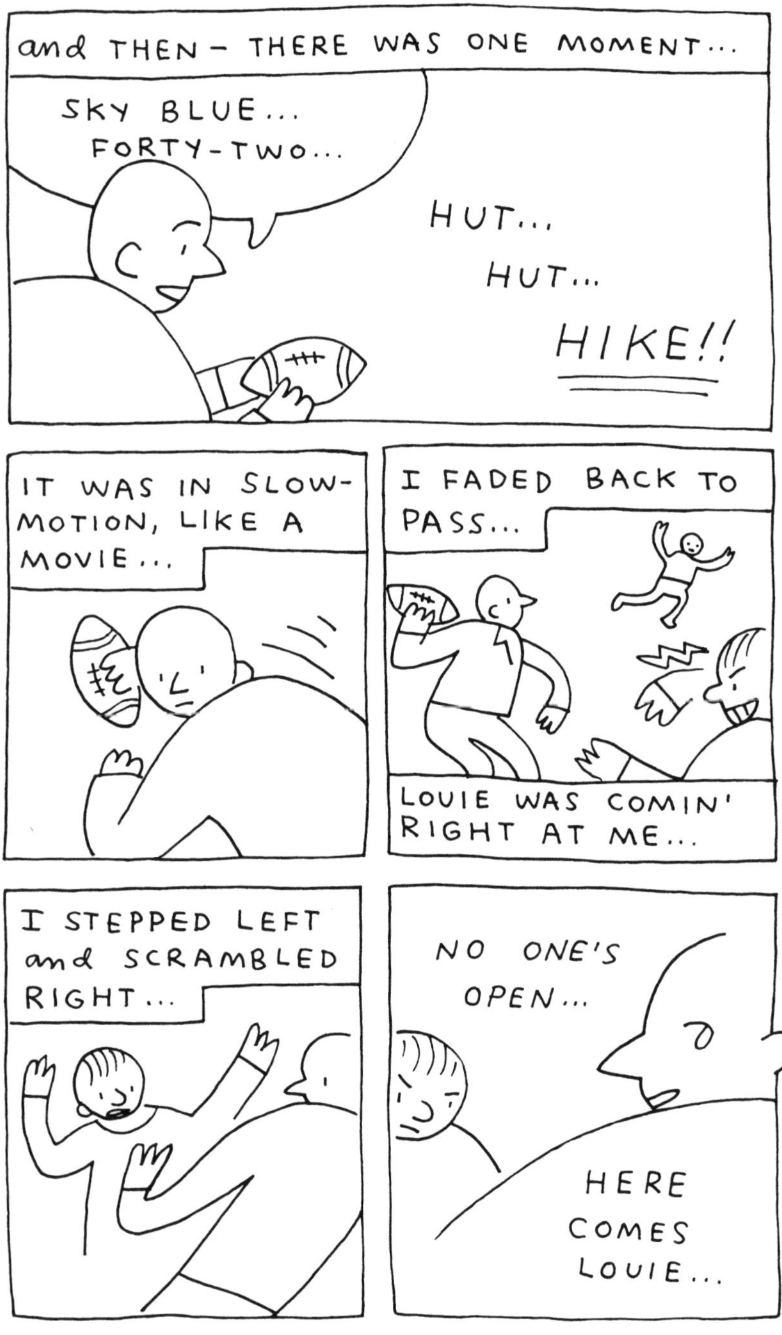
and THEN – THERE WAS ONE MOMENT...
SKY BLUE... FORTY-TWO...
HUT...
HUT...
HIKE!!
IT WAS IN SLOW-MOTION, LIKE A MOVIE...
I FADED BACK TO PASS...
LOUIE WAS COMIN' RIGHT AT ME...
I STEPPED LEFT and SCRAMBLED RIGHT...
NO ONE'S OPEN...
HERE COMES LOUIE...

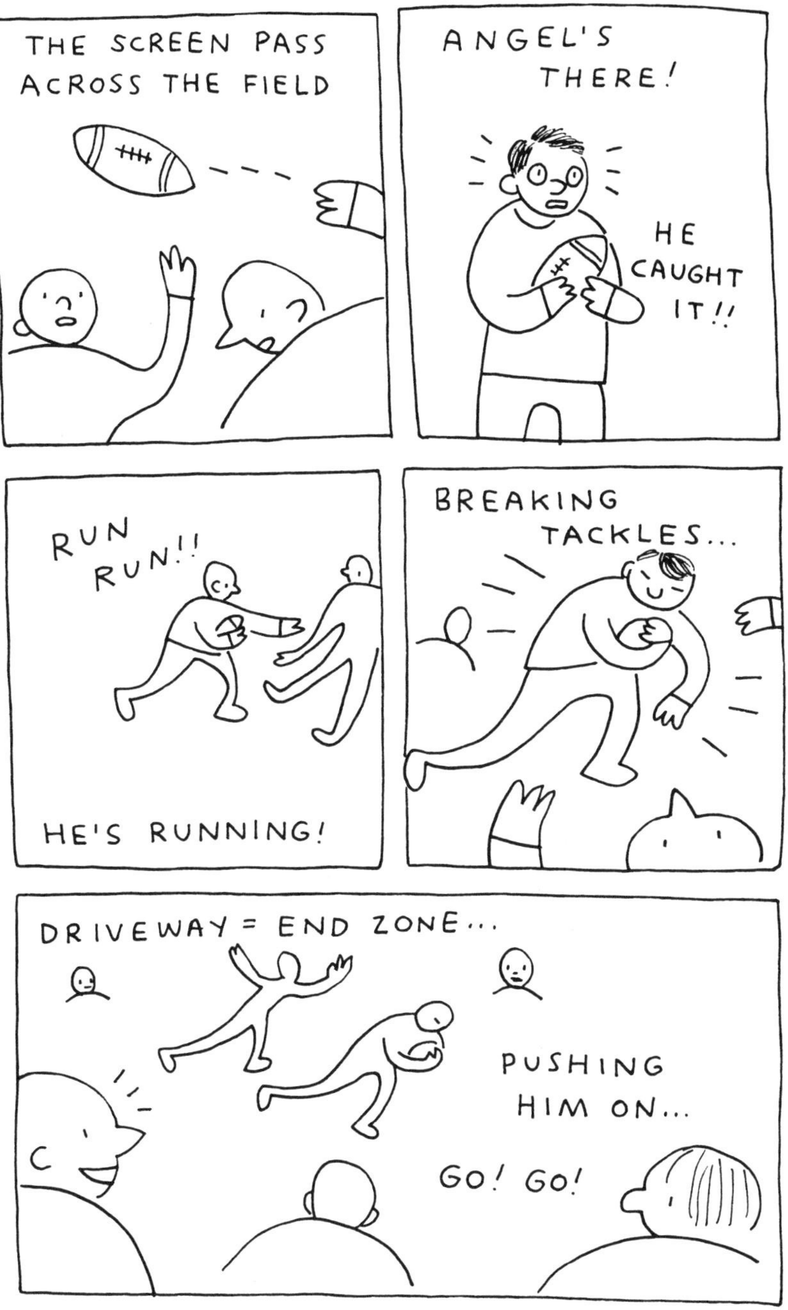
THE SCREEN PASS ACROSS THE FIELD
ANGEL'S THERE!
HE CAUGHT IT!!
RUN RUN!!
HE'S RUNNING!
BREAKING TACKLES...
DRIVEWAY = END ZONE...
PUSHING HIM ON...
GO! GO!

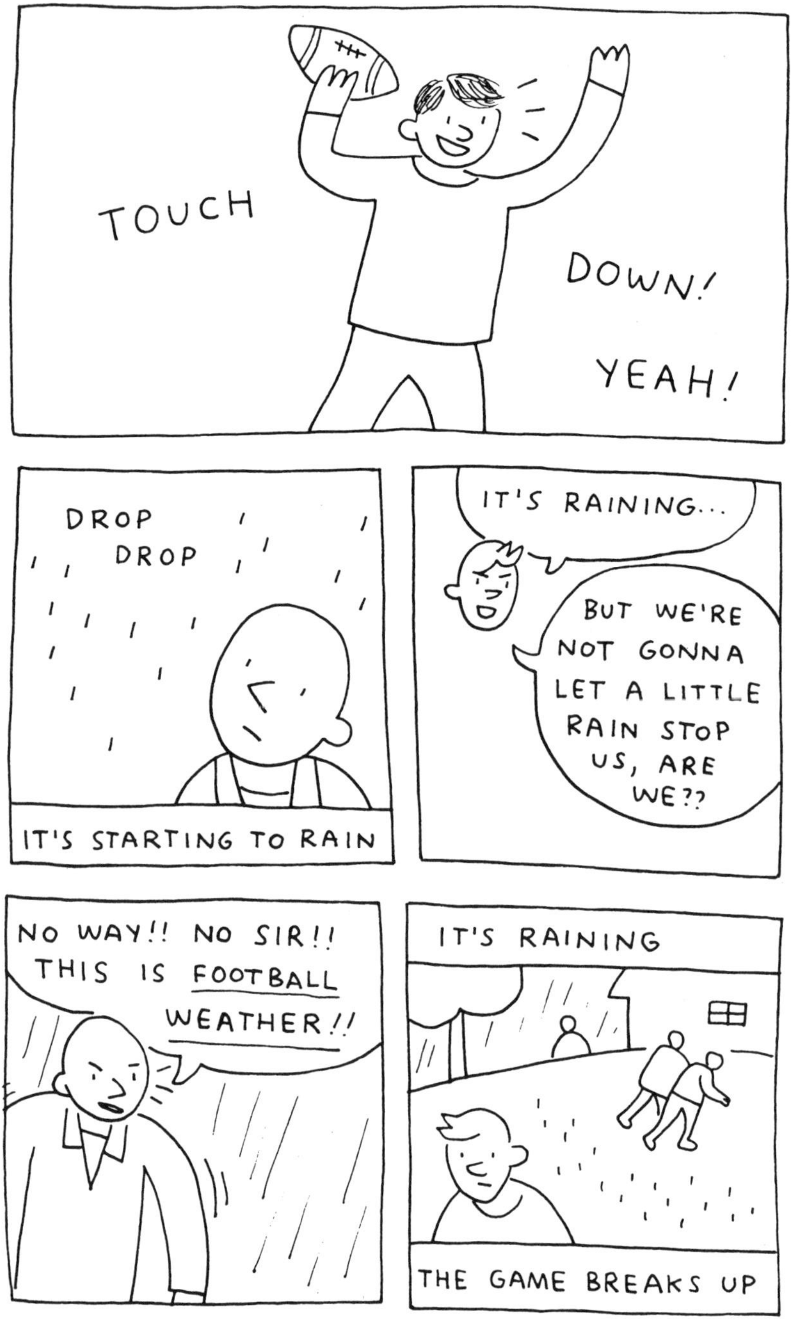
TOUCH
DOWN!
YEAH!
DROP
DROP
IT'S STARTING TO RAIN
IT'S RAINING...
BUT WE'RE NOT GONNA LET A LITTLE RAIN STOP US, ARE WE??
NO WAY!! NO SIR!! THIS IS FOOTBALL WEATHER!!
IT'S RAINING
THE GAME BREAKS UP

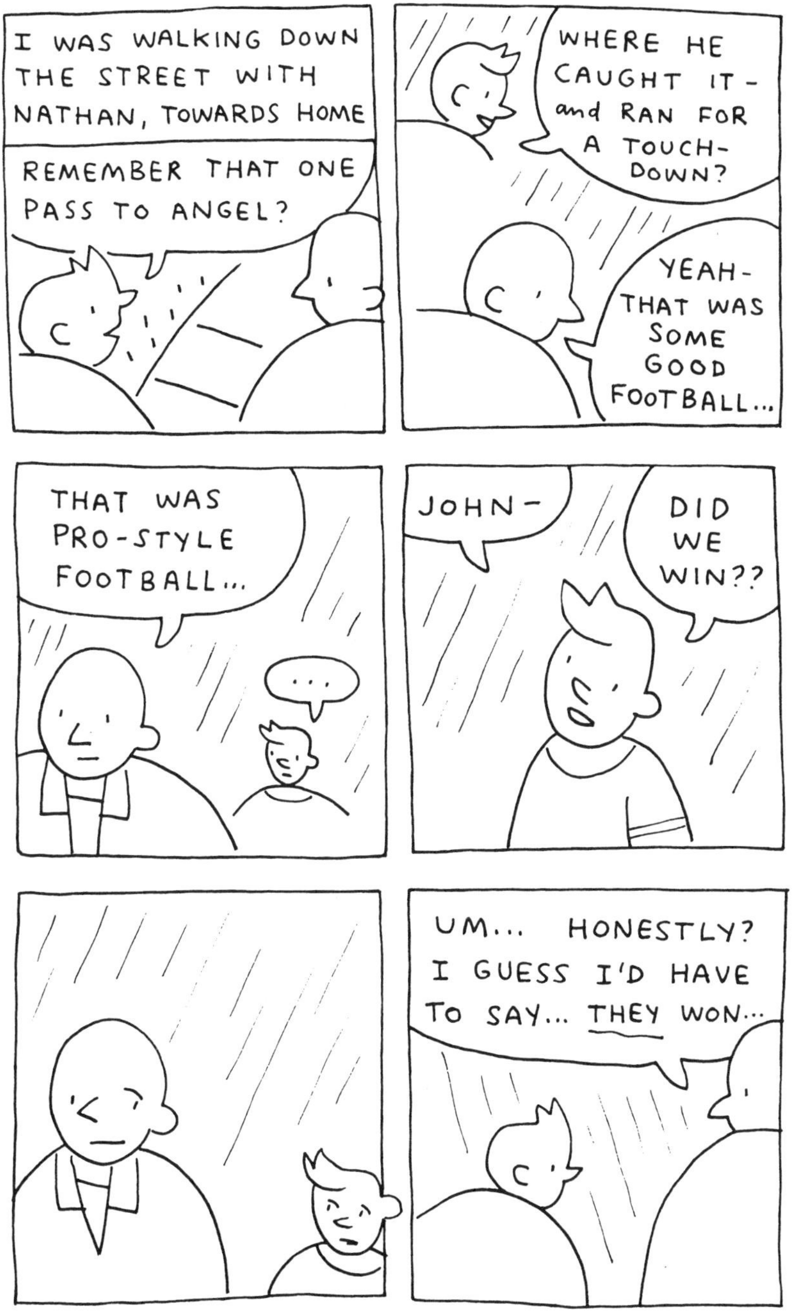
I WAS WALKING DOWN THE STREET WITH NATHAN, TOWARDS HOME
REMEMBER THAT ONE PASS TO ANGEL?
WHERE HE CAUGHT IT - and RAN FOR A TOUCH-DOWN?
YEAH- THAT WAS SOME GOOD FOOTBALL...
THAT WAS PRO-STYLE FOOTBALL...
...
JOHN-
DID WE WIN??
UM... HONESTLY? I GUESS I'D HAVE TO SAY... THEY WON...

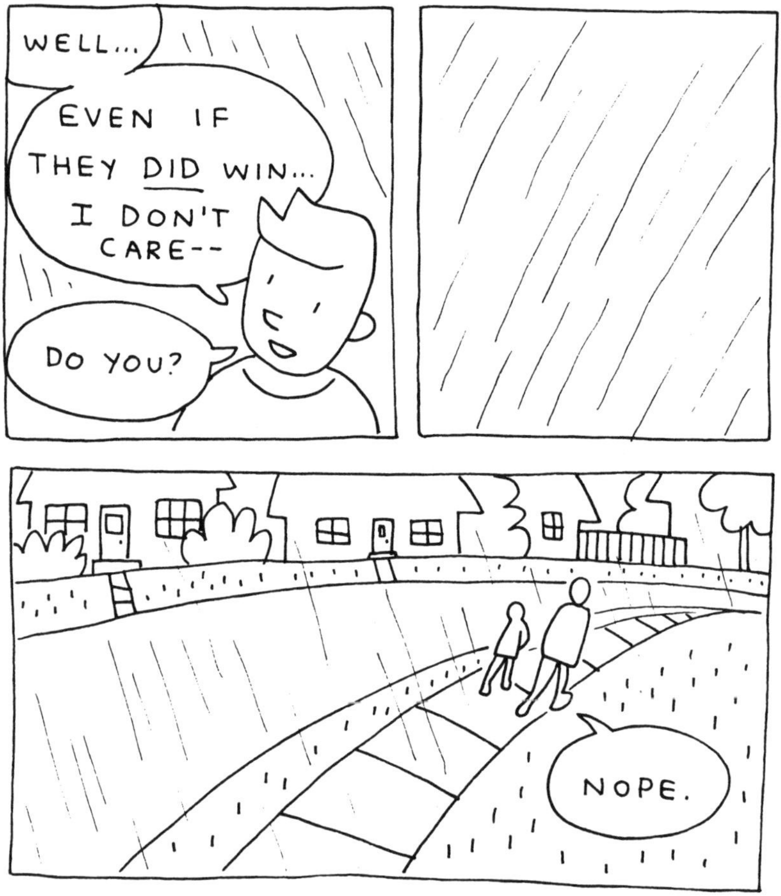
WELL...
EVEN IF THEY DID WIN... I DON'T CARE--
DO YOU?
NOPE.

FOOTBALL WEATHER
John Porcellino 2005
HAPPENED FALL 2001—
ELGIN, ILLINOIS

♡ CATCALLS ♡

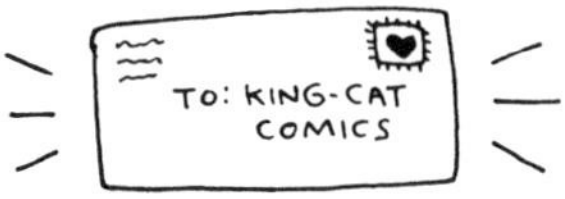
TO: KING-CAT COMICS

John,

It's true. The summer after you left, John confided in me that he didn't know why everyone called him John when his name was Jack. I eventually came to realize that his name was John, but he liked being called Jack. John Riley Abbott... Jack Riley Abbott... JackRabbott...

I remember him very well. He was my favorite person to talk to at breaktime. He always had some small bit of wisdom ready for any occasion, and told hilarious stories. When it came to women his advice was to never give up. Anyhow, when he'd gripe about his wife, he'd ask us to play "Sorry" on the radio, which meant play anything by Patsy Cline (though I think "Heartaches" is what he really wanted to hear). I loved how patient and kind he was when we were around...

I actually got to sit and talk with him at his house (over lots of beer...) We talked about art, the war, yardwork, and girls. John had a Purple Heart which I didn't know about. He was shot while marching in a convoy. He fought in the Battle of the Bulge, made out with French girls, and helped liberate a concentration camp. He saw a lot of people die, and got into all kinds of trouble with Sgt. Sven. When John was older, he dabbled in sculpture and was unbelievably good at refinishing furniture. But his breaktime stories shared with a cup of coffee were always the best.

I was glad that I got to talk with him, but I don't think his wife liked it when we drank so much beer. I remember saying "I'll have tea", and John would tell me to have a beer... "You can hack it," he'd say. I really wish I could remember all the stories and cartoons he would draw. After awhile I stopped going over as much. John had a stroke in the mid-'90's and I went over a couple more times, to mow the yard and re-set their front steps, but I eventually kind off backed off so I never really saw him the last few years. Sometimes I'd see him at the hardware store, and he always looked smaller and thinner, with that same great head of furious white hair.

I found out he had lung cancer and had been going through chemotherapy (which did nothing to his hair). The last time we talked was about a year ago, when I'd heard that he was no longer doing therapy. He had decided not to. He sounded very weak, but content. He died last spring... I'll miss the old Konky wompus...

Al Stark - Dekalb, Ill.

Blue light

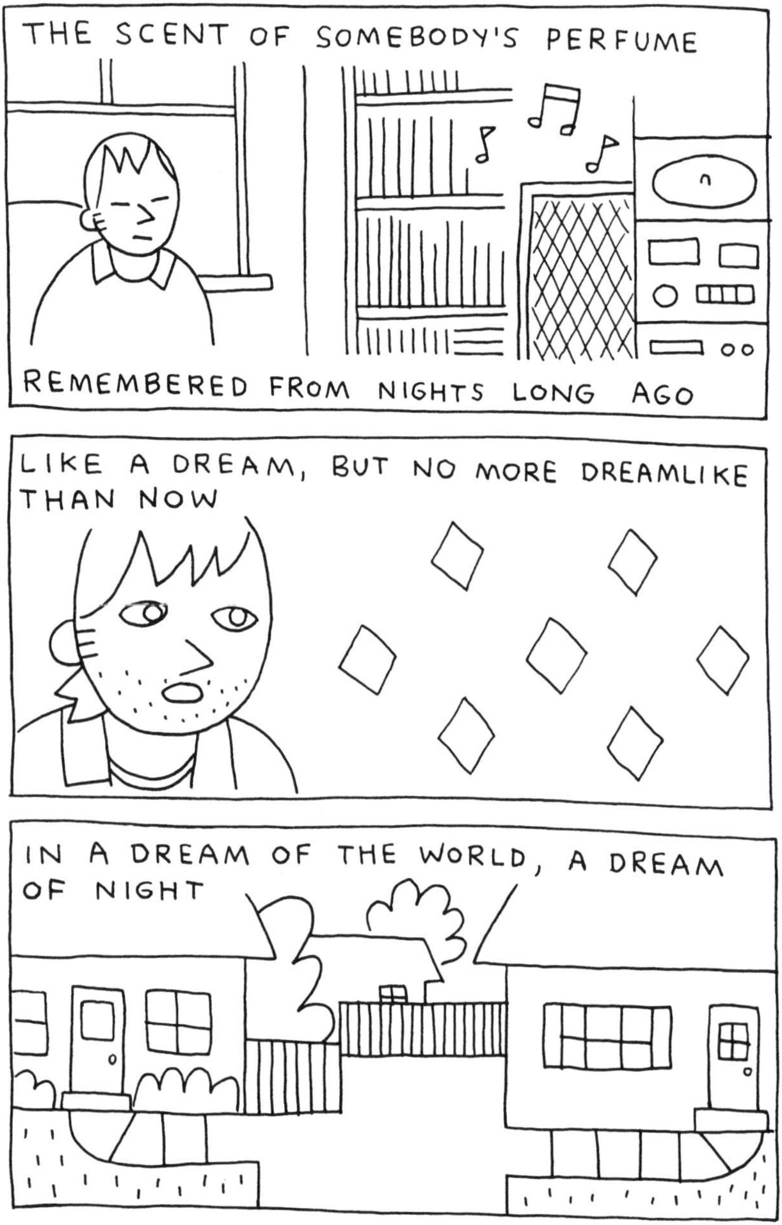
THE SCENT OF SOMEBODY'S PERFUME
REMEMBERED FROM NIGHTS LONG AGO
LIKE A DREAM, BUT NO MORE DREAMLIKE THAN NOW
IN A DREAM OF THE WORLD, A DREAM OF NIGHT

REMEMBER TOUCHING THAT ANCIENT SPACE

THAT EXISTS HERE, LIKE THEN—

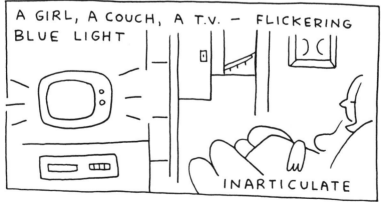

A GIRL, A COUCH, A T.V. — FLICKERING BLUE LIGHT

INARTICULATE

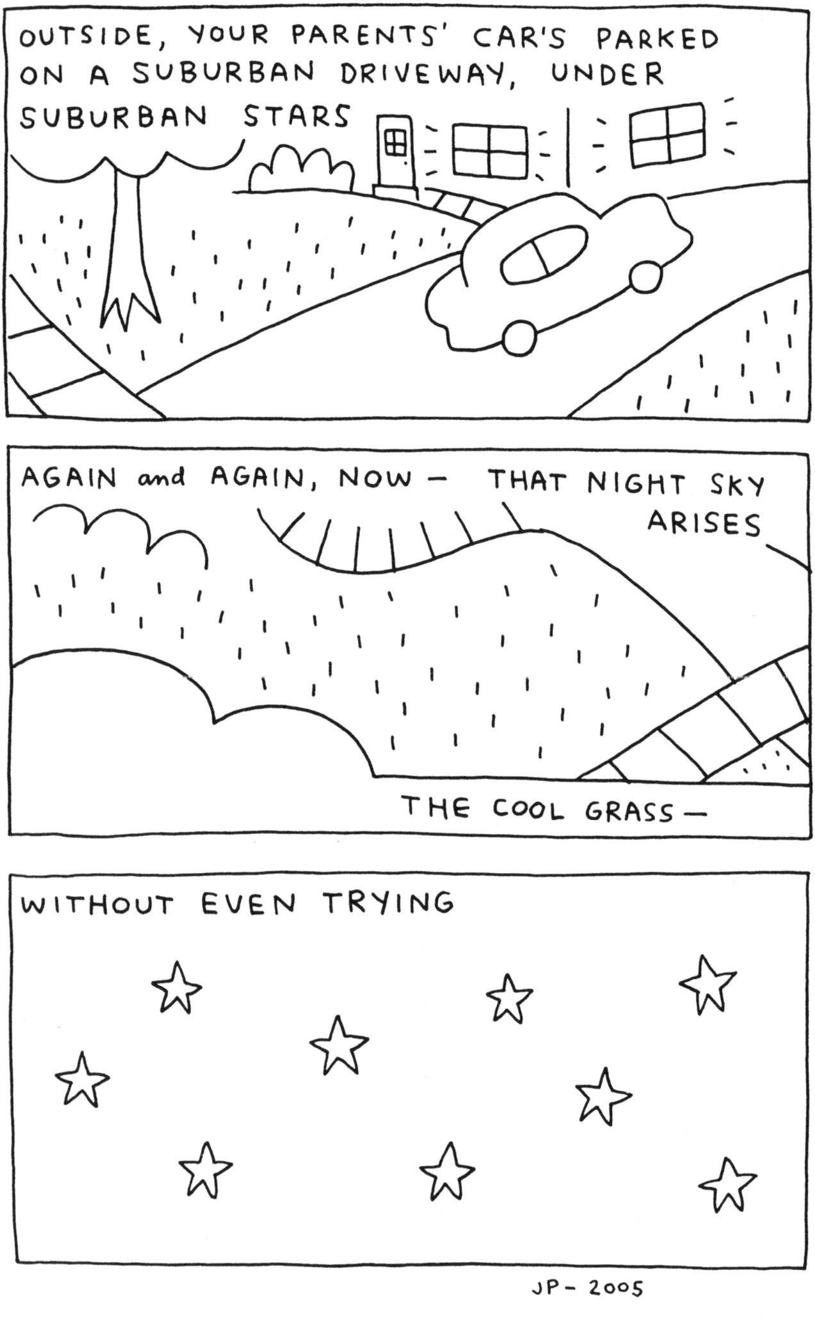

OUTSIDE, YOUR PARENTS' CAR'S PARKED ON A SUBURBAN DRIVEWAY, UNDER SUBURBAN STARS
AGAIN and AGAIN, NOW — THAT NIGHT SKY ARISES
THE COOL GRASS —
WITHOUT EVEN TRYING
JP - 2005

FREEMAN KAME

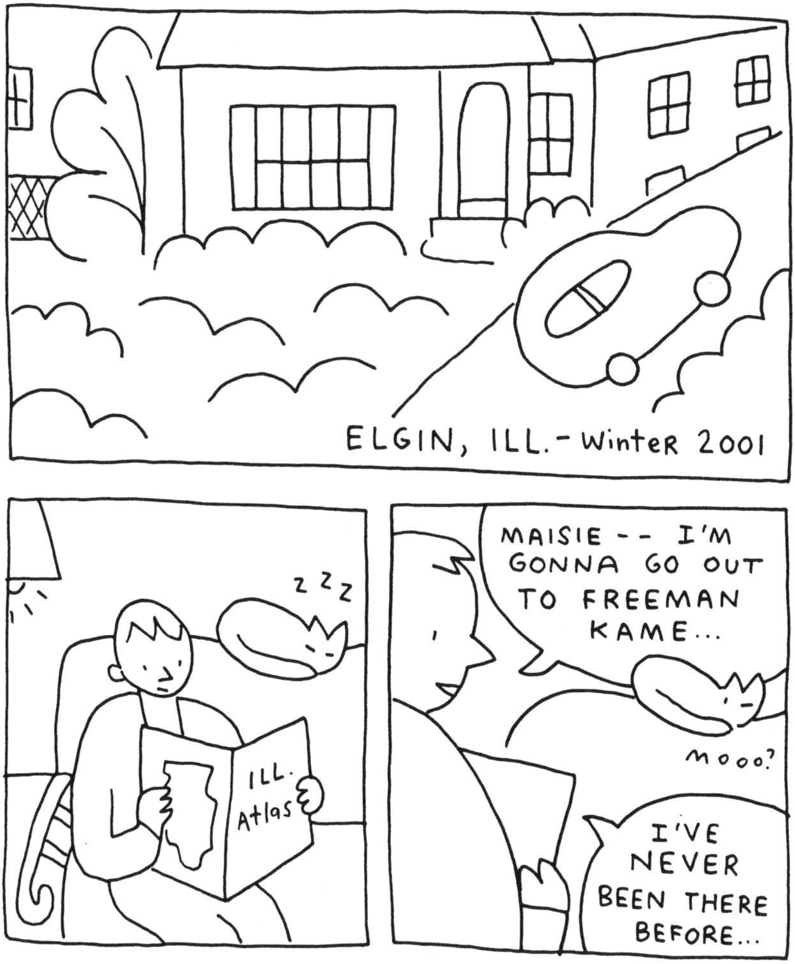

ELGIN, ILL.-Winter 2001
z z z
ILL. Atlas
MAISIE -- I'M GONNA GO OUT TO FREEMAN KAME...
mooo?
I'VE NEVER BEEN THERE BEFORE...

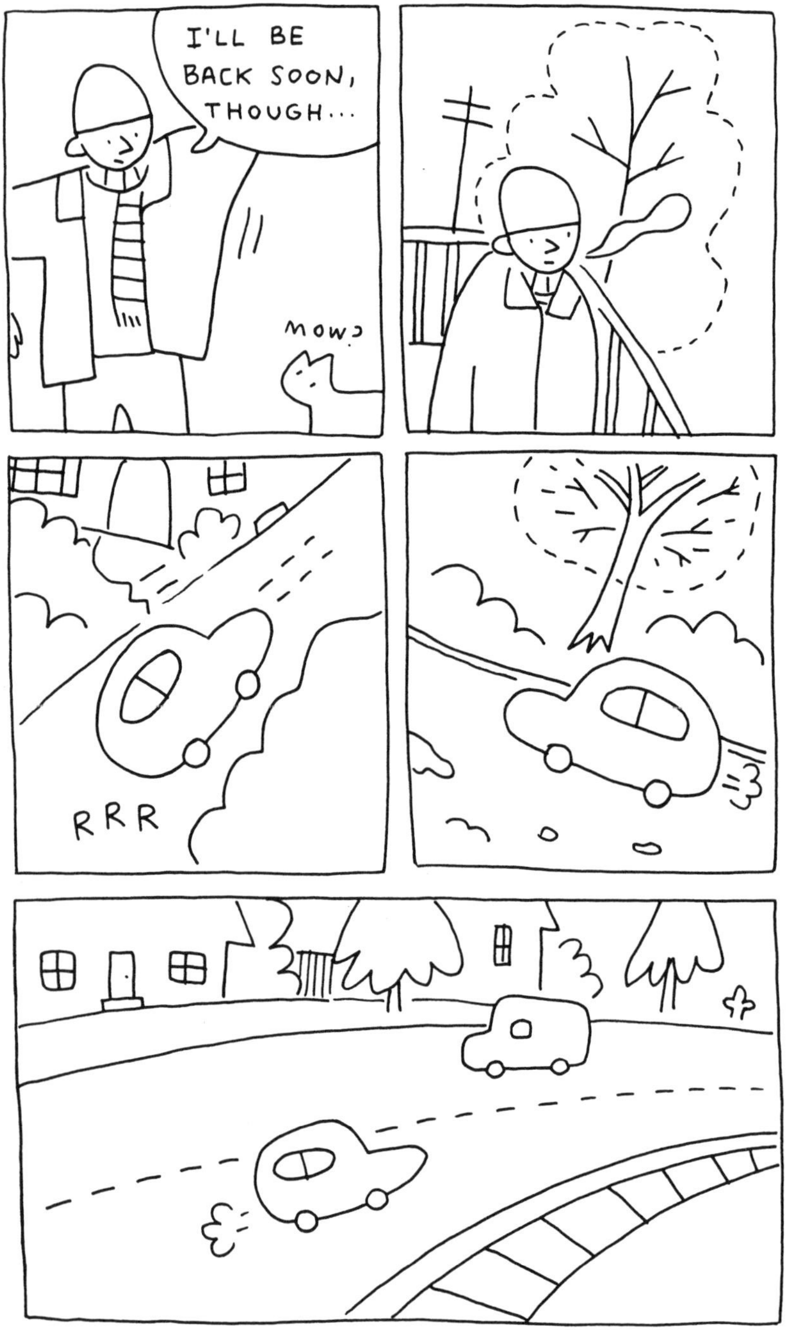
I'LL BE BACK SOON, THOUGH...
MOW?
RRR

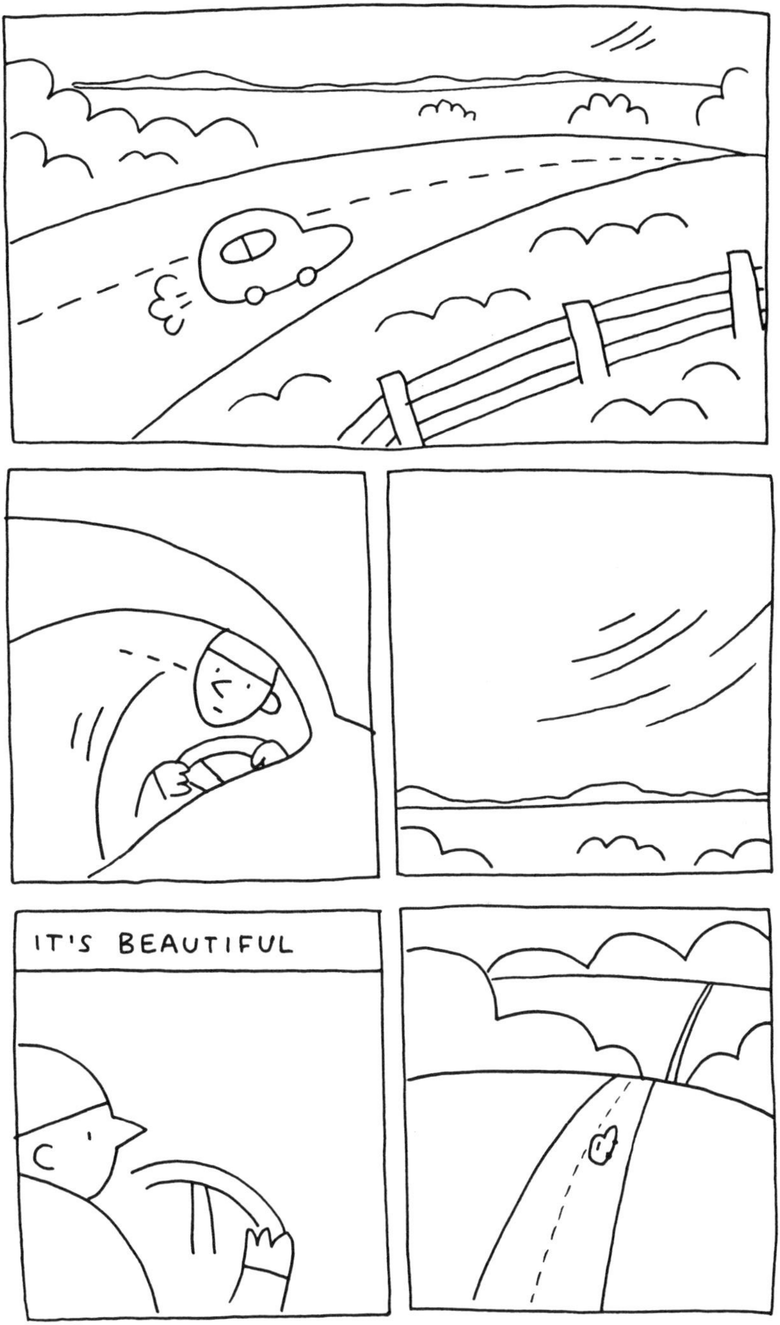
IT'S BEAUTIFUL

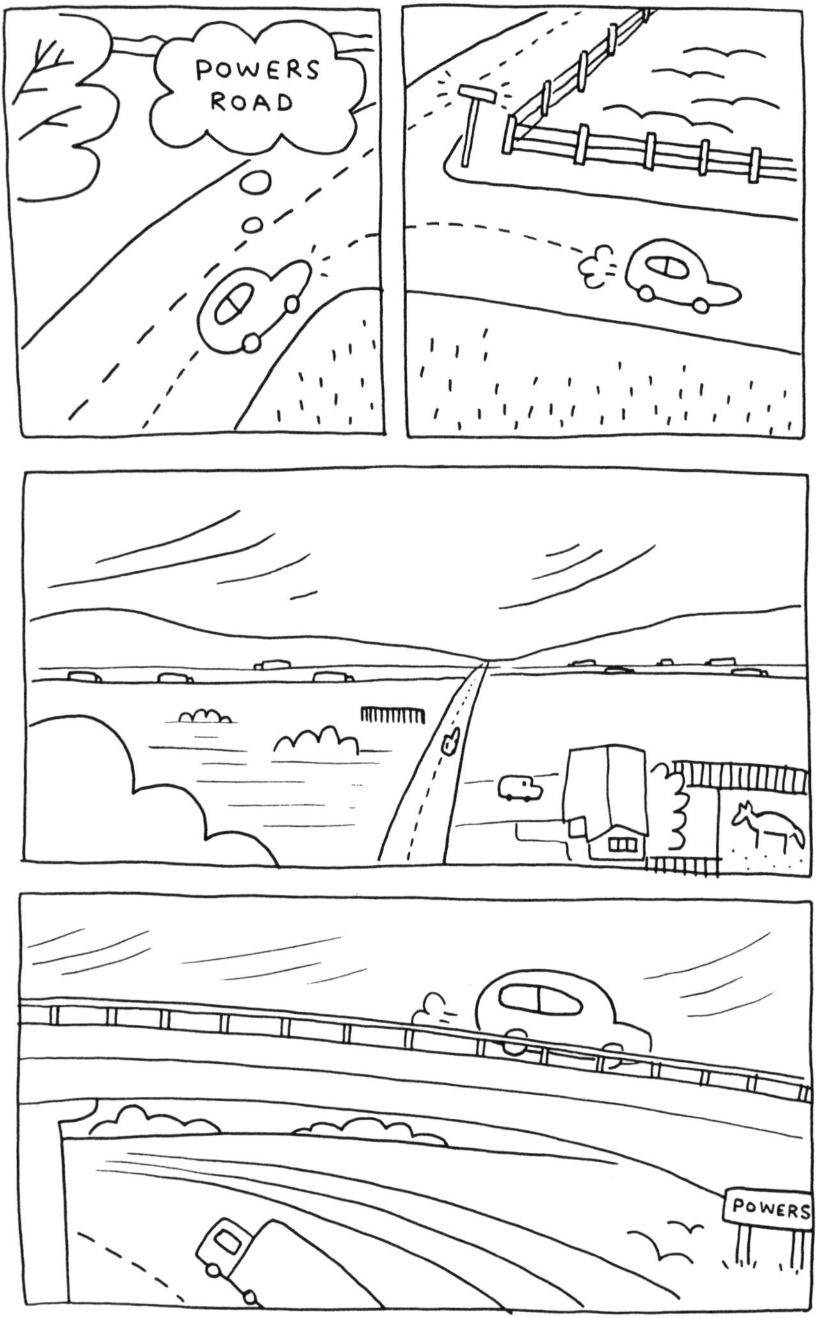
POWERS ROAD
POWERS

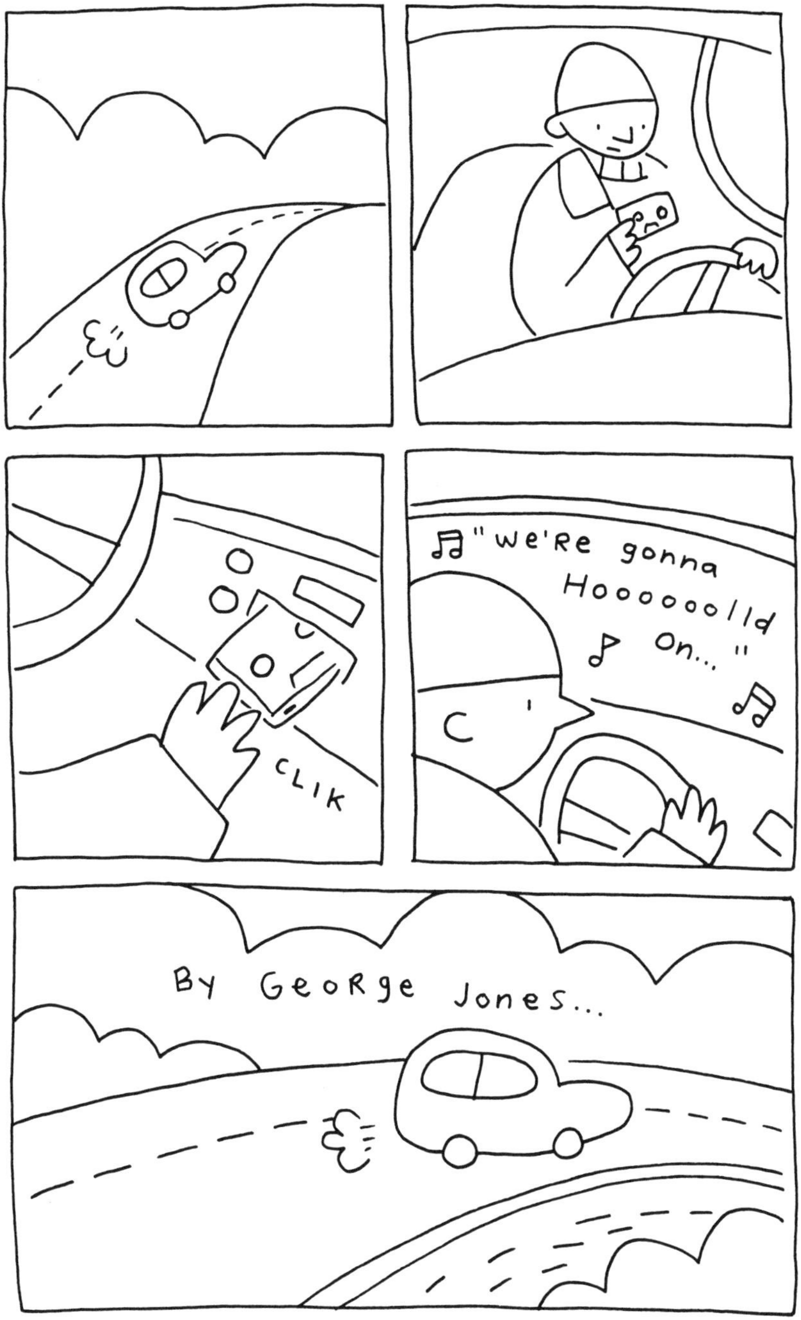
CLIK
♫ "We're gonna Hoooooolld On..." ♪ ♫
By George Jones...

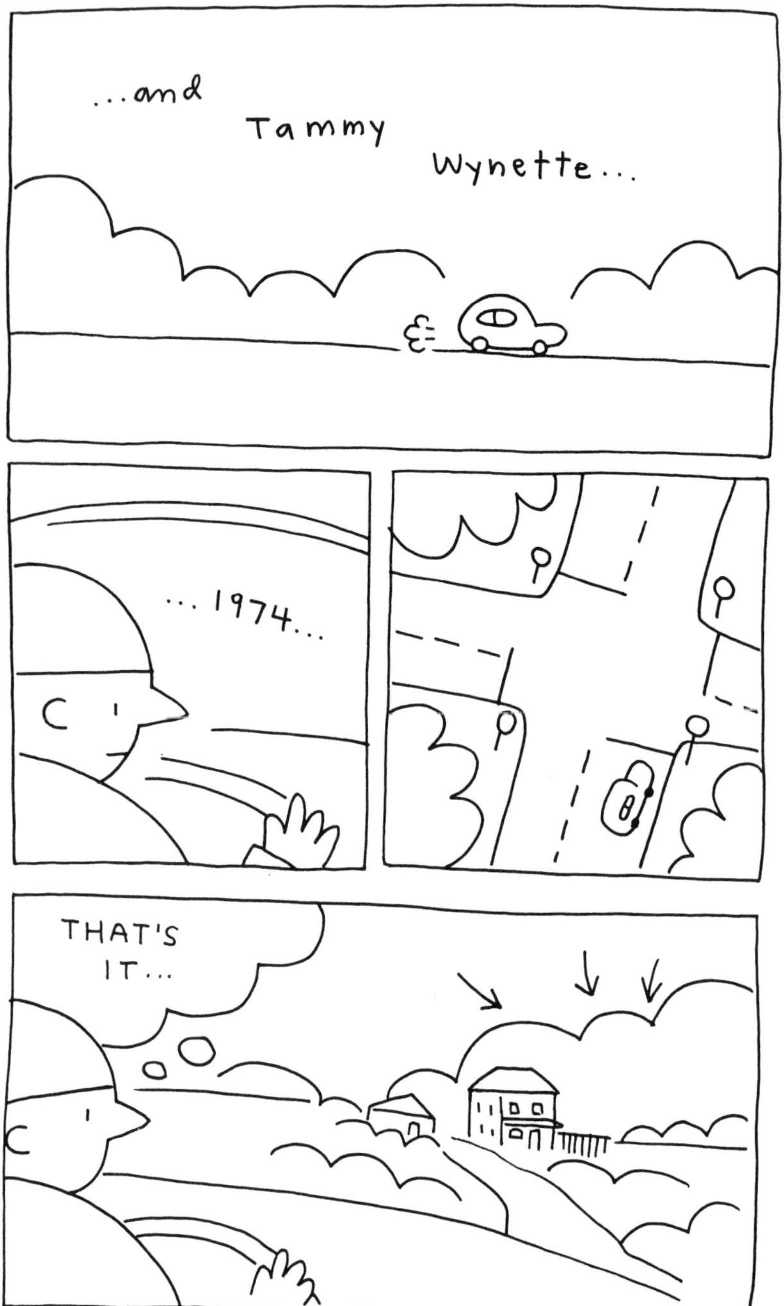
...and
Tammy
Wynette...
...1974...
THAT'S
IT...

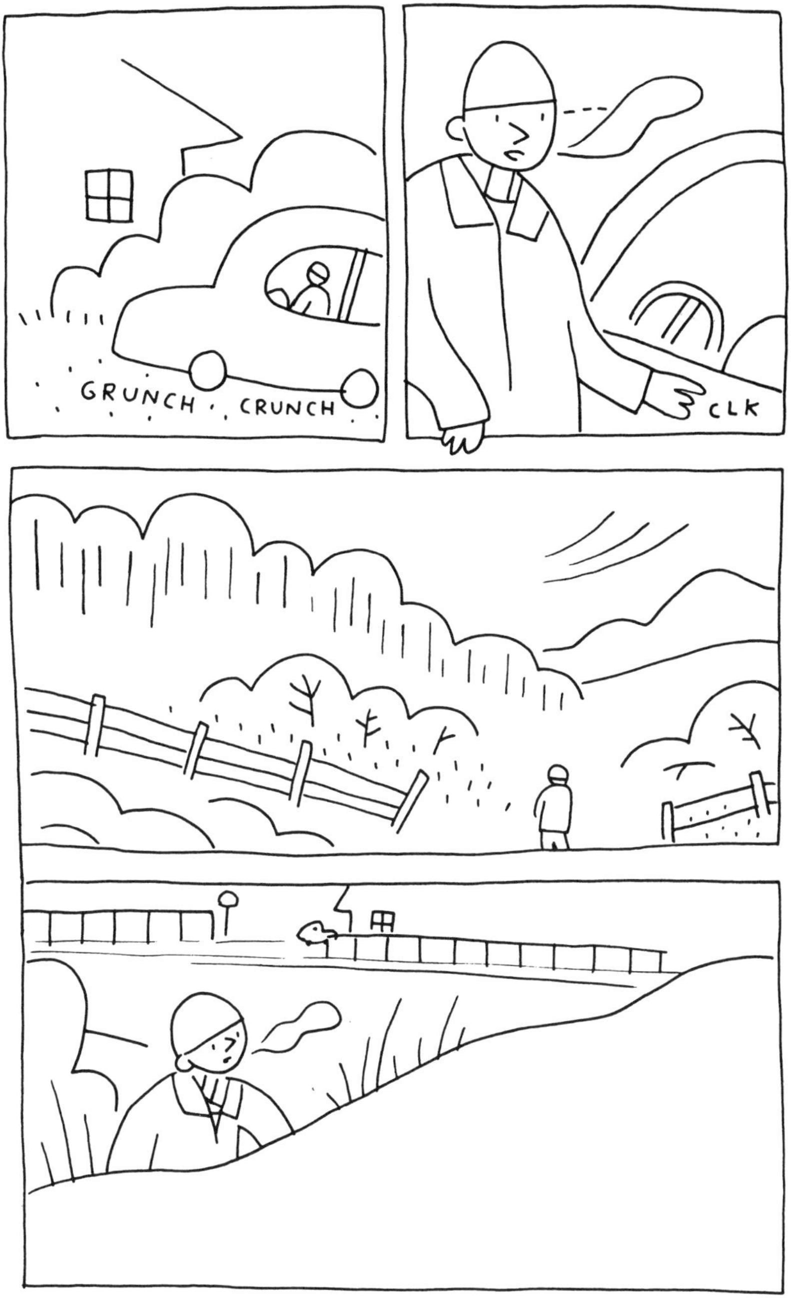
GRUNCH
CRUNCH
CLK

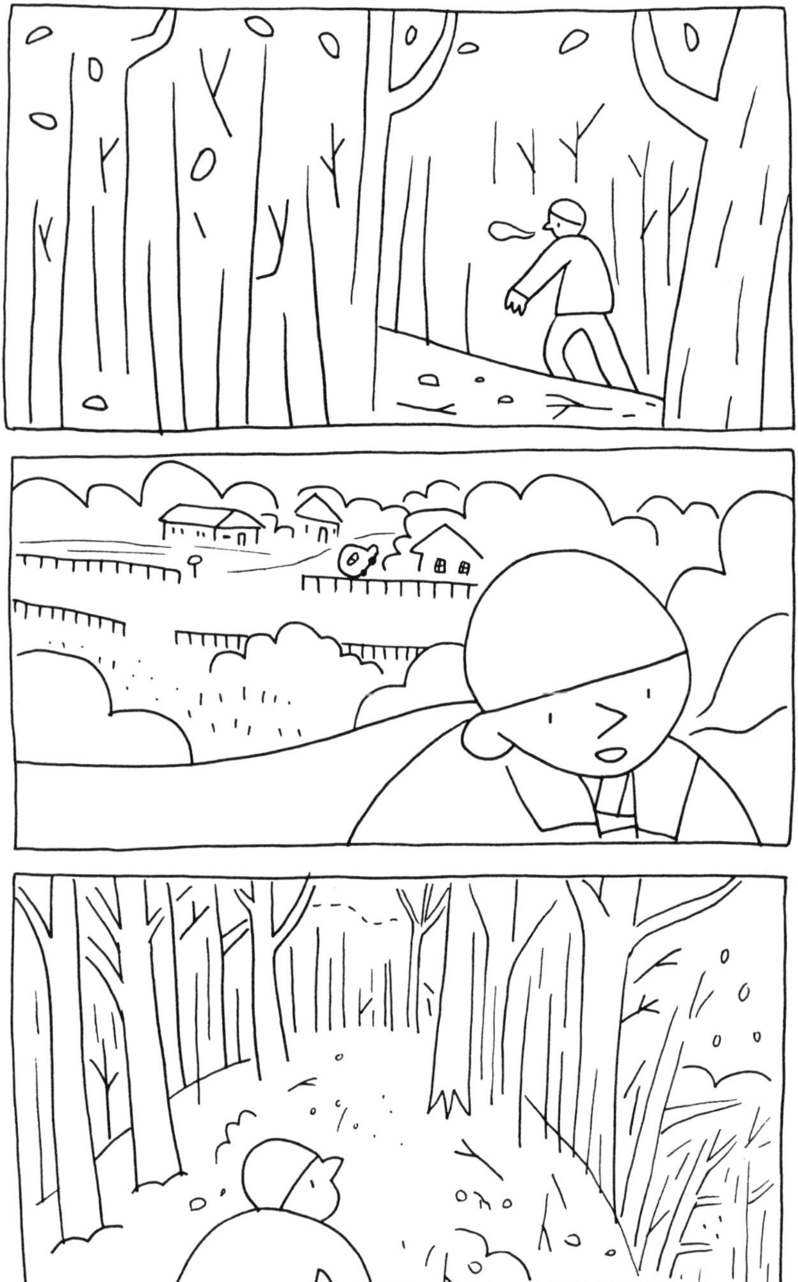

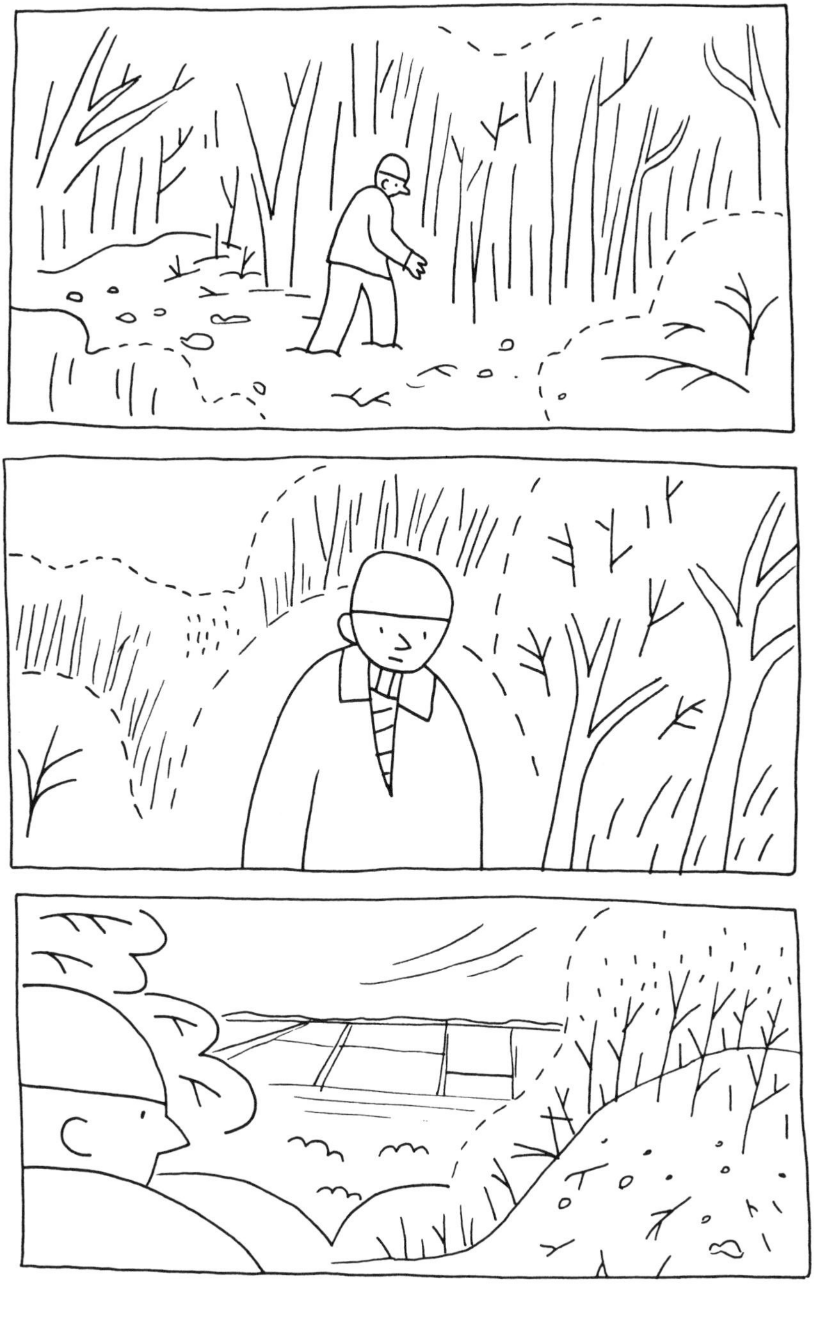

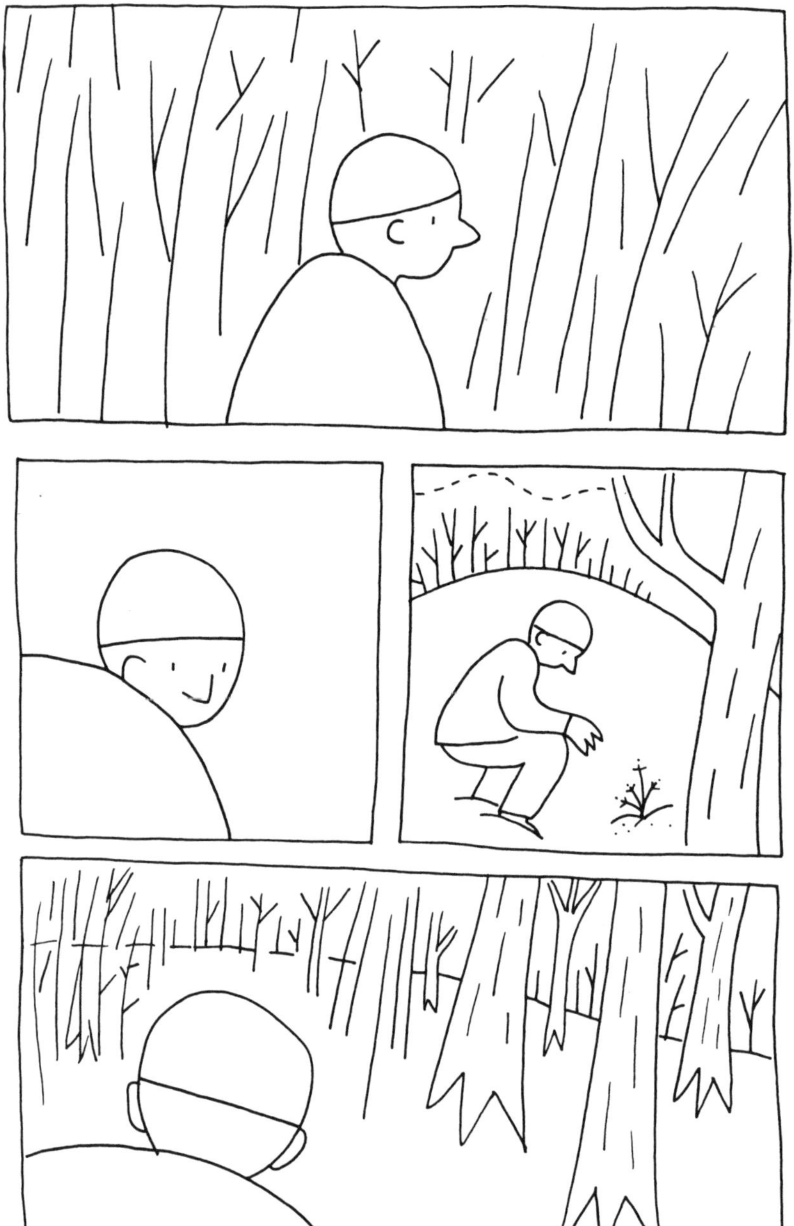

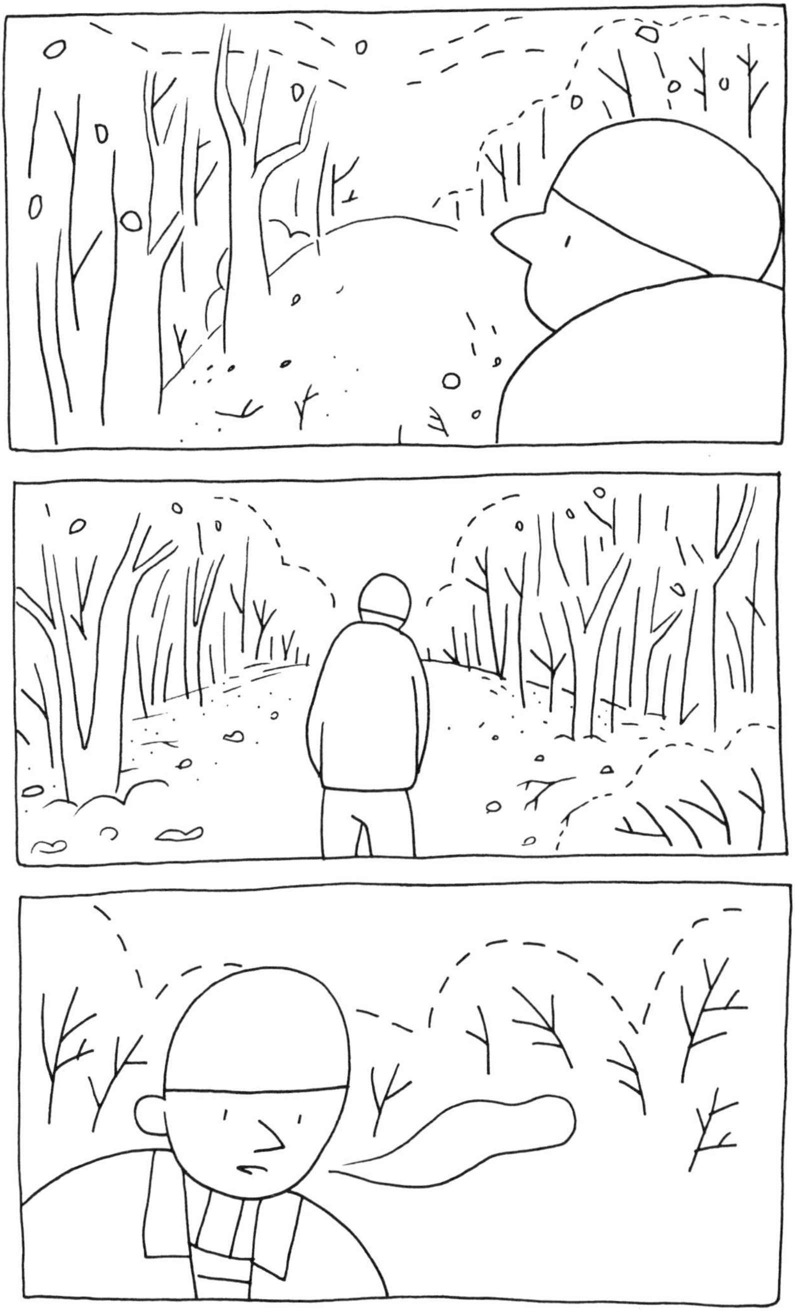

JOHN PORCELLINO
2005

Glossary of Terms

Escarbar (verb, Spanish) — to scratch around.

Kame (noun) — a ridge or mound composed of sand and gravel, formed as a result of glacial melting.

"We're Gonna Hold On" (Song) — written by George Jones and Earl Montgomery; performed by George Jones and Tammy Wynette. Reached number one on the Country Music charts, 1974.

KING-CAT
COMICS

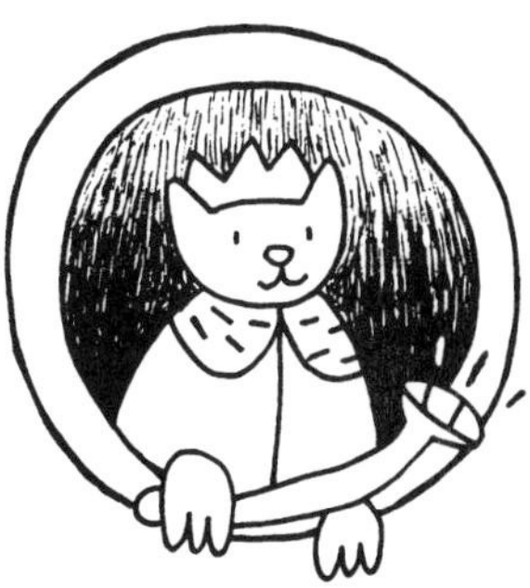

NUMBER 67 $3.00

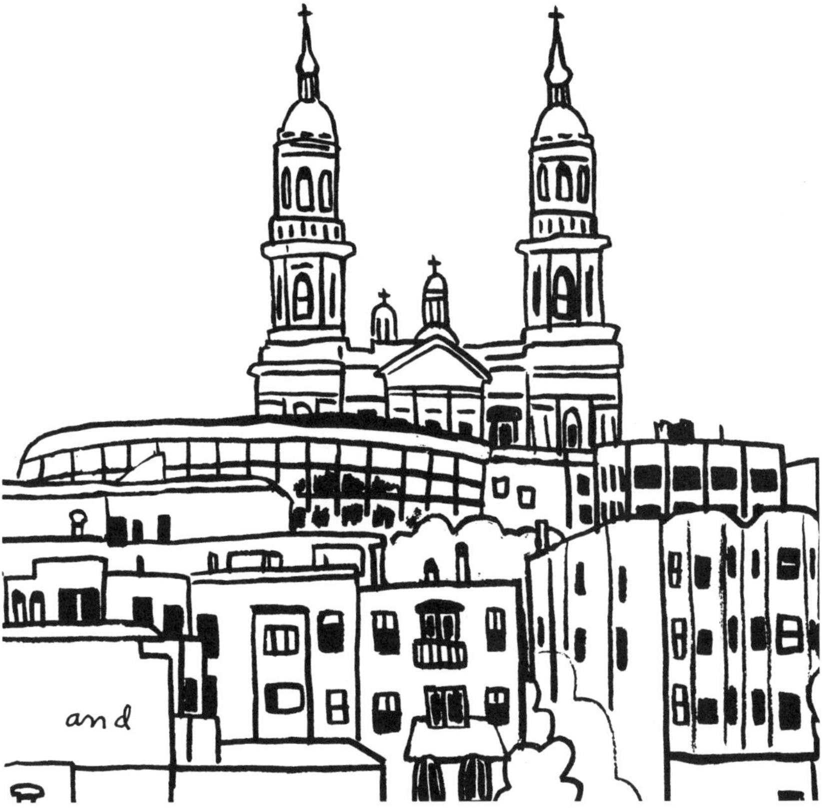
and

stories by

JOHN PORCELLINO

KC Snothose • SIXTY-SEVEN

*FOUR DAYS A WEEK I climbed up the Lone Mountain hill, on my way to work, carrying my lunch in a brown paper bag. I walked past the hospital, past the church, the chapel, the soccer fields, where I looked out across the parking lot to try for a glimpse of the ocean.

At the top of Lone Mountain I'd always glance down the alleyway toward the sea, and the Richmond spread out in waves across the hills. On exceptionally clear days I could sometimes see the Mysterious Islands, way out on the horizon, far away, and for a moment or two I'd feel very happy.

"Farallones"

Coming down the hill, then, on fogless mornings, I'd see the mountains to the north, across the bay, dusty green and gold in the distance, and I'd think about open spaces and waving grass, the California Hippie Dream. And I'd keep on walking.

Down on Geary, leaning back against the bus stop pole, I'd put my bags down and try to relax. I'd look down the boulevard – at the sky, the traffic – and the street disappearing out to the west – the Edge of America – and I'd try to relax.

I'd tell myself everything's going to be O.K., and I'd look up at the sky. Then I'd get on the bus and go to work. • • •

KING-CAT COMICS and STORIES, No. 67--
Published in Oct. 2006 by: SPIT and a HALF
[redacted]
San Francisco, CA
[redacted] - USA
www.king-cat.net

After Oct. 2006
OUR NEW ADDRESS:
[redacted]
Denver, CO [redacted]

"Nerves" (euphemism) — OCD — Post-traumatic Stress Disorder — Pyroluria

SCARED
• • •

SAN FRANCISCO. Walking in the Richmond, down wide, empty streets, pale-sunshine-pastel streets, the sky. Anza, Cabrillo, Balboa, grey sidewalks, expanse, the Ocean. 32nd Avenue.

I'm mixed-up, lost, you know — wondering, worrying, just letting things be. Then worrying some more.

I won't lie. The last three years have been hard — good — because life is good — but hard — cuz it's tough to live with this burden — Hard cuz it's tough to keep it all inside. But that's what you're supposed to do, right? Everybody's got problems. What makes you so special?

So I go on.

I wanna spill my guts, lay it out for you to see. But even writing this much is cause for embarrassment, for shame, shaking my head: "You gotta suck it up."

So I go on.

• • •

OBSERVATIONS. 4/13/06, early evening. On the path just north of the Dahlia Garden, Golden Gate Park, a SKUNK (Mephitis mephitis) approaches, black w/a pointy black face and stripe, tail raised, white-grey tail looking somewhat thrashed. It walks along the path towards me, unawares, waddling; stops to inspect a leaf, and heads uphill into vegetation, tail visible above the plants.

A woman and her baby are there, too, standing next to me. I said "Did you see it?!" I was really excited. She said: "Yeah!"

Moments later, waiting for the light to change, two PILL BUGS (Armadillidiae spp.) walking through the moss, concrete park entrance columns.   ⟶

-- Monday 4/17; approx. 5:45 PM. Walking east on JFK Drive, across from the Rose Garden— GREY-GREEN PARROT (species unknown) soars overhead high across the road, heading south towards Japanese Tea Garden, alone.

-- Late March. Heading south on Stanyan, past St. Mary's, a sudden burst of small hail, like 1-2 mm. I stood under a tree while it fell all around me for 30 or 40 seconds. Moments later, another downpour began, lasting about 15 seconds. By the time I got to Hayes Street it had all melted.

-- Early May. First appearance of CRANEFLIES (Tipula spp.) noted north of Panhandle, including one indoors, sitting on the wall above the curtains.

-- Late April '06. Behind McLaren Lodge, Golden Gate Park, a POCKET GOPHER (Thomomys buttae) peeks out of its hole, repeatedly. "Do they have good eyesight?" Misun wonders. "We must be downwind."

-- Monday May 29, 1 PM. 20th Avenue and Clement. Green HUMMINGBIRD (species unknown) buzzing around a shrubbery, chased by a bee.

-- JULY. USF - Hawk vs. CROWS.

• • •

SO WHADDAYOU KNOW - Our time here in San Francisco is almost up. Misun's graduating this Fall and anyways it's time to move along.

We've hemmed and hawed, of course, and considered and debated. We did the dishes and considered some more. And in the end we've decided to go back to Denver.

Denver's a good place- with friends and well-worn sidewalks— someplace affordable where maybe we could manage to carve out a simple, decent life for ourselves, do our work, and go on.

Still, I'll miss SF. I liked walking up and down the hills. I liked the sky. I liked the flowers and the trees, too.

I'll see you around. Welcome to King-Cat 67.

LOVE, John P.

Sleeping in the Car in L.A.

A TRUE STORY

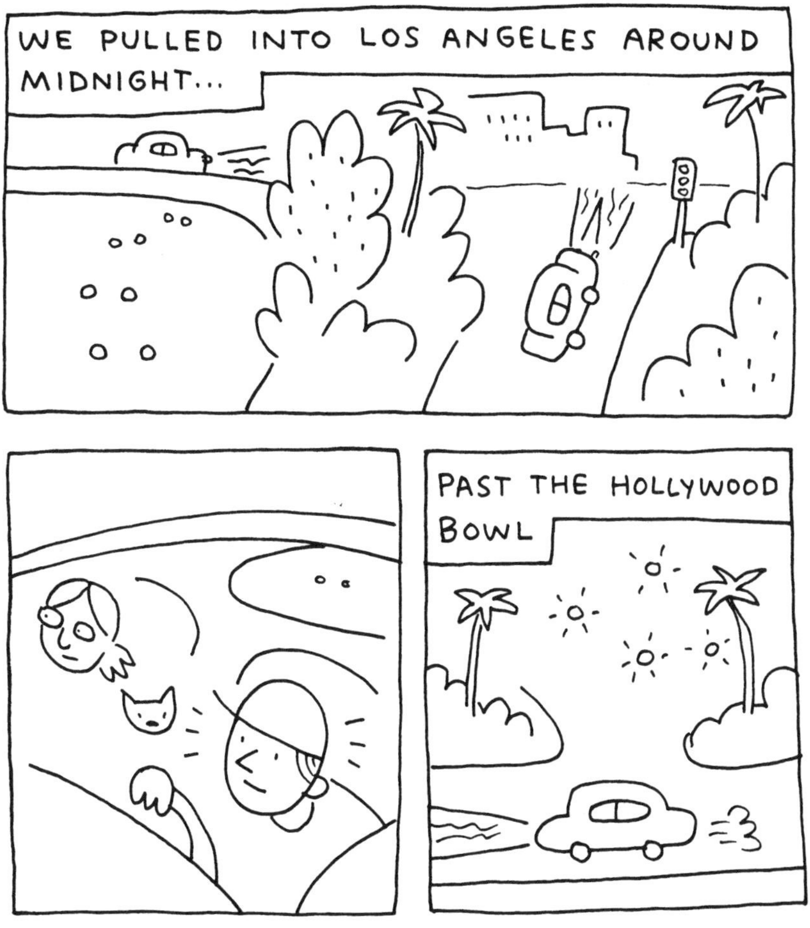

WE PULLED INTO LOS ANGELES AROUND MIDNIGHT...
PAST THE HOLLYWOOD BOWL

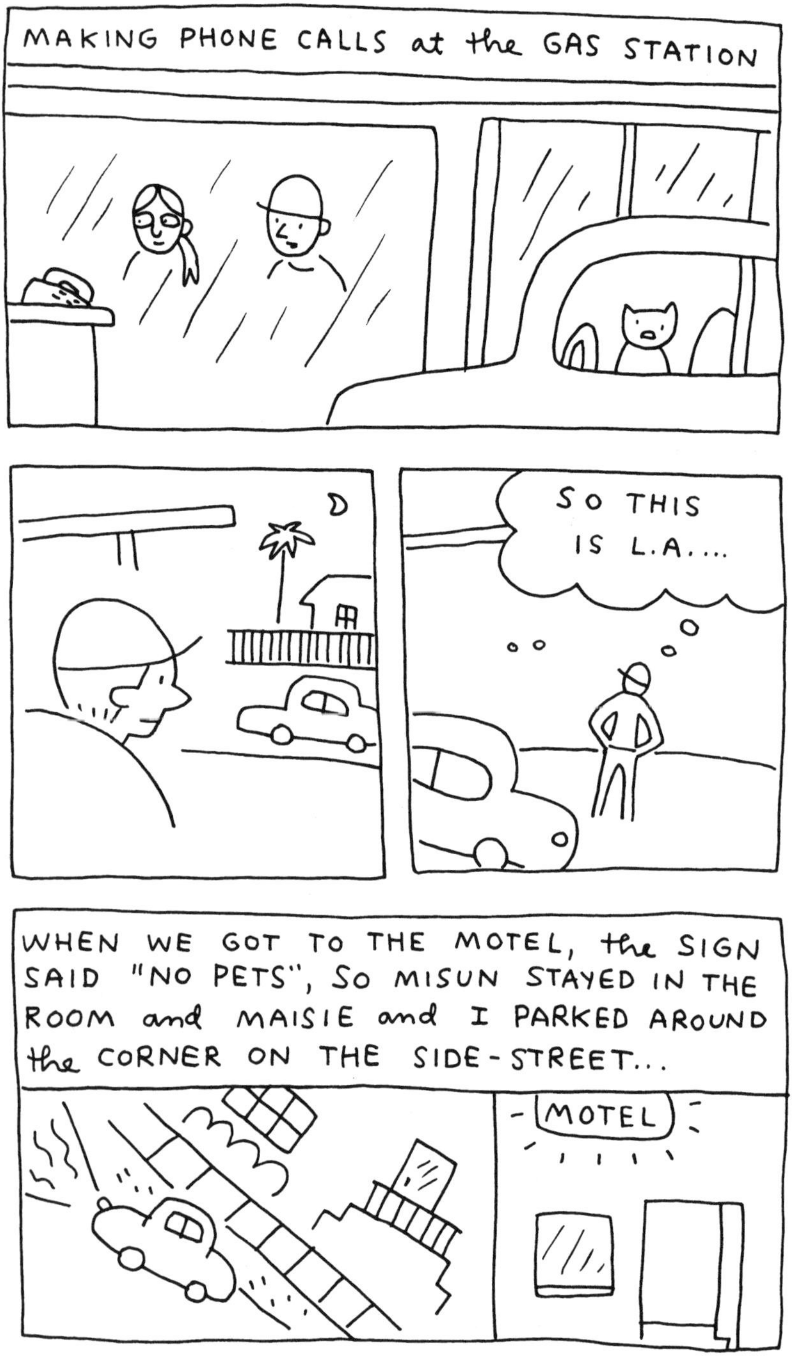
MAKING PHONE CALLS at the GAS STATION
SO THIS IS L.A....
WHEN WE GOT TO THE MOTEL, the SIGN SAID "NO PETS", SO MISUN STAYED IN THE ROOM and MAISIE and I PARKED AROUND the CORNER ON THE SIDE-STREET...
MOTEL

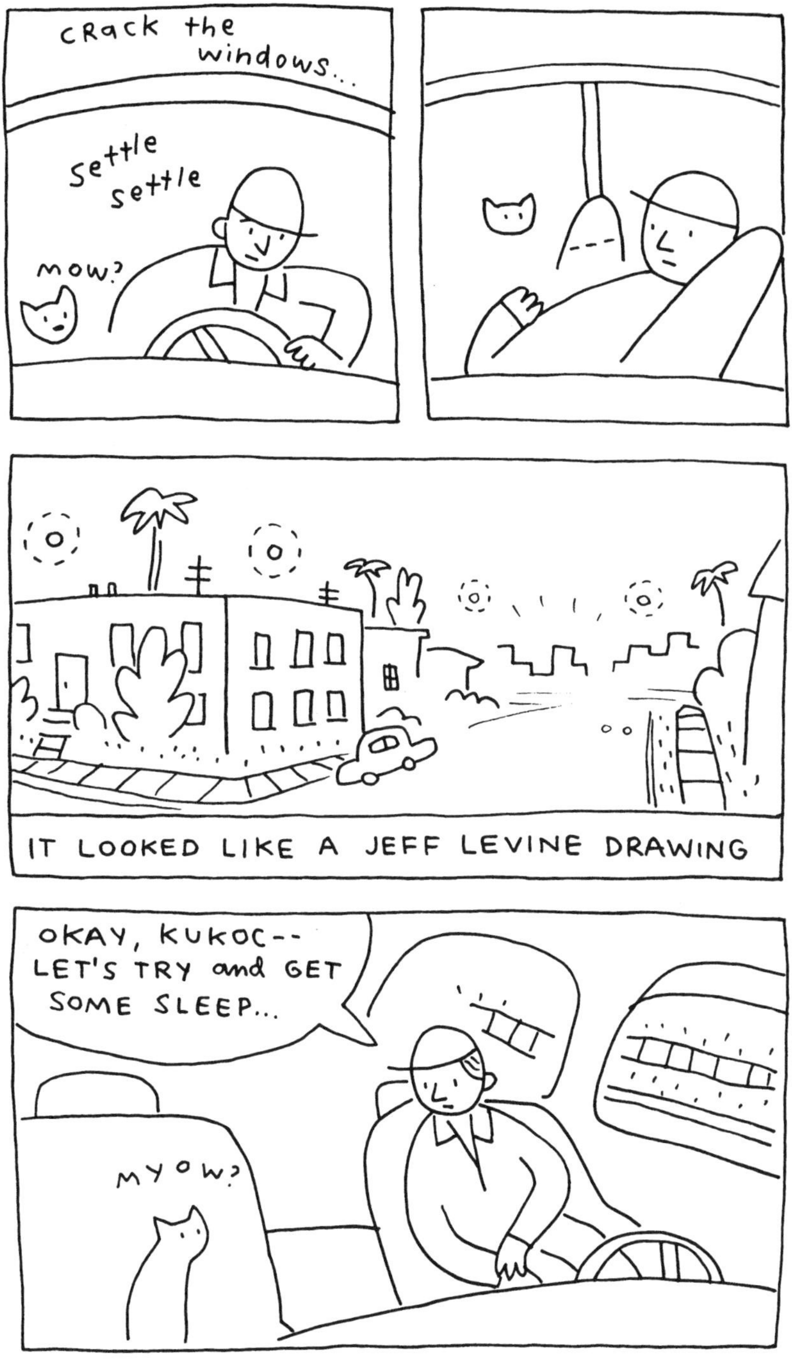
crack the windows...
settle settle
mow?
IT LOOKED LIKE A JEFF LEVINE DRAWING
OKAY, KUKOC-- LET'S TRY and GET SOME SLEEP...
MYOW?

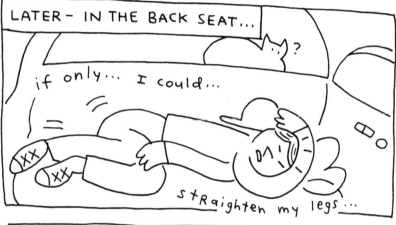

LATER — IN THE BACK SEAT...

if only... I could...

straighten my legs....

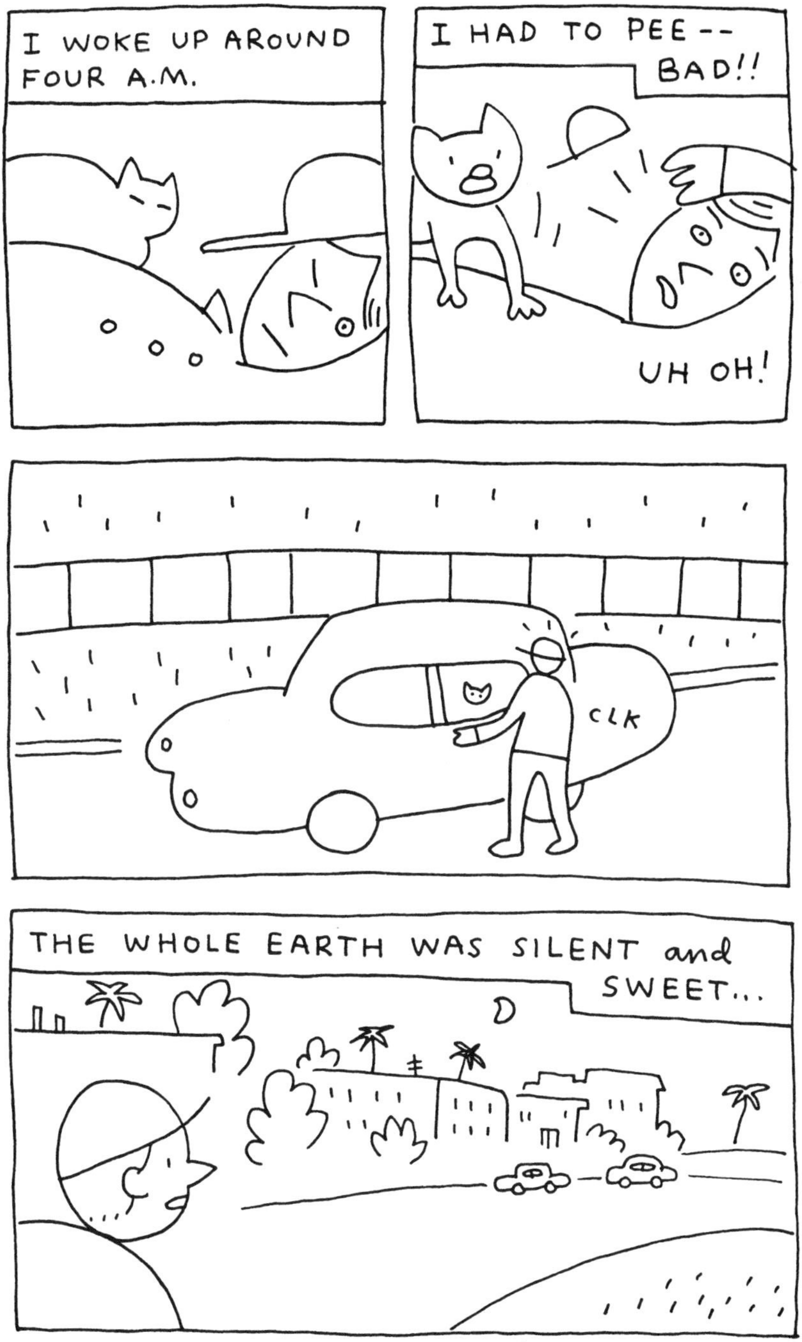

I WOKE UP AROUND FOUR A.M.
I HAD TO PEE-- BAD!!
UH OH!
CLK
THE WHOLE EARTH WAS SILENT and SWEET...
John Porcellino · 2006

WOKE UP SAD

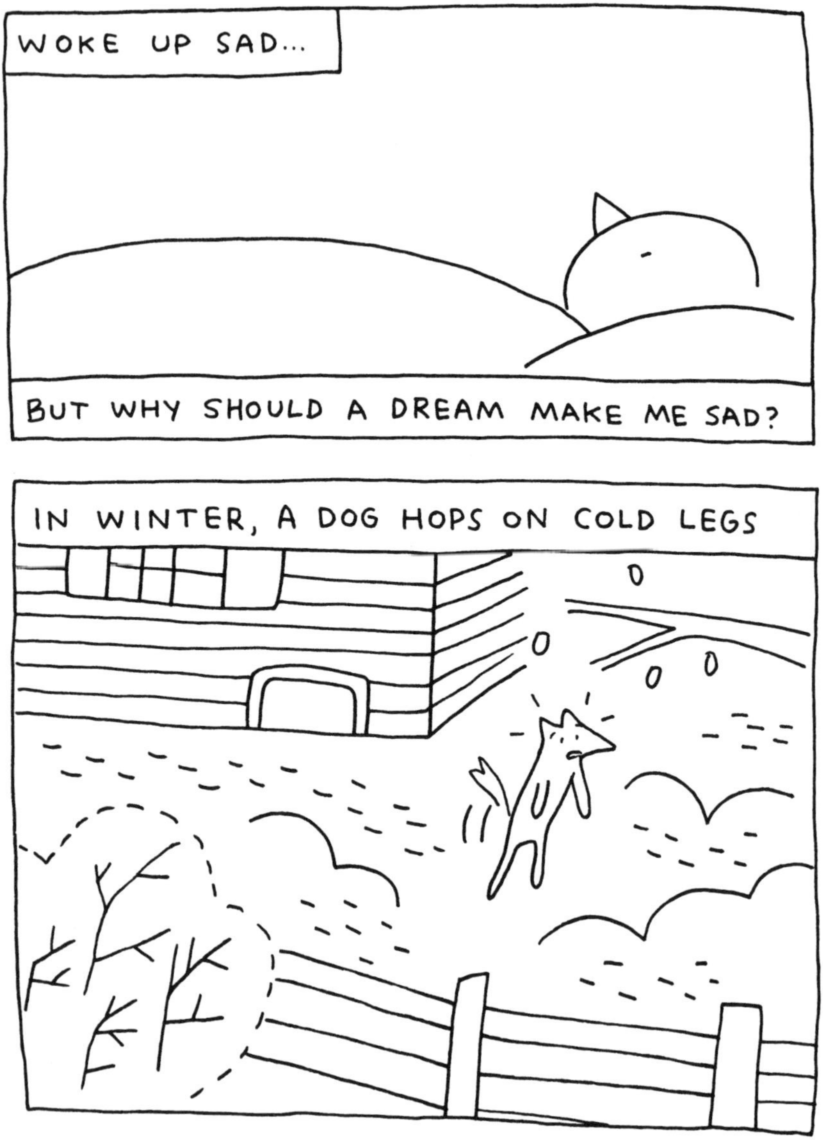
WOKE UP SAD...
BUT WHY SHOULD A DREAM MAKE ME SAD?
IN WINTER, A DOG HOPS ON COLD LEGS

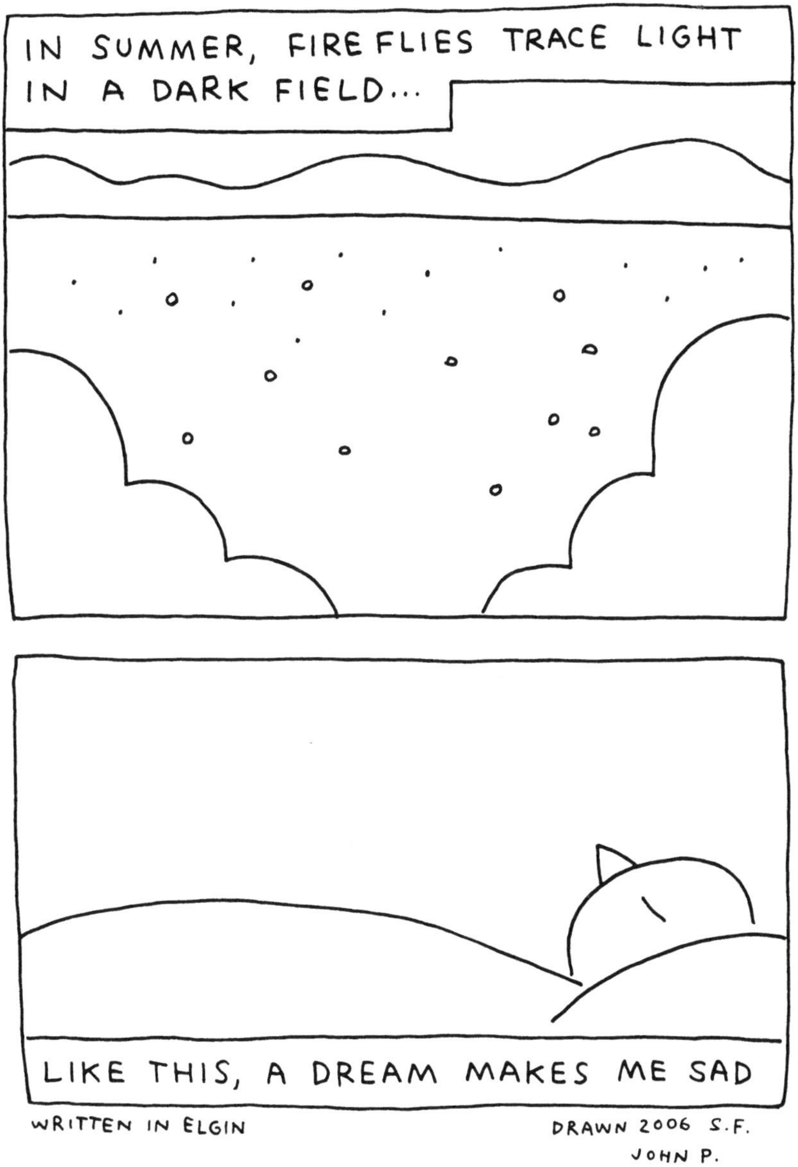
IN SUMMER, FIRE FLIES TRACE LIGHT IN A DARK FIELD...
LIKE THIS, A DREAM MAKES ME SAD
WRITTEN IN ELGIN
DRAWN 2006 S.F.
JOHN P.

Heart

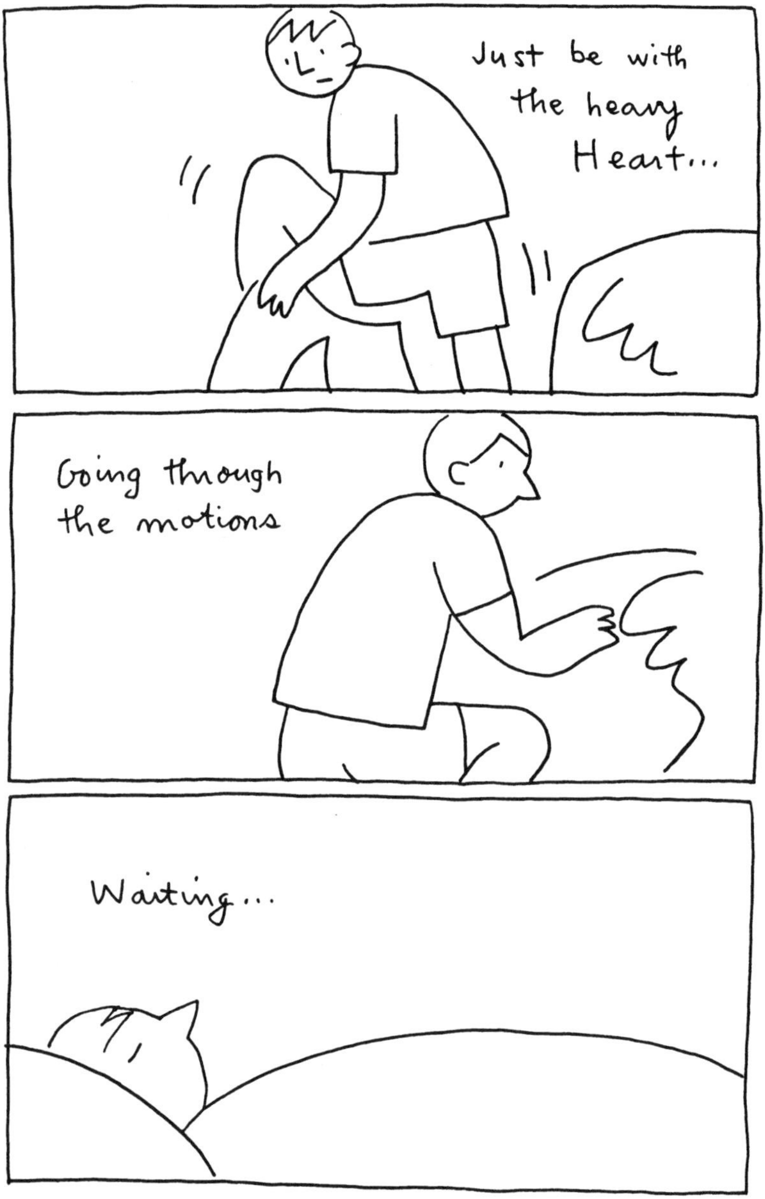
Just be with the heavy Heart...
Going through the motions
Waiting...

MAY 3RD 2006 · WRITTEN John P. 5/9

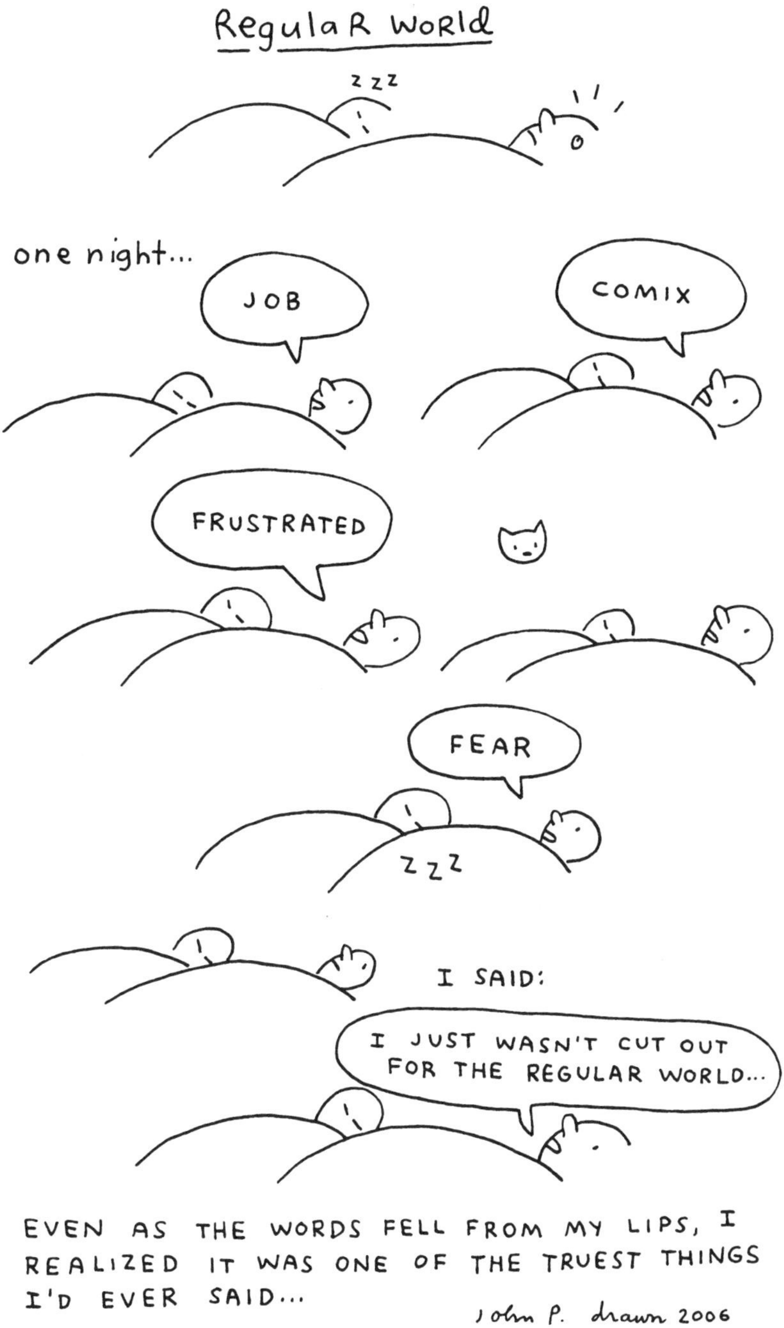
Regular World
zzz
one night...
JOB
COMIX
FRUSTRATED
FEAR
zzz
I SAID:
I JUST WASN'T CUT OUT FOR THE REGULAR WORLD...
EVEN AS THE WORDS FELL FROM MY LIPS, I REALIZED IT WAS ONE OF THE TRUEST THINGS I'D EVER SAID...
John P. drawn 2006

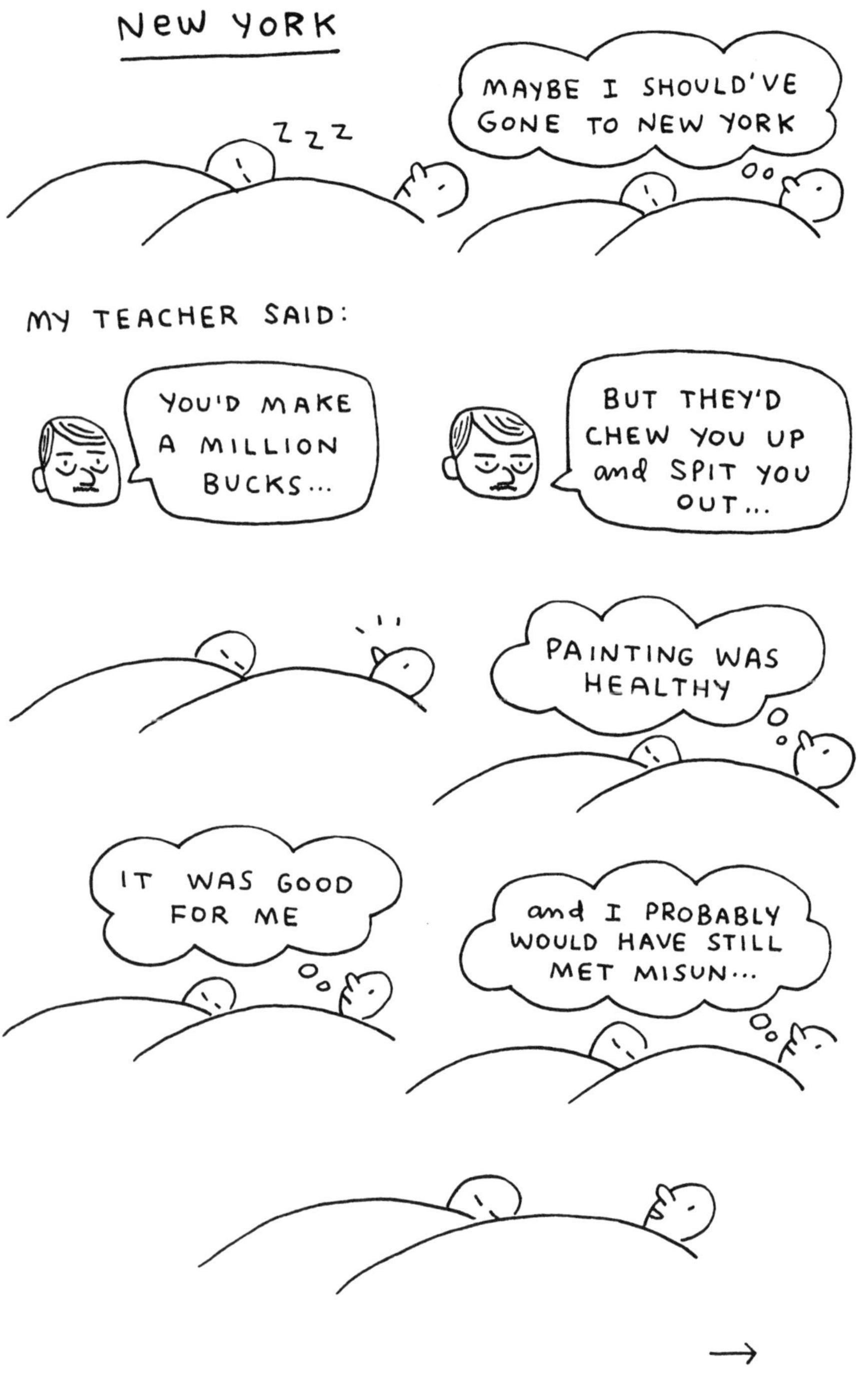
NEW YORK
ZZZ
MAYBE I SHOULD'VE GONE TO NEW YORK
MY TEACHER SAID:
YOU'D MAKE A MILLION BUCKS...
BUT THEY'D CHEW YOU UP and SPIT YOU OUT...
PAINTING WAS HEALTHY
IT WAS GOOD FOR ME
and I PROBABLY WOULD HAVE STILL MET MISUN...
→

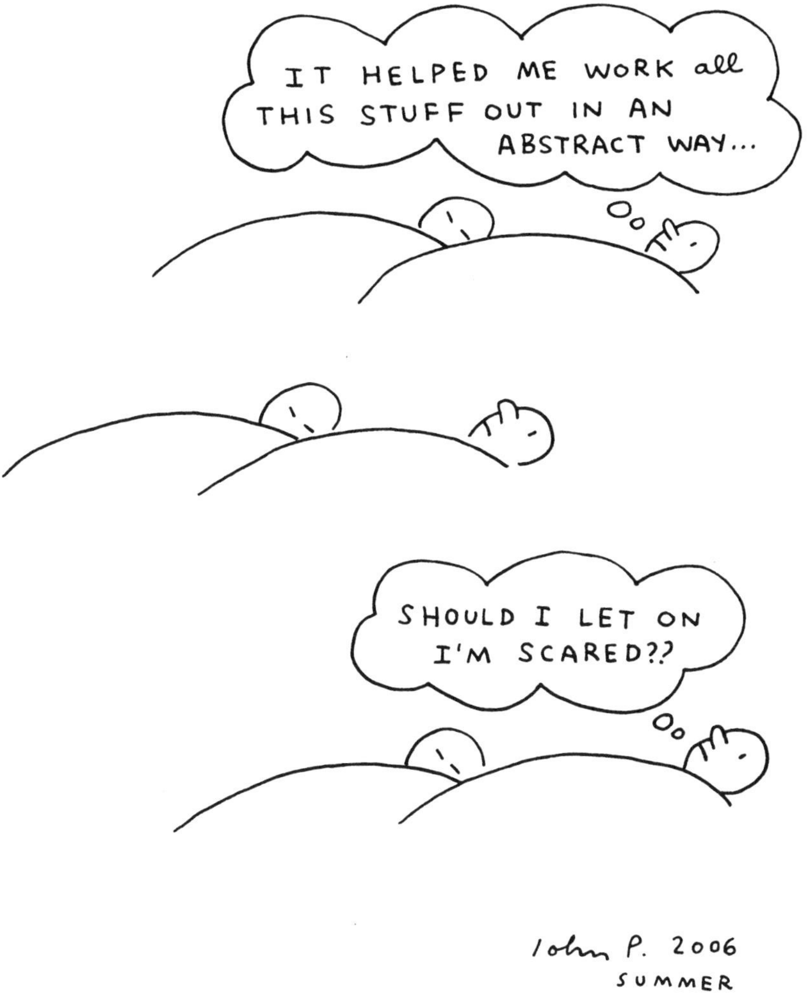
IT HELPED ME WORK all THIS STUFF OUT IN AN ABSTRACT WAY...
SHOULD I LET ON I'M SCARED??
John P. 2006
SUMMER

Teabox Advice

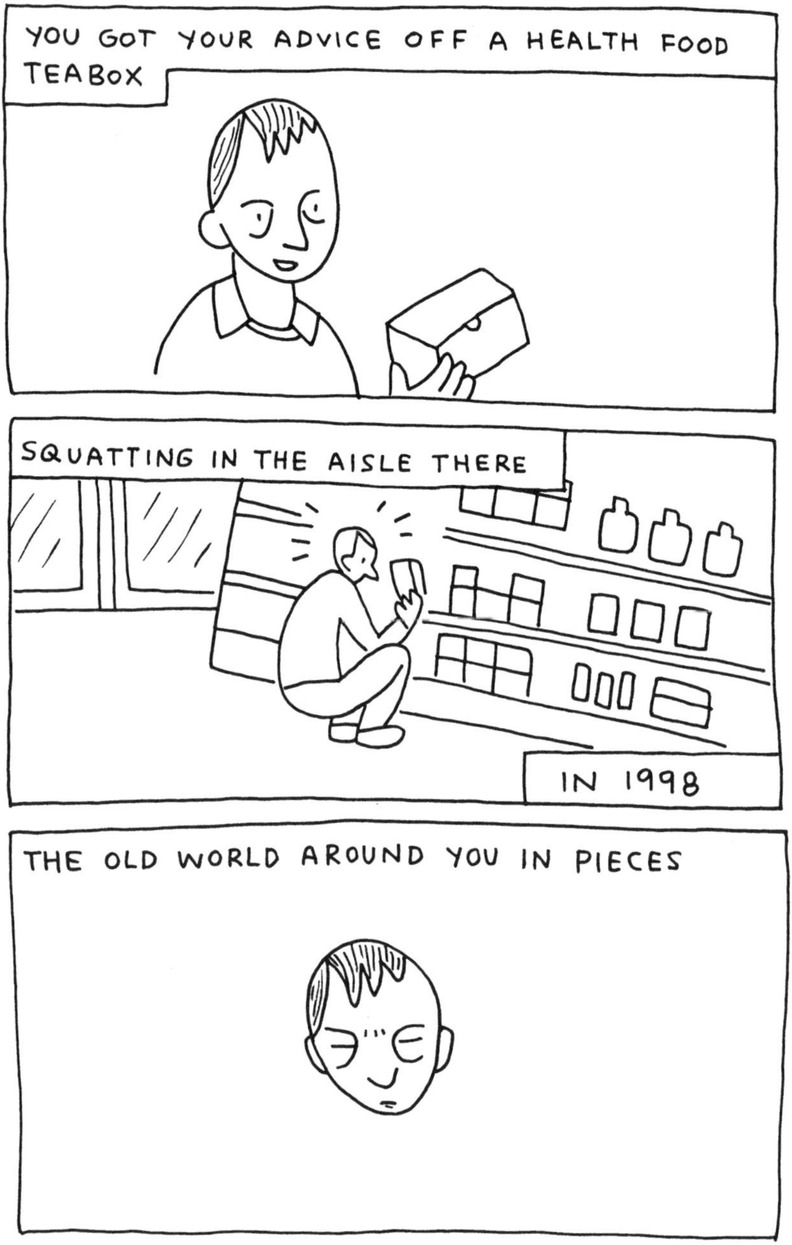
YOU GOT YOUR ADVICE OFF A HEALTH FOOD TEABOX
SQUATTING IN THE AISLE THERE
IN 1998
THE OLD WORLD AROUND YOU IN PIECES

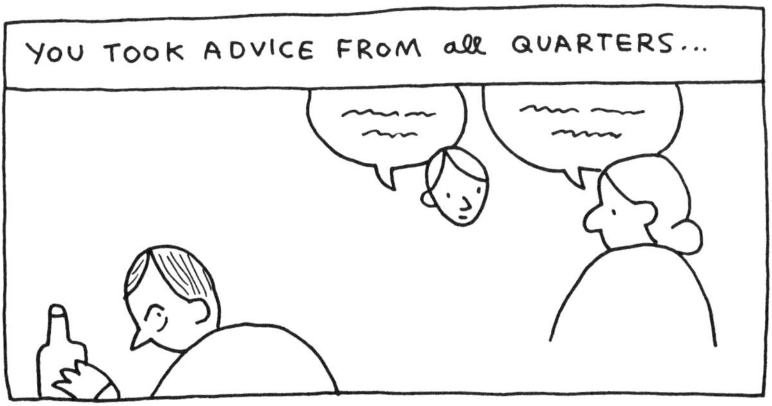
YOU TOOK ADVICE FROM all QUARTERS...

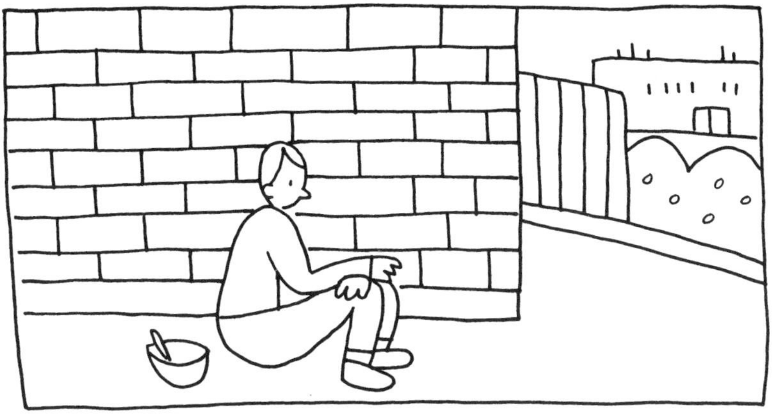

WHO KNEW YOU'D SURVIVE?

John P. MAY 2006

Hara

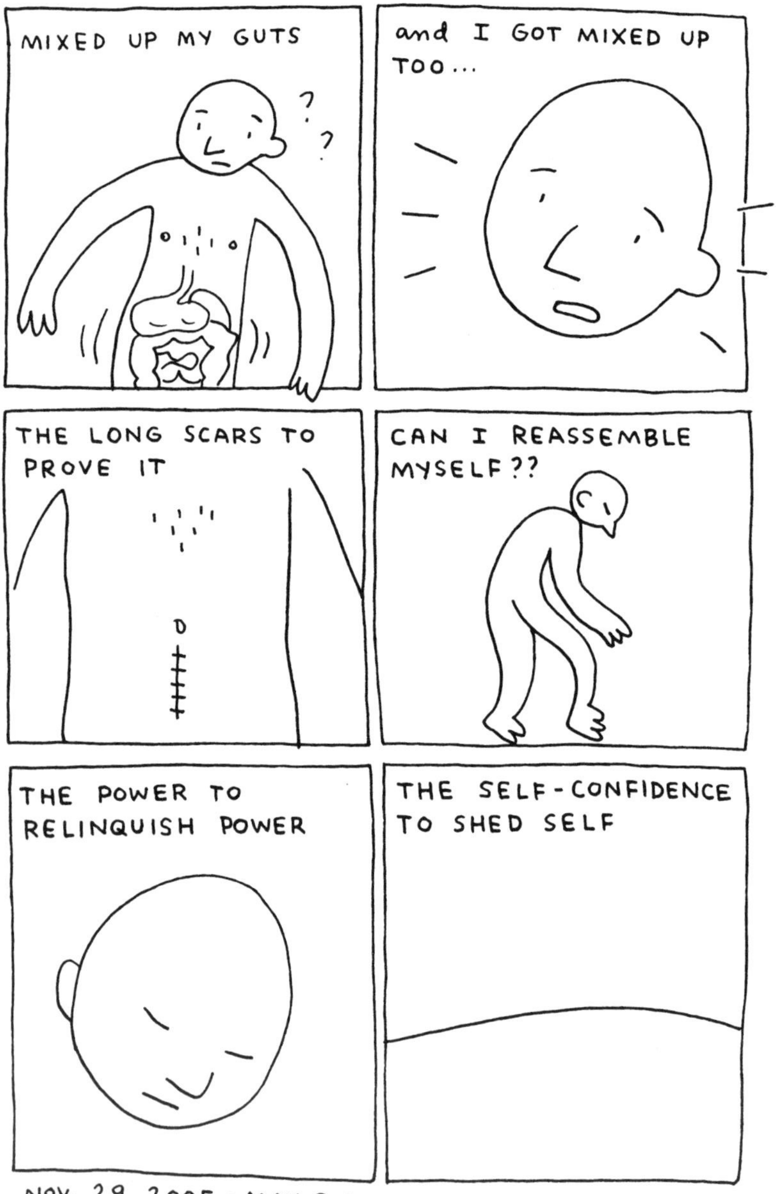

MIXED UP MY GUTS
??
and I GOT MIXED UP TOO...
THE LONG SCARS TO PROVE IT
CAN I REASSEMBLE MYSELF??
THE POWER TO RELINQUISH POWER
THE SELF-CONFIDENCE TO SHED SELF

NOV. 29 2005 - MAY 9 2006

SQUARE-HEAD JOHN

I don't know why we went to Trinidad, maybe I saw it on the map– the last town before the border. It sounded good. Carolyn and I got in the truck one day and headed out —

Down I-25, from Denver, past Pike's Peak and the Springs – past Pueblo and Walsenburg – into uncharted territory. Looking for something different.

Up ahead was Trinidad. It stood emblazoned on the mountain-top, overlooking the town, in big white letters like the Hollywood sign, only:

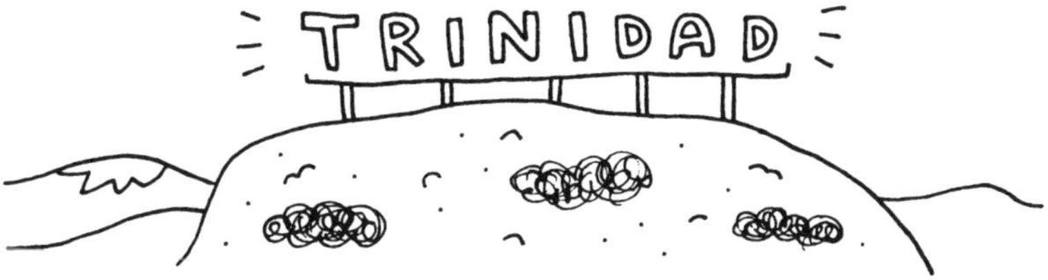
TRINIDAD

The last town before the pass, and New Mexico.

In Trinidad they had a Safeway, so we bought Potato Salad and Rolls, and ate them in the parking lot.

Under the overpass, along the River – Las Animas – the Souls – we watched as Rattle-damaged pickups blasted muffler-proof across the bridges, and the quiet, rocky water, out of sight.

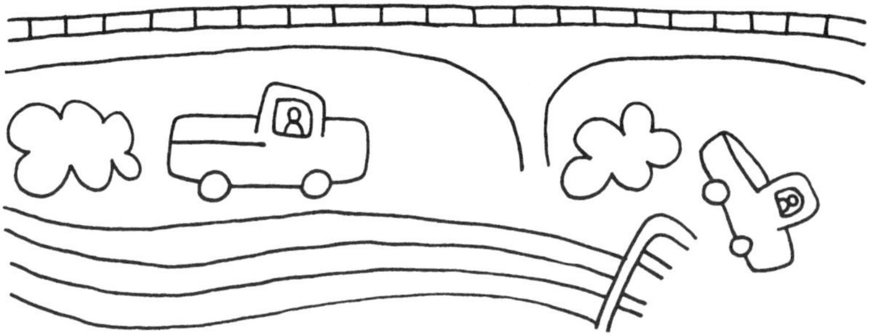

We Rambled through the town, up and down the main drag, the Red brick streets, Red brick buildings, for Rent or for sale, the sky blue with clouds.

Wandering, looking in the windows of every strange little store: the Roller Rink, the movie house, the Five and Dime, the bars and lounges.

South of town, above it all, Fisher's Peak loomed over the city, standing guard — We headed up the slope.

"Fisher's Peak"

Past little bungalows, chain-link fences, concrete posts and gravel; sitting with the sage, there, on the hill, the brush and Red earth— the Interstate and the mountains, the Red brick city, the Sun.

We came down the street again, then, or up the street, I don't Remember — but I do Remember Square-Head John's house because it was the one house covered in painted twigs, pebble sculptures, old gizmos, and the shrine to Virgin Mary.

Square-Head John stood on the porch, or out in the yard, and you couldn't help but look. He was an old, smiling Coloradan Man, weather-beaten, tan, in a baseball cap and blue jeans. Maybe he had a twig in his hands.
He said Hello.

On a wooden shelf next to the porch was a collection of his sun-bleached sculptures— painted twigs and River stones.

He explained them, that his wife forbade him anymore to go fishing with his friends, so he went out with them every morning anyway, except while they fished, he just walked up and down the river picking up driftwood and stones.

That one's my wife and I, in a boat, he said; She's afraid of the water.

Presently, his wife herself appeared at the door, and invited us all in for something cool to drink – R.C. Colas in a glass, with ice. We sat on their couch and shot the breeze.

Square-Head John said he went to the dog-track in Pueblo every weekend, but he didn't bet on the dogs. Instead, he played that coin-operated "Toy Shop" game, where you maneuver an electric crane over a bin full of stuffed animals and try to grab one and move it out of the box to take home. You know the one I mean?

Apparently, Square-Head John was a genius at that game, and he never lost. His wife laughed and stood up. Then she said, let me show you this.

She led us through a doorway, and into their bedroom. When we got inside we stopped cold...

Along every inch of wallspace, from top to bottom, and suspended from the ceiling too (hanging on an invisible support grid of wire) were hundreds of stuffed animals, of every shape, size and kind – mounted side by side to create a stuffed soft cube of a stuffed animal room.

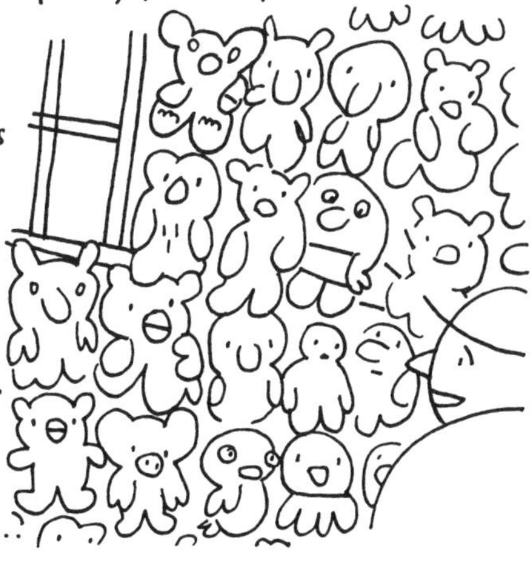

I had never seen anything like it before, and I never will again...?

Square-Head John just chuckled, and his wife sighed, affectionately.

After we finished our drinks, we went outside again, and Square-Head John walked over to the other side of the porch. They lived in a duplex house, and he walked over to the other side, which they owned too, and unlocked the door.

Inside, in the otherwise empty room, was a pyramid of stuffed black plastic bags, stacked literally to the ceiling. Each plastic bag, he explained, was crammed full with stuffed animals he had won at the track. He stored them all like this till Christmastime, when he donated them to Toys for Tots...

He opened up one of the bags and handed me a stuffed animal— a gorilla in a baseball jersey, holding a bat and a ball. That's for you, he said.

Before we left, he gave me a slip of paper with his address and his real name on it. I don't know where that paper is now, but I wish I did.

This was in '93 or so, or 1994. I never saw Square-Head John again after that, but I think of him often.

I'm writing this down, I don't know why. Just so everyone knows that Square-Head John lived with his wife in Trinidad, Colorado. He painted sticks and stones to look like people, and he was very good at that crane-grabber game.

John P. 2006 S.F.

214

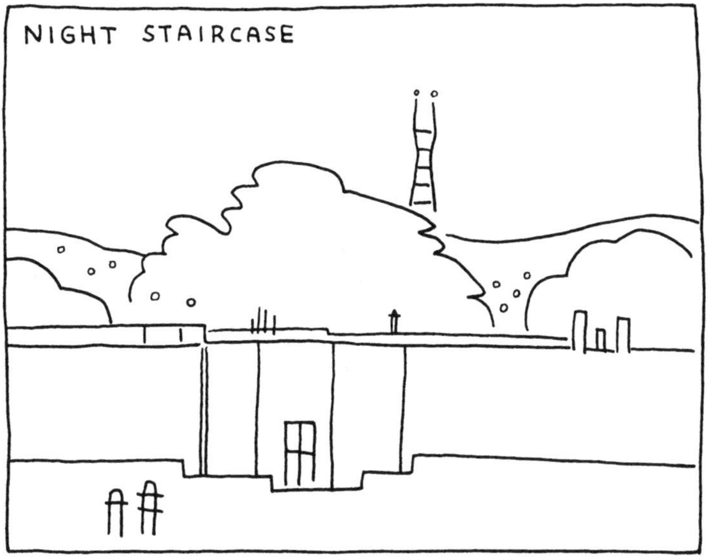
NIGHT STAIRCASE

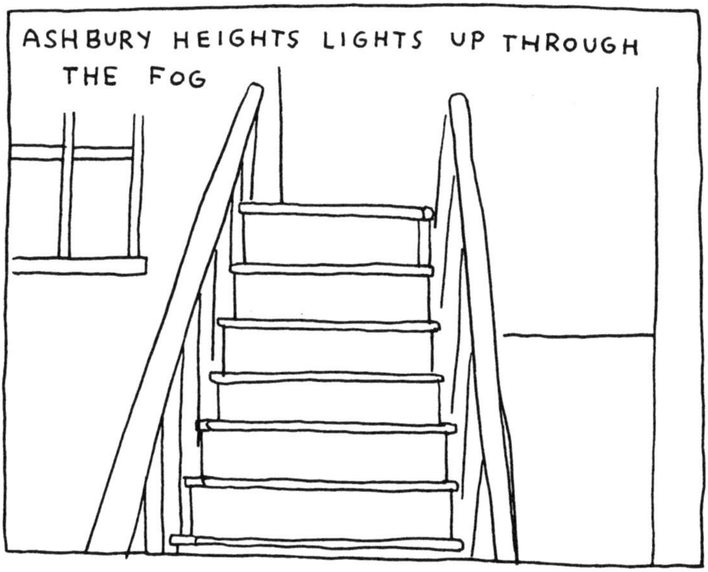
ASHBURY HEIGHTS LIGHTS UP THROUGH THE FOG

MAY 18, 2006
(DRAWN IN JULY)

SIX O'CLOCK STEPS

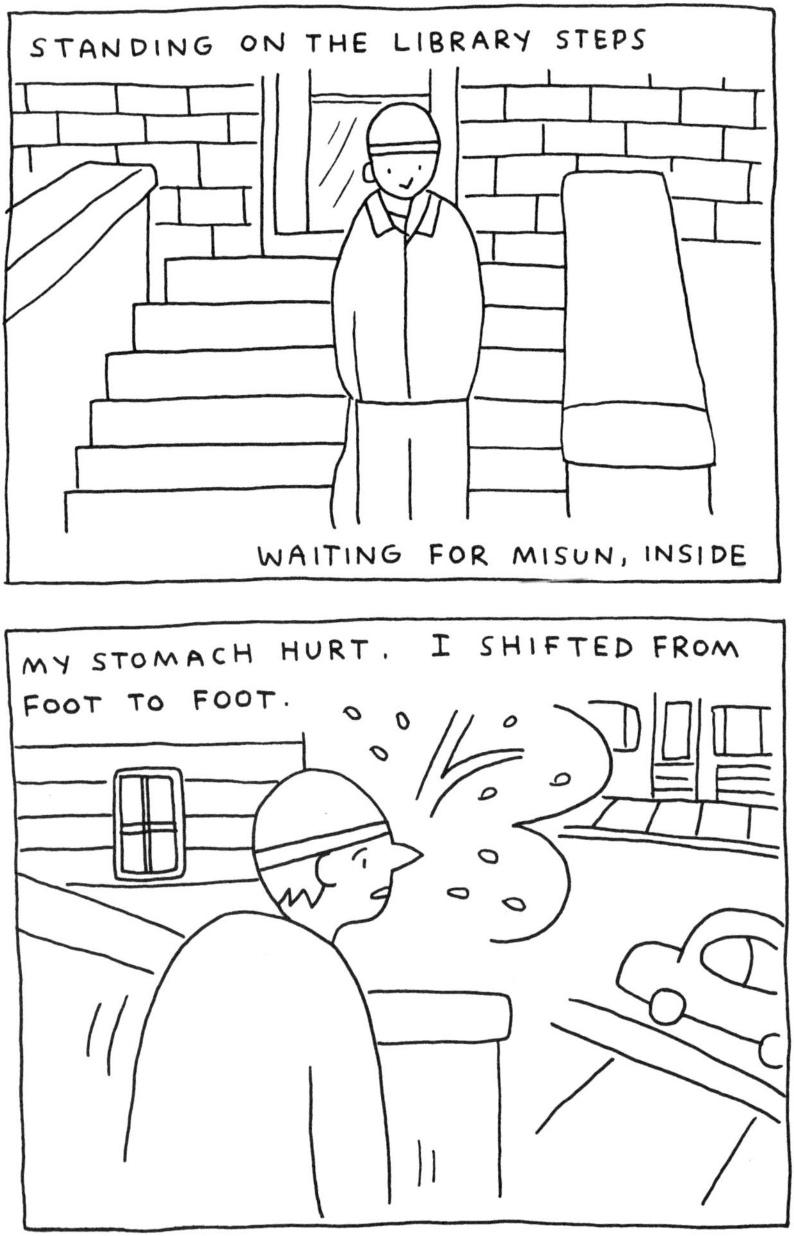
STANDING ON THE LIBRARY STEPS
WAITING FOR MISUN, INSIDE
MY STOMACH HURT. I SHIFTED FROM FOOT TO FOOT.

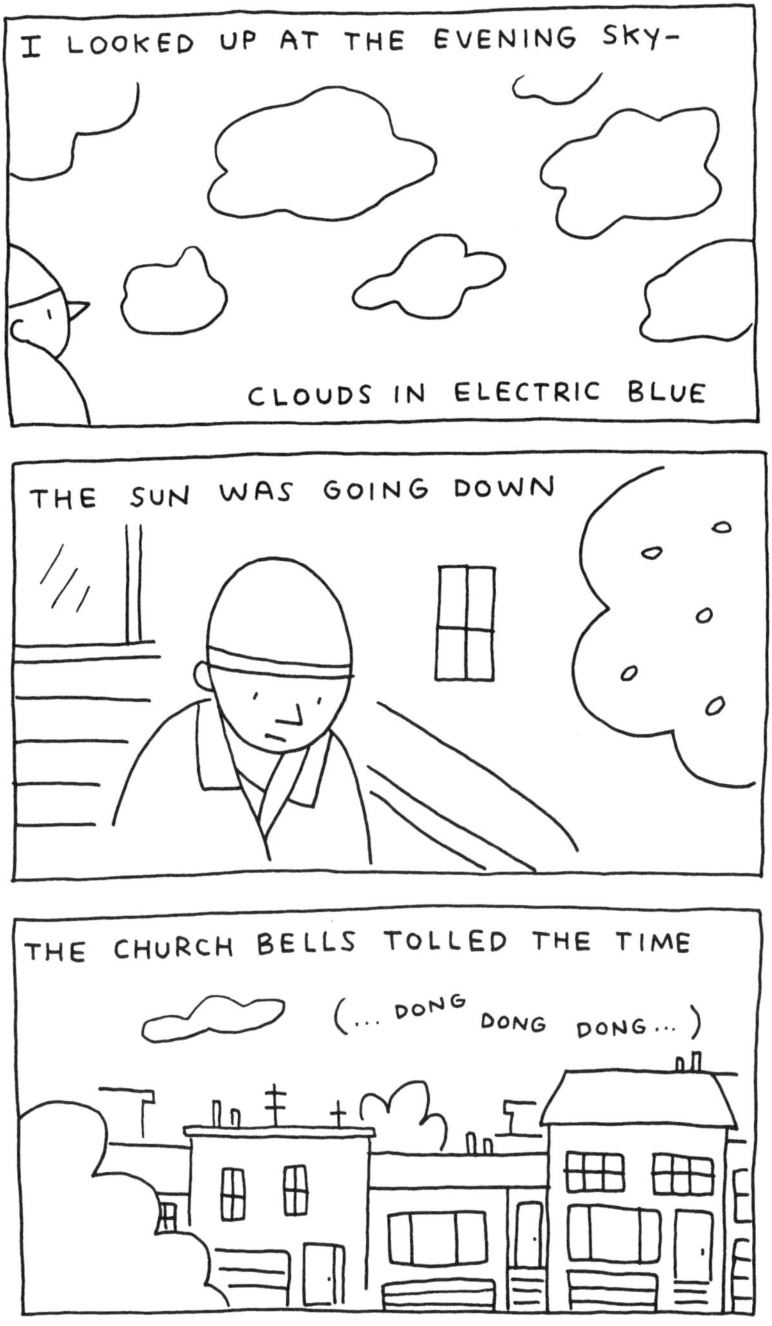
I LOOKED UP AT THE EVENING SKY-
CLOUDS IN ELECTRIC BLUE
THE SUN WAS GOING DOWN
THE CHURCH BELLS TOLLED THE TIME
(... DONG DONG DONG...)

HAPPENED 3-28-06 · REVISED 4-25 · JOHN P.

Flags

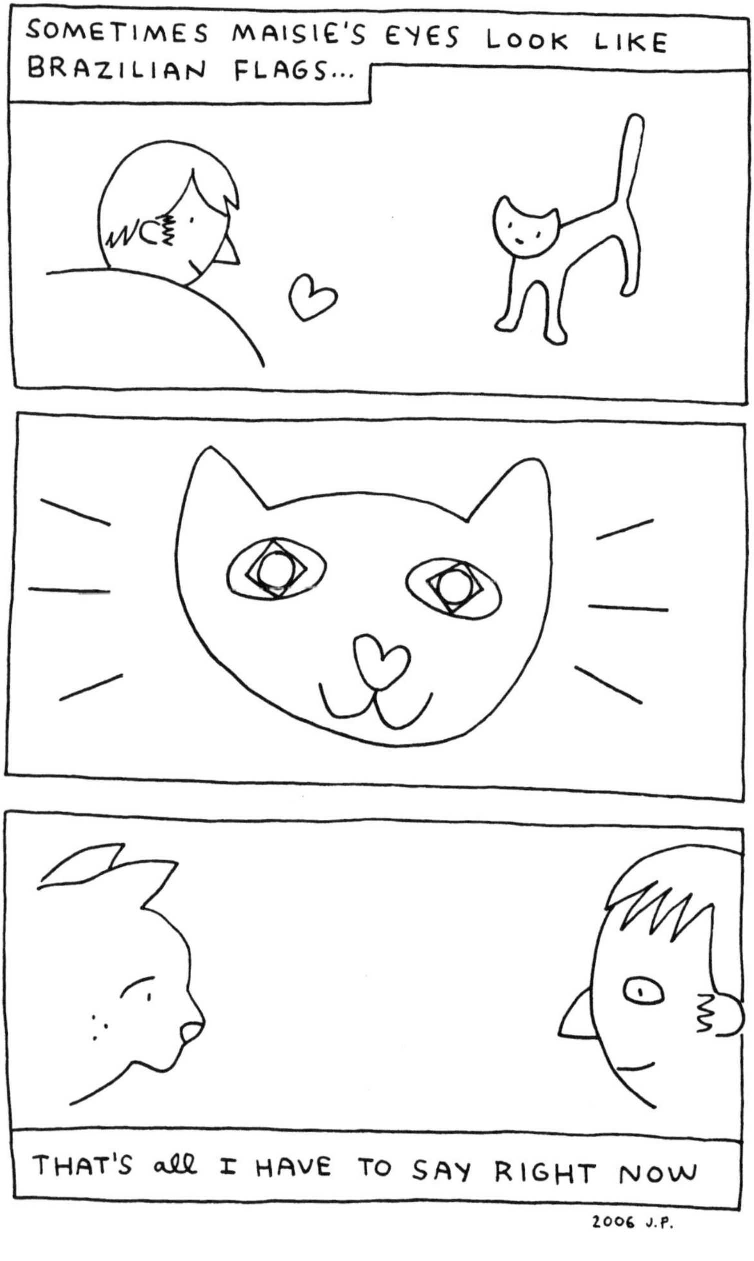
SOMETIMES MAISIE'S EYES LOOK LIKE BRAZILIAN FLAGS...
THAT'S all I HAVE TO SAY RIGHT NOW
2006 J.P.

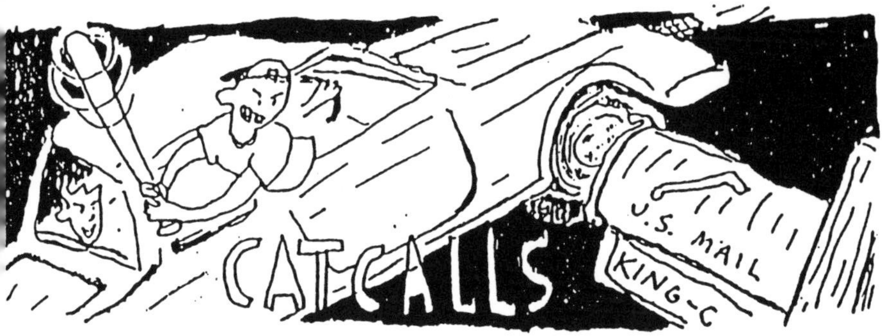
CATCALLS
U.S. MAIL
KING-C

Dear John:

... I too feel as though the internet has dealt a huge blow to the world of zines (maybe to the print medium as a whole). I think the worst part about that is that the use of the internet has really raised the bar for what it takes to disseminate info. In a zine-based media reality, all you need in order to be a magazine editor is access to a xerox machine and the U.S. Mail. Now you need to know how to maintain a website, which is pretty specialized knowledge. So we've basically handed the control of our counter-culture over to a technocrat class. And that's a huge change. I submit that the best thing about zines was the total equality of voice that was inevitable because of the absence of any pre-requisites for, or barriers to, authorship.

Gabe Galloway - Chicago, Ill.

Dear John P.

... I've been living a hermetic existence the last three years.

... Doing a lot of art work, collages, woven strips of "Vogue" mag, paper...

... The thought of you comes into my mind.

... otherwise...

... I can't think of much to say.

Shanti.

H.L. Coats - Indianapolis, Ind.

P.S.: Have you heard from Zenick?

MORE LETTERS ⟶

Hi John,

I have been prolific this year, and most of last, concentrating on black and white drawings that I sell on e-bay, but I have xeroxes of everything.

My wife and I opened a yarn shop, where we also have her knitting and my hand-painted tee-shirts, and some paintings I made. A lot of women show me their knitting projects when I'm watching the store.

Life with Paula is great. We take walks, knit and draw together, and hang out with each other as much as possible.

Peace and Love,

Jeff Zenick - Tallahassee, Fla.

John P.-

Thanks for the recent issue of King-Cat (#62). [I got this letter a long time ago; ed.] I really enjoyed the two-page spread on Catalpa trees. Interesting thing: My wife pronounces Catalpa "KAT-AW-BE" which I guess comes from the Catawba Indians. My wife also says that there were certain worms that her dad would harvest from the tree for catfishing.

John Frigo - Lafayette, Ind.

NEWS OF ELGIN from: ALICE DUBOIS

—In a parking lot I see a seagull pick something up and drop it. I walk over. It's a Hine's Lumber Carpenter's Pencil. I take it home. (I'm writing with it now).

—I see a pair of beavers one twilight in the Fox River. They look like small bears. The male eats an apple. The female stays in the water.

—I find a different trail that goes along [Rt.] 31 on the east side of the river. On it is Kane County's "only waterfall." Nearby is another stream coming out of a quarry. One day I'm wandering in the stream looking for frogs, and a baby snapping turtle floats by. I pick it up for awhile and look at it. I thought it might pinch me, but it doesn't. I think of "Minn of the Mississippi" which my father read to me as a child.

(CONTINUED AFTER TOP 40 →)

MR. KING-CAT TOP-FORTY

WINTER-SUMMER 2006

1. MY BEAUTIFUL WIFE MISUN ♡♡♡♡♡
2. MAISIE KAT ♡♡♡♡♡
3. The Beach Boys: Sunflower (Capitol Recs, 1970) ★★★★★
4. WE JAM ECONO: the Minutemen Movie DVD (Plexidisc) one of the greatest bands ever - a totally inspiring and affirming documentary, with tons of extras, inc. 3 FULL Length Concerts!
5. Flipper (!!) LIVE - !! Haight Street Fair, S.F. June 11, 2006
6. Beat This! The Best of the English Beat (Go Feet / LONDON)
7. Listening to ELO with Misun ♥
8. Walking w/ Kevin H. in S.F. (Embarcadero, NOV '05)
9. walking w/ Patrick Porter in S.F. (Geary etc) 3/22/06
10. SMiLE Concert DVD - Brian Wilson (Rhino) - Beautiful!
11. marbles Pyramid Landing CD (Spin ART) ★★★★★★★★★
12. Bob Dylan WORLD GONE WRONG (Columbia Recs)
13. Thinking about the flavor of RC Cola ♥
14. Charlie Rich Silver Linings (Epic)
15. American Primitive Vol. 2 (Revenant Records) AMAZING 2-CD set of otherworldly Old-Time music, 1897-1939. Anyone interested in America or American Music needs to hear this! Highly, highly Recommended!!
16. Everybody Hates Chris (T.V. show) - WB Network
17. My Name is Earl and The Office - T.V. shows, Thurs. nights - NBC - ★★★★★★★
18. The Definitive John Lennon 2-CD set, Capitol / EMI
19. Walden: A Fully Annotated Edition by Henry David Thoreau, ed. by Jeffrey S. Cramer (Yale Univ. Press)
20. Reading about Morton Feldman in the New Yorker
21. Walking past the Licorice Trees on Park Presidio ♥
22. GOOD FOR WHAT AILS YOU: Music of the Medicine Shows - (1926-1937) (Big Hat Records) -- Fun 2-CD collection of Travelling show music and comedy! ★★★
23. Little Fur Family by Margaret Wise Brown and Garth Williams ♥ (Harper Festival Books)
24. Van Morrison Veedon Fleece LP (Polydor, 1974) one of my new favorites!
25. The 400 Blows by Francois Truffaut (Criterion edition DVD includes "Antoine et Colette" and inspiring Director's interviews!)
26. Yellow Eyed Blackbirds (Brewer's Blackbirds?)

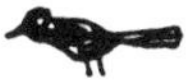

27. 2006 NBA Finals
28. The day "Unsatisfied" made me cry (by the Replacements, off LET IT BE)
29. Walking in the Richmond

MORE →

30. STUDIO A: the Bob Dylan Reader. Ed. by Benjamin Hedin (NORTON)

31. Night Train to Nashville, Volume Two. Music City R&B, 1945-1970. Every bit as good as Volume One! (Country Music Hall of Fame) (2-CD set) ★ ★ ★ ★

32. Joe Diffie "John Deere Green" song (walking around singin' it...)

33. DAE JUNG GEUM - great Korean Historical costume Drama T.V. show! (channel 32) ★ ★ ★ ★

34. Beach Boys - Good Vibrations Box Set (CAP-ITOL)

35. Roots of Rock and Roll- 1946-1954 (Hip-O) great Pre-Elvis R'n'R, country, R&B (3 Discs!)

36. YOKO ONO "Hard Times Are Over" (Song)

37. DeYoung Art museum, Golden Gate Park -
   • "Crown Point Press: The Art of Etching" (inspiring)
   • "International Arts and Crafts" (19th century DIY!)
   • "Chicano" (moving, Fun, and Enlightening)
   • "The Quilts of Gee's Bend" (genius...)

38. Sunshine   39. Hope   40. Anything else I forgot

and don't forget to ROCK ON! ♡ John P.

LETTERS (continued):

— There are mice visiting my kitchen. They steal chips of Sandalwood Bee & Flower soap and chew on them. I've tried to capture them (I sort of don't like them pooping on the counter) but they are elusive. They're cute. Sometimes I catch them in the act (of snooping for food). But they ignore the "Live Capture" traps I put out.

— Months later... I caught one of the mice (in a New Orleans beer glass) and relocated it to the Gothic church on Villa Street that the Unitarians used to use. I felt guilty for doing it, and sort of sad and lonely after kicking it out. Now the mice all seem to have departed. They left or relocated of their own volition.

   I saw Mr. Lyons the other day. He said John's living in Madison and manages a food co-op.

                    Alice DuBois - Elgin, Illinois

222

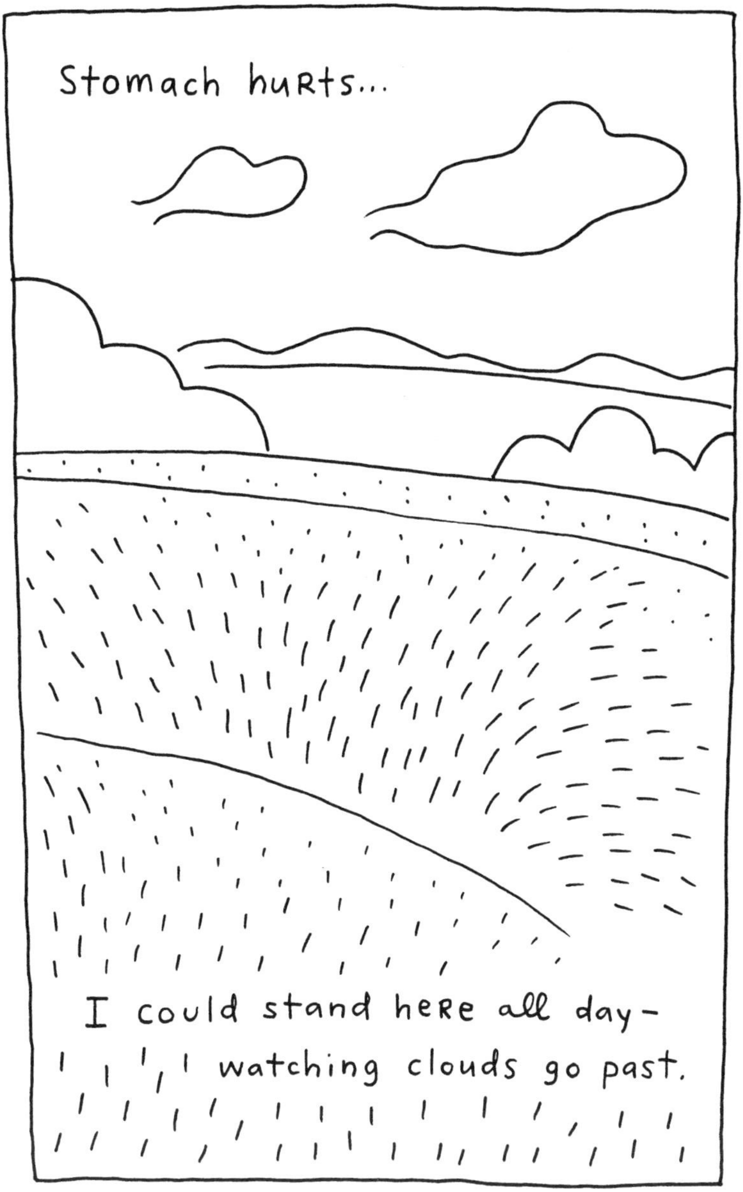
Stomach hurts...
I could stand here all day-
watching clouds go past.

BURNIDGE WOODS, ELGIN

DRAWN 2006 J.P.

CABIN FLUX

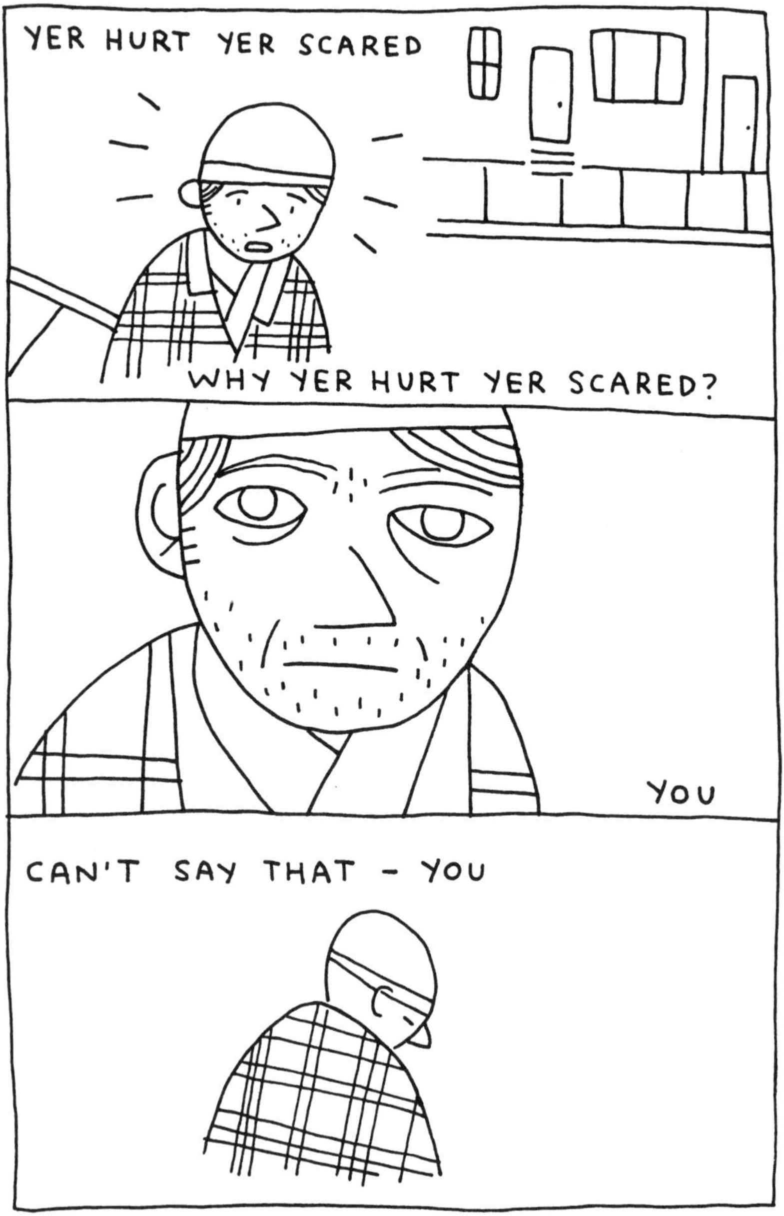
YER HURT YER SCARED
WHY YER HURT YER SCARED?
YOU
CAN'T SAY THAT - YOU

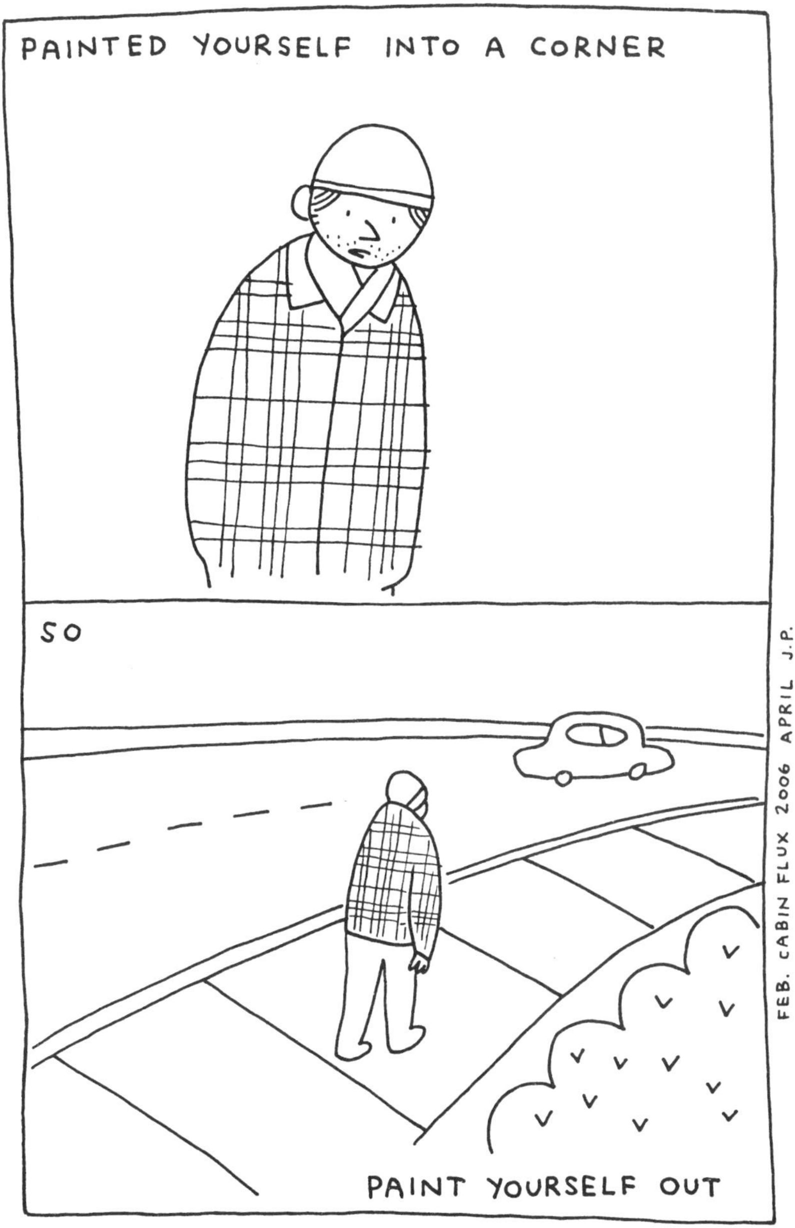
PAINTED YOURSELF INTO A CORNER
SO
PAINT YOURSELF OUT
FEB. cABIN FLUX 2006 APRIL J.P.

COURTING

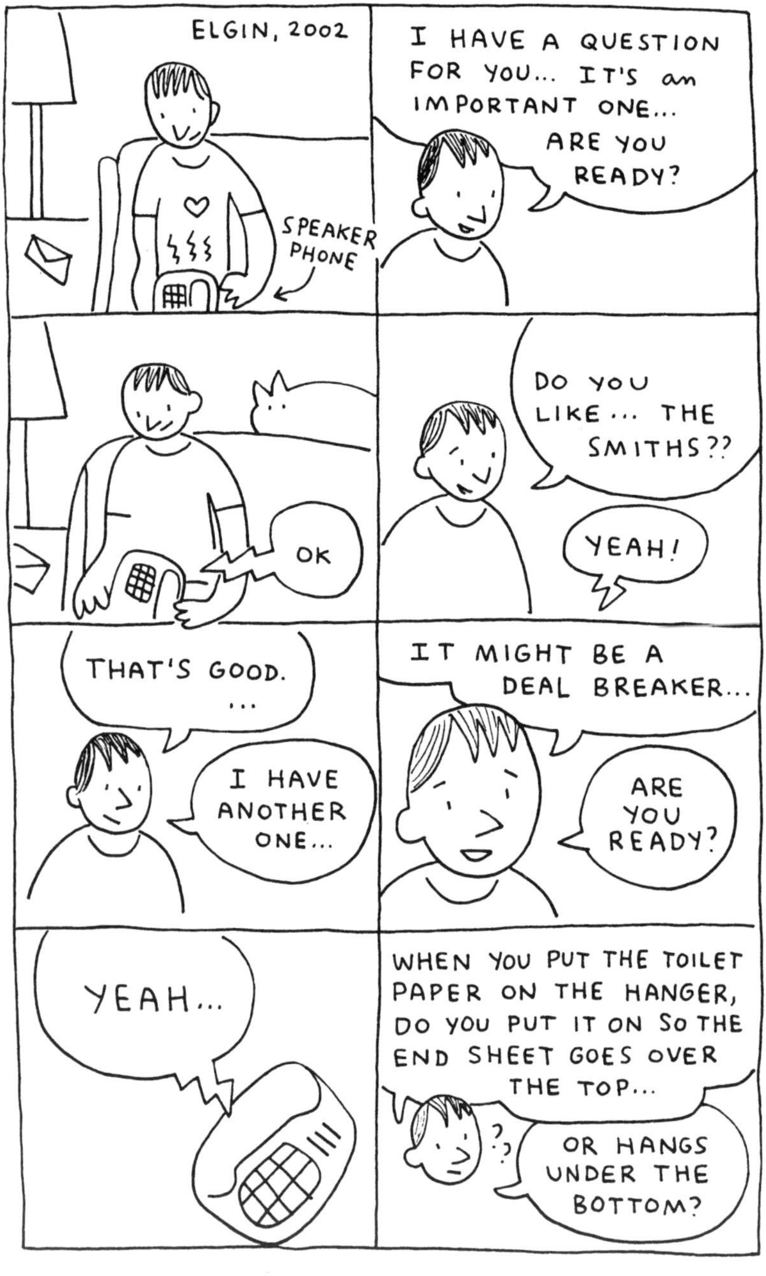
ELGIN, 2002
SPEAKER PHONE
I HAVE A QUESTION FOR YOU... IT'S an IMPORTANT ONE... ARE YOU READY?
OK
DO YOU LIKE... THE SMITHS??
YEAH!
THAT'S GOOD. ...
I HAVE ANOTHER ONE...
IT MIGHT BE A DEAL BREAKER...
ARE YOU READY?
YEAH...
WHEN YOU PUT THE TOILET PAPER ON THE HANGER, DO YOU PUT IT ON SO THE END SHEET GOES OVER THE TOP...
??
OR HANGS UNDER THE BOTTOM?

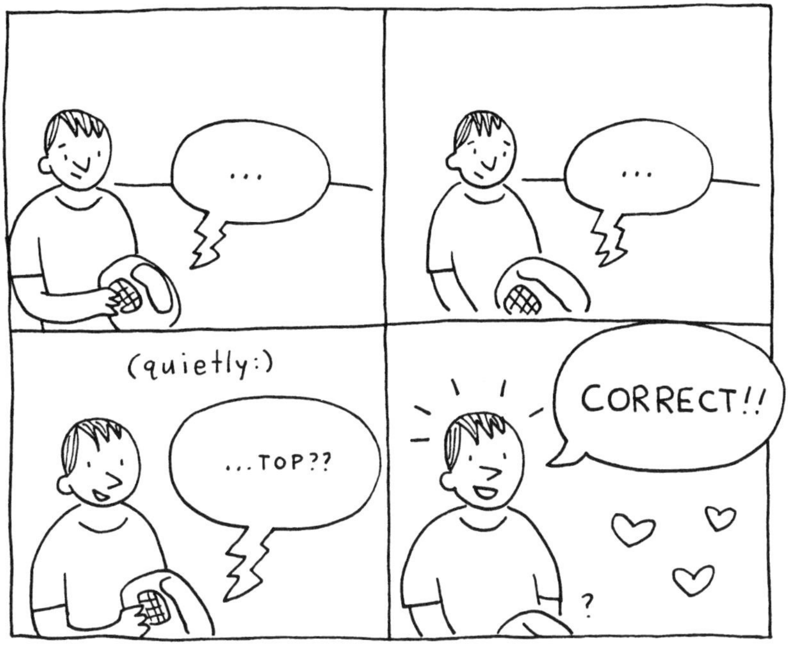
...
...
(quietly:)
...TOP??
CORRECT!!
?

HAPPENED IN SPRING 2002 ♡
DRAWN BY JOHN P., SF 2006
HAPPY ANNIVERSARY MISUN!!

Feels Like A Good Day

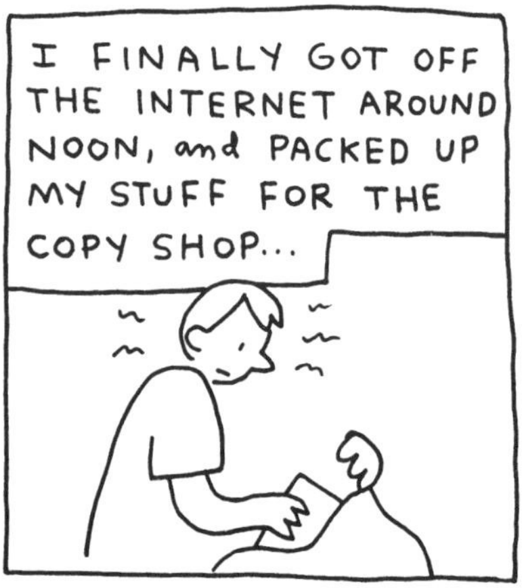
I FINALLY GOT OFF THE INTERNET AROUND NOON, and PACKED UP MY STUFF FOR THE COPY SHOP...

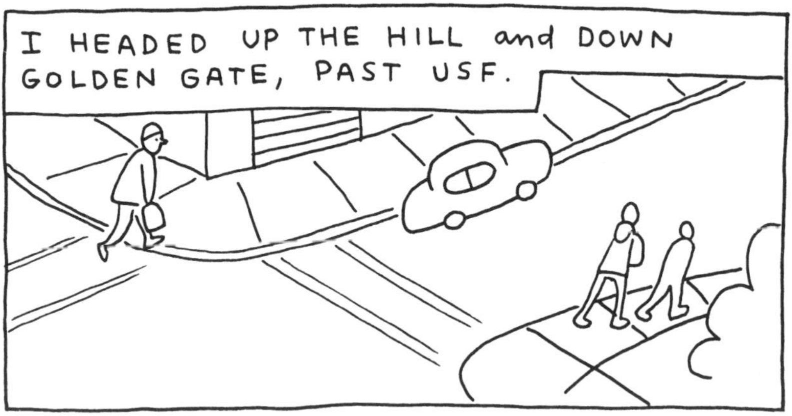
I HEADED UP THE HILL and DOWN GOLDEN GATE, PAST USF.

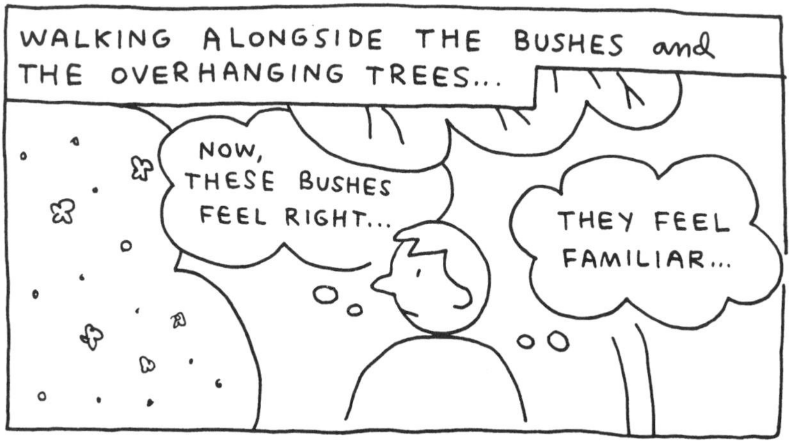
WALKING ALONGSIDE THE BUSHES and THE OVERHANGING TREES...
NOW, THESE BUSHES FEEL RIGHT...
THEY FEEL FAMILIAR...

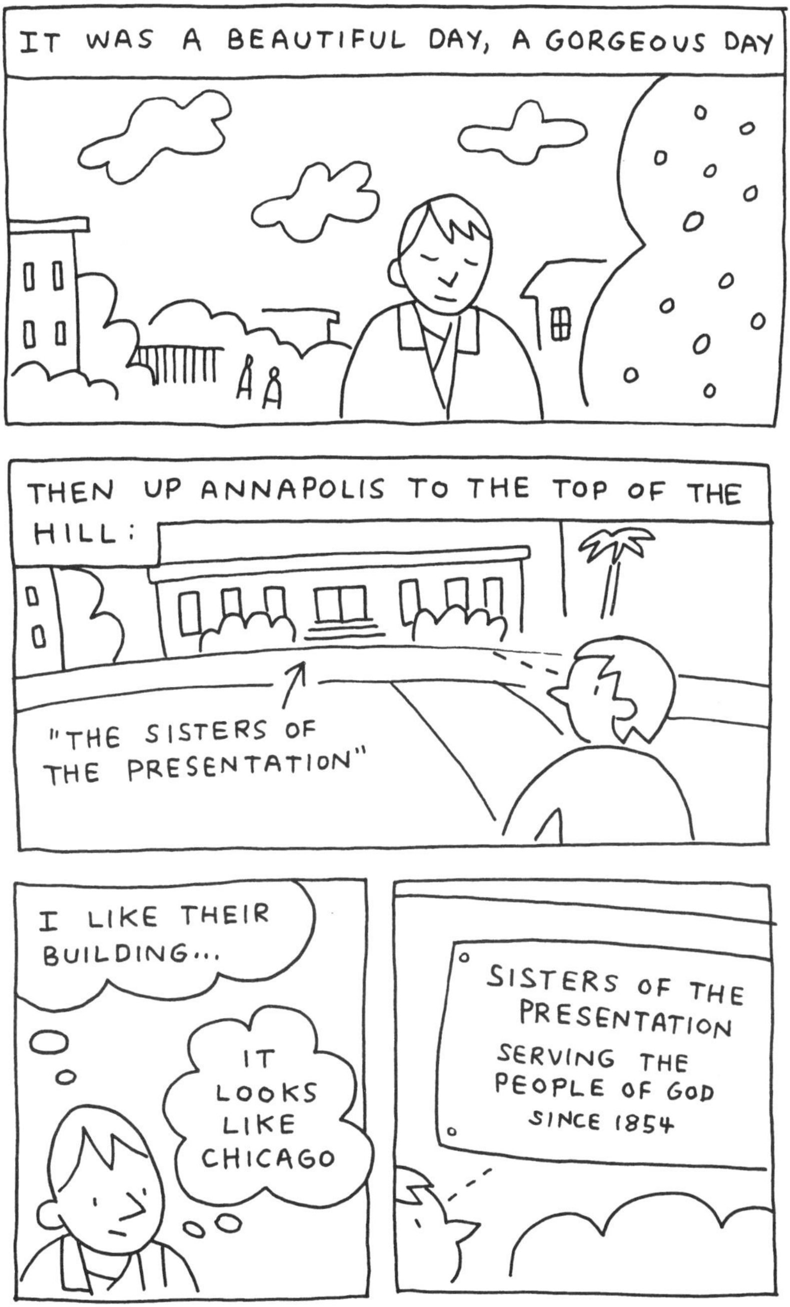
IT WAS A BEAUTIFUL DAY, A GORGEOUS DAY
THEN UP ANNAPOLIS TO THE TOP OF THE HILL:
"THE SISTERS OF THE PRESENTATION"
I LIKE THEIR BUILDING...
IT LOOKS LIKE CHICAGO
SISTERS OF THE PRESENTATION
SERVING THE PEOPLE OF GOD
SINCE 1854

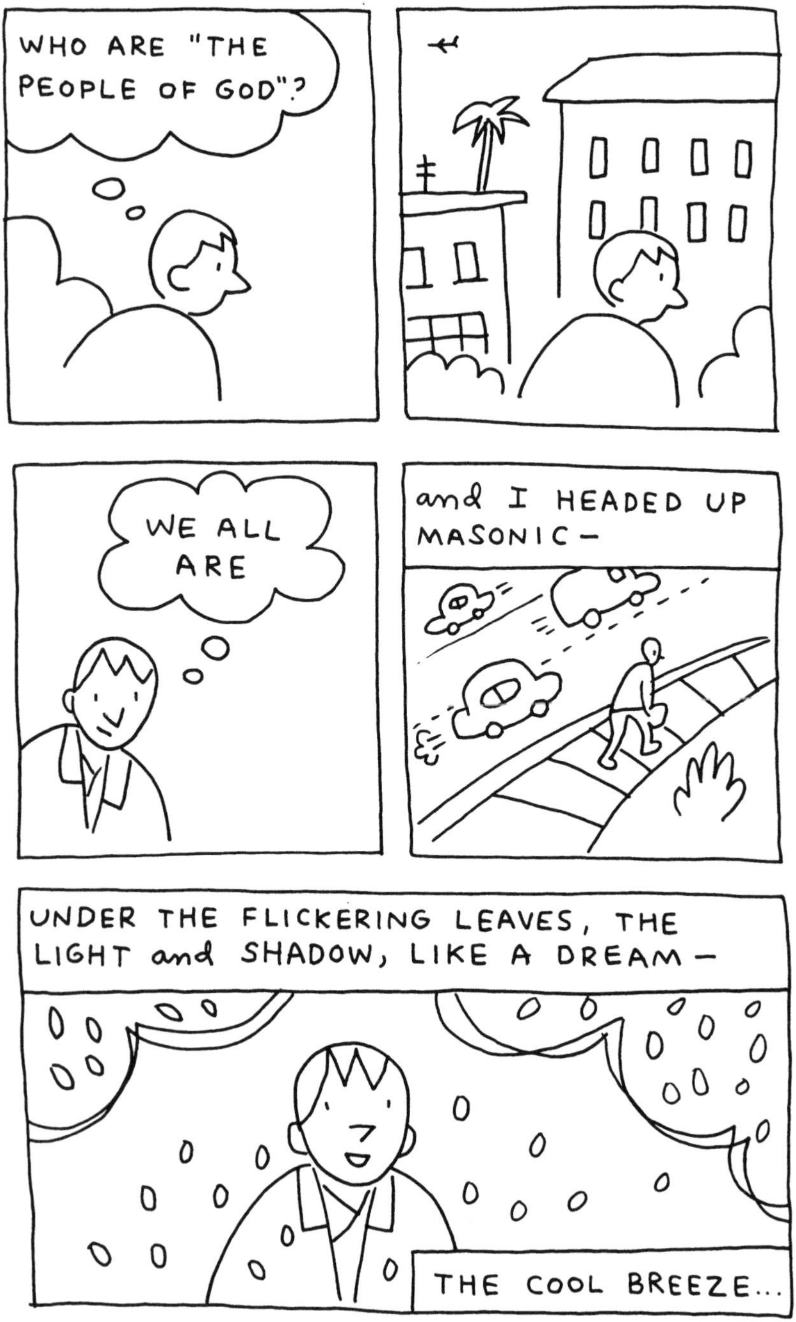
WHO ARE "THE PEOPLE OF GOD"?
WE ALL ARE
and I HEADED UP MASONIC—
UNDER THE FLICKERING LEAVES, THE LIGHT and SHADOW, LIKE A DREAM—
THE COOL BREEZE...

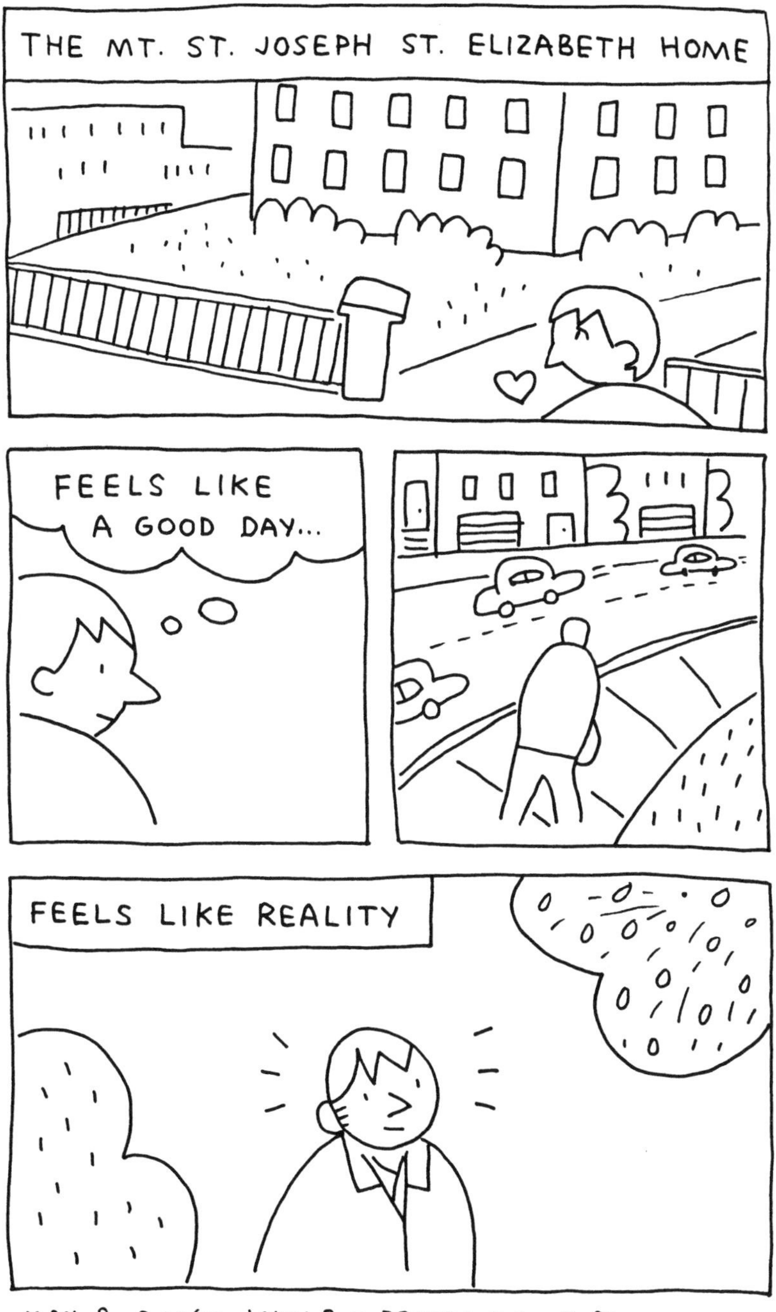
THE MT. ST. JOSEPH ST. ELIZABETH HOME
FEELS LIKE A GOOD DAY...
FEELS LIKE REALITY

MAY 8, 2006- JOHN P. - DRAWN MAY 9 ♡

EVERY day of our life—
No countdown
No waiting
—Just this

KING-CAT

COMICS and STORIES

No. 68 $3.00

BY JOHN PORCELLINO

KING-CAT SNORNOSE · 68

"SO YOU THINK YOU'RE A NERVOUS WRECK"

At the end of October (2006), we headed out on the Road again, this time moving back to Denver from San Francisco. We'd been up all day and all night packing, and most of the next day too, but finally the truck was loaded, the apartment was clean and empty. I climbed aboard with Misun and Maisie, and we pulled away, three years of a dream disappearing in the rear view mirror.

I tried to drive, but at that point we'd been up for nearly 39 hours, and when we stopped in Fairfield to buy canned beans and water, we fell asleep, in the cab, in the Safeway parking lot, our last Californian sunset dissolving around us. When we woke up, we made it another 50 miles to Roseville before calling it a night.

The next day we crossed the Sierras into Reno, and the Great Basin Desert. As usual, Maisie sat on our laps the whole time and slept. Outside Battle Mountain on a cold morning, the clouds slid down the mountainsides, ran rings around the peaks. In Elko I bought zinc tablets and Tupelo Honey... then the flats, Salt Lake, and into Wyoming.

In Rawlins, a big buck deer strode nonchalantly down Main Street during "Rush Hour", and Misun found Thai food for dinner. Standing on the windy hill above town, gassing up, looking out over November plains, I could tell we were getting close.

At Cheyenne we hit I-25 and headed south, and it felt so natural, like coming home after a long (long) weekend. The dark mountains to the west, the black prairie to the east, then city traffic and suddenly the lights of Denver spreading out before us in the clear night air. We were coming back— Denver, Colorado — what a world!

→

* * *

KING-CAT COMICS & STORIES, No. 68 ♡
for John R. and Maisie K.
LOVE

online at: www.king-cat.net

Published 10/07 by:
SPIT and a HALF
[redacted]
Denver, CO [redacted]
U.S.A.

The other day I was heading west on 32nd Avenue, when I pulled up to the intersection at Sheridan. (Sheridan Blvd. is is a narrow, congested roadway along the western edge of Denver.) I sat there watching the cars hurtling past one another, at ridiculously high speeds, motors straining, and suddenly I felt like my eyes opened to the scene. It suddenly seemed TOTALLY INSANE, and I thought to myself, "This world has become insane." — and it happened in tiny little increments, a little bit at a time, so that we never even noticed it.

I'll tell you, the last good many years of my life have not been easy. I feel weary, and beat down by life. I oftentimes despair of what the future's gonna hold for good ol' John P. But at the same time, even though I think about it all the time, I know giving up isn't an option.

I'm convinced that there's a way to live in this world — this insane world — in a sane way, with one's integrity and naturally-given good sense intact. By that I don't mean perfect. I tried perfect and it didn't work out too good. I mean simply to live out your own experience of life for real. With all the mistakes, contradictions, effort, sorrow and joy that that entails.

I feel like lately I lost sight of that. I've found myself in a deep hole of my own construction — and I wanna get out. Like the great, flawed, contradiction-laden artist Charlie Rich said — "I feel like goin' home."

Now, I don't even know if I know what "home" means anymore. It's not necessarily a physical place, right? But maybe it's that place where we feel connected to the meaning of our own lives.

Somehow I got disconnected. I got lost — and things got confused and sad, desperate and weird. I don't know exactly how it happened, but somehow I got my own life beat out of me — and I want it back.

John P. / Denver
September 2007

FRONT COVER IMAGE: BLUE MUSTARD

JOHN R.

On November 11, 2006, my dear friend John Rininger passed away, unexpectedly, in Chicago. John was a very very special person, with a beautiful, open heart. He was a remarkable artist who worked in magazines, collage, stamp art, mail art, digital art and so on. He was just an artist.

I know John struggled a lot in his lifetime, yet in later years he had a radiant strength that was really inspiring to me. He once told me that as he got older, the chord of his life simply got richer and richer.

I met John in Dekalb in the late 1980's when he worked at the Kinko's on Lucinda. He printed up early Cehsoikoes and King-Cats for me there. Once, he contributed a photocopy piece to Cehsoikoe. I reprinted it, with his name added underneath. He sent me back a copy of the zine in the mail, with no note. Under his image in the issue, he simply wrote "Name Detracts." That was it. That said a lot about John.

The last time I saw him, I was living in Elgin, and he came out on the train to visit. We had a quiet, enjoyable day. He told me how the medieval monks would sign their brilliant illuminated manuscripts "By the Hand of..." instead of using just their own names, out of humility. John had that humility about him. He saw the light amid the darkness and worked to show that light to others. I will deeply miss him.

John E. Rininger

October 8, 1961 – November 11, 2006

MAISIE
LOVE

On the afternoon of August 2nd, 2007, after a long struggle with kidney disease, our beloved cat Maisie passed away, in my arms, at home.

It's no exaggeration to say that Maisie was my best friend. We were constant companions for nearly 16 years, and we went through a lot of life together in those short years. We saw each other through a lot of beautiful moments and a lot of sorrow. Maisie always stuck by me.

In later years, I really began to feel that Maisie's prime motivator in life was Love — to give it, and receive it. By that standard Maisie lived a great life — cuz she gave, and got, so much.

She was really smart, playful, and loving. She also had an independent streak and let you know it if you were bugging her. She liked to sit in the window and look at birds, squirrels, and fish. She liked to go outside with us and smell the breeze. She liked to get her belly rubbed. Her favorite game was running as fast as she could across the room, into a plastic grocery bag that we held open for her on the floor. She'd sit inside, wild-eyed, looking out, very pleased, until a moment later she'd jump out, ready to play it again.

She had one cur-li-cue whisker.

I'll always love you Maisie kukoc!

Maisie Kukoc Porcellino

"December 18," 1991–August 2, 2007

CLOUD MOUNTAIN

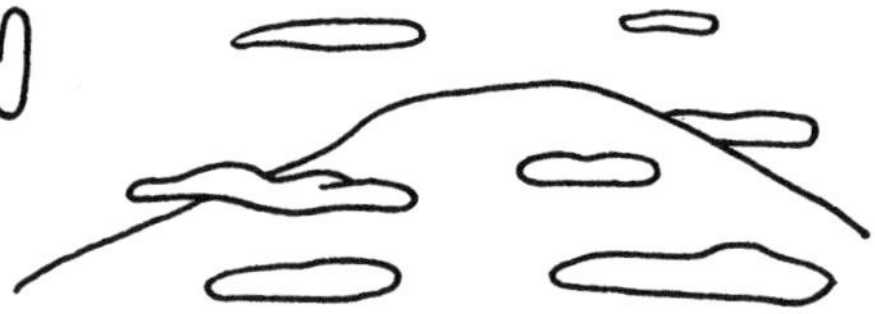

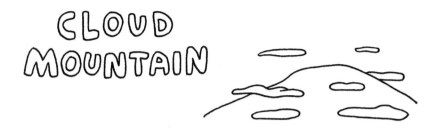

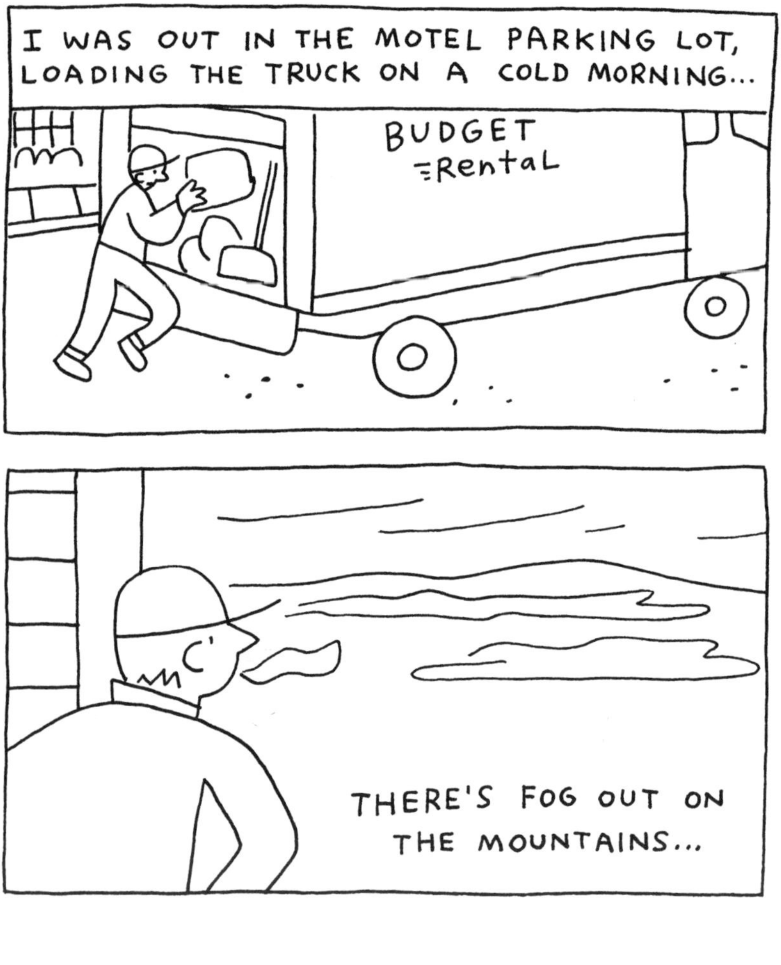
I WAS OUT IN THE MOTEL PARKING LOT, LOADING THE TRUCK ON A COLD MORNING...
BUDGET
Rental
THERE'S FOG OUT ON THE MOUNTAINS...

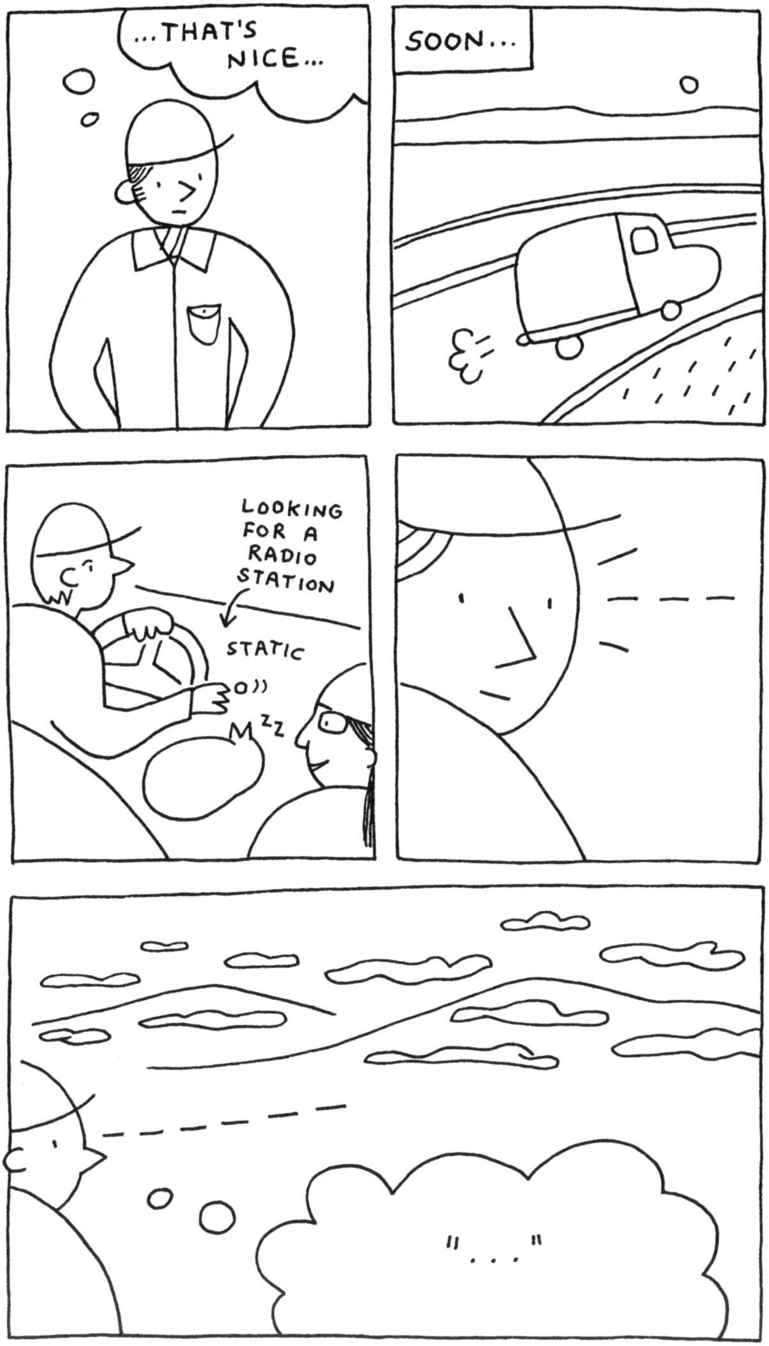
...THAT'S NICE...
SOON...
LOOKING FOR A RADIO STATION
STATIC
M zz
" . . . "

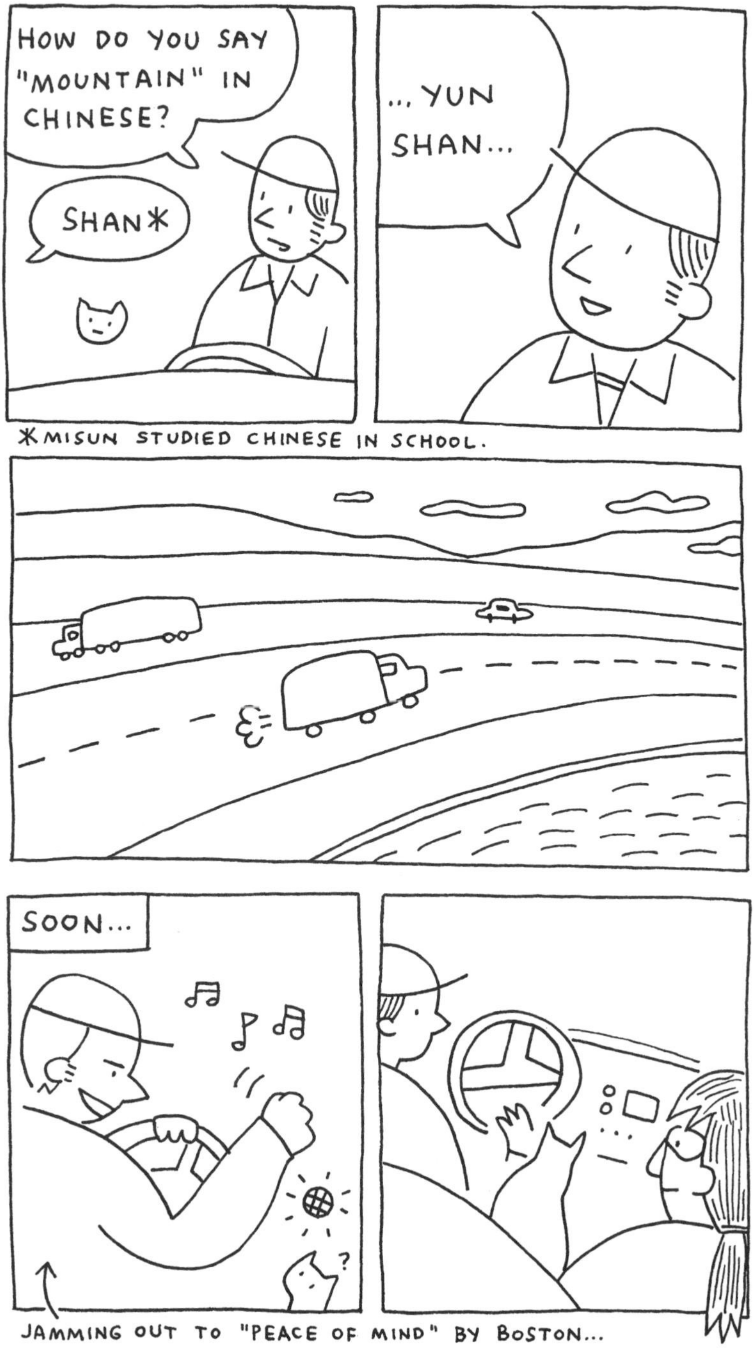

HOW DO YOU SAY "MOUNTAIN" IN CHINESE?
SHAN*
... YUN SHAN...
*MISUN STUDIED CHINESE IN SCHOOL.
SOON...
?
JAMMING OUT TO "PEACE OF MIND" BY BOSTON...

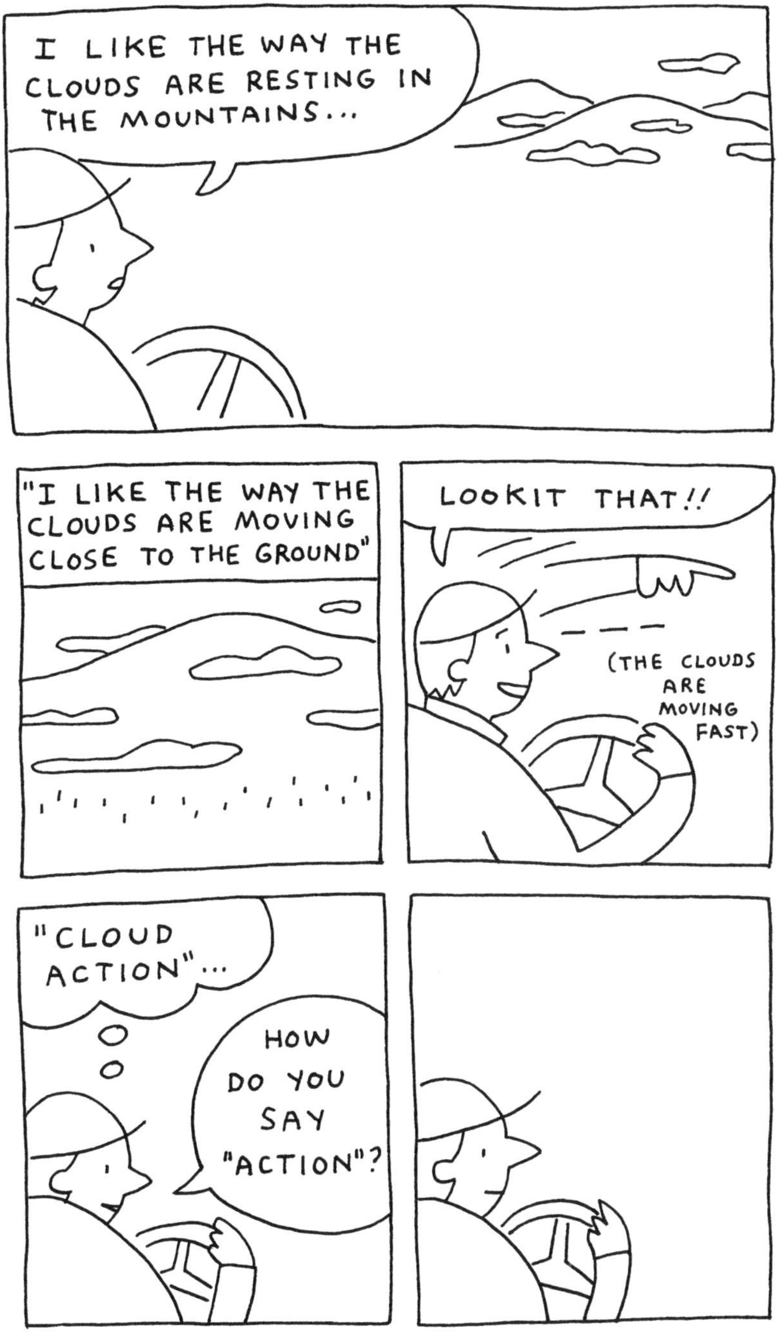
I LIKE THE WAY THE CLOUDS ARE RESTING IN THE MOUNTAINS...
"I LIKE THE WAY THE CLOUDS ARE MOVING CLOSE TO THE GROUND"
LOOKIT THAT!!
(THE CLOUDS ARE MOVING FAST)
"CLOUD ACTION"...
HOW DO YOU SAY "ACTION"?

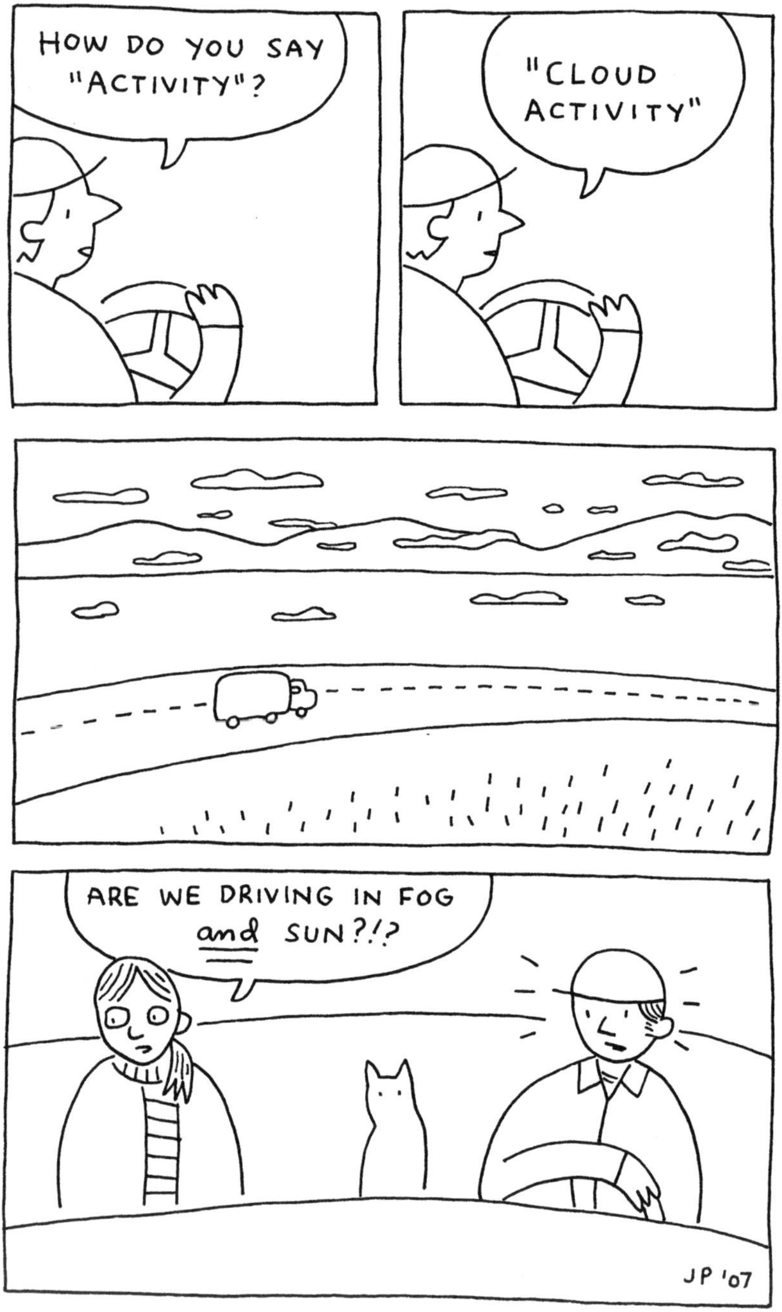
HOW DO YOU SAY "ACTIVITY"?
"CLOUD ACTIVITY"
ARE WE DRIVING IN FOG and SUN?!?
JP '07

-HAPPENED NOV. 3, 2006 OUTSIDE BATTLE MOUNTAIN, NEVADA- ♡

CLOUD MOUNTAIN PT. 2

BY JOHN + MISUN, HAPPENED 11/3/06, DRAWN 1/20/07 (10/3/07) 3:AM

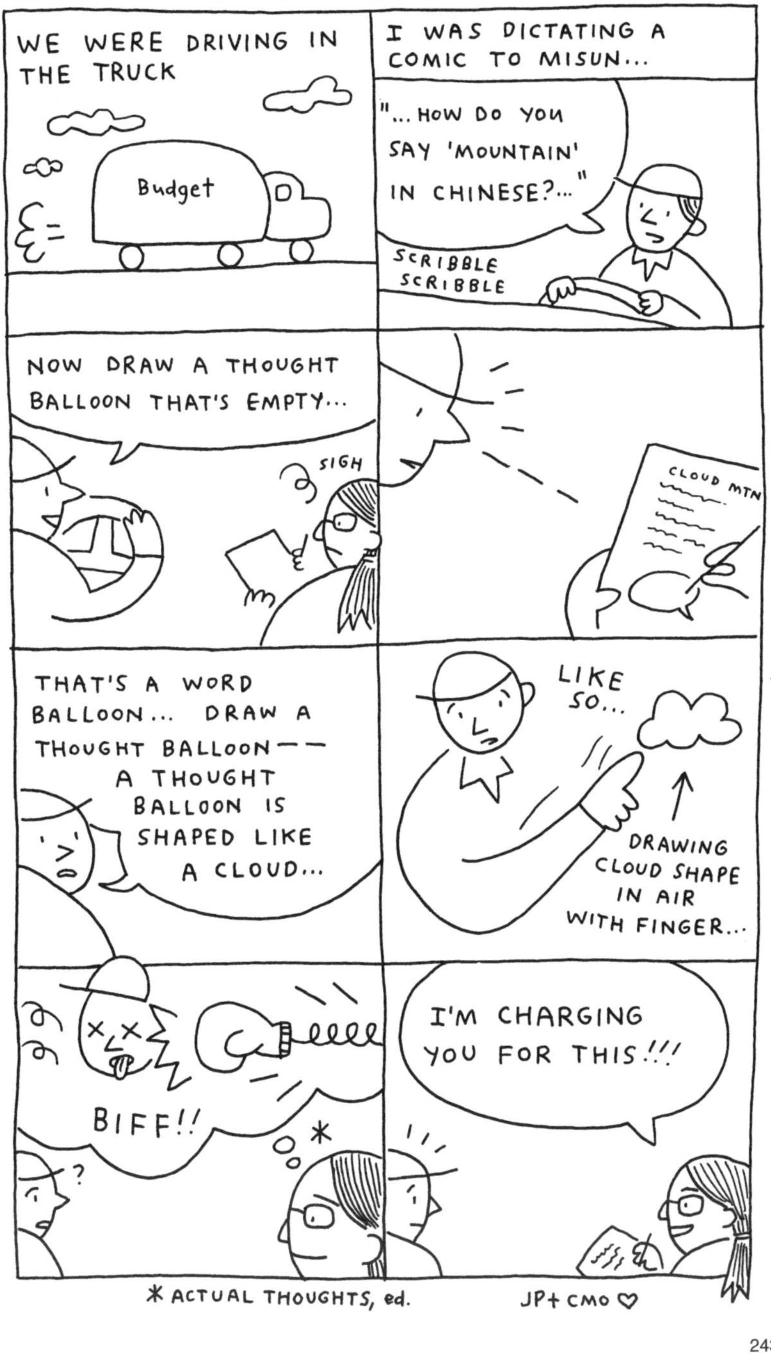

* ACTUAL THOUGHTS, ed.   JP+CMO ♡

7 WKS OF SNOW / HEAD FOR THE HILLS

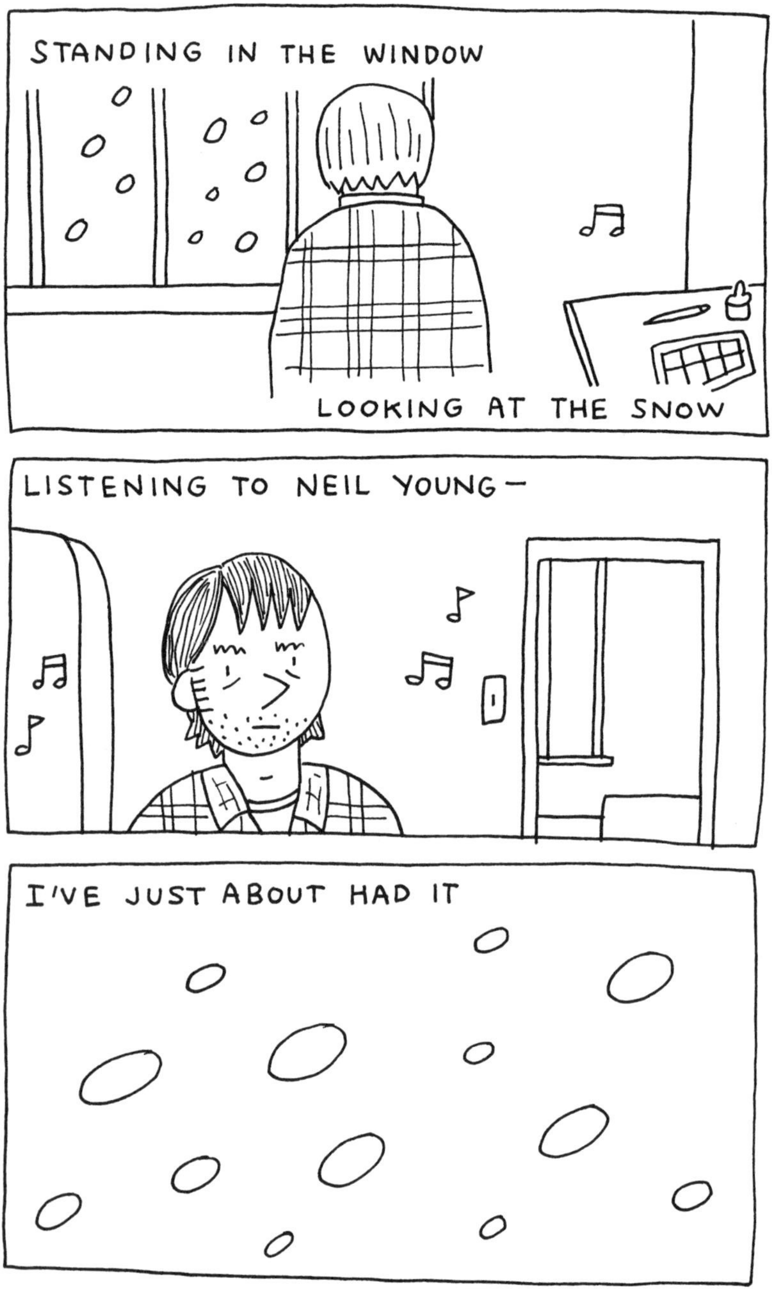
STANDING IN THE WINDOW
LOOKING AT THE SNOW
LISTENING TO NEIL YOUNG—
I'VE JUST ABOUT HAD IT

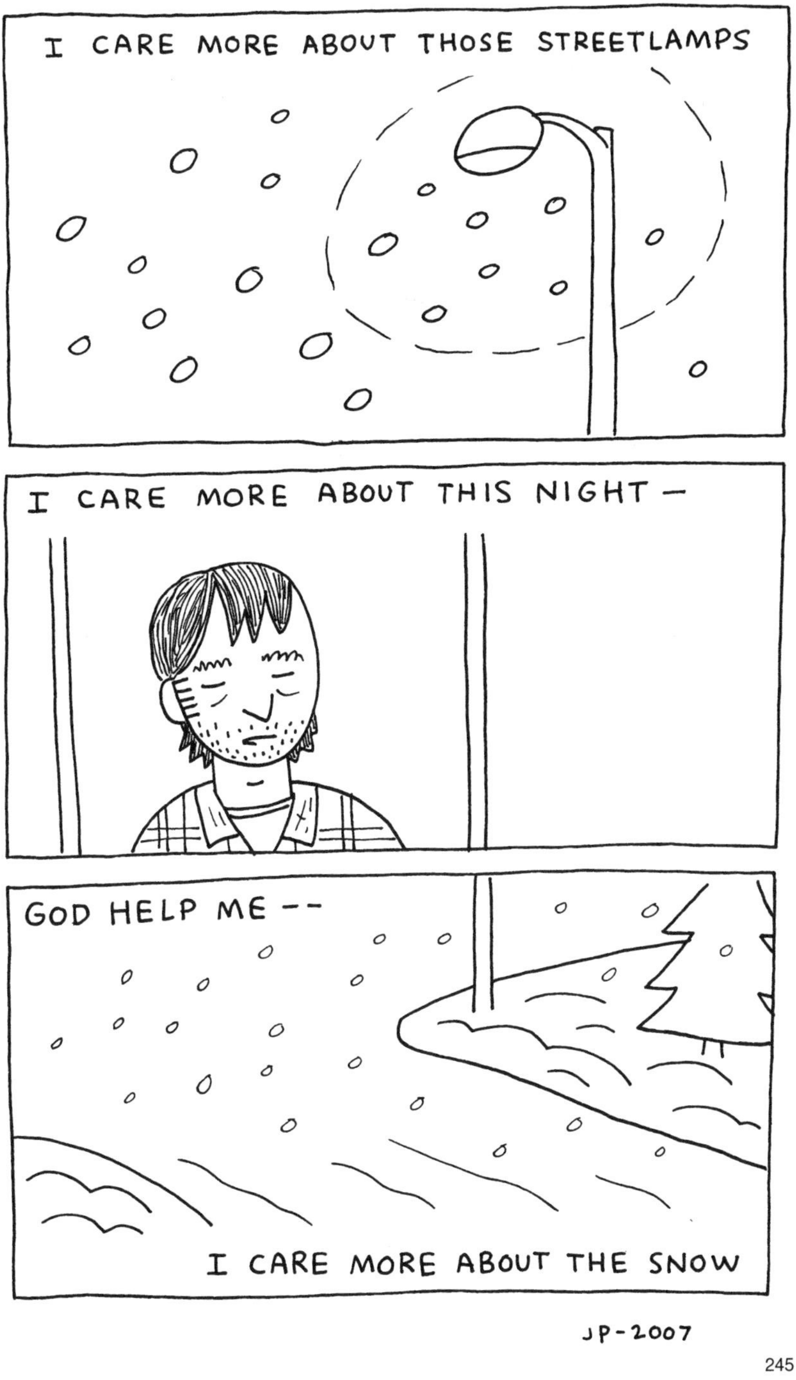
I CARE MORE ABOUT THOSE STREETLAMPS
I CARE MORE ABOUT THIS NIGHT —
GOD HELP ME --
I CARE MORE ABOUT THE SNOW
JP-2007

JOHN P. IN:

ANTHILL

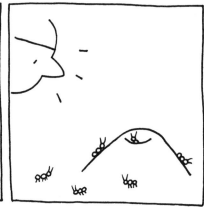

NOTHING MATTERS
EXCEPT THIS
ANTHILL

2007

JOHN P. + MAISIE ♡ IN: BREATHE...

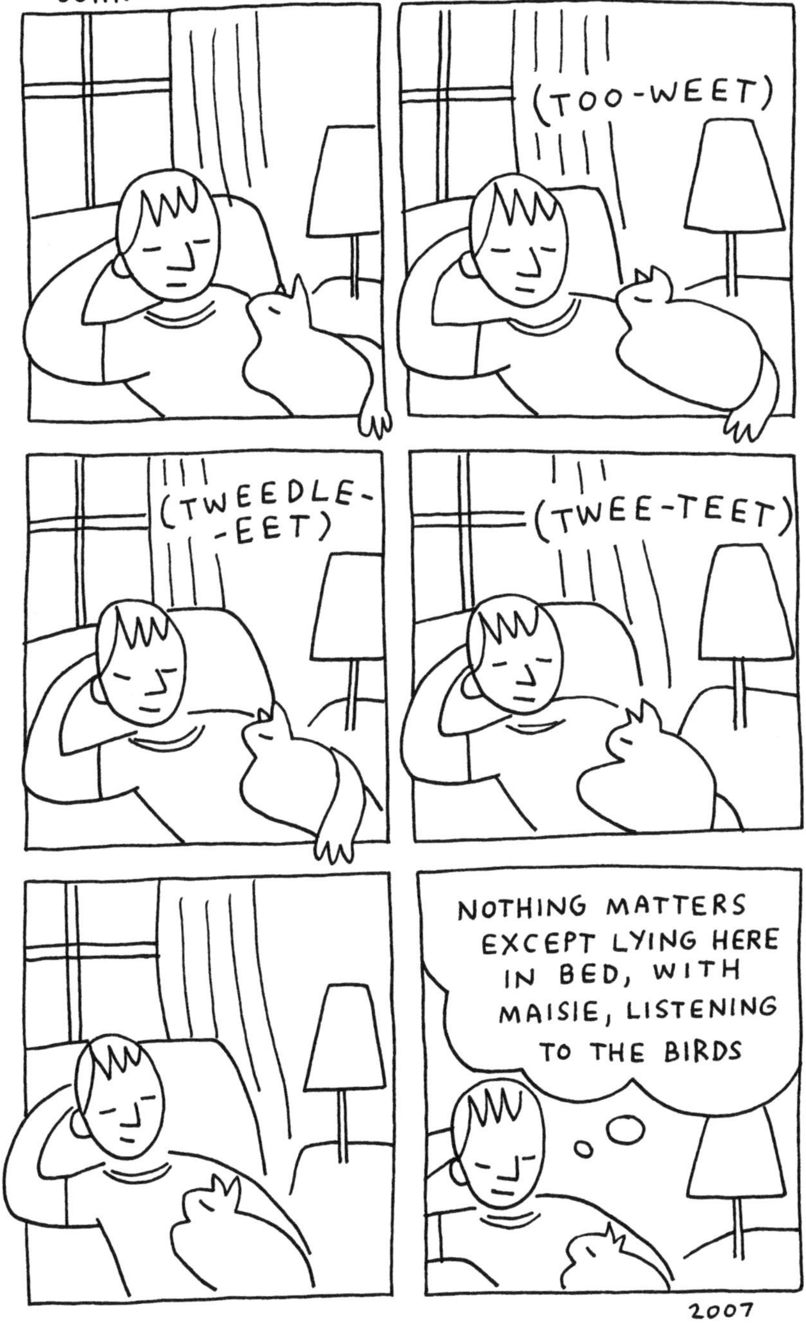
(TOO-WEET)
(TWEEDLE--EET)
(TWEE-TEET)
NOTHING MATTERS EXCEPT LYING HERE IN BED, WITH MAISIE, LISTENING TO THE BIRDS
2007

88th and FEDERAL

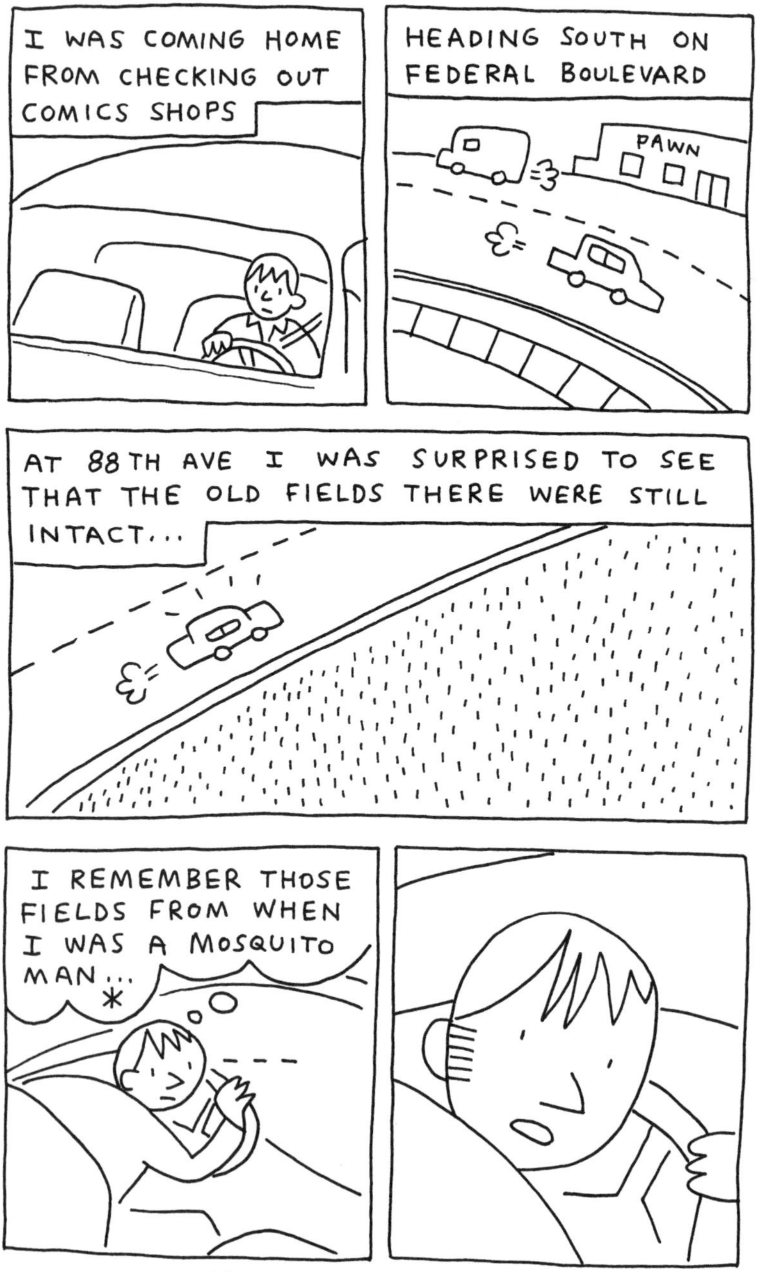
I WAS COMING HOME FROM CHECKING OUT COMICS SHOPS
HEADING SOUTH ON FEDERAL BOULEVARD
PAWN
AT 88TH AVE I WAS SURPRISED TO SEE THAT THE OLD FIELDS THERE WERE STILL INTACT...
I REMEMBER THOSE FIELDS FROM WHEN I WAS A MOSQUITO MAN... *

* Mid '90s (ed.)

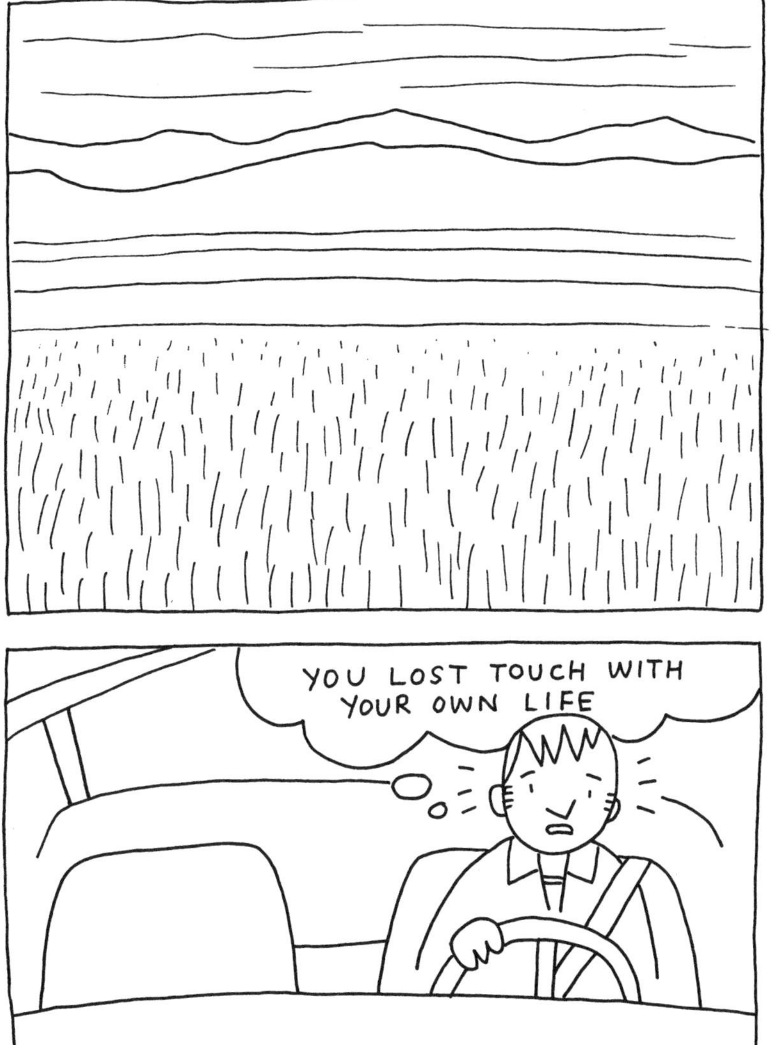
YOU LOST TOUCH WITH YOUR OWN LIFE

JOHN P. - HAPPENED
SPRING 2007

DIOGENES OF SINOPE

DIOGENES was born in Sinope, an Ionian settlement on the Black Sea (at present-day Sinop, Turkey), circa 412 B.C. At some point he was exiled from Sinope for "adulterating the coinage" and travelled to Athens, where he became a student of the philosopher Antisthenes.

Antisthenes had studied under Socrates, and had founded a "school" of philosophy called CYNICISM (from the Greek "kynikos", meaning "Like a dog."). Cynics "held the view that virtue is the only good and that its essence lies in self-control and independence." (Merriam-Websters Collegiate Dictionary, 10th ed., 1993)

The object of Cynicism was to achieve true personal freedom and self-realization within everyday life, and its adherents used unconventional methods to that end, disregarding social customs, public opinion, and popularity, as well as traditional notions of wealth and honor. Cynics turned superficial values upside-down in their quest for true value.

Diogenes, inspired by watching the adaptability of a mouse, took residence in a tub outside the Temple of Cybele, and taught there through the example of his life.

On a voyage to Aegina, Diogenes was captured by pirates, and offered for sale as a slave on the island of Crete. When asked by the auctioneer what his job skills were, he replied "I can govern men" and asked to be sold to a man who needed a master. He was sold to a Corinthian, Xeniades, who made Diogenes a teacher to his children.

Diogenes lived the rest of his life in Corinth, and died there in 323 B.C.

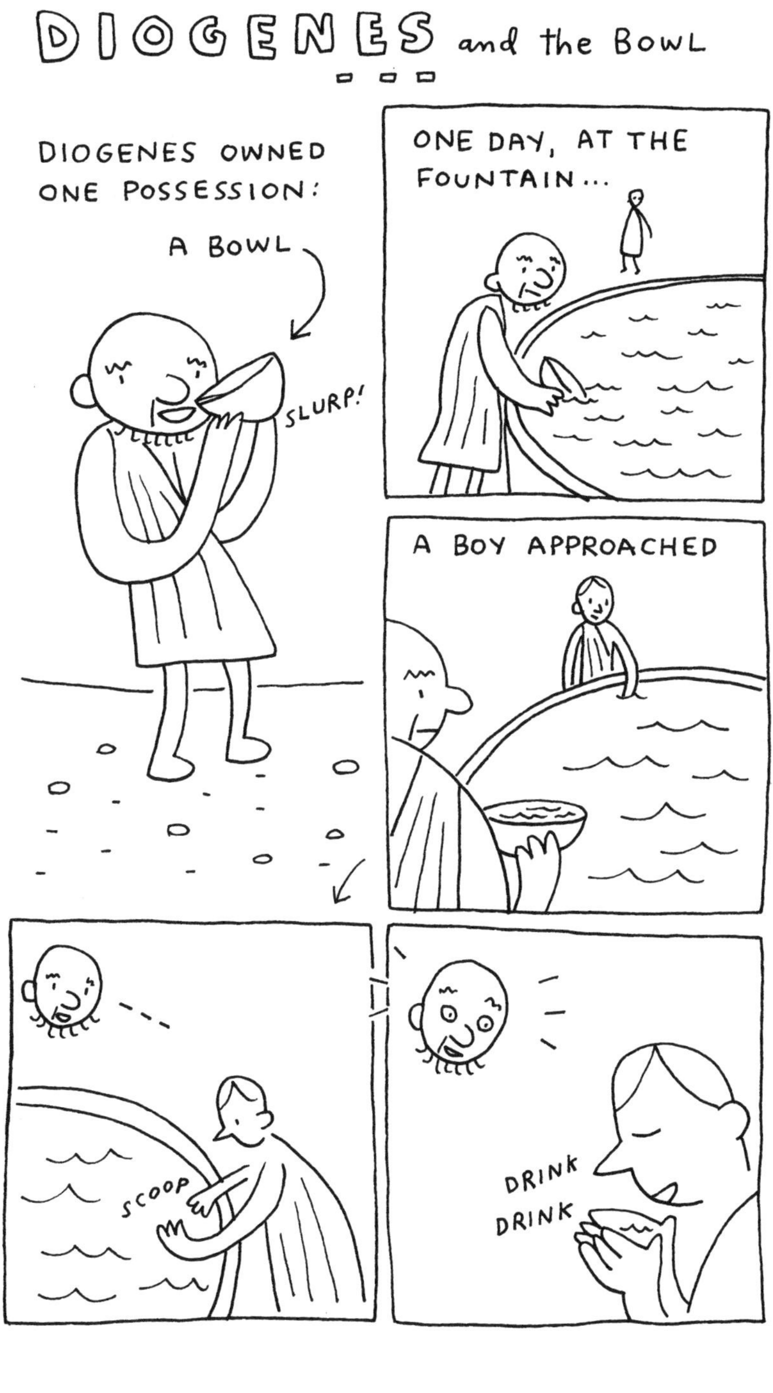
DIOGENES and the BOWL
DIOGENES OWNED ONE POSSESSION:
A BOWL
SLURP!
ONE DAY, AT THE FOUNTAIN...
A BOY APPROACHED
SCOOP
DRINK DRINK

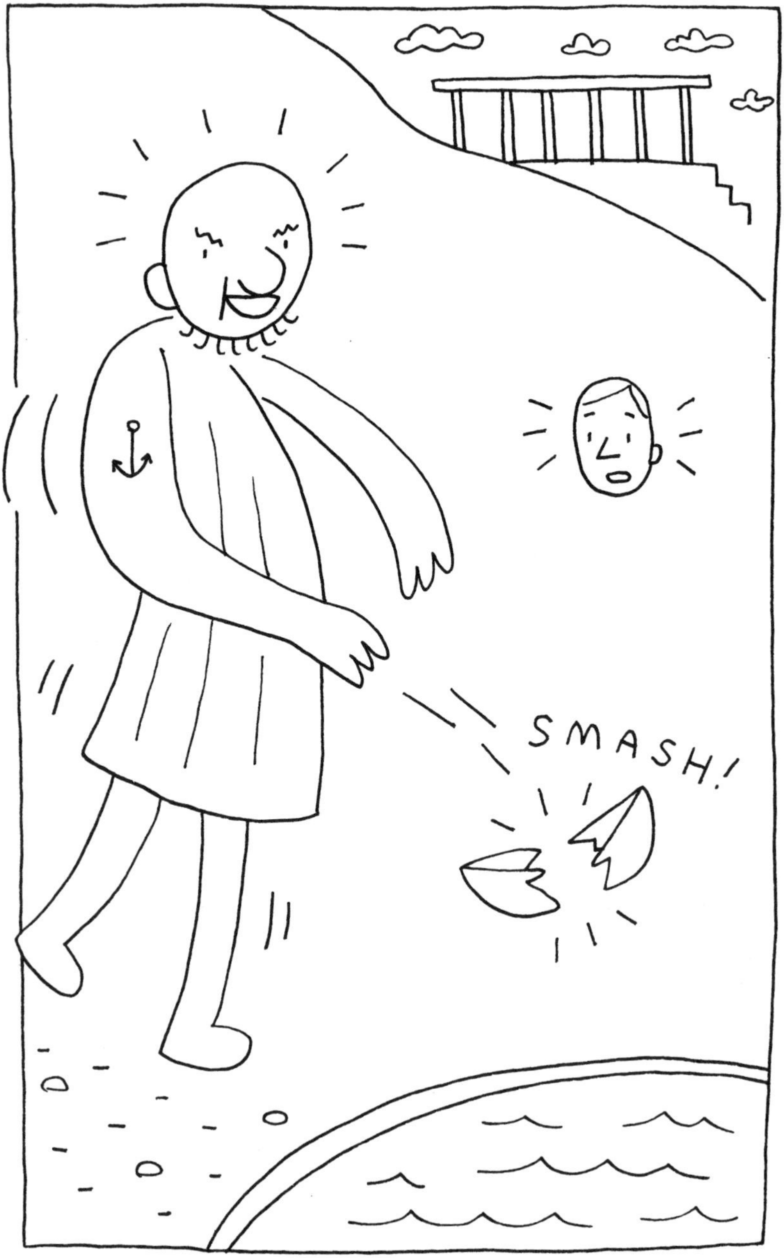
SMASH!

JP 2007

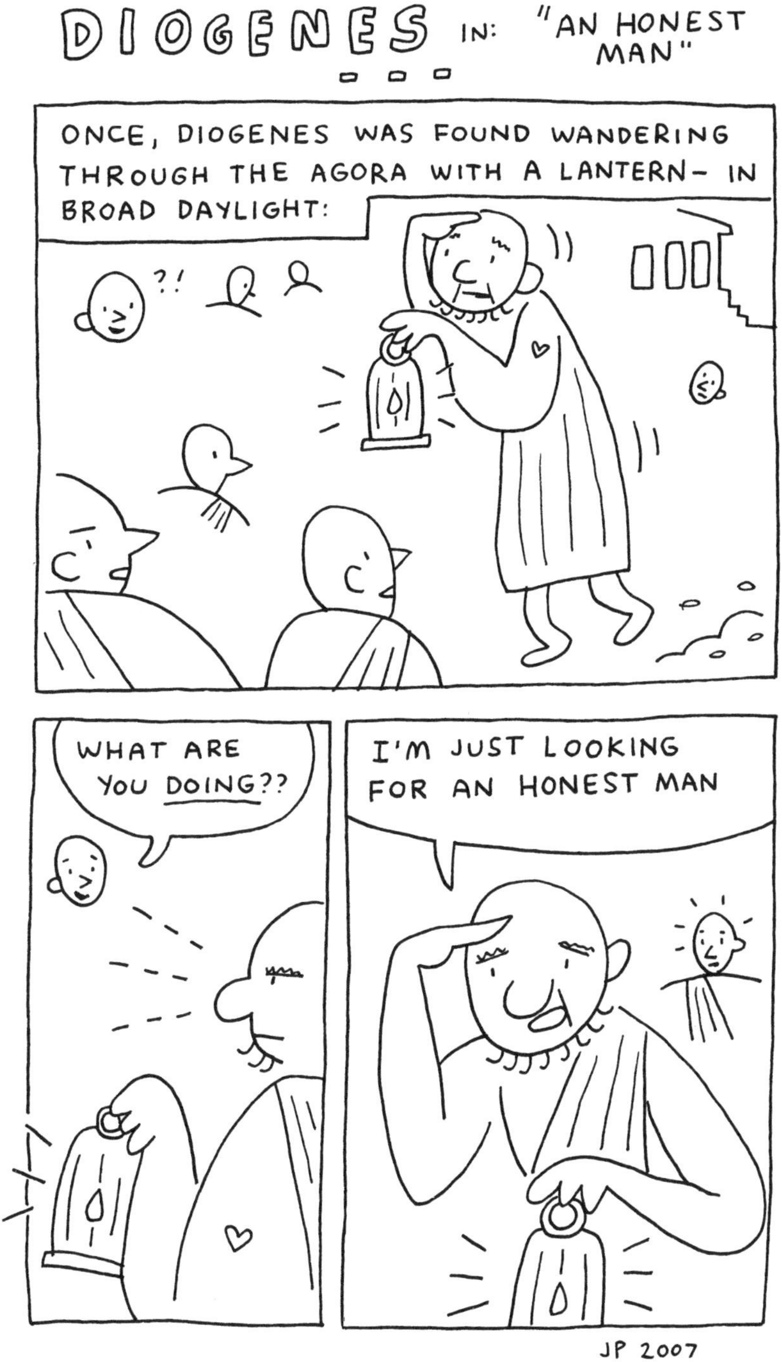
DIOGENES IN: "AN HONEST MAN"
ONCE, DIOGENES WAS FOUND WANDERING THROUGH THE AGORA WITH A LANTERN– IN BROAD DAYLIGHT:
?!
WHAT ARE YOU DOING??
I'M JUST LOOKING FOR AN HONEST MAN
JP 2007

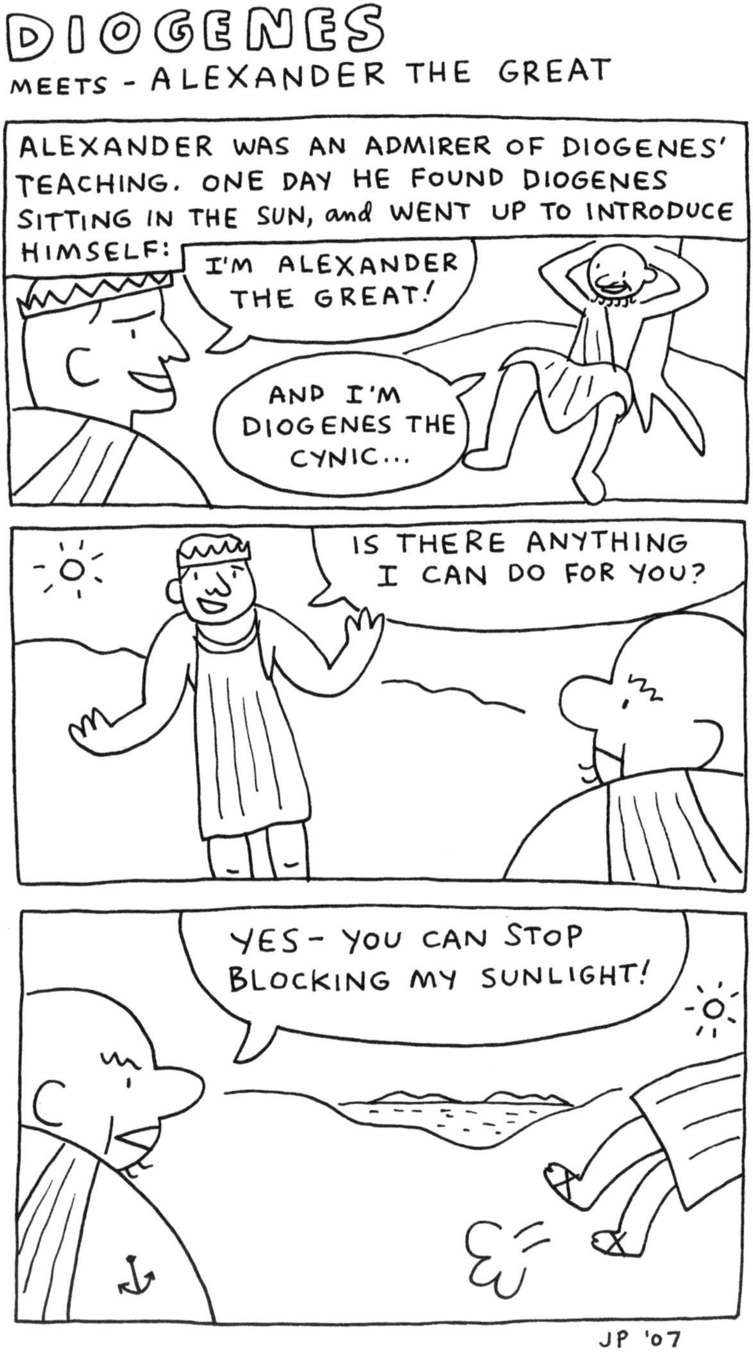
DIOGENES
MEETS - ALEXANDER THE GREAT
ALEXANDER WAS AN ADMIRER OF DIOGENES' TEACHING. ONE DAY HE FOUND DIOGENES SITTING IN THE SUN, and WENT UP TO INTRODUCE HIMSELF:
I'M ALEXANDER THE GREAT!
AND I'M DIOGENES THE CYNIC...
IS THERE ANYTHING I CAN DO FOR YOU?
YES - YOU CAN STOP BLOCKING MY SUNLIGHT!
JP '07

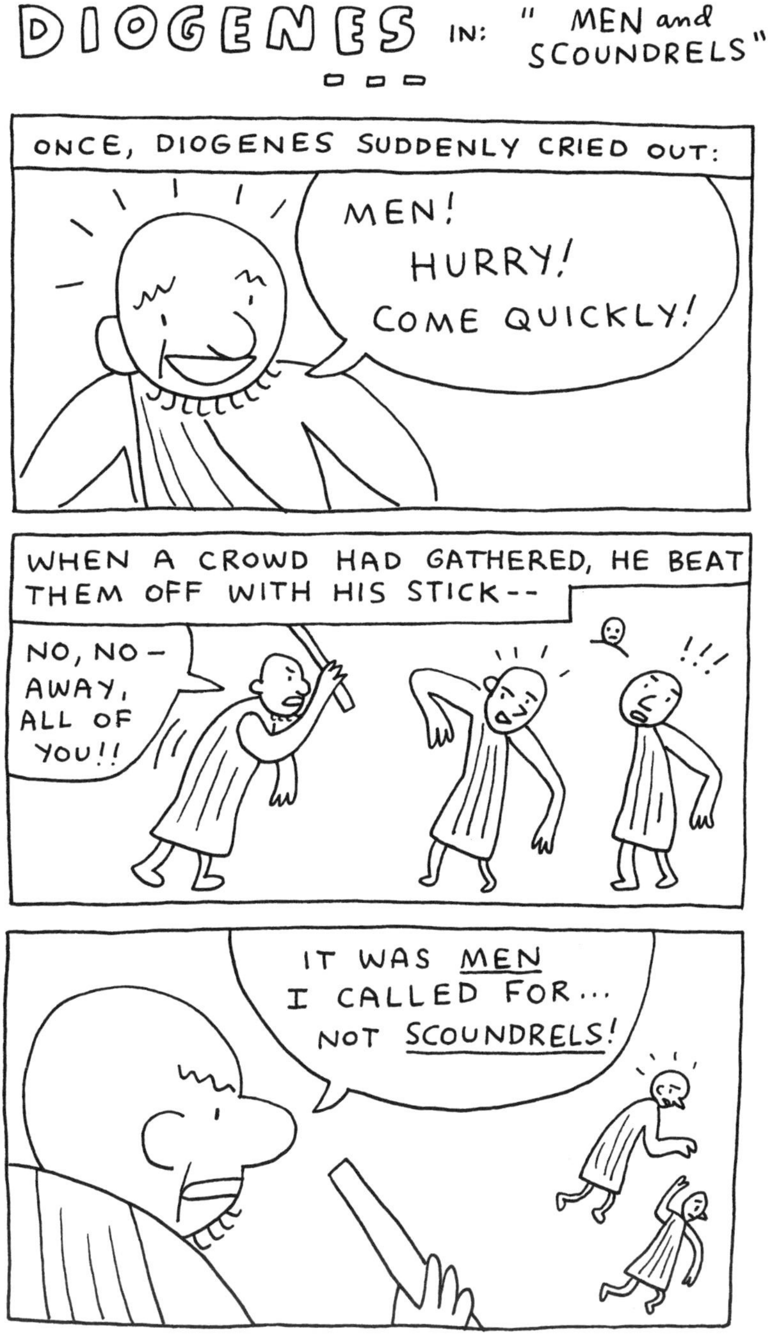
DIOGENES IN: " MEN and SCOUNDRELS "
ONCE, DIOGENES SUDDENLY CRIED OUT:
MEN! HURRY! COME QUICKLY!
WHEN A CROWD HAD GATHERED, HE BEAT THEM OFF WITH HIS STICK--
NO, NO- AWAY, ALL OF YOU!!
IT WAS MEN I CALLED FOR... NOT SCOUNDRELS!
JP 2007

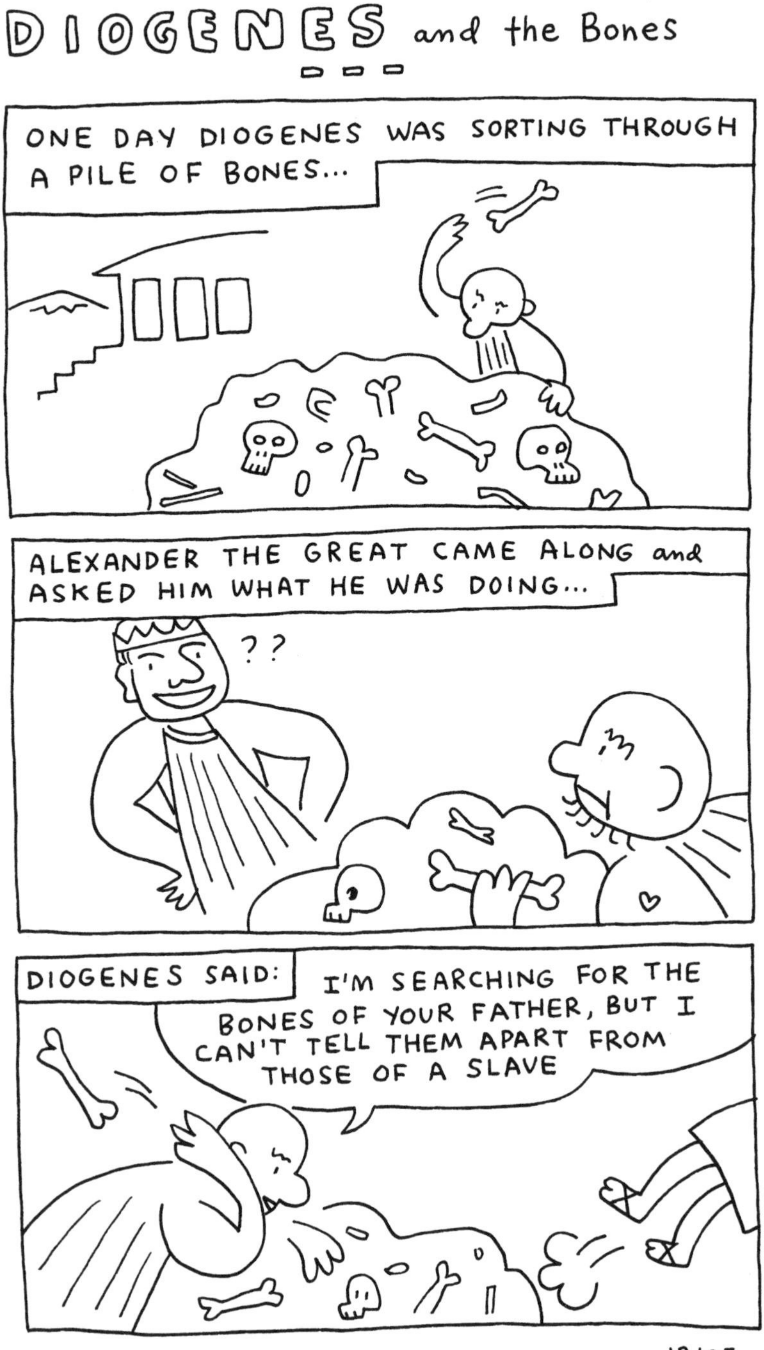
DIOGENES and the Bones
ONE DAY DIOGENES WAS SORTING THROUGH A PILE OF BONES...
ALEXANDER THE GREAT CAME ALONG and ASKED HIM WHAT HE WAS DOING...
??
DIOGENES SAID:
I'M SEARCHING FOR THE BONES OF YOUR FATHER, BUT I CAN'T TELL THEM APART FROM THOSE OF A SLAVE
JP '07

THE KING-CAT TOP-FORTY OCT.'06–SEPT.'07

SAN FRANCISCO

1. Carmelite Chapel and Monastery of Cristo Rey, Fulton & Parker
2. Thinking about the Dick Van Dyke Show
3. Bob Wills Records – AW HAW!
4. The Full Monty movie (1997, Peter Catanneo, dir.) -- ★★ CHUFFING EXCELLENT! ★★
5. Walking around STOW LAKE
6. Koret Recreation Center, USF (Bears win on Monday Night Football!)
7. Shakey Bones band – LIVE on Haight Street
8. Bob Dylan Modern Times (Columbia Recs.)
9. Nick Lowe Basher (Greatest Hits) (Columbia)
10. Elvis Presley – "Clean Up Your Own Backyard" ★★★★★
11. San Francisco! ♥

ON THE ROAD

1. Staying up for 39 Hours (?!!)
2. Truckee River Valley – Cottonwoods turning Yellow
3. Sunset in Reno
4. Rest Area of 1,000 Smells (and all of them good!): Sage, mint, chocolate, strawberry Ice Cream; Cosgrave, Nevada, 11/2/06
5. Battle Mountain Clouds ♡
6. Buck walking around Main St., Rawlins, Wyo. 11/4/06
7. Denver Lights

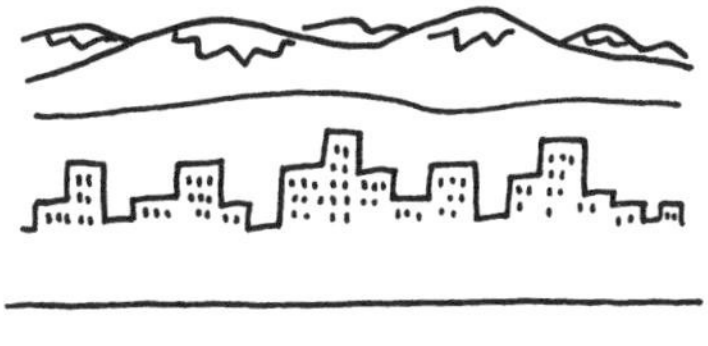

DENVER

1. Old Friends ♡
2. Blue Mustard (plant)
3. Thinking about Mark Twain
4. Denver Public Library System (and JEFFCO)
5. American Hardcore movie (Paul Rachman/Steven Blush, 2006)
6. Neil Young On the Beach (and Revisiting Tonight's the Night – "Mellow My Mind"!) (Reprise)
7. "Weeds of the West"
8. Crossword Puzzles!
9. Sketches of Frank Gehry – movie (dir. Sydney Pollack, 2005)
10. FOXES
11. The Who – The Kids Are Alright DVD and Who By Numbers (MCA)
12. TRAIN WHISTLES and THUNDERSTORMS ★★★★
13. "Land of Make-Believe / A Child's Wonder Land" Poster by JARO HESS – Brought back memories
14. That day we drove to Golden ♡
15. Walt & Skeezix book two, by Frank King – Amazing! (D+Q)
16. GO BEARS! ☺☹
17. Watching poppies bloom behind the dumpster
18. Mountains looking down over Tejon Street, Colo. Spgs.
19. Denver Zine Fest – 3/24/07 ♡
20. Crown Hill Park
21. Bats
22. Nighthawk! (8/12/07)
23. Marx Bros. A Night at the Opera & Groucho Marx – You Bet Your Life DVD (The Best Of...)
24. Bob Dylan Oh Mercy album (Columbia)

MORE TOP-FORTY:

25. Garden of the Gods (with Delaine, Lee, and Misun)
26. The Beatles "Baby You're A Rich Man" (Capitol / EMI)
27. Clear Creek Greenbelt, Wheat Ridge (Fox, Heron and Wild Licorice sightings!)
28. Mint leaves in the alley
29. Yes: the day "Siberian Khatru" came on the radio AND: FRAGILE / CLOSE TO THE EDGE (Atlantic / Rhino)
30. Steve Miller "Jet Airliner" (Classic Rock Radio)(w/Intro!)
31. POPEYE VOL. ONE - DVD Set It exists!
32. Ermanno Olmi films: GREAT! Il Posto (1961) and I Fidanzati (1963) ★★★★★
33. Pull My Daisy - Beat Film by Robt. Frank / Alfred Leslie, 1959 (I never saw it before!)
34. Pike's Peak and Turk's Head (mountains)

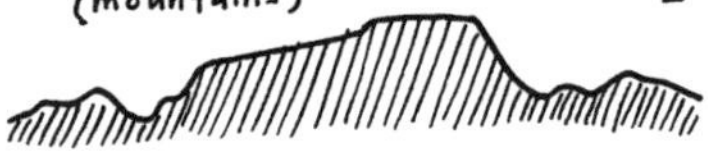

35. Sphinx Moths
36. Led Zeppelin "Out On The Tiles" (Atlantic)
37. The day "Brass in Pocket" made me cry
38. Felt Pilotes Reunion - 8/11/07 ♡
39. Walking around with Patrick Porter
40. Donal visits - 8/30 - 9/2/07 ♡
41. Andrew Goldsworthy: RIVERS and TIDES movie (2001 - dir. Thos. Riedelsheimer) ★★★
42. Zine Readings - Ft. Collins and Denver (Denver Zine Library!) ♡
43. Cats of Mirikitani documentary (Independent Lens / PBS, 2006) dir. LINDA HATTENDORF (Doc. about homeless Japanese-American artist in NYC)
44. Wild Parrots of Telegraph Hill movie - Almost made me wanna go back (dir. Judy Irving, 2004)
45. "Wild" Grapes (DENVER ALLEYS)
46. Patrick Porter Die Wanda-land CD and live performance 8/11/07 (CD on Greyday Records) ★★★★★★★★★
47. Walking / Colorado Skies
48. Brad Warner Shut Up & Sit Down book
49. Little spiders on the ceiling fan / TV antenna
50. Steely Dan "Peg"
51. Jack Kerouac - ORIGINAL On the Road scroll display, Denver Public Library
52. Robins start singing at 3:30 AM (Spring)
53. Rocky Mountain Ditch ♡
54. Home to Roost BBC TV show from the 80's! (PBS)
55. Kicking stones down Ames Street w/ Misun
56. Watching Time-Life music info-mercials w/ Misun ♡
57. My beautiful wife Misun ♡

and MAISIE KUKOC
my love

NATURE Notes

FOX SIGHTINGS —
    Visual IDs: 9 [a,b]
    Auditory IDs: 1 [c]
    Near Misses: 1 [d]

(as of 9/27/07)

a. One day I decided to go look for someplace the foxes might have a den. I thought of that one dead-end street, where the ditch is overgrown and wild, and headed in that direction. Rounding the corner, where all the cats hang out by the pick-up trucks, I saw a RED FOX sitting on the cab of one of the trucks.

I watched it for awhile until it got nervous, and climbed down, padding along the edge of the church, eyeing me warily. It looked old. I tracked it around the corner, where I saw it eat some grass, vomit, and then take off down the alley like a silent breeze.

b. One afternoon I thought to check out a nearby alley that I'd never been down before. Glancing up at the garages there, set into the hillside, I noticed a fox sitting on the flat roof of one of the garages. It looked at me, then sat down, curled up like a cat, and, covering its snout with its bushy tail, fell asleep.

c. We were awakened early one morning by a strange cry coming from the alley. It was chilling — like a human scream. Turns out it was "The Vixen's Wail," the mating call of a female fox.

d. I was coming around the corner towards home. Jane said, "Did you see that fox that just went by?" I hadn't. "It just came by; it ran down the whole block, in the middle of the street."

"WEEDS OF THE WEST"

In the Spring, weeds started coming up, even though it was still cold. I was glad to see them; they were my old friends. First was the Blue Mustard. Some people say it has a disagreeable odor, but to me it smells like Spring. Then the Flixweed, and so on.

EXCERCISE: Think about the names of plants, and apply them to your own life.

Poppies, Hollyhocks, Grapes, grow wild in the alleys. (The Grapes are so fragrant, the air smells like soda-pop.)

Misun enjoys Sweet Clover (Yellow and white), various mints.

WEED INVENTORY (partial)

- Blue Mustard — Chorispora tenella
- Flixweed — Descurainia sophia
- Shepherd's Purse — Capsella bursa-pastoris
- Common Lambsquarters — Chenopodium album
- Curly Dock — Rumex crispus
- Prickly Lettuce — Lactuca serriola
- Western Salsify — Tragopogon dubius
- Field Bindweed — Convolvulus arvensis
- Field Pennycress — Thlapsi arvense
- Russian Thistle — Salsola iberica
- Chicory — Cichorium intybus
- Puncturevine — Tribulus terrestris
- Common Mallow — Malva neglecta
- Rocky Mountain Beeplant — Clenome serrulata
- Yellow Sweet Clover — Melilotus officinalis
- White Sweet Clover — Melilotus alba
- Clasping Pepperweed — Lepidium perfoliatum
- Tumble Mustard — Sisymbrium altissimum
- Showy Milkweed — Asclepius speciosa
- Greenflower Pepperweed — Lepidium densiflorum
- Common Mullein — Verbascum thapsus
- Annual Prickle Poppy — Argemone polyanthemos

First Ladybug of Spring: 2/18/07, front yard.

If you've never seen Colorado skies, you should come out sometime and take a look.

7,000,000 birds each year are killed by the chemicals Americans apply to their lawns. (Source: Audubon.org)

There's nothing phony about the Natural World.

Sphinx moths arrive mid-summer, and hover over the Four O'Clocks.

Watching a tiny spider weave a web between the hairs on my arm.

Did you hear about the multi-acre web communally created by millions of spiders, outside Dallas? Scientists don't know what to make of it.

Reminded me of the enormous web made by dozens of big Barn Spiders on the Open/Closed sign outside the Elgin Library one summer.

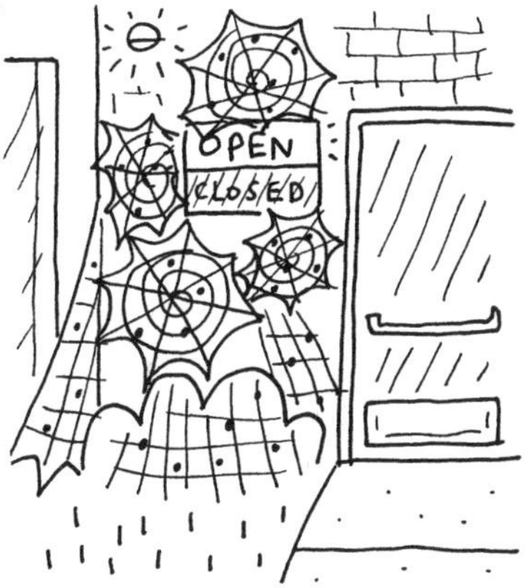
OPEN
CLOSED

Tried to grow a beard.

Following the old irrigation ditch where it goes underground, pops up blocks away, runs under the sidewalk.

Flickers, Crows, Magpies, Sparrows, Robins, Pigeons, Mourning Doves, et al.

Spring-time: Robins start singing at 3:30 in the morning, then again each evening till eleven.

Late Summer, the scent of apples rotting on the sidewalk.

SQUIRREL ACROBAT

SQUIRREL A is confronted by aggressive SQUIRREL B, on the power-line wire across the street.

"B" threatens, stamps, chatters; "A" steps back but doesn't want to give up ground. SQUIRREL B Repeatedly charges SQUIRREL A, then Retreats.

Finally, both squirrels have had enough. They Race toward each other at high speed, in what appears to be an inevitable head-on collision. I watch in disbelief as, just before the moment of impact, SQUIRREL A suddenly spins upside-down on the wire, Runs past SQUIRREL B underneath, and jumps into a nearby tree.

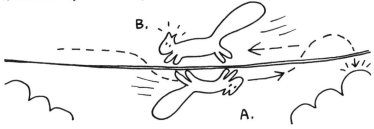

SQUIRREL B puts on the brakes and looks visibly confused.

Leaves fall.

WARM LIGHT

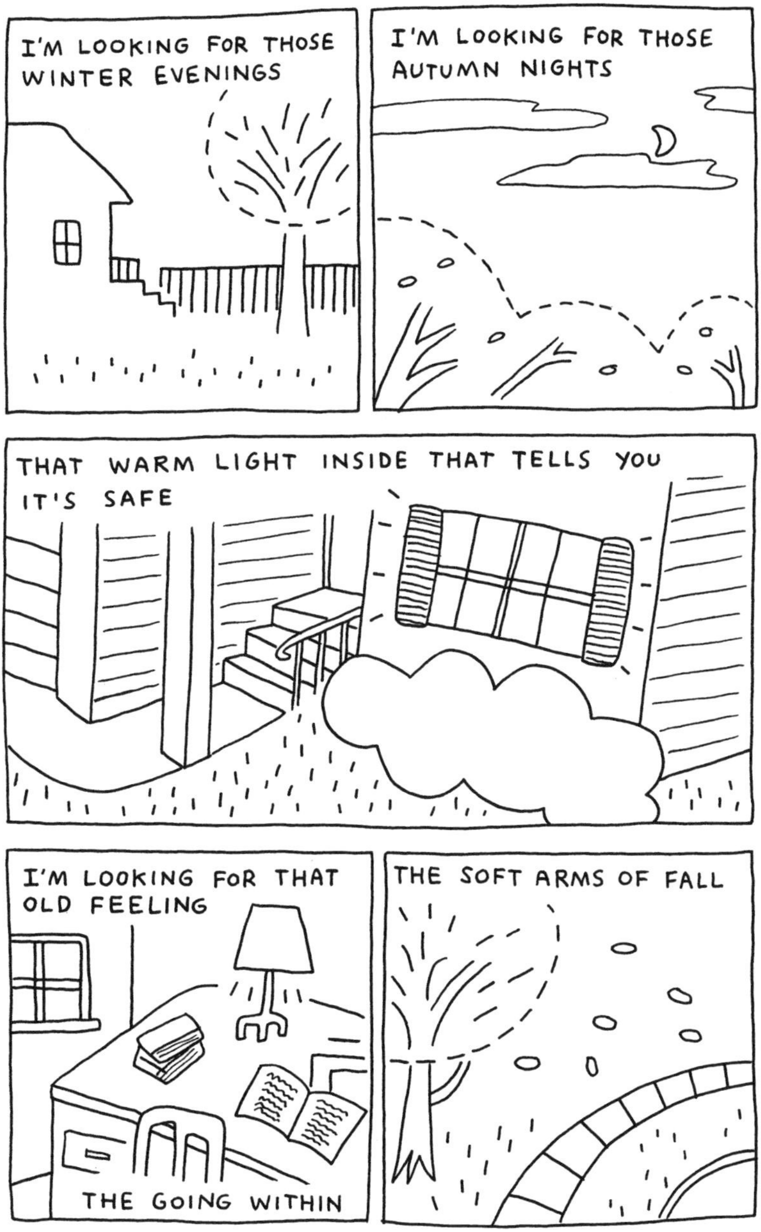
I'M LOOKING FOR THOSE WINTER EVENINGS
I'M LOOKING FOR THOSE AUTUMN NIGHTS
THAT WARM LIGHT INSIDE THAT TELLS YOU IT'S SAFE
I'M LOOKING FOR THAT OLD FEELING
THE GOING WITHIN
THE SOFT ARMS OF FALL

JP-SEPT. '07

FEEDING THE BIRDS at the FRUITFUL YIELD

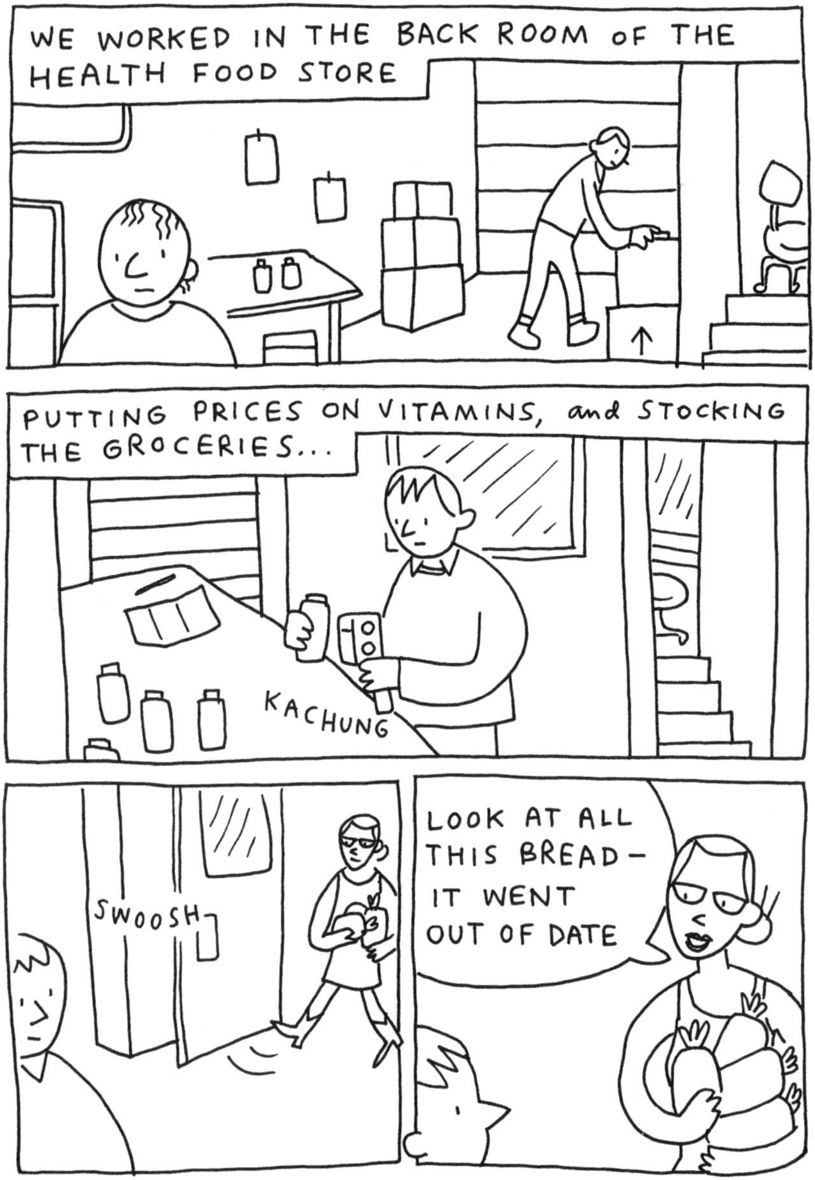
WE WORKED IN THE BACK ROOM OF THE HEALTH FOOD STORE
PUTTING PRICES ON VITAMINS, and STOCKING THE GROCERIES...
KACHUNG
SWOOSH
LOOK AT ALL THIS BREAD - IT WENT OUT OF DATE

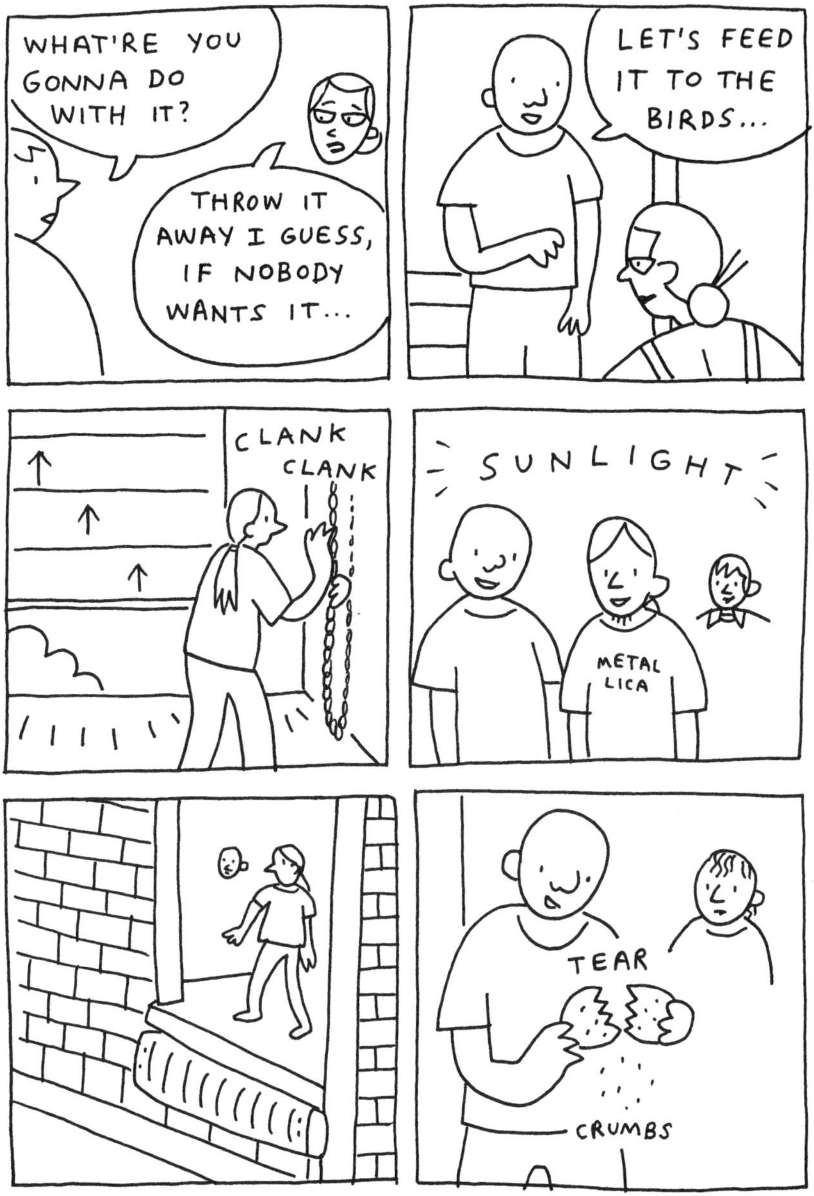
WHAT'RE YOU GONNA DO WITH IT?
THROW IT AWAY I GUESS, IF NOBODY WANTS IT...
LET'S FEED IT TO THE BIRDS...
CLANK
CLANK
SUNLIGHT
METAL LICA
TEAR
CRUMBS

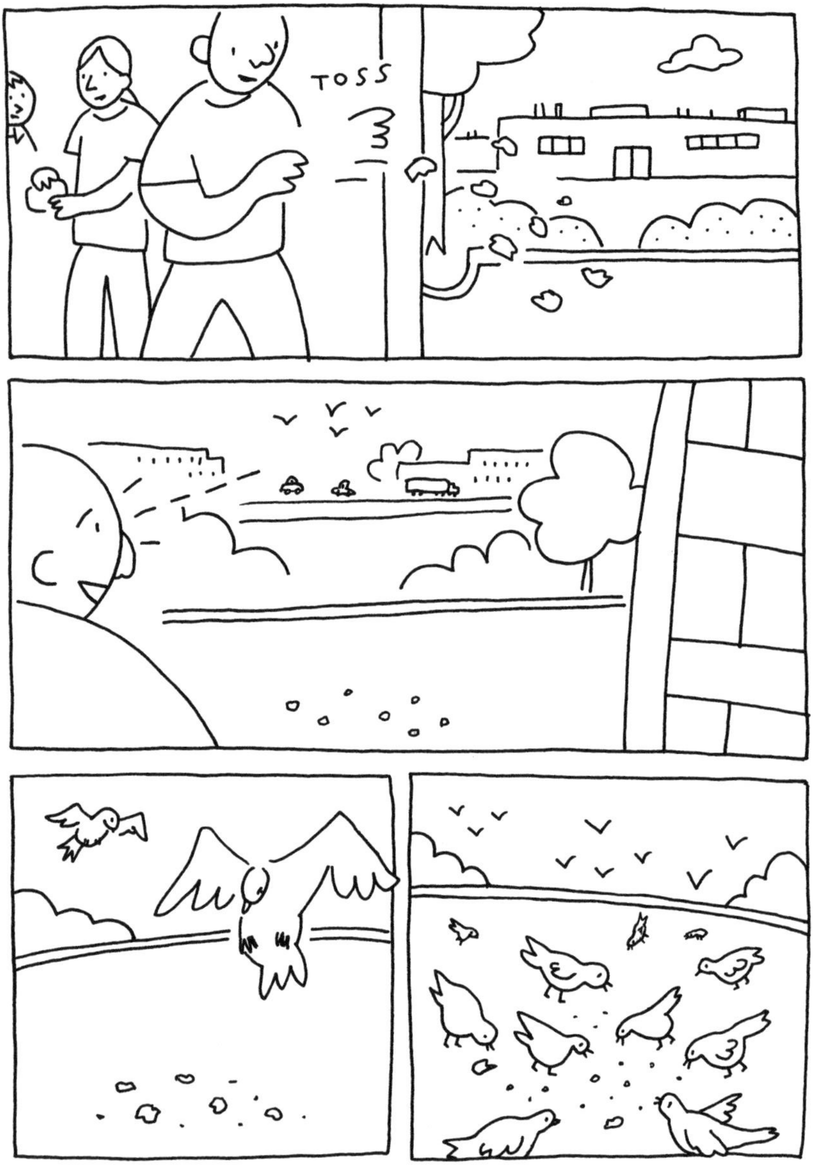
TOSS

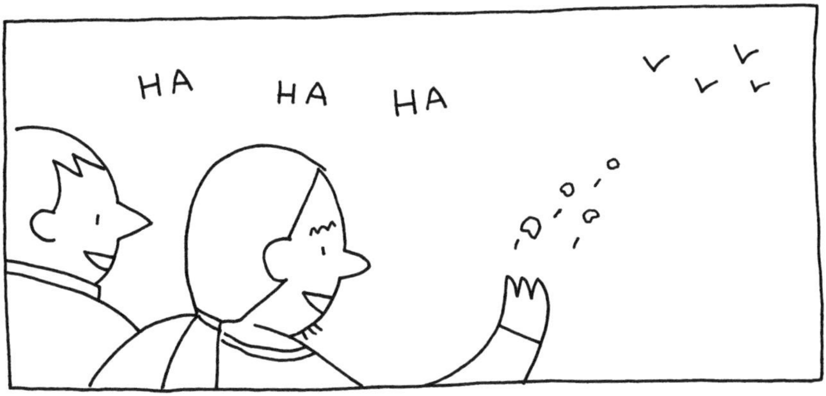
HA HA HA

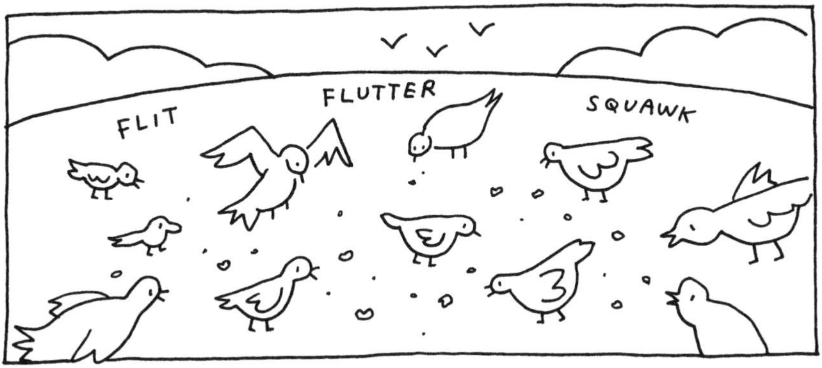
FLIT
FLUTTER
SQUAWK

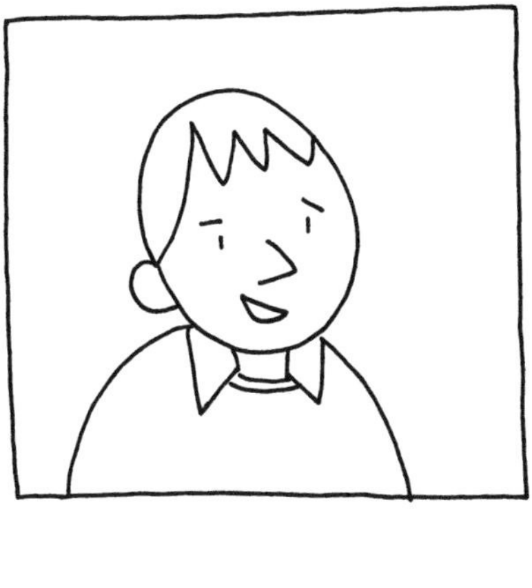

I WAS HOME.

HAPPENED 1998 · SCHAUMBURG, ILL.
DRAWN 9/19/07 · DENVER, COLO. J.P.

PURR

FROM LONE MOUNTAIN
Collecting King-Cat Comics #62-68 (2003-2007)

Notes by John P.

When the first comics included in this collection were made, I had just moved back to Denver, Colorado, with my fiancé Misun. The previous four years I'd lived in Elgin, Illinois, a few miles from where I had grown up, and there I'd stumbled my way through multiple personal difficulties, including serious mental and physical health issues, a divorce from my first wife, Kera, and several ensuing years of near solitude.

I had met Misun through the mail; she was a reader of my comic-zine *King-Cat*, and we had mutual friends in Denver. I was at an impasse in life, and Misun was showing me a way forward. We decided to move back to Denver (I'd lived there from 1992–1998), where it was sunny, cheaper than Chicago, and where she could continue her training in Traditional Chinese Medicine. I was heartbroken to leave Elgin, but after the strain of the previous couple years I was also looking forward to a fresh start and being able to focus on my comics work again, due to the lower cost of living.

At the time of our move, I was in the grip of a crippling case of obsessive compulsive disorder, one that had made it essentially impossible to draw my comics without a great deal of suffering (see also *Map of My Heart* and *The Hospital Suite*, from Drawn & Quarterly, 2009 and 2014, respectively). In this regard, relocating to Denver did me good. In Colorado's sunny climate, I felt the stories that had earlier been buried by anxiety begin to make their way back to the surface.

#62: August 2003.

Cover. 212 North Melrose Ave., Elgin Ill., where I lived from November 1998 through December 2002. This little Sears Roebuck kit house on the west side of town, built in 1925, was the closest thing I'd had to a home since childhood. (Kevin Huizenga taught me how to get the Zip-a-Tone® effect in Photoshop™.)

King-Cat Snornose, including Corrections and Clarifications.

[**Standing There Sweating**]. While I lived in Elgin I sat with a Zen Buddhist group and studied formally under my teacher, Susan Myoyu Andersen Roshi. This is just a memory of one Tuesday night after sitting, standing in the parking lot talking to Roshi.

March. You can see from the inscription that I drew this comic a mere five days after the fact. This was a sign that things were getting better—I was drawing more often and more freely. By the way, they did in fact have kites at Ace Hardware® that day.

Long Day. Upon our arrival in Denver I got a job at another health food store, but it was cheap enough to live there that I only had to work three days a week. This was like the perfect ratio for me—it got me out of the house and forced me to interact with people, but also left me enough free time that I started to develop some creative momentum. Drawing was becoming enjoyable again, especially compared to those last years in Elgin when my struggles with OCD made creative work almost impossible.

Fabyan Street Bridge. I was already trying to make sense of what I'd experienced while living in Elgin. Back there, there was so much personal history, each street corner, each lamp post and sidewalk crack felt imbued with memory and time. In panel two I'm remembering working in the area as a Mosquito Abatement Man during the 1980s; in panel three I'm remembering my solitary Friday nights in Elgin, driving down to Geneva to compulsively buy CDs and books in a desperate bid to fend off loneliness.

Although I loved Elgin, in my four years there I never met a single person to call a friend.* Even so, I sentimentally wanted to live there the rest of my life, in my little Sears kit house, and fantasized about becoming a beloved Elgin art-

---

*True to form, one week after arriving back in Denver I received not one, but two letters from cool artists living in Elgin, who had just discovered my presence there and wanted to know if I could meet up sometime.

ist, documenting and celebrating my adopted hometown. But it wasn't to be. One time, after my first book came out (*Perfect Example*, 2000), I sent a copy to the Elgin *Courier-News* in the hopes they might review it or do an article, like "Local Boy Does Good." Instead I came home one day to an answering machine message from the Arts Editor, telling me in no uncertain language that her newspaper would never do anything to help promote such "filth," and how appalled she was that I would think a decent, family publication like theirs would ever allow itself to be in any way associated with such depravity. Well, it's funny now (very funny!), but at the time it only underscored the all-consuming loneliness and self-disgust I felt.

Pai-chang's Wild Ducks. One of my favorite Zen Stories, I always thought this epic three-parter was a hoot.

[The Sound of the Birds]. Perhaps my favorite feeling in the world is a fresh spring breeze coming in the morning window, coupled with the sound of the birds.

Catcalls. As of this writing, Al still works at that hardware store.

King-Cat Top Forty. Two books listed here were instrumental in the course of the next few years of my life. *Depression Free Naturally*, by Joan Mathews-Larson, was based in part on the research of Carl C. Pfeiffer (*Nutrition and Mental Illness*), and these books sent me down a path of self-care that would ultimately save my life.

Filler® Presents:. At the health food store, I was introduced to that earnest musical genre known as "Coffeehouse Rock."

Facial Hair Funnies® Presents "I've Got a Beard".

Catalpa Trees. One of the hardest things about going back to Denver was leaving my family behind in Illinois. My health problems had made me acutely aware of our mortality, and in my mind we were all always getting older. I had cherished the time I'd been able to spend with my mom and dad back home, from Tuesday Night dinners together to football on my couch on Sundays, and it was hard to give up. This story is just trying to look forward and look back at the same time.

[Good Times Bad Times]. Another love letter to home.

Trombones No. One. Mung Bean soup.

Pingree Grove. Nighttime Encounter with the Void.

Back Cover. The bend in Route 20 at Pingree Grove, Illinois (map).

In between issues 62 and 63, we made the sudden decision to move from Denver to San Francisco, where Misun could attend one of the premier acupuncture schools in the country. Again, I was heartbroken and scared. I loved Denver, and San Francisco seemed so very far away from "home." (Not to mention that because of my health issues I couldn't fly, so a trip to see my parents would be a grueling multi-day journey.) But we went.

OCD is a disease of familiarity. New surroundings, while fear-inducing at first, often-times relieved my symptoms— everything was fresh and hadn't yet taken on a multi-layered patina of anxiety. So those early days in SF were open and free, and the creative spirit of the city inspired me.

#63: (August 2004).

Cover. Palm Tree, Bernal Heights, San Francisco.

King-Cat Snornose including Plum Blossoms.

Hardy Mums. Dispatches from the Endless Void.

Stuff. *From The Gateless Gate (Mumonkan)* Case 20: "Shogen Osho asked, 'Why is it that a man of great strength does not lift his legs?'" To which Mumon added this verse:

Lifting his leg, he kicks up the Scented Ocean;
Lowering his head, he looks down on the fourth Dhyana heaven.
There is no space vast enough for his body—
Now, somebody write the last line here.
(Translation by Katsuki Sekida)

One time I was visiting the Denver Zen Center, and was talking to Danan Henry, the teacher there. I was telling him at length about my health problems, and as I went on and on he could sense my anxiety rising. When I finally finished he simply said, *"But don't you see? Nothing happened."*

Mr. Sicko-Face.

California Road Trip: Itinerary and Highlights.

Great Western Sky. Living out west, it was easy to see the expansive desolation of the world. It simultaneously scared me and covered me like a blanket.

The Bottle and Me. This was a comic that I'd originally drawn for the long-lost original issue #61 of King-Cat (see *Map of My Heart* notes). At that time my OCD prevented me from publishing it, due to a panel in which it seemed like I was blaming the origins of my drinking on a past girlfriend. Anyhow, I shortly lost all the pages that I'd drawn for that issue. So now, in SF, I redrew it from memory, and omitted the questionable passage.

King-Cat Top Forty.

[The Flowering of Branches]. I was studying Nutrition in a mail-order course during these years.

Barbers I Have Known. One of the Elgin artists who contacted me after I arrived in Denver was Alice DuBois. She later gave her copy of King-Cat #63 to Jerry the Barber, and he got a kick out of it.

Transfers. This comic was originally untitled, but I always called it "Transfers." I've rectified the situation here. *"Stop checking— there are absolutely no flaws."* — Hongzhi Zhengjue [Book of *Equanimity* (*ShōyŌrŌku*) Case 48]

Like a Pigeon. Likewise this comic was originally untitled.

"Mayfly" Incident. Title undoubtedly plagiarized from Jenny Zervakis' *"The Cicada Incident,"* Strange Growths #7, 1993.

Size, Location and Position of the Heart. Starring Fast Charlie (the neighborhood cat) and Matisse's *The Two Sisters*.

Back Cover: Sutro Tower. I loved this kaiju and always wanted to make a coffee table book called *One Hundred Views of Mt. Sutro*. Did you know that Sutro Tower is not actually on Mount Sutro? I do, now.

In April of 2005, my worst fear came true, and my Dad passed away suddenly of an abdominal aortic aneurysm, back home in Illinois. Watching him walk to his car that last day in Elgin, after he helped us pack up our moving van in 2002, did in fact turn out to be the last time I ever saw him.

#64: (July 2005).

Cover: Dad. From a Family photo.

[Epigraph].

[Dad].

The Cat on the Sidewalk. Loss and Time.

Baoche's Universal Action. Based on an excerpt from Dogen Zenji's *Genjokoan*, translated by Anzan Hoshin Roshi and Yasuda Joshu Dainan Roshi.

The Tops of the Trees.

Fifty-eight. On Golf Road (Illinois Highway 58), between Elgin and Hoffman Estates, were vast swaths of forest and field that I'd explored since I was a kid. My home.

Memories of My Dad. The poem "Do Not Stand at My Grave and Weep," originally written in 1932 by Mary Elizabeth Frye (1905–2004), has a very interesting history and provenance. (Google it sometime.)

Biding Time. Living in SF had started to lose its charm. All I was was homesick.

April 5th—Park City. We were driving east on I-80, trying to make it home before my dad passed away. This was the last night my dad and I were both in the world.

Endless Bright World.

The Monk. After the initial honeymoon period in SF, my OCD got worse and worse. To combat the anxiety, I would walk. I would just get out of the apartment…and move. Through nearby Golden Gate Park, or sometimes just with no destination. I'd walk from Stanyan to the ocean, trying to burn off the fritzing, haywire energy coursing through me.

One of my main walking spots was the "Rhododendron Dell," a small, trashed former garden east of the Science Building in Golden Gate Park. It was mainly weeds and wildness, and muddy paths, and it reminded me of home. I would walk its circular paths again and again, counting each lap, then reverse direction to go counter-clockwise, and turn around again, and try to turn my bleeding, fraying mind off. One time I saw a monk.

[Sunlight Slips Through Cracks in the Buildings…]. I was at a point in my life when I was always leaving.

April 7th—Western Illinois.

Dream.

[Yellow Flowers]. Lo and behold, in five years' time I found myself living ten miles from these power lines.

Dad's Drawing.

After my dad's death, I found myself drawing more than I had in years, and produced the next few issues in rapid succession.

#65: (October 2005). Places.

Inside Front Cover. A quick look at a map will tell you that Iowa and Kansas don't actually touch each other.

King-Cat Snornose.

Iowa City. Basement drunks.

DeKalb '91–'92.

Scott County Memories. My OCD brutalized me on this one. I drew and redrew, and whited out and then redrew and then erased and redrew that last panel until the paper nearly had holes in it.

King-Cat Top Forty. #37 should read, "*Los Angeles, CA 7/14 – 7/19.*"

Country Roads—Brighton. Actually, it *did* turn out that way…five years later.

North Alfred Street. I was obsessed with getting the text on these pages to look "just right" (thanks, OCD!)—which meant printing out dozens of copies to use as masters, trying to get the text lined up perfectly straight, with no specks, and no toner drop outs. I printed so many copies that I ran out of toner, and then found that they no longer made cartridges for our ancient printer. So after printing every copy I'd have to remove the cartridge, shake it, put it back in, and print the next one.

Then I would go over each page with a magnifying glass looking for specks, and whiting them out. (One thing I've learned about despecking is: the more you despeck, the more specks will appear. Like literally, new specks will continue to appear as long as you keep looking at the page.) I'd also examine each printed character and look for any spots where the toner may have dropped out, or gone down imperfectly, and then using my magnifying glass and a 005 Micron, I'd attempt to fill in missing serifs, etc. Friends, and readers, I beseech thee: do not do this.

Back Cover: A scene from Iowa, off I-80.

KING-CAT
COMICS & STORIES
NO. 65 $3.00
BY JOHN PORCELLINO

Complete (partially unused) drawing for potential wraparound cover, King-Cat #65

#66: (December 2005)

King-Cat Snornose.

Las Hojas. Jacob puts on a long sleeve shirt between panels 5 and 6, page nine, and removes it again on page eleven.

Catcalls.

Blue Light. Teenage Love Affair.

Freeman Kame. There is a large radio tower off Powers Road, at the interstate, so for years I mistakenly thought it was called "Tower Road." It was at the last second I realized my mistake, and corrected it in time to print the comic. Thanks Mapquest®!

Glossary of Terms.

Back Cover.

As the fall of 2006 approached, our time in San Francisco was coming to an end. Misun was graduating from Acupuncture school, and without her financial aid there was no way we could continue to live in the Bay Area. In our three years there I'd come to love the city, of course (how could you not love it?), but I was ready to move on. The last few weeks I'd take the bus downtown and look at the bay, or wander along Ocean Beach, hike the Presidio; ride the Geary bus back and forth and back and forth, trying to soak it all in.

We made plans to move back to Denver. I finished up *King-Cat #67*, and sent the files to my beloved old printshop in Colorado; when we arrived back in town, there they were, waiting for me.

#67: (October 2006)

Cover: Lone Mountain View. In SF, we lived at Hayes and Shrader, at the foot of Lone Mountain. I'd walk up it every day on my way to work. At night the flood-lit towers of St. Ignatius looked down over the neighborhood, and I'd walk up and down the hills, up each side street and down the next, pacing, pacing, trying to maintain.

King-Cat Snornose. My OCD was insidious, infiltrating every aspect of my life, and I invested an enormous effort in trying to keep it hidden. I wanted so bad to just come clean, to spill the beans, admit I was a failure, a monster, a casualty. But I was too afraid even of that. Life had taken on the feeling of a nightmare, where any horrible thing could happen at any moment, and it was always your fault. I tried desperately to find some sanity in nature, in little details, in laughing at myself, but it was hard. (For more information about this time, please see my book *The Hospital Suite*.)

Sleeping in the Car in L.A. Once, a long time ago, I wrote a comic called "Security Lunchbag" [see *King-Cat Classix*], about the joys of sleeping in a car. When you're sleeping in a car, in LA, with your cat, you are like a sandwich in the world's most cozy, safe lunchbag. And all is well. And all is always well, forever.

Woke Up Sad. The Japanese poet Kobayashi Issa wrote: "*This world of dew is a world of dew, and yet...and yet...*"

Heart. Years of illness, both mental and physical, were taking their toll.

Regular World.

New York. For my wonderful teacher Ben Mahmoud. (I still think about it now and then.)

Teabox Advice. The quote is "*There is some pleasure in being on board a ship battered by storms when one is certain of not perishing.*"—Blaise Pascal (off a Celestial Seasonings box)

Hara. "*In the medical tradition of Japan, hara refers to the soft belly, i.e. the area defined vertically by the lower edge of the sternum and the upper edge of the pubis and laterally by the lower border of the ribcage and the anterior iliac crest respectively.*"—Carola Beresford-Cooke, *Shiatsu Theory and Practice: A comprehensive text for the student and professional.* Churchill Livingstone, London, New York, Tokyo 1996, p.235 (via Wikipedia).

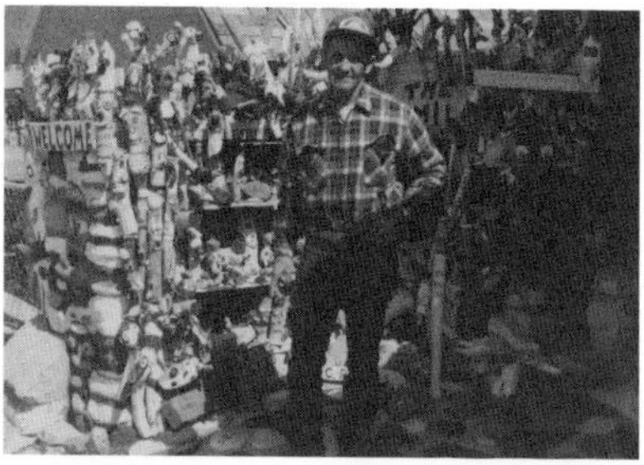

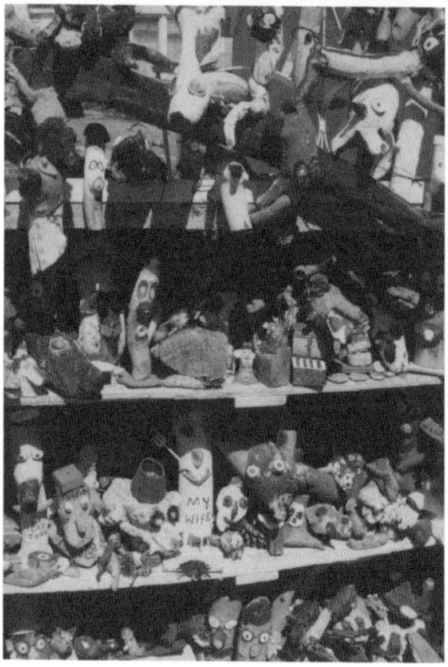

MY WIFE

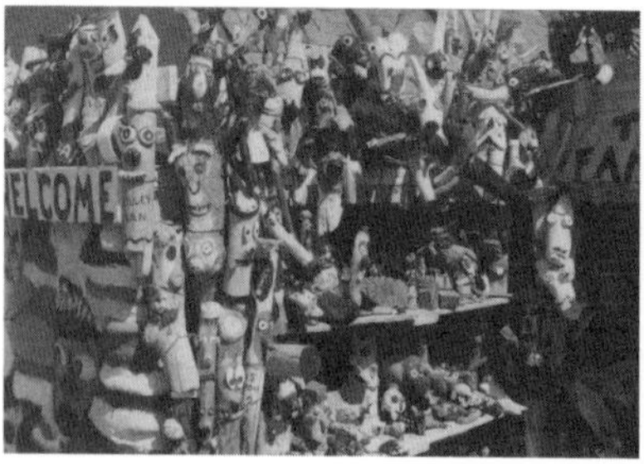

Photos of Square Head John and his artwork

Square-Head John. The Mystery of Square-Head John was finally solved in King-Cat #69.

[Night Staircase]. The Sutro Tower makes one last appearance.

Six O'Clock Steps. Park Branch Library, 1833 Page Street.

Flags. I have nothing to add.

Catcalls.

King-Cat Top 40. Those two records, *American Primitive Vol. Two* and *Good For What Ails You*, really changed my life, opening up whole new vistas of thought and exploration for me. Highly recommended.

Unused photo reference for "Night Staircase," King-Cat #67

[Stomach Hurts…]. My favorite place on earth.

Cabin Flux. Fighting back.

Courting.

Feels Like a Good Day. Out walking, in sun, hand in glove with the universe.

Back Cover: Every Day of Our Life/Bay Bridge. Last days in SF. As usual, despite my struggles, I felt sad to be leaving, sad for another part of my life to be ending.

Once we returned to Colorado, things were rough. Rents had gone up quite a bit in the three years we'd been away, and apartments were hard to find. We lived in a motel for the first few weeks and then finally found a place out in the West Highlands at 31st and Vrain.

That fall there was a blizzard every Thursday for seven weeks straight. With no car, in this semi-suburban part of town, we pulled my cheap luggage cart with a cardboard box strapped to it four miles roundtrip, through snowdrifts, to the Safeway for groceries. Truthfully, it was so rough it became kind of fun. (See also: "*Teabox Advice*" note.)

Living in the Highlands was lonely. And my anxiety was at its worst. I began walking again, obsessively, through our new neighborhood at night—up one street, down the next, gazing out at the lights of the city spread below, my head on fire.

In the spring of 2007, while working on my first King-Cat collection for Drawn & Quarterly (*King-Cat Classix*), I suffered my second nervous breakdown. If you've ever had a nervous breakdown, you know there can be a kind of peace that follows it, as your system is simply too shorted out to respond anymore. During this peace I began drawing my next book, *Thoreau at Walden* (Hyperion Books, 2008). Working daily, and so intimately, with the life of one of my biggest heroes, Henry David Thoreau, helped me begin to emotionally accept my situation, and move forward. When *Thoreau at Walden* was complete, I began work on the next *King-Cat*.

#68: (October 2007)

Cover: Blue Mustard. Blue Mustard (*Chorispora tenella*) is one of the earliest flowering weeds of the Colorado plains.

King-Cat Snornose: "So You Think You're a Nervous Wreck."

John R. I love you.

Maisie Love. Right before we left San Francisco, Maisie had become very ill and was diagnosed with kidney failure. We nursed her for the next eleven months, but in August of 2007 she passed away. (I love you, too.) (For Maisie's full story, please see King-Cat #75.)

Cloud Mountain.

Cloud Mountain Pt. Two.

7 Wks of Snow/Head for the Hills. During this period of massive depression, I checked out *On the Beach* by Neil Young from the library, and listened to it on endless repeat for several weeks straight. Lawyer's Note: DO NOT ATTEMPT THIS AT HOME.

Anthill.

Breathe.

88th and Federal. You can never step in the same river twice.

Diogenes of Sinope. I think it was John Hankiewicz who turned me on to Epictetus' *Enchiridion*. That

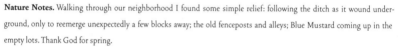

Back steps and loading dock area of the Fruitful Yield, Schaumburg, Illinois. (See also: "Ant Crossing," King-Cat Classix [King-Cat #61])

led me to Diogenes, and like many, in him I found a new hero.

Diogenes and the Bowl.

Diogenes In: "An Honest Man."

Diogenes Meets Alexander the Great.

Diogenes In: "Men and Scoundrels."

Diogenes and the Bones.

King-Cat Top Forty.

Nature Notes. Walking through our neighborhood I found some simple relief: following the ditch as it wound underground, only to reemerge unexpectedly a few blocks away; the old fenceposts and alleys; Blue Mustard coming up in the empty lots. Thank God for spring.

Warm Light. This was a grueling one. I drew it three times I think (OCD) until I got one that was "acceptable." I remember that shaky feeling of dawn coming up and you're still drawing and all your blood has run cold, but it's done.

Feeding the Birds at the Fruitful Yield. The Fruitful Yield was a health food store I worked at during my time in Elgin. I still have recurring nightmares about it.

Back Cover: Maisie.

After #68 I was at a crossroads. Things had been bad for a long time. My anxiety had destroyed any chance I'd had at a normal life, my friends and family were starting to die around me, and the strain was beginning to show in my marriage to Misun. In the spring of 2008 we found a nicer, bigger apartment (one with insulation!) in downtown Denver, and moved again. It was a chance to start over a bit, to have a fresh go of it and really try to figure out a way to make things better. Little did I know that the upheaval was just beginning.

WARTS

WHEN I WAS IN HIGH SCHOOL I GOT WARTS ON MY FEET

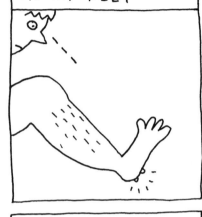

PROBABLY FROM WALKING AROUND THE POOL IN GYM CLASS, BUT WHO KNOWS?

TRYING NOT TO GET A BONER

I WENT TO THE DOCTOR and HE CUT THEM OFF WITH A KNIFE

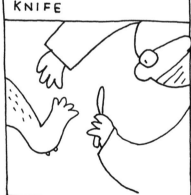

AFTERWARDS, I LAID ON THE COUCH and LISTENED TO BEATLES RECORDS

JOHN P. DRAWN 1/11/03

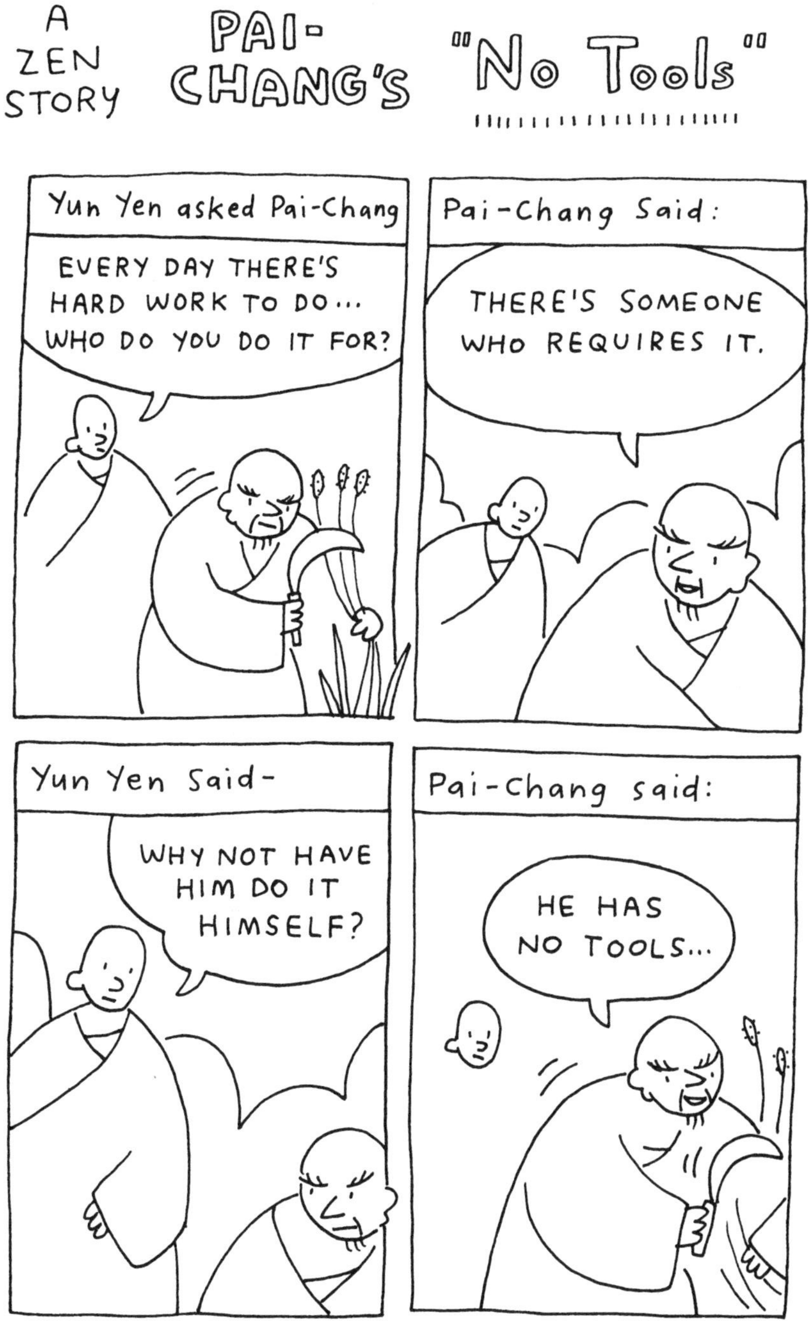

A ZEN STORY
PAI-CHANG'S
"No Tools"
Yun Yen asked Pai-Chang
EVERY DAY THERE'S HARD WORK TO DO... WHO DO YOU DO IT FOR?
Pai-Chang Said:
THERE'S SOMEONE WHO REQUIRES IT.
Yun Yen Said-
WHY NOT HAVE HIM DO IT HIMSELF?
Pai-chang said:
HE HAS NO TOOLS...

✌ CIRCUS PEANUTS

ONE MORNING WE WERE HEADING OUT TO PICK UP MAISIE at THE VET'S...

MISUN WAS EATING HER BREAKFAST AS WE DROVE

SHE SAID:

GOD MADE BANANAS...

I SAID

GOD MADE MONKEYS TO EAT THE BANANAS...

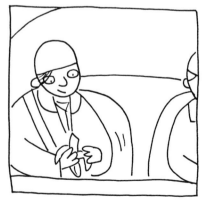

GOD MADE FINGERS — TO PEEL THE BANANAS...

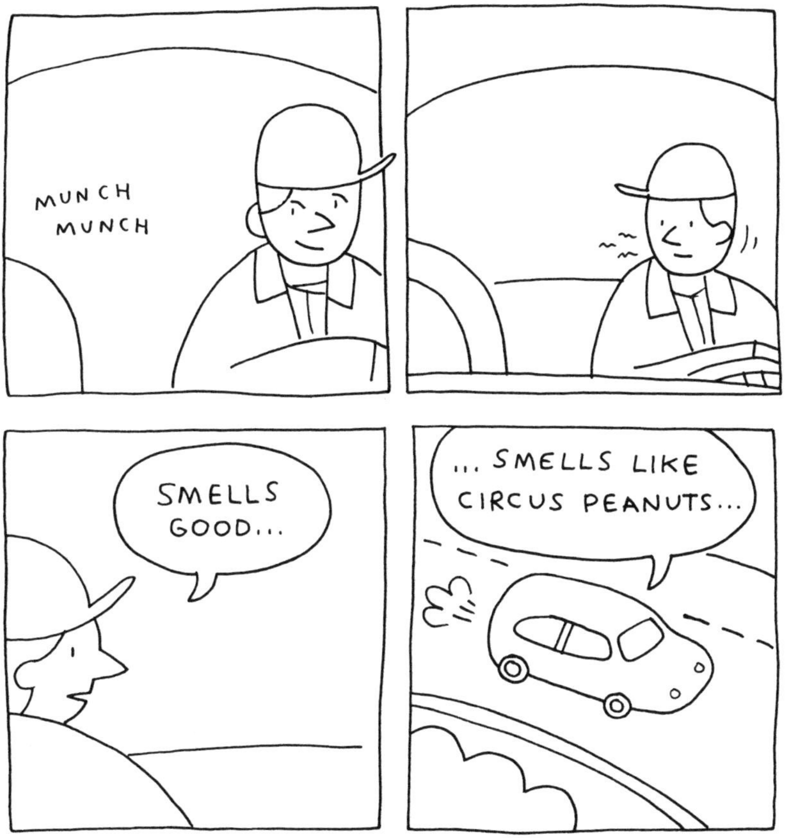
MUNCH
MUNCH
SMELLS GOOD...
... SMELLS LIKE CIRCUS PEANUTS...

HAPPENED SUN. APRIL 4
DRAWN 4/12/04 - John P.

OUTSIDE-IN

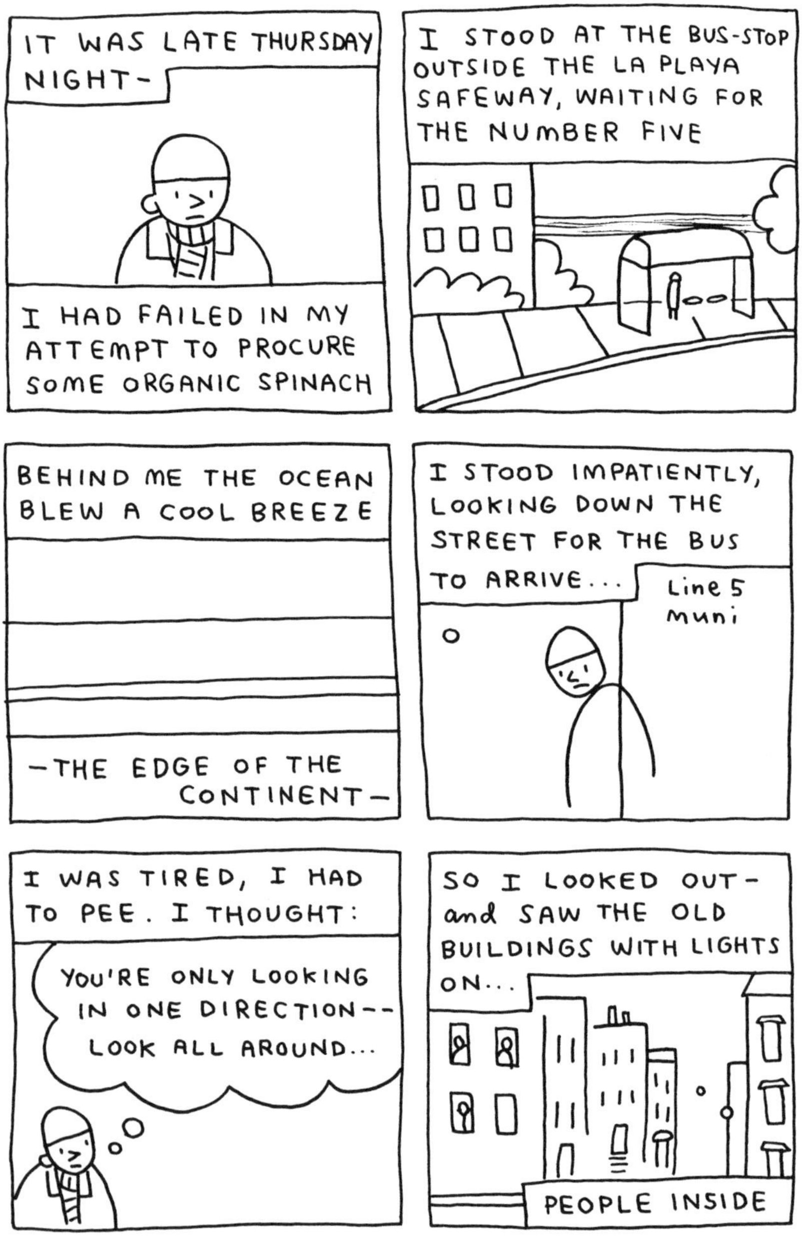
IT WAS LATE THURSDAY NIGHT-
I HAD FAILED IN MY ATTEMPT TO PROCURE SOME ORGANIC SPINACH
I STOOD AT THE BUS-STOP OUTSIDE THE LA PLAYA SAFEWAY, WAITING FOR THE NUMBER FIVE
BEHIND ME THE OCEAN BLEW A COOL BREEZE
-THE EDGE OF THE CONTINENT-
I STOOD IMPATIENTLY, LOOKING DOWN THE STREET FOR THE BUS TO ARRIVE...
Line 5
muni
I WAS TIRED, I HAD TO PEE. I THOUGHT:
YOU'RE ONLY LOOKING IN ONE DIRECTION-- LOOK ALL AROUND...
SO I LOOKED OUT- and SAW THE OLD BUILDINGS WITH LIGHTS ON...
PEOPLE INSIDE

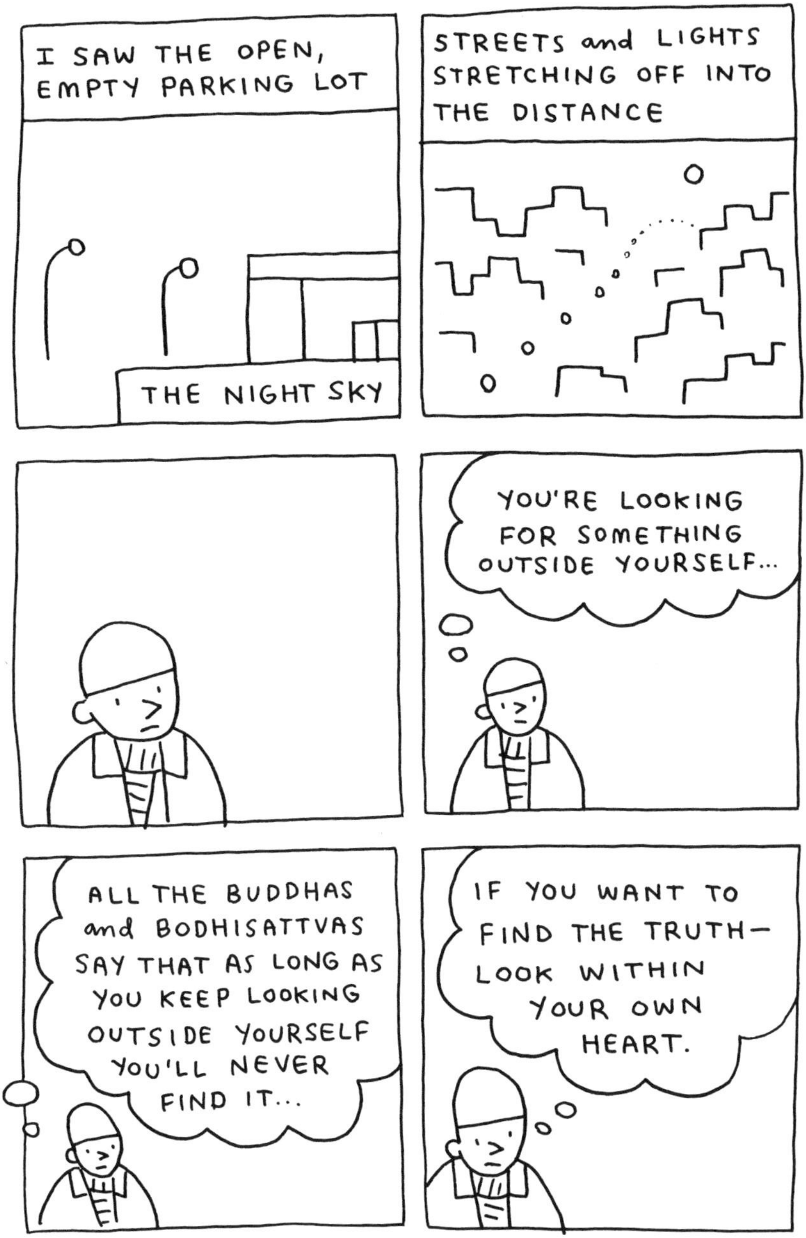
I SAW THE OPEN, EMPTY PARKING LOT
THE NIGHT SKY
STREETS and LIGHTS STRETCHING OFF INTO THE DISTANCE
YOU'RE LOOKING FOR SOMETHING OUTSIDE YOURSELF...
ALL THE BUDDHAS and BODHISATTVAS SAY THAT AS LONG AS YOU KEEP LOOKING OUTSIDE YOURSELF YOU'LL NEVER FIND IT...
IF YOU WANT TO FIND THE TRUTH— LOOK WITHIN YOUR OWN HEART.

HAPPENED 3/3/05 DRAWN 3/29
(REVISED 8/24/14 INKED 4/23/17)

MOSQUITO SURPRISE

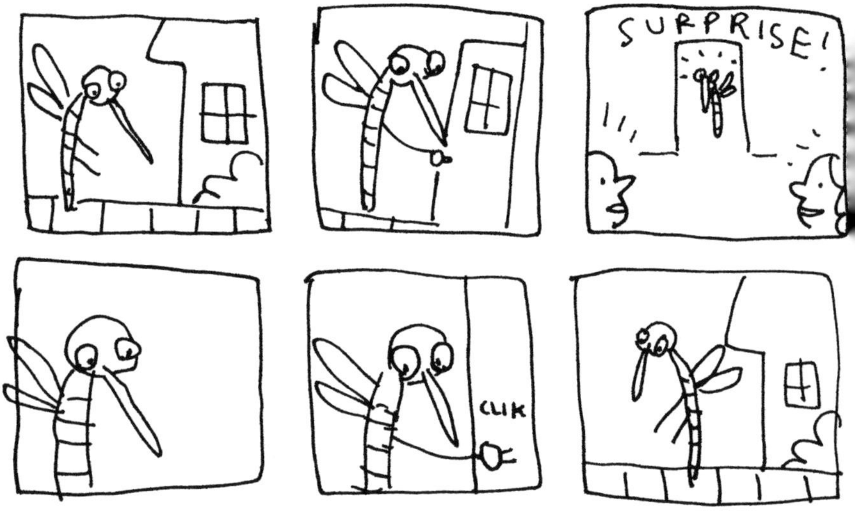
SURPRISE!
CLIK

John Porcellino

3
POEMS
ABOUT
FOG

BY
JOHN PORCELLINO

fillmore Street

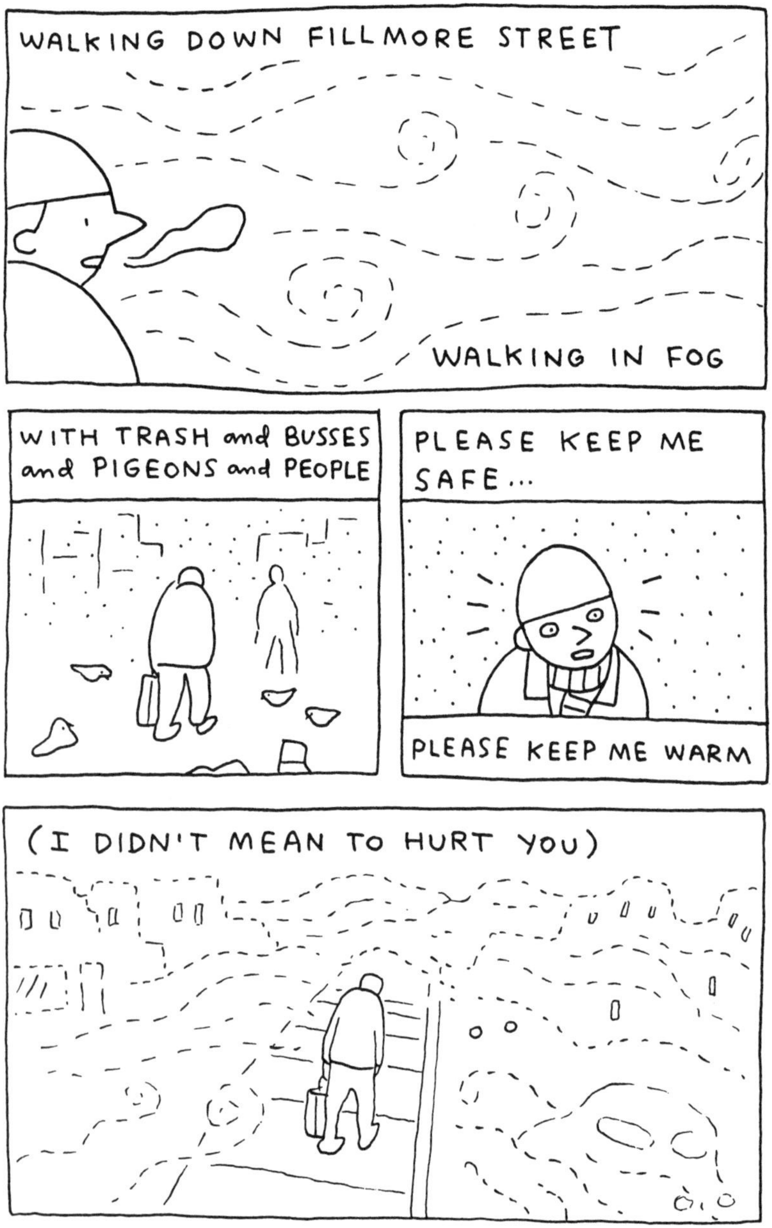

WALKING DOWN FILLMORE STREET
WALKING IN FOG
WITH TRASH and BUSSES and PIGEONS and PEOPLE
PLEASE KEEP ME SAFE...
PLEASE KEEP ME WARM
(I DIDN'T MEAN TO HURT YOU)

SUMMER 2004 · DRAWN MARCH 29, '05

San francisco

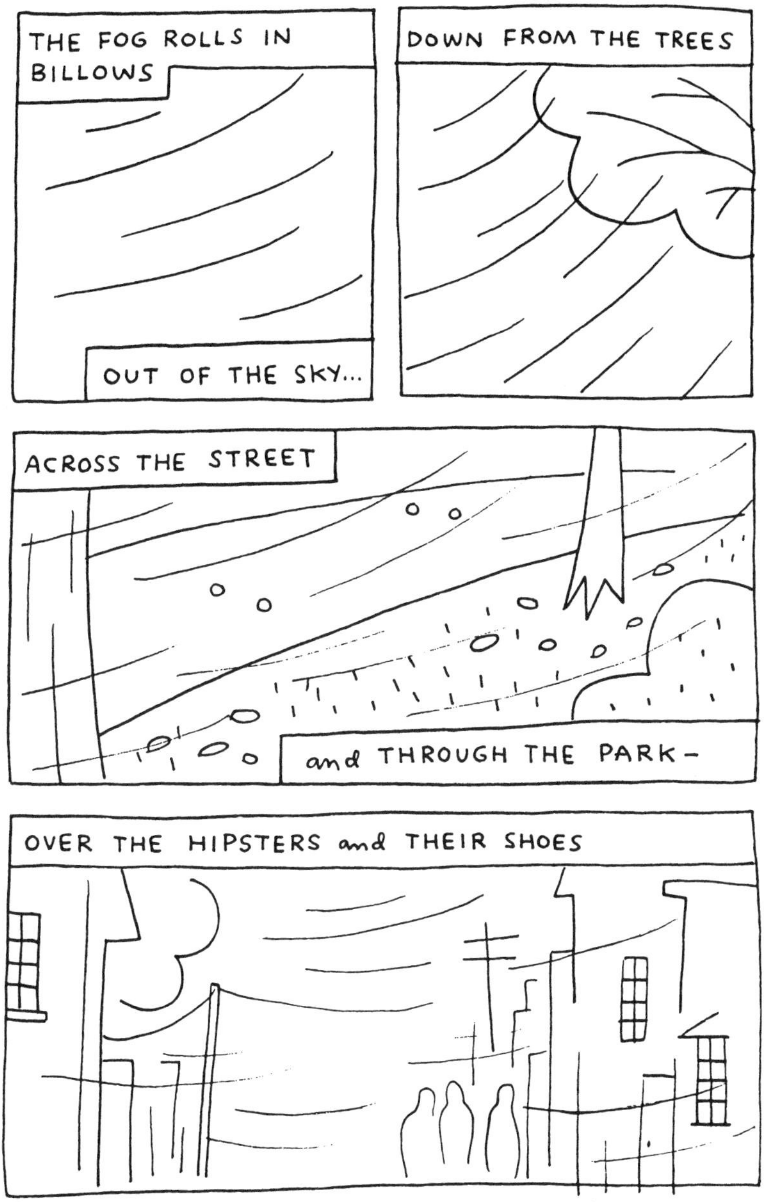
THE FOG ROLLS IN BILLOWS
OUT OF THE SKY...
DOWN FROM THE TREES
ACROSS THE STREET
and THROUGH THE PARK–
OVER THE HIPSTERS and THEIR SHOES

J.P. OCT. 21, 2005 - drawn MARCH '06

Downs and Yards

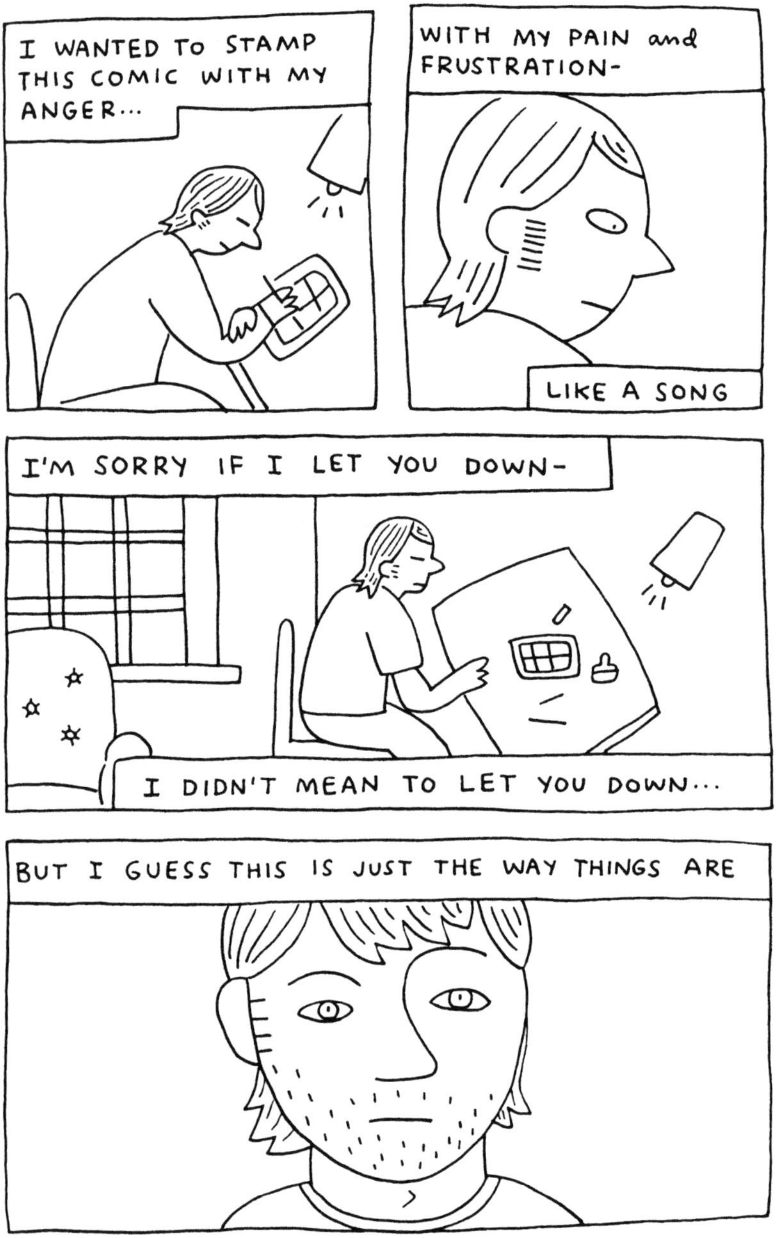

I WANTED TO STAMP THIS COMIC WITH MY ANGER...
WITH MY PAIN and FRUSTRATION-
LIKE A SONG
I'M SORRY IF I LET YOU DOWN-
I DIDN'T MEAN TO LET YOU DOWN...
BUT I GUESS THIS IS JUST THE WAY THINGS ARE

OUTSIDE, THE ANNOUNCER CALLS DOWNS and YARDS
THE FOGHORN BLOWS
INSIDE, THE DAYS are GETTING SHORTER...
IT'S FALL AGAIN

BUT I'M LOST.

OCT '05 – MAR '06
DRAWN MARCH '06 J.P.

The ones that Everybody knows

JOHN PORCELLINO

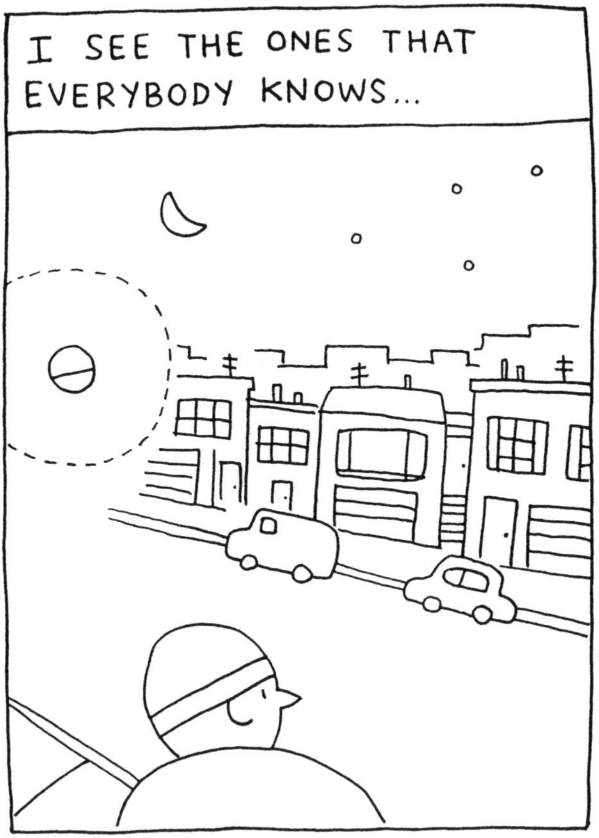
I SEE THE ONES THAT EVERYBODY KNOWS...

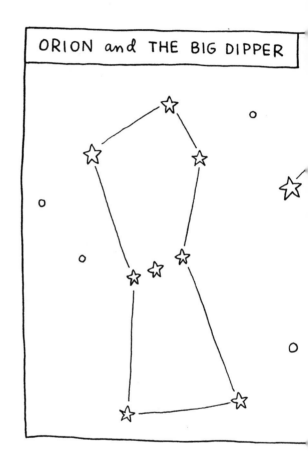

ORION and THE BIG DIPPER

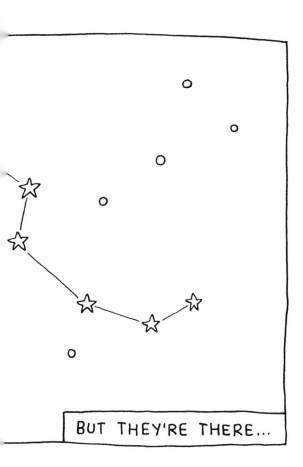

BUT THEY'RE THERE...

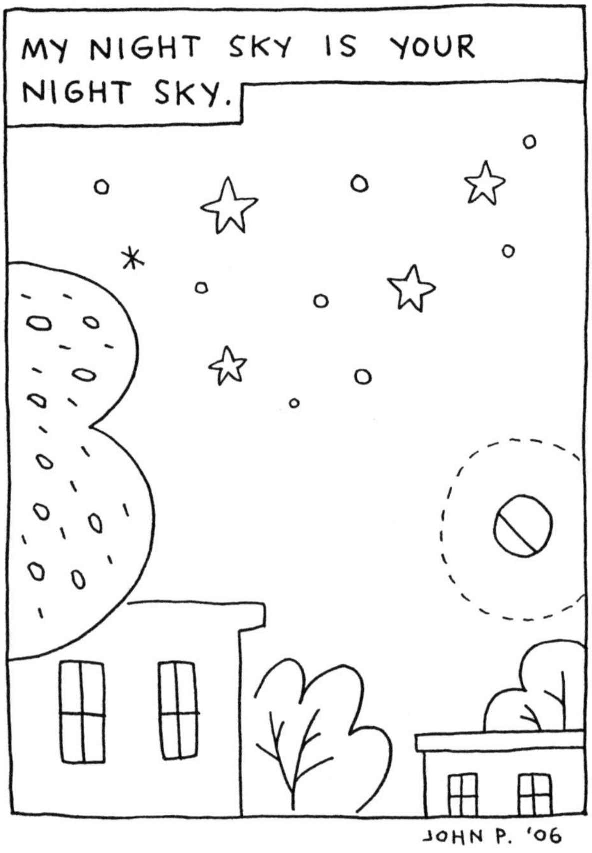
MY NIGHT SKY IS YOUR NIGHT SKY.
JOHN P. '06

Cloud Mouse

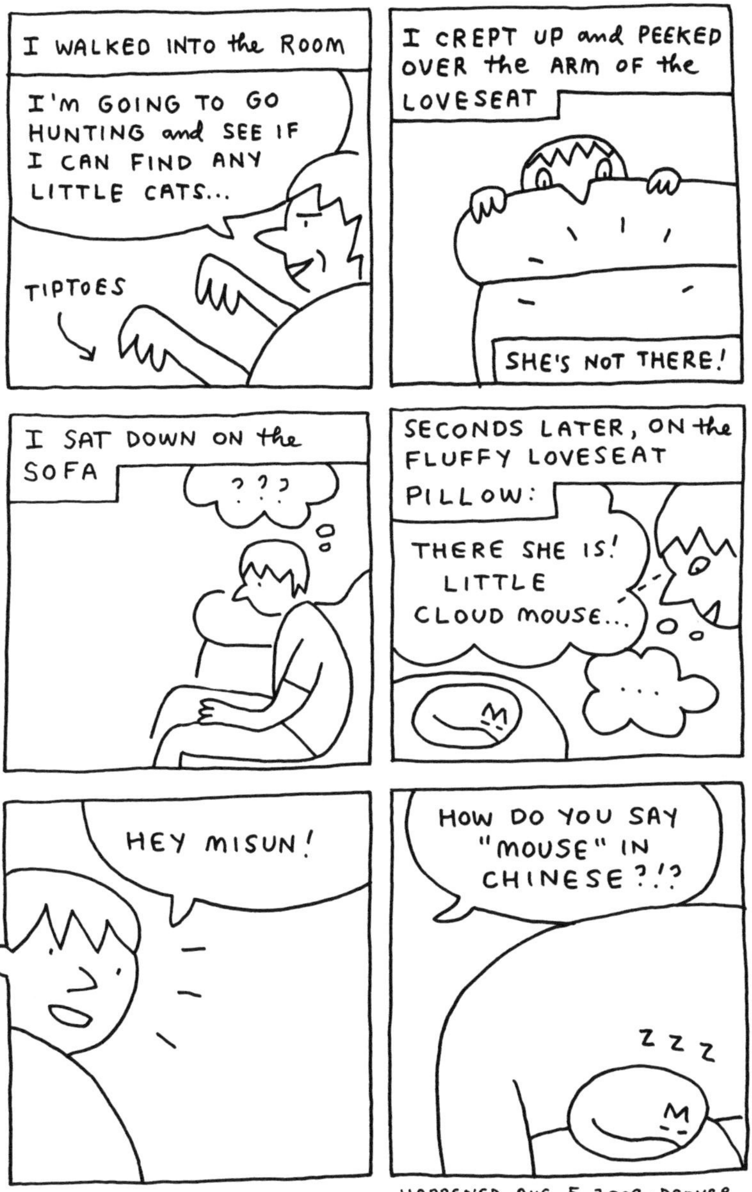
I WALKED INTO the ROOM
I'M GOING TO GO HUNTING and SEE IF I CAN FIND ANY LITTLE CATS...
TIPTOES
I CREPT UP and PEEKED OVER the ARM OF the LOVESEAT
SHE'S NOT THERE!
I SAT DOWN ON the SOFA
???
SECONDS LATER, ON the FLUFFY LOVESEAT PILLOW:
THERE SHE IS! LITTLE CLOUD MOUSE...
...
HEY MISUN!
HOW DO YOU SAY "MOUSE" IN CHINESE?!?
Z Z Z

STARRING CHARLI(E) the CAT

HAPPENED AUG., 5, 2009 · DENVER
DRAWN APRIL 7, 2017 · Beloit J.P.

BONUS COMICS NOTES

Hippie Girl (Drawn in 2017). By 2006 I had become a coiled snake of anger, fear, and resentment, but I did my very best to hide it. Or repress it, or squash it down where I hoped nobody would be able to see it. Of course that just ended up eating me alive from the inside out.

Warts (January 2003). This was the first comic that I drew after arriving back in Denver. The change of scenery had loosened the OCD's grip on my creativity, and after this one the ideas poured forth. I don't know why this comic went unpublished till now, I guess the OCD hadn't loosened *that* much. (Previously unpublished.)

Pai-chang's No Tools (2003). Another outtake from King-Cat #62. Based on a translation by Norman Fischer. (Previously unpublished.)

Circus Peanuts (April 2004). Outtake from King-Cat #63. (Previously unpublished.)

Outside-In (May 2005). I really struggled with this one. The original pages are a mess of blue lines, eraser smears, and teardrops, and sat in a box unfinished for almost ten years. Apparently in 2014 I found them again and revised a few lines, and just like that they were good to go. (Those meds really help.) I inked them in 2017, especially for inclusion in this book. (Previously unpublished.)

Mosquito Surprise (Circa 2005). Drawn at a party at Minty Lewis and Damien Jay's house in the East Bay. (Previously unpublished.)

3 Poems About Fog (2006). In the spring of 2006, the Alternative Press Expo was coming up, and I quickly whipped these comics into shape and made a little zine. This was one of the earliest comics of mine I scanned and prepared in Photoshop, and consequently when it came back from the printer I realized I had screwed up the margins on the cover: the cover text was supposed to be centered but instead skewed left an inch or so. So in a fit of inspiration I pulled out a pair of scissors and cut the extra space at the right edge into the shape of fog clouds. Eureka! **Fillmore Street** is where I worked, in a little health food store in Pacific Heights. I'd take the 21 Hayes bus to Fillmore and then walk the rest of the way. **San Francisco:** Living near Haight and Ashbury gave me an intimate glimpse into the world of trendy footwear. I remember I was really (OCD) afraid to publish this comic, for fear that I'd offend all the San Francisco hipsters with expensive shoes. C'est la guerre. **Downs and Yards:** We lived a few blocks from Kezar Stadium and on Saturday nights I'd sit in our apartment and listen to the announcer call games over the loudspeakers, and the fog horns, and there was something comforting about that.

The Ones That Everybody Knows (April 2016). I had so much fun making *3 Poems About Fog* that I made this little jobber for the Alternative Press Expo that year too, about walking in my neighborhood at night to relieve my anxiety. And all the while, as Frank Sinatra once sang, "I thought about you."

Cloud Mouse (Drawn in 2017). This is a story I found written on an envelope in a box of old junk. It's from the period shortly after this book ends, but I thought it was cute and it references one of the comics collected here, so there you go.

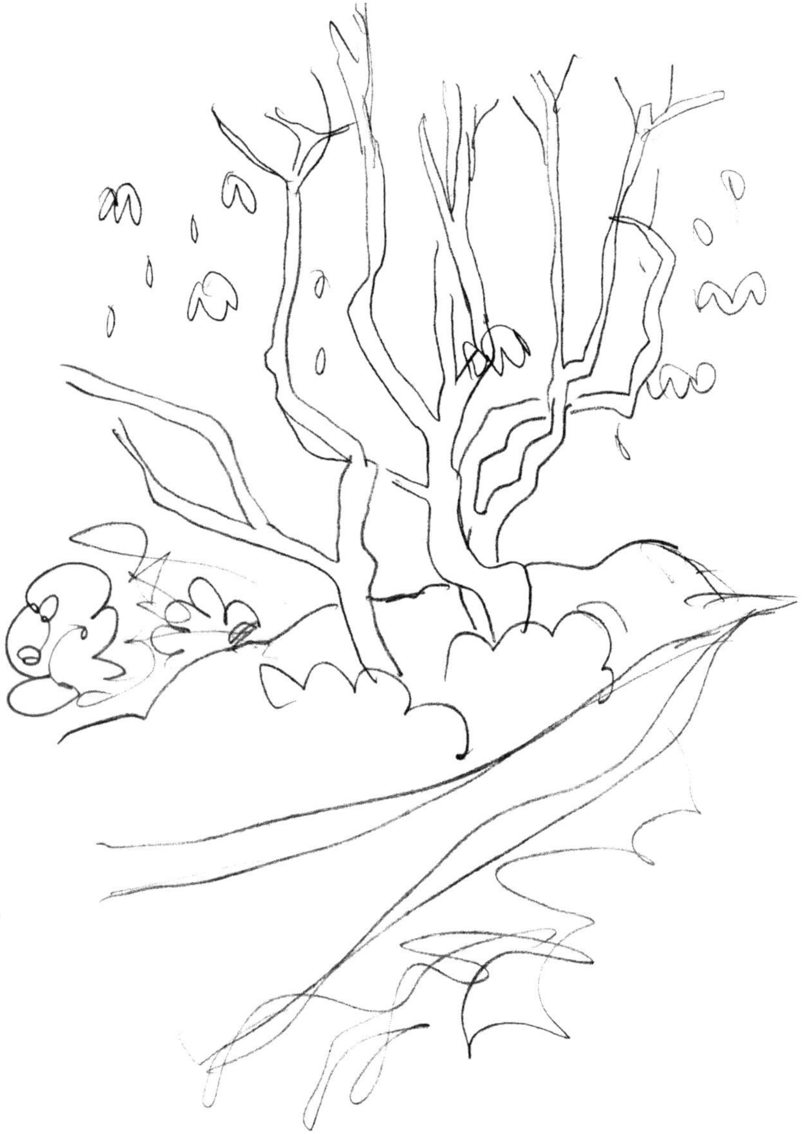

Path – Rhododendron Dell
March 1, 2005

March 1, 2005

INDEX OF TITLES

FEB. 7
2005

John Porcellino was born in Chicago, Illinois, in 1968. He wrote and photocopied his first zine in 1982, at the age of fourteen. In 1989, Porcellino began writing his celebrated *King-Cat* mini-comic series, which has been ongoing for more than twenty-five years, winning acclaim from *Time*, *Entertainment Weekly*, *USA Today*, *Punk Planet,* and the *Globe & Mail*. His work in *King-Cat* has been translated into French, German, Italian, Spanish, and Swedish.

Porcellino is the author of *Diary of a Mosquito Abatement Man*, *King-Cat Classix*, *Map of My Heart*, *Perfect Example*, *Thoreau at Walden*, and *The Hospital Suite*. He lives in Beloit, Wisconsin, with his girlfriend and two cats and two dogs, and continues to produce new issues of *King-Cat* on a regular basis.